THE BUXTON HYDRO

THE BUXTON HYDRO
(SPA HOTEL)
THE STORY OF THE SPA TOWN'S BEST KNOWN HYDROPATHIC BETWEEN 1866 AND 1974

PETER LOMAS

ASHRIDGE PRESS/COUNTRY BOOKS

Published by Country Books/Ashridge Press
Courtyard Cottage, Little Longstone, Bakewell, Derbyshire DE45 1NN

Tel/Fax: 01629 640670
e-mail: dickrichardson@country-books.co.uk

Cover Pictures
Front: Buxton Hydro
Back: St. Anne's Crescent
Courtesy of Buxton Museum

Printed and bound by: HSW Print

CONTENTS

INTRODUCTION

On the 9th March 1849 as the Reverend James Shore, Minister of Bridgetown Chapel, Totnes, finished preaching his sermon for the evening service at the Countess of Huntingdon's chapel at Spa Fields London and descended the pulpit he was arrested by two officers of the Court of Arches in near riotous conditions. They pushed through the shocked and protesting onlookers to arrest and transport him to Exeter jail.[1]

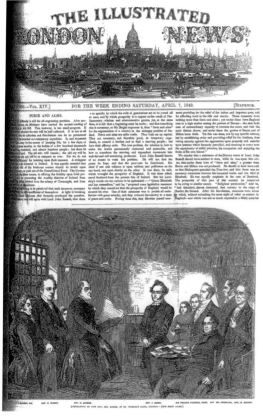

Imprisonment of James Shore
Illustrated London News, Bath Library

One might have suspected that he had committed some evil crime but instead this humble minister had been the victim of Henry Phillpotts, the tyrannical high church Bishop of Exeter, who had pursued him through the civil and ecclesiastical courts on one of Phillpotts personal vendettas. Ostensibly Shore was prosecuted for failure to pay the bishops costs of the litigation, but in reality it was for preaching the Gospel without a licence from the Bishop at Bridgetown chapel on a question of conscience and attempting to secede from the established Church of England. Shore was the first clergyman to be prosecuted for attempting to secede from the Church of England and officiate in his own chapel as a non-conformist minister since the Reformation and his adherence to the principles of serious religion, as evangelism was then known.

In the view of Shore's numerous

---

1   Grayson Carter *Anglican Evangelicals: The Protestant Secessions from the Via Media, C.1800-1850* Oxford 2001
    p373

supporters, this dispute with Phillpotts led him to become momentarily one of the most celebrated religious figures in England, a martyr to ecclesiastical despotism and oppression.

He was to remain in prison for three months at considerable cost to his health receiving many distinguished visitors and followers. He was eventually released after much debate and publicity in the national and local press concerning the injustice of his plight.

His case prompted the introduction of the Clergy Relief Bill providing legal protection for seceding clergyman and he became an important cause celebre in English evangelism his case adding to the crisis of confidence, which seized not only evangelism, but also the Church of England, itself in the mid-19th century.[2]

These events not only helped to form the Free Church of England and to expand the non-conformist movement but also had the unlikely result of the setting up in the 1860's of what was to become one of the largest Hydropathic Establishment in the Midlands which after his death was carried on by his grandson H.R.P. Lomas (H.R.P.) in the late 1890's and early 1900's.

Buxton Hydro 1899

H.R.P floated the business in 1899 for the sum of £130,000 (in today's terms 8 million pounds) only to fall from grace in 1941 as a result of a downturn of the business after the First World War reflecting a similar decline in Buxton's fortunes at the same time. He led a colourful and rich life as is evidenced by the diaries and accounts of his exploits in the local press. He was an example of a benevolent Victorian entrepreneur.

---

2 Grayson Carter p379

CHAPTER 1

THE REVEREND JAMES SHORE – TOTNES

Shore was born in 1805 in Dorset being the third son of a corn merchant (later spa owner), Thomas Shore. He graduated at Sidney Sussex College, Cambridge and married Susanna Gream in 1827 by whom he had three daughters; Julia, Isabella and Emily. He was ordained deacon in 1828 to serve as curate at the parish of Berry Pomeroy, Devon. He became Minister of the Chapel-of-Ease at Bridgetown on the outskirts of Totnes and stayed there until 1862 during which time he became entangled with the notorious Henry Phillpotts, Bishop of Exeter.

The Bishop entered upon his tenure of the Bishopric of Exeter in 1831 and his jurisdiction encompassed the eastern border of Devonshire and reached to Land's End in Cornwall and the Scilly Isles. In every town and village his corporation possessed an office – a church, an agent or propagandist – a Rector, Vicar or Curate. All were engaged in contending for the souls, or influencing the minds of the layman around them. They possessed a common code of morals and a common procedure of worship. Many of the clergy the Bishop appointed direct, but some could be appointed without

James Shore 1840's
History of the Free Church of England

Henry Philpotts 1840's

9

his permission.[3]

When Phillpotts arrived in Exeter in 1831 he regarded the church as "his ploughed field, on which he could sow what corn he liked, in neat drills from between which the weeds could easily be hoed out and from which birds were to be scared away, if necessary, by gunshot. He had no intention of leaving his neighbour's field alone; he was a habitual trespasser, who claimed a right of way whenever he chose to trample or poach."[4]

His physical appearance on his arrival in Exeter was described; "*a face at the same time interesting and terrible, the face of a man in the prime of its life, with hair already becoming thin, an intellectual rather than a bulging forehead, restless twinkling eyes, a proud arching nose and a rat trap mouth whose corners drooped in line with a crescent of deep wrinkles extending from his nostrils to his chin. He betrayed energy and impatience.*"[5]

Phillpotts knew of his unpopularity and at times took measures to protect himself from it. He admits in a letter to his secretary and solicitor, Ralph Barnes, to be "*cautious… in admitting adverse newspapers to my table, yet the caution has not prevented me from learning of the extreme unpopularity of my appointment to Exeter.*"[6]

1831 sawPhillpotts as the victim of the Guy Fawkes system of burning effigies of clergyman. Phillpotts knew his reputation and took action by requesting protection from the 7th Yeomanry Cavalry who filled the palace in Exeter, whilst the crowd in the Cathedral Yard burned Phillpotts in effigy; "*hollow turnip as head and candle as nose, clad in mitre and lawn sleeves*"[7]

At that time the church in Exeter was suffering the same malaise as that which had overtaken other corporations. Attendance at the Churches fell off and the way was left open to Wesley and his successors to preach regeneration, and it was to dissent that many of the poor and middle classes turned for spiritual help and comfort. Naturally the clergy resented itinerant preachers wandering about their parishes, and the methods of some of the later revivalists were open to ridicule by those who did not share their fanatical ideals. In fact dissenters were often as unpopular as Roman Catholics, and the emancipation of both stirred up immense feeling throughout the country in the eighteenth century. Unfortunately, the established Church was far too complacent to recognise the danger it was in and lost many of its members before it began to put its house in order. But an unexpected reprieve came in the form of a great revulsion of feeling against the horrors of the revolution in France, and anyone who had a stake in the land began to support the Church on principle.

A.N. Wilson in *The Victorians* states "*For Tories of the old School, the lesson was simple enough: start to dabble with religious freethinkers, or to question the aristo -*

---

3   RS Lambert *The Cobbett of the West* Nicholson and Watson 1939 p36
4   RS Lambert p40
5   RS Lambert p35
6   R Newton *Victorian Exeter 1837-1914* Leicester University Press 1968 p20
7   Owen Chadwick *The Victorian Church Part One:1829-1856* London: SCM Press Ltd 1997 p22

cratic system, and before long you find a guillotine erected; you find kings having their heads chopped off; you find the reign of terror and Robespierre."

It was felt that the Church was the only institution which could preserve order in a disintegrating society. The man responsible for putting new life into the see of Exeter was Phillpotts.

His predecessors had done little or nothing to improve the low standards in their diocese, and rock bottom was probably reached in the closing years of the 18th century. In county parishes two Sunday services with one sermon, or occasionally two, and a *"Sacrament Sunday"* three or four times a year, were all that were considered necessary. Unfortunately even these were not always held in every parish due to plurality and non-residence. At this time in Devon about 45 per cent of the incumbents were non-resident and over 48 per cent of the benefices were held in plurality.

The evils of sinecures, pluralism and non-residency flourished in the country. When the Duke of Wellington offered Phillpotts the Bishopric in Exeter, Phillpotts had 18 children to provide for and persuaded the Duke that not only should he have the income of the Bishop of Exeter at £3,000 but he should also keep the income from the Durham rectory at £4,000. At this point in time the country was restless with discontent against church abuses. The parishioners of Stanhope had petitioned against the proposed plurality, and some of the Exeter clergy had protested against Phillpotts appointment. It was especially hypocritical of Phillpotts as he determined to rid his diocese of pluralism, his war cry being "reside or resign" but nevertheless his strong-arm tactics appeared to get results on this issue.

Many of the clergy connected with the cathedral held livings in other parts of the country which they rarely visited, leaving their duties to be performed by poorly paid curates who were paid between £40 and £150 per annum, whilst the Bishop earned £3000 and the Dean £2,000. Many fellow clergy had similar fat absentee livings. This must have left a sour note in the minds of the curates.

Parts of the diocese, especially in Cornwall, were strongholds of non-conformity. Not only did these dissenters labour under many legal disabilities, exclusion from universities, no right to burial in consecrated ground by their own ministers, no right to registration of births, deaths and marriages except in parish church registers, they were also cut off by a social gulf from the main body of the Church of England adherents. Ministers kept to themselves and were regarded as a lower order of beings by the Orthodox Church. The only bridge between the Anglican and dissenting ministers was provided by the evangelical revival. Many of the best clergy in the diocese were evangelicals and they were willing to collaborate with their non-conformist brethren, not only on questions of public morals but often over the promotion of causes like the abolition of slavery.[8]

Bishop Phillpotts had much of this on his mind, especially as the previous Bishop of Exeter had been seen as elderly and feeble.

He looked to the disappearance of dissension, in which category he included

---

8   RS Lambert pp 36&37

Totnes 1840

Roman Catholics and non-conformists, with the final goal of a national church. He also saw that unorthodoxy, individualism, and innovation were traits, which he wished to reduce.

Phillpotts had written a series of violent tracts[9] on current matters of public controversy. He was a zealous supporter of the tractarian movement begun in the 1830's. He defended their views on baptismal regeneration, sacramental grace, high churchmanship and ritualism.

Prior to Exeter Phillpotts had been preferred to the various fat livings of Durham and, through his friendship with Lord Eldon, ending up with the living of Stanhope-on-the-Wear, one of the richest in the whole of England.[10] But he was anxious for further promotion and in 1829 the Tory ministry under the Duke of Wellington changed its mind and decided to emancipate the Roman Catholics. Phillpotts notorious for the zeal which he had opposed any concession to the Catholics also changed his mind and backed the Emancipation Bill. He went down to Oxford to vote for the government candidate, Sir Robert Peel, at a critical by-election.

Bishops were often appointed because of services rendered either to the Whigs or Tories, who in their turn gave promotion to those who supported their views.

In the Totnes area the 11ᵗʰ Duke of Somerset owned a considerable amount of land and had built many houses. He also had become friendly with the Reverend James Shore. In 1832 the Duke erected a church in Bridgetown designed to seat 700

---

9   Series of publications beginning in 1833 voicing several Abglican academics' unhappiness with the lack of seriousness with which the establishment regarded its religious duties. Known as Tractarian or the Oxford Movement.

10 RS Lambert p39

worshipers, but was unaware that it was necessary to obtain a licence from the Bishop of Exeter if it was to be used for Anglican worship. The Duke and Phillpotts met in August 1832 to discuss the options available. The building could be either a chapel-of-ease within the parish of Berry Pomeroy whereby the responsibility for providing services and a right of nominating a minister would belong that to the vicar of Pomeroy or it could be a chapel taken out of the parish and the Duke could acquire the patronage upon provision of a suitable endowment. The Duke was more concerned about patronage of the chapel than about its legal status and Phillpotts was determined, quite rightly, to ensure the financial stability of the chapel in the future.

Phillpotts refused to consecrate the chapel until the Duke had agreed to establish a suitable endowment. There followed acrimonious negotiations and finally Phillpotts agreed to license the building as a chapel-of-ease provided that patronage be held by the vicar of Berry Pomeroy and the Duke agreed to provide an adequate endowment as soon as possible. When the endowment was established the Duke would then have the right of appointment of a minister. Ralph Barnes, the Bishop's secretary and solicitor, drew up the agreement and the licence was granted on the 9th November 1832. John Edwards, the vicar of Berry Pomeroy, at the request of the Duke then appointed his curate, James Shore, as Minister of Bridgetown. The chapel was now open for worship.[11]

Preferment was a matter of goodwill or good connections, and politics entered into the picture as well, as Shore was later to find out.

In 1834 John Edwards died and the Duke nominated the Reverend Edward Brown as his successor with the understanding that Shore would continue at Bridgetown. Brown continued until 1843 when he exchanged a living for that of Monkton Farleigh, Wiltshire held by the tractarian William Burrough Cousens.

The Bishop discovered that in 1834 Brown had not provided the bishop's registrar with the required nomination for Shore to serve as minister at Bridgetown and it appeared that Shore had been preaching at the chapel without a valid licence. Brown insisted that he had completed the necessary paperwork when he was appointed. Phillpotts informed Shore that he could only continue at Bridgetown by acquiring a new nomination from Cousens. This provided Phillpotts with an excuse to commence his attack on Shore.

Phillpotts saw Shore as a rebel cleric. Shore had fallen foul of the Bishop in 1841 over the choice of a new incumbent of the parish of Chudleigh when he had put himself forward as one of the initial four candidates. He withdrew prior to the election but was afterwards publicly accused of publishing a handbill supporting Wilmot Palk, the evangelical candidate opposed to the Bishop. Palk was appointed and Shore was summonsed to the Bishop and criticised for his disloyalty. The Bishop had attempted to forestall the appointment of Palk in the courts, lost the case, and suffered the public humiliation of his candidate not being appointed, all, according to the Bishop, because of Shore's action.

---

11   RS Lambert p133

Cousens took up residence in Berry Pomeroy in October 1843 and having been advised by Phillpotts "*to take especial care whom you appoint as your assistant curate at Bridgetown*" had a meeting with Shore and informed him that the nomination was no longer in his hands as the Bishop had made arrangements to replace Shore as minister at Bridgetown.[12] Shore was at a loss to understand this because he had just received two separate requests from Phillpotts asking him to secure the nomination from Cousens as soon as possible.

Shore went backwards and forwards between the two parties but soon realised he was being deceived by both Cousens and Phillpotts. In his meeting with Cousens on 16th October 1843 Shore with some justification lost his temper declaring that he was being driven out of the Church, since he could not support his wife and children if he lost the £200 paid to him by the Duke. He then said that he would continue to officiate without the Bishop's licence, and that there was nothing else to do since he was being driven out of the church.[13]

The Bishop eventually told Shore that the whole difficulty really arose from the Duke's original failure to endow the chapel

Shore then received a note from the Bishop prohibiting any further services at Bridgetown. He obeyed the order and closed the chapel; it remained closed for the next five months. Shore now faced losing his income and ruin.

During this time Shore received offers of preferment elsewhere, but he felt he had to refuse such offers as insinuations were surfacing in the locality about his character. Shore then consulted the Duke of Somerset who offered to remove the chapel from the jurisdiction of the Church of England if that would allow Shore to continue as Minister.

Shore was sincerely attached to the Church of England but reluctantly agreed to secede out of concern for the spiritual welfare of his congregation especially as they were under the care of a Tractarian incumbent. In addition, Shore believed that Phillpotts would use his influence to make it difficult for Shore to secure employment elsewhere with all the attendant poverty that this would bring to himself and his family.[14]

Shore's family must have been feeling the strain and in a letter from his daughter, Julia, on the 26th January 1844 she refers to the imminent reopening of the chapel and her doubt in her faith in God.

Letter from Julia Berry Shore to her father the Reverend James Shore, Bath.

---

12   RS Lambert p135
13   RS Lambert p155
14   Grayson Carter p.363

Bridgetown.
January 26th.
1844.

My very dear Papa,
I am highly delighted at the prospect of seeing you next Friday and I hope you will return quite well. I am very glad to hear that the chapel is likely to be opened shortly. It is a very sad thing its being shut so long but I trust that the Lord will help the trial and make us value it more when it is reopened; we never value our privileges till they are taken from us. Oh how often have I been at to the House of God in anxiety as a form and become as others did but I trust if I am permitted to go again I shall be enabled by God's assistance to go in a very different frame of mind.
I trust the Lord has begun the good work in those things which I formerly liked, now I take no pleasure in and the things which I used to dislike now I take the greatest delight in, such as prayer, reading the word of God and Christian conversation. I have for some time wished to tell you my state of mind knowing that you would be very happy to give me any advice, but I have never had the courage to introduce the subject, I shall ever have cause to remember last year with thankfulness as the year in which I was brought to the knowledge of the truth.

My very dear papa,
Your sincerely attached and very affectionate daughter.
Julia Berry Shore.

Psalm 23."

Shore was in Bath at the time attending one of his many meetings around the country to put forward his case to the public.

Shore then informed Phillpotts that he would resume his preaching at Bridgetown chapel even though this meant secession from the established Church.

The Bishop warned Shore that it was impossible to continue in this manner as both Canon and civil law forbade the secession of any clergyman who had been episcopally ordained. Shore ignored this threat to prosecute him if he attempted to secede and prepared to recommence services at Bridgetown.

In February 1844 eight hundred members of the Bridgetown chapel petitioned the Duke of Wellington to reopen the chapel who was only too willing to comply, and on the 26th of that month the building was registered under the Toleration Act 1689 as a Dissenting meeting-house. The number of signatories on the petition bore witness to Shore's popularity within the community.

Shore informed Phillpotts that he now regarded himself outside the authority of the Church. Phillpotts promptly revoked Shore's licence to officiate in the diocese. Three days later Shore recited the oaths and signed the required declarations under the

Toleration Act of 1689.[15]

Shore wrote to Phillpotts asking if there were any further procedures to go through in order to lawfully secede from the Church. This request was ignored and the Bishop's secretary politely informed Shore that he could not preach anywhere without the licence of the Bishop.

On 14th April 1844 Shore reopened the chapel as the first congregation of the Free Church of England.

The canon law on which Phillpotts was relying read "*no man being admitted a deacon or minister shall from henceforth voluntarily relinquish the same, nor after - wards use himself in the course of his life as a layman upon pain of excommunication*", so once a minister always a minister (of the Church of England).[16] In the 17th century it was intended to bind the clergy for life to the church the intention being to prevent indiscriminate secessions undertaken in an attempt to escape episcopal discipline and it would help to avoid rival religious bodies within the parish.

No attempt had previously been made to enforce this canon in the 18th century. It is ironic that it was alleged that the Bishop himself was consistently breaking canon law by "*deserting his episcopal residence in the cathedral city; habitually altering the wording of services to suit his fancy; persistently bestowing his patronage upon his relations; and repeatedly usurping patronage rights belonging to others*".

As a result of Shore's continued preaching without a licence at Bridgetown chapel charges were instituted against him in the ecclesiastical courts at the instigation of the Bishop.

Shore considered ignoring the summons but believed he might be committed for contempt of court and therefore appeared before the commission at the Seven Stars, Totnes arguing that he was now a Dissenter and exempt from the jurisdiction of the church.[17]

The commission rejected his claim and he then appealed to the Court of Arches. The Court dismissed Shore's claim stating that "*both the spirit of the canons and common sense opposed the notion that a clergyman could voluntary renounce his orders*".

---

15 Grayson Carter p364
16 Grayson Carter p365
17 Grayson Carter p366

Chapter 2

SHORE'S IMPRISONMENT

Shore's harsh treatment had given him the support of many non-conformists and several Anglican clergymen who went about the country speaking on his behalf and a fund was raised to help him. At the same time other places in the Exeter diocese were seeing the effects of the growing ritualistic movement and on Good Friday 1844 the parishioners of Ilfracombe were dismayed to see the interior of their church draped in black, considered a sure sign of Romanism. Changes to the normal Protestant services and the use of new rites and ceremonies caused great anger. A local gentleman built a church and Protestant liturgical services were provided for those who felt endangered by the growing encroachment of Romanism. On hearing of the events in Bridgetown the congregation at Ilfracombe threw in their lot with the Free Church of England and in December 1844 Shore formally opened the building as a Free Church of England chapel, and he continued to preach for the week until Christmas.[18]

In due course Shore appealed to the Court of Queen's Bench, which on 11th November 1845 granted a rule nisi for prohibition. The case was referred back to the Court of Arches who exempted Shore from seceding from the Church of England but charged him with, "*publicly preaching prayers, according to the form prescribed by the Book of Common Prayer and of preaching in an unconsecrated chapel without a licence.*"

Shore was then admonished to refrain from such ecclesiastical offences in the future, which not only was in breach of the rules of the diocesan but would also now violate those of the court; in addition there came the reminder that he was still a clergyman, "*from which office he cannot of his own authority relieve himself.*"[19]

The proceedings were reported in full in *The Times*.

Three days after the ruling Lord Brougham introduced a petition on Shore's behalf in the House of Lords stating that the law was unfair in constraining a man who had once taken upon himself the Orders of the Church of England to remain for ever a minister of that church. It was particularly hard since the Bishop of his diocese had set his stamp on him and marked him down as a man unworthy to minister in the church, had revoked his licence, thus brought him and his family face to face with starvation.

Phillpotts dismissed the action by denying any wrongdoing and dismissed Shore as a disobedient malcontent of little significance. He blamed the ailing Duke of Somerset

---

18 www.bible-christian-heritage.co.uk/jameshaw.htm
19 Grayson Carter p367

for failing to keep his promise to endow the chapel.

The Duke's son quickly leapt to the defence of his father claiming in the House of Lords that the statement by Phillpotts was a deliberate falsehood; he continued *"there was no such engagement. The Duke never did agree to endow the chapel, and the licence was not granted upon the Bishop's receiving any such assurance… The Bishop has not only made a charge diametrically contrary to the truth, but he has made a malicious charge, for the purpose of giving a false imputation to the individual in question. Why has this Bishop, from first to last, agitated this whole country on religious passions? If I look to the addresses and charges of other Bishops, what do I see? I see them entreating more men calmly and carefully to make allowance for other's feelings on religious questions, to exercise mutual forbearance. When I see one man alone blundering on and disturbing the church, I have to say it is a most unfortunate visitation for this county, that he should be its Bishop. I shall now leave him to the ignominy he deserves. It is not I alone that show he has made this gross perversion of the truth; it is in his own secretary's letter."*[20]

Dangerous words to use if said outside the privileged arena of the House of Lords. These words did not escape the notice of Thomas Latimer, the editor of *The Western Times*, based in Exeter, who had been a long time opponent of clericalism. His biography shows the struggle between himself, the radical editor and the militant High Church Bishop culminating in a libel suit in 1848 when the first successful plea of justification[21] by a defendant was allowed. It was a contest between two rival methods of propaganda, pulpit and press. Latimer pleaded the cause of the curate, the yeoman, the farm labourer and the*"underdog"*. He championed the cause of the freedom of the Press

Phillpotts' unpopularity was growing apace not only amongst his own clergy but also amongst Conservative laymen.

He had established himself in a *"marine villa"* near Torquay and his continual absence from Exeter was resented.

Latimer had pursued Phillpotts with determination and saw the statement in the Lords by the Duke's son concerning Shore as an opportunity to ridicule Tory and high church intolerance.

Latimer, in his role of defender of the working clergy against the oppression of their ecclesiastical superiors, had followed Shore's case from its earliest beginnings, his indignation gradually increased as he saw the poor curate being harried from pillar to post by the Bishop and the courts. He had already published editorials in Shore's favour, and supported the fund, which was being raised for him. Towards the end of 1845, however, there had been a lull in his criticisms of the Bishop. For Latimer himself had secured election to Exeter Town Council as representative of St Petrock's ward and was busy with his new duties there; furthermore, the Bishop had lost one of his sons, Lieutenant Phillpotts, killed fighting the Maoris in New Zealand. So for some

---

20 RS Lambert p138

21 i.e. that the matter published was true and that it was for the public benefit that the matter should have been published in the manner and at the time it was published

months *The Western Times* left Phillpotts alone, until in May 1846 the Lord Chief Justice decided against Shore's appeal and his fate was sealed. Almost immediately on top of this came the attack on the Duke of Somerset.

At this stage a public campaign to protest against Shore's prosecution was made to encourage Parliament to enact relief for seceding clergyman.[22]

On 13th April 1848 five thousand of Shore's supporters held the first of several rallies at Exeter Hall London and other gatherings were held in large cities in England and Scotland. One of the speakers in London declared that "*by God's help, there should be a church in which Bishops should not be able to play such pranks*".

A meeting was held at the Public Room, Broadmead, Bristol at which there were three thousand persons present.

Shore's case continued unabated. His appeal to the Judicial Committee of the Privy Council heard on the 24th August 1848 was rejected and three documents were issued: a prohibition against officiating or preaching within the province of Canterbury, a writ to pay the Bishop's costs in the Court of Arches and the Privy Council.[23] Sir John Dodson in his judgment declared that a priest, although a seceder from the church, may be committed to prison for contempt of court for preaching as a dissenting minister.

Naturally, Shore was disappointed by the Privy Council's ruling. He had hoped that the publicity would have persuaded the Council to overturn the ruling of the Court of Arches.

In early 1849 a warrant was issued for his arrest on the grounds of failing to pay £186.14s 2d being the Bishop's costs in the Privy Council.

Serving Shore with a warrant for his arrest in Bridgetown was out of the question, as this would inevitably have led to a violent confrontation between the officers of the court and Shore's supporters. Shore continued to preach wherever he was called by God and in early March tested this assertion by accepting an invitation to preach at the Countess of Huntingdon's chapel at Spa Fields in London.

The ecclesiastical authorities intended to arrest Shore in the act of preaching at Spa Fields and on 9th March 1849 two officers of the Court of Arches quickly slipped into the back of the chapel, and, in one of the more dramatic religious confrontations of modern times, waited until Shore had finished his sermon and had begun to descend from the pulpit, then arrested Shore amongst the shocked and protesting congregation and transported him to Exeter jail.[24]

Shore then wrote a letter to the Reverend T E Thoresby, Minister of Spa Fields, "*I am at last to be incarcerated for contempt of court they say, for non-payment of the Bishop's costs – but really and virtually for preaching the gospel outside the established Church. Indeed I have not the means of paying the costs, and even if I were able to do so I should still be under contempt of court for preaching the gospel, and*

---

22   R.S. Lambert p.136
23   Culling Eardley *An Appeal to the Country on behalf of Revd. Shore* 2nd ed. Torquay 1849 pp 26&27
24   Grayson Carter p373

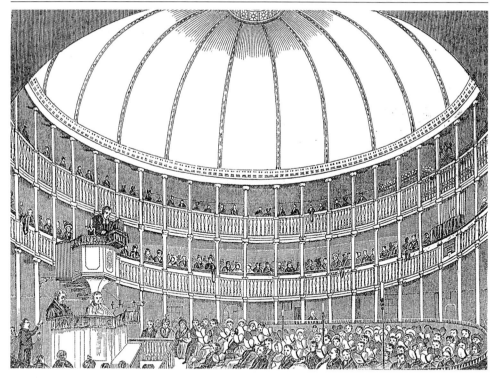

Spa Fields Chapel

therefore will still be kept in prison."[25]

Thoresby rushed off to place an announcement in the next edition of *The Times*. Phillpotts was greatly annoyed by this public rebuke and subsequent sensation, and ordered Barnes to issue a statement denying Shore's allegation and assuring the public that the reason for the arrest was merely Shore's refusal to pay outstanding court costs.

To the public, Shore had seceded as a matter of conscience, and Phillpotts had concocted a series of legal obstacles in an attempt to prevent this from occurring. The officers of the court had invaded the sanction of a non-conformist chapel to arrest and imprison Shore for nothing more than preaching the gospel, in addition, even if Shore paid the costs, he would still be subject to continued arrest and the imprisonment for preaching without a licence.

From his Exeter jail Shore defended himself against the allegations by publishing a strong attack on Phillpotts and upon the discrepancies within the explanation. Shore claimed that Phillpotts had withheld many of his most important letters.

The Illustrated London News of 7th April 1849 produced a drawing of Shore in prison attended by his followers.

The drawing shows Shore's wife and daughters visiting him in prison as well as the

---

25 Vaughan *History of the Free Church of England* 1960 p33

Deputation to James Shore in St. Thomas's jail, Exeter
Bath Library

other dignitaries. It cannot have been easy for the family with the publicity and the strain which it must have put on Shore.

It was reported in *The Times* that some of the Reverend Shore's sympathisers went so far as to take their children to him for baptisms, which he actually administered in the jail.

Punch published a cartoon of Phillpotts under the heading "*Church Mouse*" with a poem as follows:

The Church Mouse's Petition (after Sir Joshua Reynold's "Musicipula")

> *Oh! Here a Reverend captive's prayer*
> *Indurance vile that lies,*
> *Nor let a Bishop's heart be shut*
> *Against a Debtor's cries.*
>
> *Fly here, my Lord, immured I sit,*
> *Behind this prison grate,*
> *Cast at thy suit in costs, whose sum*
> *Exceeds my small estate.*

Cartoon from Punch – the Church Mouse

If e'er thy breast has horror felt
Of bigot's stake or chain,
Let not thy prosecuting ire
Seceding SHORE detain.

Oh! Do not yet more deeply stain
Thy somewhat dingy lawn,
Nor triumph that so poor a prize
Within toils is drawn.

The free donations of my flock
My scanty means supply,
And why should thine intolerant heart
My pulpit's use deny?

The cushioned desk and sounding board
Were made for all and each;
Let every clergyman enjoy
The common right to preach.

The well-taught theologian's mind
Man's conscience will respect;
Regard all creeds with liberal eye,
And hope for every sect.

Should e'er the times, as some forbode
Of faggot and of flame
Return, and Smithfield, as of yore,
Its mitred victims claim;

Beware, my Bishop, lest in turn,
Thou feel the zealot's rage:
And, being roasted, call to mind
SHORE in his dungeon-cage!

Or, though thou to the martyrs fate
May'st not be doom'd to share,
For once let Pity bid thy heart
A prostrate victim spare.

So, in thine ever stormy See,
May peace at length be found;
And harmony and concord well
Where strife and wrath abound.

So may'st there never go to law,
Thyself the cost to bear;
Thus in thine own hot water boiled,
And caught in thine own snare.

The Bishop's costs payable by James Shore
Christian Times

Whilst in jail Shore's health began to deteriorate and his friends and supporters felt pressure to pay his costs and secure his release. The sum was gathered and delivered to the court on 23rd May but Phillpotts then insisted Shore pay a further sum of £124.10s. for additional costs which was paid under protest by the committee in London which had been formed for this purpose.

A week later Shore was released.

Shore then returned to his ministry in Bridgetown declaring, *"I shall occupy the same ground and preach the gospel as I did before and if the Bishop feels it to be his conscientious duty to carry out the laws of his church, I shall, of course, be soon committed to prison again. I hope I shall be able to preach to my congregation... next Sunday."*

This he did and remained there unmolested by either the ecclesiastical courts or Bishop Phillpotts for some years. He also continued to appear at public meetings up and down the country bemoaning his ill treatment and gradually gave up this activity to preach full time at Bridgetown.

On March 30th 1851 the religious census reveals that the morning service had 320 attendees and 422 at the evening service. He was obviously a popular preacher had the support of the majority of his parishioners.

There was much debate in the ecclesiastical press over the Shore affair, on the one hand *The English Churchman* condemned Shore as a deserter and traitor to the establishment cause and went on to admit that the main reason behind Phillpotts' prosecution of Shore was his opposition to an evangelical clergyman at Bridgetown; on the other hand *The Christian Times* stated that the Bishop's enmity towards the evangelical clergy lay at the foundation of all the cruel and unmanly proceedings against Shore.

Phillpotts' conduct of the affair would appear to have been strictly correct but his known views and severity attracted widespread interest in the case, some would say exceeding its merits, except to emphasise the Bishop's continuing unpopularity.[26] It is doubtful, however laudable his intentions were, that the means Phillpotts implied to achieve his ends were not the best. Each encounter left his opponents except Latimer, defeated and resentful. Though it may have been necessary to resort to legal action to enforce discipline at that time, yet Phillpotts so often appears as delighting in vindictive pursuit of small fry, with cunning ferocity and ruthlessness.

Shore's case at least might have been settled without such harmful publicity, had Phillpotts called for a little goodwill between Cousens and his colleagues. But he seemed not to care what was man's opinion of him so long as he was technically correct in his procedure.

In the meantime Phillpotts continued his old litigious ways and died in 1869 at the age of 91.

Henry Phillpotts – in old age
Daily Telegraph

In his obituary in *The Times* of 20th September 1869 it was stated "*whilst at Stanhope he had become active both as a clergyman and county magistrate, preach - ing on Sundays the duty of submission to "the powers that be", and enforcing and illustrating his teaching by the committal of poachers and other offenders on weekdays. One of the Bishop's clergy stated that "his aptitude for this kind of business was very remarkable; that he seemed possessed by intuition of that which to others was a matter of laborious study", and that the magistrate's clerk used to aver that "Mr. Phillpotts could always tell what was in an Act of Parliament before he read it, and even before it came out". He published*

---

26 GCB Davies *Henry Phillpotts* SPCK 1954 p226

many pamphlets, political, religious and controversial. The Edinburgh Review stated that he lived in perpetual hot water, and lived to be far more feared than loved even by those whose cause he espoused."

Phillpotts has been described as "*brilliant, scathing and cordially detested*", "*pugnacious and unpopular", "lacking in those characteristics which the world expects from a clergyman in high office – tolerance, loving kindness and common politeness," "it is not possible to study his career or to read his charges without gaining a rueful affection for this elephant trampling so conscientiously amid the porcelain... but if his ability and integrity and force of character are confessed, it is impossible to credit him with prudence or delicacy, impossible not to feel that his nomination to the bench was unwittingly the hardest knock to the English churches ever struck by a Tory minister of the Crown.*" Litigation was his great hobby and one of his sons said he must have spent between £20,000 and £30,000 on this activity.[27]

The diversity of opinion on Henry of Exeter reflects the complexity of his character.

The Shore saga, combined with the surplice riots in Exeter, led to many Free churches being formed and in 1863 the formal constitution of the Free Church of England was registered in the High Court of Chancery. The church still exists and it has 27 churches throughout the United Kingdom.

---

27 Exeter *Flying Post* 12th February 1963

CHAPTER 3

TOTNES – THE LATER YEARS

In 1852 Emily, Shore's eldest daughter, married John Bulteel whose father, H B Bulteel, was the former high Calvinist curate of St. Ebbe's, Oxford. He was a friend and supporter of Shore, who had also seceded from the Church of England.He was a happy-go-lucky character, a cheerful extrovert who in his early years as an undergraduate started a Town and Gown riot[28] during the disturbances over the treatment of Queen Caroline. He had a well-earned reputation as a *"rather wild young man"*[29]

H. Bulteel

In 1823 he was appointed to a fellowship of Exeter College. He became a priest in 1825 and, in 1826, Curate-in-charge of St. Ebbe's where he was a popular preacher of conventional Evangelical doctrines.

During this time he married Eleanor Sadler, known as *"the pastry Cook's daughter"*. Dons were not allowed to marry so he abandoned his academic career and in those class-conscious days this was much frowned upon.[30]

In February 1831 he was due to preach the University Sermon and word got around that he would not mince his words. His criticism of the church infuriated the Bishop and the dons, whom he accused of being willing to give false testimonials for unsuitable candidates for Holy Orders, accused the bishops of being chosen by ministers of the Crown, politicians who might not be Anglicans and spoke in favour of disestablishment being the only way of putting matters right.[31]

In the summer of that year Bulteel went on an evangelical tour of the West Country

---

28 The relationship between Oxford University and the city of Oxford has history spotted with outbreaks of rioting and violence.
29 Grayson Carter p.253.
30 Vivien Allen *The Bulteels: the S tory of a Huguenot Family* Phillimore 2003 p.180
31 *The Oxford Dictionary of National Biography* HB Bulteel, Timothy LF Stute

propounding increasingly anti-clerical ideas. He called on all evangelists to secede en-mass from the established Church and affiliate with the Free Church of England. He went on, "*the high handed Bishop of Exeter, Phillpotts, has deprived more clergyman of their licences than perhaps all other bishops combined and was the living embodi - ment of everything incurably wrong with the Church of England.*"

Naturally, in displaying his views so forcibly, the Bishop of Oxford, Bishop Bagot, had previously withdrawn his licence.

The ex-don also became a thorn in the side of the Anglican establishment and supported Shore in his fight with Phillpotts, even publishing a poem entitled "*Old Tamar's Remonstrances or Protestant Rymes for Anglican Times, a ballad by Once A Priest*". In a short preface, he wrote that "*the Bishop of Exeter, had succeeded in bringing to the jail of St Thomas the Reverend James Shore, for the costs incurred by the bishop in prosecuting him in the ecclesiastical courts, after he had retired from the established Church and made the declarations of a dissenting minister… Had not the author been fully persuaded for a long course of years that the people of God are all priests, one as much as another, and that all other priesthood on earth, whether in Rome or England, is a wicked imposture: and were it not that the present times afford a melancholy proof of the power of priestly delusion, these lines most probably had not been written; but when error and guile are being so abundantly employed in high places, to deceive, enslave and ruin the souls of the simple, he deems no apology necessary for delivering his protest against them.*"

Bulteel's son, John, was born on the 13th September 1830. He was a complete con-trast to his father; a civil servant for 45 years, he was well thought of by his superiors. He disagreed with his father's religious ideas returning instead to the Church of England.[32]

John and Emily moved to Windsor where they had one son, Henry James. Shore's other daughter, Isabella, married Thomas Lomas, a second clerk in the Admiralty, in June 1858 Henry Bulteel officiating at the ceremony.

Thomas was born in Rochester, Kent and had two brothers, William and John. He and John were educated at Bexley Hall Place School in Kent. Dickens is said to have

Hall Place Park – School of Thomas Lomas 1841

---

32 Vivien Allen p.82

taken it as his inspiration for Scrooge's school in "*A Christmas Carol*"!

During Thomas' time at the Admiralty he received a letter from the Admiralty thanking him for his services during the Chartist demonstration in London. The authorities had feared that there might have been violence and all the main buildings in Whitehall were heavily protected. At Somerset House a portcullis had been built; the roof of the Bank of England was parapetted with sand bags, and guns mounted through the apertures; all the prisons in the central London area were reinforced with additional arms and soldiers. 1848 was the year of revolution throughout Europe, the government was therefore right to take precautions although the Chartist movement lost its momentum soon afterwards.

Thomas also attended the Duke of Wellington's funeral.

Thomas Lomas 1840's

Invitation to the Duke of Wellington's Funeral

*Letter to Thomas from the Admiralty
11th April 1848*

In 1858 Thomas and Isabella also moved to Windsor and their only son, Herbert Reginald Pomeroy Lomas (HRP), was born on 13th April 1859. One year later Isabella died of tuberculoses in Windsor on 15th April 1860 aged 22.

Henry Bulteel wrote a letter of condolence to his friend James Shore and arranged to preach the sermon at Isabella's funeral.

"Letter from H.B. Bulteel to Revd. James Shore on death of Isabella

Crescent,
Monday April 16 1860

My Dear Friends,

I thank the great God, and most kind and merciful Father, that the painful struggle has closed at last, and ended in a glorious victory – earlier in the morning than his son arose when he triumphed over death he has given your dear Isabel to triumph through the power of his Resurrection, and has drawn her up to pass a never ending Lord's Day with himself in heaven.

I felt very well assured that if he did not restore her to bodily health he would not suffer her to depart without showing her none of himself and his salvation than that she had as yet seen, and now my wish and prayer with regard to her in case recovery was not to take place has been granted – and I cannot but bless the Lord, and feel grateful to him for what he has done.

But how with regard to yourselves? I have not been a witness to the sufferings, as you have. I have not watched over the day and night like you – I have not had my heart rung by seeing her agonies, without the possibility of rehearsing them in the least – these are the things which in addition to the closeness of the parental tie chase the poor sufferor so near that it is like parting with your own Isabel when she is recovered – all this has fallen to you both – deep is the wound you have received, and long perhaps you may continue to feel it – but there is the healing hand – the deep mercy, the long suffering love, the enduring loving kindness, and the unchanging faithfulness of him with whom you have to do, and who had and will have to do with you.

I feel I can only commit you into his hands entreating him to uphold you in your trial, and though it be a fiery one, you may feel that by it you have only lost your bonds, and that your sad walk is at liberty.

According to the desire intimated in John's letter this morning I shall, if the Lord wish, go to Totnes on Friday, and stay there till the Sunday is over, and preach for you on that day, as I so soon expect to see you I will add no more at present but send united love to you and sympathy with you and remain.

Affectionately Yours,
H. B. Bulteel."

Isabella's death must have left Thomas devastated and he and the young HRP returned to live with Shore and his wife.

On the 13ᵗʰ August1862 Thomas married Isabella's sister and Shore's youngest daughter, Julia.

Both canon and civil law as it stood prohibited the marriage of a deceased spouse's sister so they were married in Neufchatel, Switzerland. However, it was a fairly common practice for the deceased's sister to marry the spouse if there were young children of the first marriage as this was invariably the best thing for the children. The Deceased Wife's Sister's Bill, as it was known, caused much distress in the early 19ᵗʰ century. It was only in 1907 that the Act was passed. E M Forster commented *"some feared the Bill would break up the home by transforming beneficent aunts into hostile and partial stepmothers"*. Ironically, Phillpotts had been a vigorous opponent of the Bill calling it the *"Incestuous Marriages Bill."*!

Marriage certificate of Thomas Lomas and Julia Berry Shore

No.157. Neuchatel, Switzerland
In the year 1862 on 13ᵗʰ August at half-past nine in the morning before us Louis Barbier, officer of the civil state of Neuchatel are convened:

Thomas Lomas, Esquire, originally from Rochester in the county of Kent, England, living in Neuchatel, born on 21ˢᵗ December 1824 at St Margaret of full age, son of the late William Lomas, Esquire, living at his home in Edmonton in the County of Middlesex, England and of Matilda nee Baker, his spouse proved to us the death of Susanna Pomeroy, nee Shore, who died on 15ᵗʰ April 1860 shown in a death certificate obtained at Windsor in the County of Berkshire dated the 17ᵗʰ April in the same a year, of the one part;
Julia Berry Shore, without profession, originally from Berry Pomeroy, and the county of Devon (England), living in Neuchatel born on 25ᵗʰ May 1828 at Berry Pomeroy, of full age, daughter of the Reverend James Shore MA, minister of the chapel at Bridgetown, Berry Pomeroy married to Susannah nee Gream, his spouse, of the other part,
Which we have been requested previously to officiate the celebration of the marriage in consequence of the publication required by law, publication which without objection would stop the authorisation of the contract of marriage, in the Republic of Neuchatel in the year 1860 in accordance with the chapter of the law, the acts, rules and rights respectively of the spouses; we have after - wards asked the future spouses if they wish to become husband and wife and each of them have replied previously and affirmed; we have declared in the name of the law that Thomas Lomas and Julia Berry Shore be married. The several pages of this document are to be deposited in the archives under number 157 and registered in London. Signed in the town hall of Neuchatel in the presence of John Lomas, aged 36 years, brother in law and Charles Turnell,

Professor, aged 62, witnesses at Neuchatel witnesses to the document signed by us after having it read to us.

Thomas Lomas   Mr. Lomas

Julia Berry Shore   Chares Turnell

L Barbier

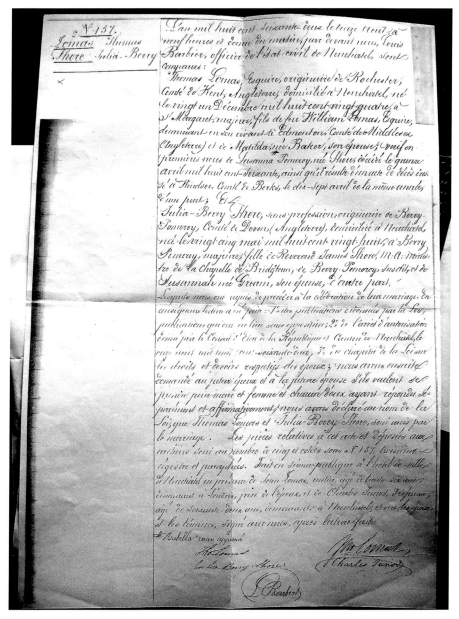

Swiss marriage certificate of Thomas and Julia Lomas 1862
Neuchatel Local Records

At this time Totnes was being fractured by conflict and discord but Shore stayed at Bridgetown until the middle of 1862 and formally resigned in April 1869, the duties at the chapel between 1862 and 1869 being carried out by his deputies. *The Totnes Times* of 16th April 1869 stated "*The Church of England prayers have from the commencement been regularly used, and the change therefore will not be so striking – it will merely be from a Free Church, using the Church of England services, but not under the control the bishop, to a Chapel of Ease under Berry. Any clergyman of the neighbouring parishes, however, or clergyman from any part of the kingdom, will now be able to take part in the services, and a future Bishop of Exeter may even preach from the pulpit at Bridgetown chapel!*" The chapel was finally consecrated as an Anglican chapel of ease in 1888.

The furore over the Shore affair was immense but short-lived in that once he was released from prison it died down just as quickly as it had arisen and one might have assumed that he would have continued to live the rest of his life in Bridgetown in obscurity, but this was not to be the case.

CHAPTER 4

DERBYSHIRE BECKONS

Shore's health had suffered greatly from the stress caused by his brush with Phillpotts and in particular his arthritis caused him a good deal of pain. His children were aware of his state of health and urged him to take a break from the Chapel.

Letter from Emily F. Bulteel to her father the Reverend James Shore, Totnes

Gascoigne Terrace
July 30ᵗʰ/52

My very dear Papa,
I most sincerely do wish you many many happy returns of your birthday, and hope that you may be restored to better health. I trust you will like the whip which we have had such great pleasure in getting for you.
I do hope you will be able to get someone to take the service at the chapel so that you may be able to go with Mr Bulteel. I think it would do you so much good. I feel sure you require rest and change. With best love, again wishing you many happy returns of the day, in which John most cordially unites, I remain
My very dear Papa
Your most affectionate daughter
Emily F. Bulteel

Letter from Julia Berry Shore to her father the Reverend James Shore, Totnes

10 Gascoigne Terrace,
July 30ᵗʰ/52

My dearest Papa,
Although far from home, I cannot allow your birthday to pass without wishing you many happy returns of the day; may every blessing, spiritual and temporal, attend you, and may you long been spared to your attached children.
Isabel will give you a small token of our love, which I hope you will like, and find useful.
Mr. Bulteel is thinking of going abroad for a week or two and wishes you to accompany him, pray do so if you can in any way get a supply for the chapel, I think it would do you a great deal of good, you require a change of air and scene, and rest.
With best love, believe me,

My dearest Papa,
Your very affectionate daughter
Julia."

Shore may have become disillusioned with the Church and, from seeds sown in childhood, appeared to find a new direction in his life. His father, Thomas, was a corn merchant in Dorset and in 1814 he purchased Nottington Mill, near Weymouth. James would have been 9 at the time and grew up there with his 7 brothers.

Over a number of years Thomas acquired several fields, extending to the damp pastures and willow beds of the valley floor, including the site where there was a sulphurous spring. As was often the case with millers, Thomas became involved in lengthy litigation over water rights which was well documented in the local press.

Nottington's sulphurous spring was known about as far back as 1719 when local farmers found their sheep, cattle and dogs were cured of scab and mange. Local people also drank the water which was said to cure various ailments. A stone wall was later built around the spring to prevent the cattle treading there. In the 1770s and 80s there was an upsurge in sea water and mineral water treatment. Weymouth was becoming a fashionable resort and George 3rd stopped at the well to drink the water on several occasions.[33]

Shore prospered both as a farmer and miller and by 1829 was in a position to develop the spa. The proposed octagonal building was to contain hot baths, a pump room and suitable accommodation for those invalids who preferred using the mineral-water at the fountain head. He had the spring analysed by Alexander Barry, Professor of Chemistry and Natural Philosophy of Guys Hospital.

In the meantime James Shore's chronic rheumatism grew worse and as The Reverend Thomas Binney, one of Shore's supporters who visited him in prison (see drawing in *The Illustrated London News*), had attended Smedley's Hydro in Matlock in early1862 as a patient, it may have been his recommendation to seek a cure that prompted his visit to Matlock, now accessible by rail.

In Europe the application of water in the treatment of fevers and other maladies had, since the 17th century been promoted by a number of medical writers. In the 18th century taking the waters became a fashionable pastime for the wealthy classes who toured the resorts around Britain and Europe to cure the ills of over-consumption. In the main treatment consisted of promenading, baths and the repetitive quaffing of foul tasting mineral-water.[34]

Many believed that the powers of medicinal well waters had to be taken "*in situ*", the owners of the wells encouraging such a belief. However, at the end of the 19th century almost all surviving Spas boasted they could provide waters of the mineral composition of most, if not all, the major Spas of England and the Continent.[35]

---

33 DMH Reeby *Weymouth's Spas Nottington and Radpole* 1994 p.23
34 James Bradley Marguerite Dupee, and Alastair Durie *Taking the Water Cure: The Hydropathic movement in Scotland 1840 to 1940* Business and Economic History volume 26 No.2 Wellcome Trust 1997
35 Peter J Neville Havins *The Spas of England* Hale and company 1976

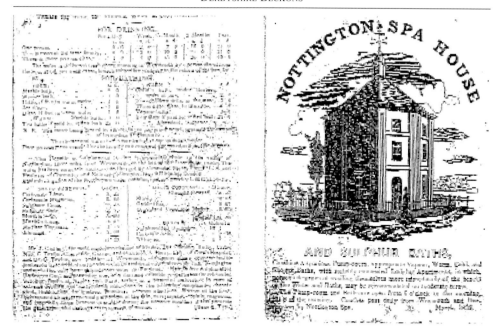

Brochure for Nottington Spa

Spas were not Hydropathic centres in the 19th century. Hydropathy in the 1820s was an entire medical system based exclusively on the internal and external application of water. The creator of hydropathy was Vincent Priessnitz based at Graffenburg in the Silesian Alps Austria who experimented with different methods, firstly upon local livestock and then his willing neighbours. He discovered a new formula of a cure centre grafted on to a hotel.

In an age when medical practice was dominated by the use of entic and astringent drugs, combined with bleeding and leaching – hydropathy's appeal was based on the spiritual and physical properties of water, and the benefits of healthy air and plain diet.

People flocked to Graffenburg from all over Europe amongst whom was Captain Claridge who published an account of his visit in 1842 and lectured throughout England.

Members of the public and a few medical practitioners were enthusiastic but the bulk of the emergent medical profession were less so. Many vocal critics linked hydropathy with other forms of medical quackery – homeopathy, mesmerism (hypnosis), phrenology (study of the shape of the human skull in order to draw conclusions about particular character traits and mental faculties) professional self-advertisement, and the sale of patent medicines.[36]

The Lancet professed to be at war not with water but with quackery. Apothecaries and pharmacists resented hydropathy for the same reason they reviled homeopathy;

---

36 Bradley p.427

namely that it set out to discredit the use of drugs and encouraged people to think that they could get well without putting that hands in their pockets. In the 1840s several well-known people died in the hands of hydropathics and prosecutions were instigated. In addition the water doctors themselves contributed strongly to their own disrepute by consistently exagerating their claims to cure grave diseases which were seen to be untrue.[37]

In 1842 doctors James Wilson and James Gully established institutions treating both resident patients and outpatients at their Hydros in Malvern. They were the first to put hydropathy on a thorough footing. They were firmly entrenched as its leading practitioners, but many less dedicated men moved into set up practice and trade on their reputation. They set up gimmicks to attract clients as for example, "*medical mesmerist and magneto electician*". Hydropathy was then run by men who had to be both hydropathics and businessman, hence the conflict and the proliferation of new-fangled "*treatments*" to attract clients. Gully and Wilson could afford to be high-minded in the treatment of their patients and from the start had imposed strict discipline on their patients. People such as Wordsworth, Darwin, Florence Nightingale and Dickens were patients and had enough self discipline of their own to accept that asked of them by the hydropaths.

The patients of mid-Victorian England were largely members of the new bourgeoisie, flooding to the Hydros partly because it was the fashionable thing to do and partly to be cured as quickly as possible at least inconvenience to themselves. Many were disappointed that the cure had not lived up to their expectations. After attending one of the newer Hydros they had been surprised to discover that after a round of heavy meals, heavy-drinking, tempered only a little by the occasional hot bath and the casual game of billiards, they had not experienced any great improvements to their health. The true hydropathic cure took time and whereas the earlier patients had been prepared to spend up to two or three months at a Hydro, then most likely, to go on to another, maybe on the Continent, the whole process being in the nature of a "*sabbatical year*" really only to be indulged in by the wealthy.[38]

Adverse medical opinion and a disappointed public combined to bring the whole practice of hydropathy into disrepute.

Some of the older establishments retained their curative thrust, but for an increasing number the title "*Hydro*" merely implied that they aimed to be respectable, comfortable and a cut above the general run of hotels.

However, by the end of this period the Hydros were servicing medicine and tourism. The baths, douches, packings and poultices were a small part of a larger package selling rest, recuperation, sociability and the allure of country surroundings. They had become a hybrid. Over this period fewer and fewer guests came as patients, more for a holiday and a tonic. Gradually the resident physician's post became less central to hydropathic operations and gave way to one who visited on a daily basis.

---

37 E S Turner *Taking The Cure* 1967 p.193
38 Havins p.140

More and more attention was made to the provision of both indoor and outdoor activities, such as tennis courts, croquet lawns or golf courses and entertainments including billiards, charades, and tableaux vivants.[39] Full time lady entertainers were employed and their enthusiasm and skill was of much importance to the guests.[40]

By the late 19th century the typical Hydro had developed into a more substantial undertaking treating thousands of patients annually for a week at a time in a large purpose-built building with lavish facilities under the supervision of fully trained and qualified medical practitioners and staff. At the peak of the movement there were over 50 Hydropathic hotels in Britain, of which the best known was Smedleys at Matlock in Derbyshire and Ben Rhydding near Leeds which was opened by Dr Macleod in 1843.[41]

By this time Hydros had become much more relaxed places to stay. At one time there was an assumption that Hydros were temperance institutions and that a basic tenet of hydropathy was that the consumption of alcohol was unhealthy. Some Hydros remained adamant on the principle of abstinence but the reality was that a blind eye was turned, even where the prohibition was total, bottles being smuggled in, or refuelling at licensed premises in the locality. The Hydros generally remained temperance and they were at the opposite end of the cultural spectrum from the "*g a y*" continental spa hotels: the province of non-conformist clergy, missionaries on furlough, maiden aunts and sober professional people.[42]

Despite the increasing emphasis on leisure the Hydros remained to a greater or lesser degree committed to providing hydropathy. Changes occurred in medical theory and practice which allowed an increased emphasis on both climatic location and leisure facilities, and new hydrotherapeutic techniques. No longer was hydropathy a "*cure all*" but became one part of the orthodox therapeutic regime, geared particularly to rest, and the cure of gout and rheumatism. In the late 19th century hydropathy combined the emphasis of rest, fresh air and a plain and healthy diet with the newly emerging medical technology of the rotgen rays, ultraviolet light and electrotherapeutic and galvanic treatments.

Into this world Shore found himself as a patient in 1862 where he received great benefit and relief from the treatment. So much so that he moved up to Matlock permanently with his wife, firstly assisting Smedley and then running his own Hydro at Matlock House until about 1865. Here and at Smedley's he "*qualified*" himself in the art of hydropathy. He had already learnt a considerable amount about homeopathy and the two branches of alternative medicine suited Shore perfectly. His experience in spiritual matters helped to make him a suitable candidate for running a hydropathic establishment.

Smedley actively encouraged people who worked for him to set up in the

---

39 Living Pictures – group of silent motionless persons in imitation of well known works of art or dramatic scenes from history or literature.
40 Bradley p. 431
41 Bradley p.432
42 Alastair J Durie *The Business of Hydropathy in the North of England 1850 to 1930* University of Leeds p.39

hydropathy business on their own.

Feeling perhaps that there were greater opportunities elsewhere, Shore moved to Buxton in 1865. The first railways arrived in Buxton on the Midland line in 1863 and the town was looking forward to increasing prosperity and to becoming one of the most popular places as a holiday resort in the country. The coming of the railways ceased the decline of Buxton in the early 19th Century resulting in a great increase in population and building. Access was now much easier for the new middle classes, whereas previously coaches had brought in scores, hundreds arrived by train.

From 1850 Buxton had begun to grow from a village to a busy and fashionable spa, although criticism had been made by observers of the shortage of good, comfortable accommodation.

Initially, hydropathy was not recognised as a significant medical facility in the town because members of the medical profession placed such great faith in the medical efficacy of the Buxton mineral water and natural gases.

However, in about 1866 James Shore laid the foundations of the soon to become famous Malvern House Hydropathic and Homeopathic establishment in Hartington Street, Buxton. The first building provided accommodation for 40 patients.[43]

Being a shrewd man of business and a close thinker Shore entered into the Buxton enterprise with zeal.[44]

Malvern House 1866

---

43 Trevor Marchington *The Development of Buxton and Matlock since 1800* unpublished theses.
44 Buckley *Modern Buxton* 1886.

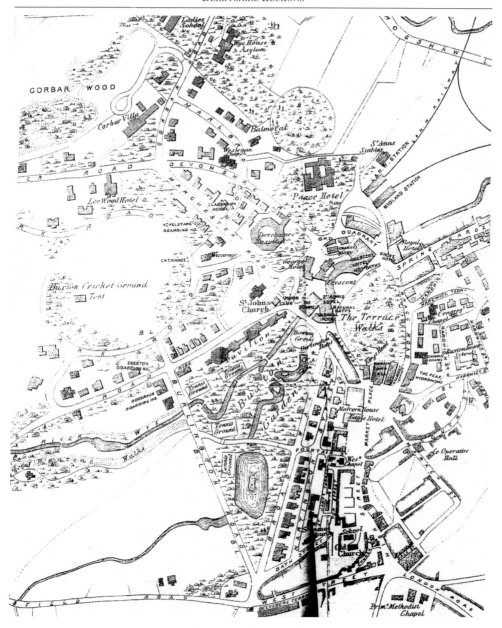

Map of Buxton 1860's
Buckley's *Modern Buxton*

Royal Hotel 1860s
Courtesy of Buxton Museum and www.picturethepast.org.uk

This was one of the first hydropathic establishments in Buxton and so successful was it that Shore took a lease of the Royal Hotel in Spring Gardens (built in 1849) as a hydropathic to be run in conjunction with Malvern House. He also purchased Street House farm 6 miles south of Buxton to supply Malvern House and the Royal with fresh vegetables and farm produce.[45]

On 14th July 1868 Shore's wife Susannah died. It is interesting to note that the death certificate shows her being the wife of James Shore, "*independent minister*". The certificate was altered on 30th July to show James Shore "*minister of Bridgetown church*". He formally resigned in 1869, some years after leaving Bridgetown. It cannot have been easy for her during the Phillpotts era being the wife of a clergyman having spent time in prison, and the feeling of disgrace which she must have had quite apart from having to support him during this turbulent time.

In the meantime Thomas Lomas had taken a big step by resigning from his position in the Admiralty so that he and Julia could assist Shore in Buxton.

On 5th October 1870 *The Buxton Advertiser* carried an advertisement for both the Royal Hydropathic and Malvern House establishments, the latter advertisement showing Mrs T. Lomas as the lady superintendent at Malvern House. Both advertise-

---

45 Grayson Carter p.377

Thomas and family 1865   *HRP 1867*

ments show divine service on Sunday at Malvern House: "*morning at half past 10 o'clock; evening at half-past 6 o'clock. Open to the public*". Shore himself conducted the services and occasionally visiting ministers would be invited to preach, as did the Rev. W. Haslam, Rector of Beckenham, Norfolk, when on 11th February 1871 he gave an evangelical address. "*Christians of all denominations are welcome*" so ran the advertisement in the Buxton Advertiser. The services at Malvern House continued for a time after Shore's death, Thomas presiding over the services and HRP playing the organ.

In 1868 Shore founded a branch of the Free Church of England in Buxton and subscribed £150 to the Church in 1873.[46]

The 1871 census shows James Shore (Independent clergyman) as the head of the household at the Royal with approximately 50 visitors and Thomas head of the household at Malvern House with hardly any visitors at all! Could it be that James had persuaded all the guests to stay at the Royal? In 1871 HRP, who was 11 years old, was shown as a boarder at Ashford House, Upton, Cheshire

The Buxton Advertiser, in common with many holiday towns, provided a weekly list of visitors for a number of years and from this it is possible to see who stayed at the Royal and Malvern House. On 14th September 1867 the numbers at Malvern House were 36 and from September to October Thomas and his family are shown as staying

---

46   Grayson Carter p.378

Malvern House 1872 – first extension
Jean Askew

at Malvern House. They did not reappear on the list of visitors until June 1868 and stayed until July 1873. There is no mention of the Lomas family again until the 12th September1874. The reason for their absence was that they had been "*sent away*" due to a disagreement which was alluded to in Thomas's letter to his sister in law, Emily Bulteel, in1875 after the death of James. (See post.)

Meanwhile Shore continued to prosper and became a respected businessman in the town.

In view of Shore's continued success the first of many extensions was built in 1872.

In January 1873 Thomas and his family moved from Buxton to Tyne Avon, Clifton, Bristol and HRP attended Clifton College (opened in 1862) on a daily basis.

On 20th January 1874 HRP, who was 15 at the time, began keeping a diary when he first attended Clifton College, the diary ending on 18th September 1876 after the family had again moved back to Buxton. (*See Appendix 2 Diary of HRP*)

The diary begins with his first days at Clifton College but his attendance was sporadic due to illness and the fact that the family stayed in Windsor before moving to Buxton.

HRP's stepmother, Julia, taught him Greek and gave him piano lessons. His love of music, especially the piano, was encouraged by Julia. They "*had music*" virtually every evening.

HRP 1873

Victorians attending church
Illustrated London News

Like many Victorian families, they took religion seriously attending church twice on Sundays (occasionally 3 times), HRP making various disparaging remarks about the sermons he hears. One can also assume that he was reasonably intelligent having a discussion with Miss Tucker on the 8th February 1874 about *"Infant sprinkling and the Prayer Book"* by Robert Govett, a brilliant English pastor who in 1844 resigned his curacy forming a non-denominational church in Norwich. This theme of a non-acceptance of the established Church carries on through out the diary showing the effect that the Reverend Shore had on the family.

In February, Thomas and Julia took HRP to Windsor to consult Dr Harper and he was told *"he had better not go to school"* which *"he was very glad of"*! He had previously boarded in Cheshire whilst his parents were assisting Shore in Buxton.

HRP refers to Uncle John Lomas[47] and Grandmamma (Matilda Lomas) who were Thomas's brother and mother and who at that time were living in Windsor. The Lomas and Bulteel families were close at that time and there are frequent references to the Bulteels in the diary. HRP Thomas, Julia and her sister Emily, John Bulteel and the Reverend Shore and his wife were all buried at Bridgetown cemetery, Totnes, again showing the strength of feeling that the families had for James Shore.

After a brief visit to Bristol they returned to Windsor and HRP describes various processions in which he sees Queen Victoria looking *"most extremely cross"* and *"of course John Brown was there"*. He obviously enjoyed the proximity of royalty and the

---

47   See Family Tree Appendix 5

pageantry involved. There is a full description of the return of "the Ashanti troops".

On 2nd April another brother of Thomas and his wife, William and Sarah, came to stay with Thomas and family in Windsor. Their son, Alfred, who took HRP to visit London Zoo, was later to become a director of the Buxton Hydro and the two cousins were obviously good friends.

Thomas took HRP on holiday to Devon on 18th April including a visit to Totnes where they attended a service in Bridgetown chapel sitting in the Duke of Somerset's pew. HRP enjoyed the holiday with his father which helped to bond their relationship.

The last entries for June 1874 relate to the end of their time in Windsor and between 15th June 1874 and 8th January 1876 there are no entries, the pages having been torn out.

During that period Thomas and family returned to Buxton to assist running the Shore ventures and it is mere conjecture as to why the pages were torn out, but the reason could be that HRP may have experienced the traumatic event of witnessing the death of his grandfather during that period. From an early age HRP was fond of Buxton; he saw a lot of his grandfather and was probably spoilt by the guests and staff. On 7th February 1874 he writes "*I hope very much we shall go to Buxton*".

CHAPTER 5

THE DEATH OF JAMES SHORE

In July 1874 the Lomas family were back in Buxton, all differences between Thomas, Julia and the Rev. Shore having been resolved. They stayed at Mrs.Rogers establishment in Broadwalk rather than Malvern House. One week later Thomas's brother, John, and his mother joined them, so it was obviously meant to be a permanent move.

On the 15th August James Shore, Thomas, John, H.R.P and two ladies were riding on horseback to Street farm and *The Buxton Advertiser* takes up the story.

"The Buxton Advertiser
Saturday, August 15th, 1874.
Melancholy Accident.

Sudden Death of the Rev. James Shore.
A startling illustration of the proverbial uncertainty of human life experienced in this neighbourhood on Wednesday last. It was a splendid morning, one of those fine fresh days, after heavy rains, which compensate for the dull past and tempt to long rides and rambles over the hills. A pleasant party left Malvern House about 11 o'clock consisting of four gentlemen and two ladies, on horse - back. The gentlemen were the Reverend James Shore of Malvern House and the Royal Hydropathic establishments, his son-in-law and grandson, Mr Thomas Lomas and Master Lomas; and Mr John Lomas. They rode along the pleasant breezy uplands of the London Road indulging in an occasional halt and arrived at the higher ground near the well known "Duke of York" Inn, shortly after 12. It was here, when they were quietly walking their horses, which were not "blown" or tired, when the party was separated in groups, and Mr Shore with his grandson was riding about 15 or 20 yards in front, that his horse was seen to trip or stumble, and Mr Shore was thrown over its head, falling on his left temple on the hard road. Mr John Lomas immediately rode to his assistance, dismounted and attempted to raise him; but seeing the frightful injuries, immediately remounted and road back to Buxton for Medical aid. Mr Thomas Lomas whose attention had been preoccupied by an approaching carriage, did not see the fall but rode up directly afterwards. Mr Shore was insensible, and bled from nose and mouth. Restoratives were sent from the neighbouring Inn, but they could not be administered; and Dr. F Turner and Mr Flint, Doctors, of Buxton, who happened to be out on professional duty in the district, coming up

almost immediately, after a brief examination pronounced him dead. Anything more sudden and awful cannot be imagined, and when the sad intelligence was brought to Buxton it created the greatest consternation at both of the large establishments which Mr Shore controlled, and spread over the whole town and district. The body was moved to the Duke of York Inn, from whence it was brought, with the instigation of the coroner, to Malvern House in the evening. Mr Shore was about 70 years old.

An Inquest was held at Malvern House on Thursday by the coroner, when the above facts were put before Dr Turner by Mr John and Mr Thomas Lomas corroborated by James Bringloe, coachman to Mr Shore; it also appeared that the horse which bore Mr Shore had been purchased only the day before and had been ridden several times; that he went easily and comfortably with it but that his coachman had cautioned him that it had a stiff knee and was therefore not safe on its legs. It was also elucidated in evidence that Mr Shore habitually rode with a loose rein. The verdict was "accidental death." The remains will be removed today to Totnes, in Devonshire where the interment will take place.

Mr Shore has been in Buxton 12 years, and has conducted his large business with considerable administrative ability; but while displaying all the shrewd - ness and care necessary to a man of business, he has been most remarkably liberal and charitable as a citizen, and many will miss his kindly help. His career has been a very remarkable one, and, in early days, he was subjected to much persecution by the late Bishop of Exeter."

Shore's death certificate shows his occupation as a Free Church Minister and the cause of death "*a fall from a horse*" after a Coroners inquest held on 13th August 1874.

Grave of James Shore

The obituary refers to James Shore having lived in Buxton for 12 years, but in fact Buckley's Modern Buxton states that Malvern House was founded in 1865 not 1862.

The Buxton Herald and Gazette of Fashion, The Derby Mercury and *The Totnes Times* also gave full obituaries.

The body was taken down to Totnes and a description of the funeral in *The Totnes Times* reads:

"The funeral took place on Sunday last, the cortege leaving Totnes station about half past one, and all along the route to Bridgetown Church, and cemetery – where the interment took place, a large number of tradesmen of the town, and others, many of whom had been attendance at Bridgetown church under the deceased's ministry, added to the procession; and by the time the body arrived in the church the sacred edifice was half full. The deceased was born to the grave by eight members of his old congregation, and besides the hearse there were two mourning coaches, which contained the following members of the family: – Mr George Shore (brother of the deceased), Mr Bulteel and Mr Lomas(Sons-in-law the deceased), and masters Harry Bulteel and Herbert Lomas (grandsons of the Deceased); Mr Walton and Mr John Lomas, family connections; and Reverend F H Hole. The funeral service was impressively read by the Reverend W Watkins, Minister of the church. In the evening the same Rev. gentleman delivered an able funeral discourse, with the view of improving the occasion and administering solace to the bereaved. In the course of his remarks he alluded feelingly to the sad event of that day – a funeral of one whose lot it had been to minister for many years in that building, and warned others as to the danger of living unprepared for death, which might occur at any moment, as in the case of their departed friend, who, in the full vigour of life and his usual spirits, by an accident, was suddenly called to his account; contrasting the difference of living a life of preparedness with being unprepared for the great and soemn change, he enlarged on the reward in store for the Righteous. The church was fully attended and the services throughout appropriate to the occasion, one of the hymns (no. 170 A.& M.) being "Thy will be done" . In the absence of the organ, Mr F Holman, organist, played "The Dead March in Saul" on the harmonium, as the congregation were departing."

There then followed a description of Mr Shore's ministry and persecution, concluding with

"During the time the suit against him was going on the congregation at Bridgetown Church stood nobly by their pastor, for on the commencement of the proceedings in August 1841, a meeting of Mr Shore's friends was held, when a committee was appointed to collect subscriptions towards his defence. Of this committee the late J Derry, Esq. was Chairman; the late E.Luscombe, Esq. (then Mayor of Totnes), Treasurer; and the Committee comprised Messrs. T Michelmore, Boardman, John Windeatt, F. B. Cumming, J D Searle, J D Moysey and others; and whilst Mr Shore was in gaol at Exeter, a crowded

*meeting of his friends was held at Bridgetown, when a petition to Parliament
and an address to Mr Shore were unanimously agreed upon. The address and
petition was signed by upwards of 800 persons, the former being presented to
Mr Shore whilst in prison, by Mr Derry; and the latter presented to parliament
by Mr Bouverie, MP. Many other friends from Totnes visited the Rev.gentleman
whilst he was in prison*
*On Mr Shore being let out of prison, he addressed meetings in all parts of
England (one of which held at Exeter Hall, London, was attended by between
3000 and 4000 persons), and raised a strong feeling in his favour."*

The description of the funeral in *The Buxton Advertiser* read:
*"Early on Saturday morning, the body of the late Mr Shore was removed from
Malvern House to the railway station, and at 10:20am the immediate friends of
the deceased, with J Walter and J Lomas Esq., accompanied the body to Totnes.
The interment took place at 1.30 on Sunday. Every mark of respect was shown
to their former pastor and friend, by the inhabitants of the locality. About 120
formed into procession and followed the corpse to the grave. There was a large
gathering in the church and at the cemetery. Some may have been drawn to the
scene by the sad end of the man they had formerly known; but many others
came and notable amongst them, the old men, to shed a tear over the grave of
him who had in former days preached to them so effectively the word of life.
Special sermons were preached on Sunday in the Malvern House Church,
appropriate to the mournful occasion, by the Rev.W Bailey. The attendance at
the evening service was unusually large. At the request of several of the
hearers and residents of Buxton, Mr Bailey has consented to print the evening
sermon. We expect to have it ready on Saturday, and shall be glad to receive
orders for it."*

The *High Peak News* wrote about religious intolerance *"It is hard to realise that but
25 years past that there was religious intolerance of such a deep tenacity that even
hardships were practised which reflected but small honour on a country which vaunts
forth to nations her moderation of character."*

His will, dated 7th September 1873, appointed his brother, G N Shore, his son-in-
law John Bulteel and Isaac Walton, bank manager,[48] as executors and trustees.

After making various small bequests, he gave to Miss Ann Atkins, the matron of
his hydropathic establishments, an annuity of £50. Miss Atkins is shown in the list of
visitors for some time after Shore's death and was therefore also appreciated by
Thomas and Julia.

Thomas and John Bulteel were to receive the sum of £4,000 previously lent by
them to Shore.

The business of hydropathy carried on at Malvern House was to be given to HRP

---

48   Manager of the Buxton branch of the Sheffield and Northern Bank.

on his attaining the age of 30. The trustees were empowered to run the business and directed to employ HRP until he was 30, half of the income to go to Julia and the other half to Emily until HRP reached 30, with the proviso that if the trustees should, on HRP attaining the age of 25, consider him to "*have sufficient habits of industry and application to conduct and manage the business*", then they were to transfer the business to him absolutely.

After the business had been transferred, Julia and Emily were to receive an annuity.

On 23rd March 1875 letters of administration, with will annexed, were granted to Julia, all the other executors having renounced probate of the will, presumably because the estate was well- nigh insolvent and they would have no interest in running Malvern House on behalf of H R P.

Shortly after the grant was issued on 27th March, Thomas wrote a long letter to John and Emily in an attempt to defuse the tension that had arisen since Thomas and family had first come to Buxton to assist Shore.

"Malvern House.

My Dear John and Emily,
We have hitherto refrained from correspondence not wishing by any hasty words to add to the complication of matters, for I would not believe it can be the wish of either family to live otherwise than in a friendly spirit. Now that the court of Probate has granted to Julia a Limited Probate to administer the estate till it comes into my legal possession, it is time for us to write, and I shall endeavour to do so in a kind and friendly spirit.
Before I enter on business arrangements, I am enforced to reply to some of the charges that have been brought against us, and also give our estimation of the value of the "letter" which is put forward as the ostensible cause of all the mischief. Well then, as to this "letter", I will show you personally that, although it was written at the time with a measure of consideration, it was none the less done in a hasty spirit. No man with the intelligence of Mr. Shore would have done so an uncivil an act, as to send a letter of this nature to his daughter to keep over the head of an elder sister, and to coerce trustees in their duty. The proper course, had he calmly reflected, would have appeared to him to have given instructions to the trustees verbally or more properly by letter, or what could have been more easily done and more correct to have left a written memorandum to that effect attached to his will.
I know it was quite thought that Mr Green who had received the instructions from Mr Shore to make the will, would have now something to say, indeed it was represented to us as the one thing John decided that he should be sent for. We yielded to the urgent appeal, although I at the time said I thought it was unnecessary expense. Emily questioned him in accordance with her wish, to which he had nothing to say apart from the will, and without reference to it. I must be admitted to say that it was a subject of some pain to us, that this letter

should have been in his possession at a time when we were endeavouring to serve you in the true spirit of a friend. You will remember that in November 1873 Mr Shore asked us to sign a Bank guarantee. I find now from the correspondence that he had previously written to you, that you very properly declined to do so, from the promise you had made your late father. He then wrote to me, and I told him, "But at the same time, if you wish help from the Bank, should Malvern House not pay its expenses this winter, I shall be happy to sign the present form if Bulteel will also do so. In all things we have acted together and I shall not wish to dissociate myself ". At Christmas we went to Buxton. Mr Shore spoke to me about the matter, and told me Mr Watson could give me particulars about it. I saw him and thinking that it might cancel the feeling of anxiety Mr Shore manifested of you, because you refused to sign, "alleging that he has done so much for you both and that now you refused to do this little matter for him", I told Mr Watson for that reason I would sign one to the amount of £500 and payable within the year.

Afterwards when I told Mr Shore, "I hope that the Bulteels will be in the same position as ourselves", alluding to the yearly allowance, not knowing at that time that he had bound himself to pay your rent, he expressed himself so strongly that I did not again refer to the subject. Moreover, when we were at Windsor afterwards, I saw your uneasiness at the turn of matters. I counselled you what you should do just before the rent of your house became due, and so I pencilled you out a letter which reminded Mr Shore that he had signed the lease of your house which led him to send you a cheque for the rent, and so was the means unexpectedly to you of making matters straight again. The kindly spirit this manifested Shore, without hesitation in assisting, has been the principle of our acting all the time that we have resided here in close connection with Mr Shore. We could most easily have feathered our own nest for he had frequently said "those that serve me, I will serve". So much for the reception of the "letter", now for the reason of it

It will appear to any careful unbiased mind that it is a considered and arranged one preceding out of a subject at hand. On 17th September 1873 I had a very friendly letter from Mr. Shore, but on 21st October a very unpleasant correspondence commenced. At that time Emily was staying at Buxton. It was all about dear Herbert. The principal subjects of grievance were, that we would not consent, while he was so young, to his being at Malvern House without one of his parents, that he does not stay at your house on his way from Budleigh to Derby, and that we did not allow him a second time in the quarter to come away from his studies at Derby to come to Buxton. The last letter of the correspondence, a letter of yours, was written on 27th October 1873, on the very same day as a letter to Emily. Everyone knows that Mr Shore was peculiarly a man that did not like to be thwarted; he wanted to have Herbert under his own control in a large establishment where he could have had little or no control over him, for Mr Shore had not time for his many personal arrangements. No parent should be allowed to surrender his pastoral duties over his own child. So much for the motive that prompted the "letter", now as to the formation. Much has been said of the inappropriate words of command expressed herein, but surely with relatives like ourselves, and with all who were intimate with Mr Shore, it would seem unnecessary to bring proof to show that such was always his style of writing when annoyed. He was an impulsive man, very easily disturbed, and when so put out, always expressed himself in an exaggerated and extreme manner. I say with us, who were so well acquainted with him, we can want no proof of what we know so well. Look at the manner in which he expressed himself about you because you would not sign the guarantee, this Mr Walter knows for he explained himself to him. But I can give you proof for I happen to have a copy of a letter to the Assessor of Taxes at Bakewell, which he sent to me in the spring of last year. I find these expressions – "outrageously unjust" – "shamefully unjust" – "an outrage on common honesty" – "outrageous charges" – "shameful injustice", and he says at the end "I wish this letter to be laid before the commissioners, as I might have to send a copy to Somerset House". I merely mention this therefore to show that he often expressed himself even more strongly then he felt as the occasion required.

We had an affectionate invitation to Buxton in the spring of last year, and on the first occasion that Julia went to the Service on Sunday, Mr Shore said to her "I am very glad to see you here again", putting much emphasis on "here". He had also told Mr Walter that he wanted to make an alteration in his will in respect to Thomas Lomas. It was also quite arranged that he would have accompanied us to Llandudno in the autumn. This shows that all unkind feeling had passed; that having written the letter he had either not the courage to withdraw it, or which is quite possible, for his memory of late was very bad, he had forgotten it. He had previously forgotten whether your lease was signed, and asked Julia at Christmas time to find out who had signed it. But to my mind he evidently wished to cancel the effect of that letter by an alteration in his will. He had left no verbal instructions with anyone that we should not be the managers; on the contrary, the expectation of all people is that we shall not only be so, but are the proper persons.

Another subject has been dwelt upon, our removal. We left Malvern House at the request of Mr. Shore when he could spare us; we did this on purpose that it might be his own act, so that it might not be said afterwards that we left an old man in the midst of strangers and so neglected a parent. The immediate cause of our leaving was because we differed from Mr Shore in the manner in which he dealt with a poor afflicted gentleman that had gone somewhat deranged. Yet we had the sympathy of nearly all the visitors, who learning what had transpired, spontaneously drew up a testimonial to present to us which was signed by 14 of the 18 visitors in the house; and most of the four approved but had not the courage to sign. It being, however, represented that if the testimonial were presented all that signed it would be immediately sent away, it *was withheld; but a copy was given to us; and the original was to be had on our sending for it. We have sent for it and this is the testimonial, "we the under - signed ladies and gentlemen at present residing in Malvern House beg, before we separate, to tender our cordial and sincere thanks to Mr & Mrs. Lomas for their unswerving kindness and attention to our every comfort. We also wish to express our admiration and approval of the judicious and Christian conduct displayed by them during their recent trying circumstances and we cannot too highly commend the charitable forbearance exercised by them towards a stricken fellow creature".*

Besides this a sum of £10 was hastily subscribed and sent to us, and further I would quote from a few letters I happen to have by me; "Your friends have more delights to have the opportunity of offering a trifling remembrance of how much they all appreciate your constant efforts to add to their comfort as well as the interest of the House". "We think Mr. Shore has made a great mistake in parting with you". "I have a vivid remembrance of the pleasant time I spent in Malvern House with Mr. Lomas and yourself, and only wish now that you are back again." "It quite cheered me to see you were both back again". These are from persons who from position and ability are well able to form a judgment. If it was necessary, I could on application, multiply this to a great extent.

All this time we were at Malvern House, about 4 years, there was an under-current of mischief going on by certain persons for their own ends; things were represented to Mr Shore in a very different light from what they were. Mr Shore was a man of kindly spirit, but he listened to, and was led by controlling women who endeavoured to have their own way over an old man.

The reviews of this ten years since Mr Shore resided in these parts tell us, that disturbances have existed more or less all through it. There was the case of Wilcox, then Dr. Daybell of whom Mr Shore spoke in the highest terms, also many more that assumed different positions after them. People have been dealt with in a stringent manner and sent away abruptly. Shall it be a matter of wonder that the same hand should remove us for no one has maintained their position with Mr Shore, except the Williams, and even they notwithstanding they were with him nearly 25 years, all but sent away.

I do not dwell upon this subject from morbid sentimentality to bring to memory the acts of a departed man, for it would have been rather my spirit to have cast into the oblivion of time any defects in him, which are common to our humanity, for the best of us have nothing to boast of, but on the contrary much to grieve over and lament. Even were I so disposed, nothing can alter the blessed rest he now enjoys. But I am enforced to refer to these matters in vindication of the truth. With this part of my subject I close, I now come to business matters.

Julia will proceed forthwith to carry out the Probate as speedily as possible and shall pay the many claimants as soon as we are able. We shall send you a balance sheet, showing the condition of the estate and also a cheque for such half of the amount of profits that may be divisible on Malvern House. Julia is now making arrangements with Mr Bailey to take charge of the Royal, as last year. The condition of the inside is very bad, and there are great many things that must be done to make the place acceptable to visitors. She will forthwith attend to this. It would have been well if we could have had it open by Easter but in consequence of this long delay, that cannot be.

She has been in correspondence with Mr Nelson as to the Matlock mortgage. [49] They have paid me one ¹/₂ years' interest, which I have paid into the Bank, and wished to know whether we would continue the mortgage after March. I told him we should call in the mortgage, and requested he would be prepared to pay it off. I also wrote in February to Mr Stooly to tell him that we should pay him off his £2,000. I did not write before, because I had no authority, but in consequence of the delay I thought it prudent to do so, so that we shall only have to pay four months' interest beyond what we should have had to pay if we had given six months' notice in due time. This is a loss the estate will have to suffer in consequence of the unsettled state of things. We intend out of the balance of the money that may be due from the estate, supposing there will be about enough, to pay off Mr Stooly and the interest. The £4,000 I should put into the government securities in John's and my name; when I am prepared to do so, I will let you know. The £50 a year to Miss Atkins for the present will be paid out of the receipts from the Royal.

Julia has given Mr. Catchpole six months' notice to leave. He is no use either in the pulpit or in the house, and is not liked. This is therefore an unnecessary expense that can be avoided. I can take the family worship and Mr Bailey, and others will supply the pulpit, in the same way we have been arranging lately. There will be no disposition to disturb Miss Atkins as matron, on the contrary to show her every kindness as a matron of the establishment has come to expect. As Miss Larkins is going to be married she will give up, and has partly given up playing. Herbert who plays the organ very nicely, has played several evenings and will play one part of the service and Julia the other.

There is a matter that seems to have caused some unpleasant feeling, which is that the Estate, being in debt, none of Mr Shore's personal effects can legally be divided. We have been thinking that an arrangement of this sort might be made. Emily and Julia might select a few articles that they would like, to about the same value, with a written undertaking that if he who comes in possession should require them, they will be given up, or the money value, according to the valuation, paid for them. In this way I think the difficulty may be overcome. If Emily therefore will come and see what she wants, or will let Julia know, they can be sent. Julia intends for your own satisfaction, to let you have a half-yearly balance sheet e.g. at March and July and she will appoint Mr Watson,

---

49   When Shore sold Matlock House Hydro he probably allowed the purchaser to pay only part of the purchase price, the balance to remain outstanding under mortgage to Shore.

Auditor, at a remuneration of £5-5 a year. He will audit the accounts from time to time. Julia intends to make the late Mr Shore's bedroom a consulting room; for it is too hot for anyone permanently to occupy. She will therefore remove such things from Kenilworth for that purpose. Dr. Bennett will have regular days and hours of attendance.

Now in respect to our stay here, I know it is considered from a conversation that has occurred that we should pay, as others. The prosperity of the house during the winter is much indebted to our stay here, for it is not a thing of theory but one of fact that visitors will not remain in a house when there are only servants. Besides which we have had many things to do which necessarily falls to us, because no matron can do them. The House this winter will about have paid its cooking expenses, notwithstanding the unsettled state of matters which have prevented some from coming. We should not have thought that under these circumstances any expectation of payment would have arisen, bearing in mind that you have a benefit out of the estate of Mr Shore which you can claim legally, whereas what he would have done, and promised to do for us has no virtue in consequence of his death.

Yet we prefer to err on the right side so have therefore, on reflection, determined to charge ourselves £3.30 shillings a week from the 1ˢᵗ January to 31ˢᵗ March 1875. Herbert is entitled to be in the house. It cannot be supposed that we are anxious to have the heavy duty and responsibilities of the management of two Establishments, the very charge of the money department would be quite enough for most people, as I know by experience. For in the space of nearly four years, I received about £2,000 and we paid mostly everything besides. These are duties which devolve upon us, which personally, and especially from what has transpired, I would gladly have been quit of, but my son's interests I cannot pass over. I hear, again it may be thought, that we should be reaping too much advantage out of the Estate in living here free, notwithstanding the heavy duties that devolve upon us, nevertheless we desire to carry on the right side, and shall therefore pay you over and above your half-share of profits on Malvern House £50 a year so long as Julia's Probate is in force.

It will be our duty to reduce the amount of debt. In a letter of 27ᵗʰ October 1873 on the debt Mr Shore writes, "if I am spared a year or two longer, this I trust will be paid off. This I am desirous of doing in order to leave it to Herbert with - out encumbrance".

I would not suppose that there can be any feeling of jealousy in respect of Herbert's position under the will. It simply assumes that because he was willing to take charge of such an establishment and thus perpetuate the memory of Mr Shore. Harry had the first claim, and would certainly have been chosen had he so desired for I frequently have heard Mr Shore speak to that effect. It is not out of place here to mention that it had been considered in time past that Herbert should take his third of the £4,000 as his mother's, a right to which certainly he was entitled. Doubtless if I had urged the justice of this claim, it could have been so arranged but I prefer in all things that men should make their own bequests. If therefore he should appear to have a benefit, which after all must be dependent on his own exertions, it is clear it is a claim to which he is justly entitled.

In conclusion, I have endeavoured to put before you the simple truth in all matters. I am not aware that there is a single point that I have advanced that is not strictly true, for I have given this subject due consideration, the truth of such is evidenced to by the correspondence quoted which I have attached to a copy of this.

I have only to add that we hope that when either of you or Harry should wish a change, that you will come, and we shall be happy to receive you free of cost to yourselves. Of course other members of the family will have to pay as visitors. And we hope also that in view of the difficulties that surround the administration of the estate, that all animosity and unkind feeling will subside, and that the future will be to us all one of harmony and peace.

Believe me,

My Dear John and Emily, Yours affectionately,

Thomas Lomas.

P.S. Since writing the foregoing I have received a letter from Mr Nelson in which he says he expects to be able to pay the interest due on the "25" in the course of the next 10 days, and as they are arranging to consolidate their mortgages to expedite their payment of the £4,500, he wishes to have copies of such papers as we hold. I have told him that the deeds are with Messrs. Brookley Wright and Man, solicitors, Macclesfield. I have also sent a copy of this letter to Mr Woolley asking him to ask his Solicitors to forward the information if asked for, at the cost of Mr Nelson. This request as usual to whom they wish to pass on the mortgage."

The letter sets the scene perfectly and is remarkably businesslike, although Thomas may have painted the picture blacker than it was in reality. Nevertheless, Shore was not perhaps the businessman that the Buxton townsfolk believed, having had to obtain loans from his sons-in-law. However, the letter only shows one side of the story. The Buxton List of Visitors shows that when Thomas and Julia were running the Malvern and Shore was at the Royal there were many more visitors staying at the Royal.

CHAPTER 6

THE YOUNG H R P

HRP's diary continues from 8th January 1876 when the situation at Malvern House had settled down.

Buxton at that time was expanding both in terms of development and its reputation. In James Croston's *"Buxton and its Resources"* in 1873 he describes a morning scene;

"An hour before everything was still and silent; now all is life, and gaiety, and fashion. Visitors are thronging from all points; the lame and the halt are slowly hobbling on towards the baths; others are indulging in their morning draught of mineral water, or aiding the effect by promenading to and fro along the colonnade; others, again, are toiling up and down the steep Hall Bank, or sauntering along the walks on St Anne's cliff; and here and there you may see a group of laughing, merry-eyed youngsters, in the charge of a coquettish-looking nursemaid, disporting themselves upon the turfy slopes; but the number of children is small, comparatively – rheumatism and lumbago being among the ills that juvenile flesh is seldom heir to. Gay companies, in equally gay looking equipages, start every now and then from the doors of St.Ann's and the Old Hall to enjoy a forenoon airing; and people of a less aristocratic class are bargaining with the owners of one-horse chaises for a drive to the Lover's Leap or the Cat and Fiddle; whilst in Spring Gardens knots of eager pleasure-seekers are gathered round the "Peverel of the Peak", bent upon a ride over the bleak and dreary moors, to see the multifarious wonders that Castleton displays. Literature seems to be in favour with the stay-at-homes; the benches and rustic seats invitingly placed upon the gravelled walks are, for the most part, occupied by elderly gentlemen and their dames, many of whom are leisurely perusing the daily papers, or wading through the Advertiser's list of visitors, and noting what new arrivals there have been since the Herald issued its long array of names a couple of days before. Cornhill appears to be in the ascendant with the beaux, at least such of them as are not occupied in staring unmeaningly at the moving panorama of beauty and fashion, – and light fiction has its peculiar charms for the belles. Just now a couple of bewitching damsels are tripping away from the library to seek the shady retirement of the Serpentine Walks, intent upon storing their minds with the rich fund of information to be gleaned from the "Cousin's Courtship" or the "Minister's Wooing". The fine arts, too, have their attractions, as is manifest by the group of loungers who are

contemplating the cheap engravings and lithographs of Derbyshire scenery exposed to view in the stationer's window; whilst, close by, a country couple are expressing in plain, blunt phraseology, their opinions of the personal appearance of the noble, knightly, and scientific personages with whose portraits Mr Bentley, the photographer, has liberally adorned the entrance to the hot baths. At 11 o'clock, the hour when the band plays, approaches, the throng every moment increases; bustle and animation are everywhere apparent; clouds of muslin, silk, and lace pass continually before the eye, and the unclouded sun pours down a flood of brilliance that adds immensely to the gaiety of the scene – even the spar shops seem to experience the cheering influence, and their owners look more than ever determined to inveigle the money out of the pockets of visitors."

This was a far cry from only 30 years previously when Granville revealed Buxton's stagnation. Although it had a *"fragrance of aristocracy"*it was *"a very dull place, lacking amusement and even more society in its present apparent desertion"*.

He suggested improvements for Buxton, a more elegant pump/well room with smart female attendants. He suggested that the DukeofDevonshire, who owned most of Buxton, might provide a promenade room in the form of a Grecian temple on the hill top fronting the Crescent.

The Duke responded to some of the criticisms and wanted to improve Buxton's own reputation. When he sold off properties he acted as an unofficial planner by imposing restrictive covenants preventing development unless he approved the plans. In 1871 he provided the land for Buxton's great enterprise, the Pavilion Gardens, including the elegant pavilion. Edward Millner, the London landscape gardener and garden architect, designed it and also transformed the central area of the Serpentine Walk with two miles of walks and five bridges. New waterfalls were made, two lakes joined, many trees and shrubs planted and a bandstand made for the town band which in various forms played throughout the year. The Duke had also given more and more of the Crescent stables to the Devonshire Hospital with the final great extension in1881 when the half acre circular interior space was roofed over by the largest single open dome in Europe.

Buxton had tended to rely on the Duke for expansion of the town but in 1873 it began to free itself from ducal tutelage. An Act empowered the Local Board to construct water and gas works, and attempts were made to extend the season and encourage visitors to come at Christmas and Easter.[50]

The Buxton Improvements Company was formed in 1870 for the purpose of making the town more self-sufficient rather than relying so heavily on the Duke.

A roller skating rink had recently been opened in the Pavilion Gardens and HRP tries '*rinking*" with limited success at first, but by the second day he had mastered it

---

50 Phyllis Hembry *British Spas from 1815 to the Present* Athlone Press 1997

Roller-skating in Buxton 1870s
Courtesy of the Board Collection and www.picturethepast.org.uk

and became very enthusiastic. Roller-skating was somewhat of a craze throughout England at the time and was making a fortune for those setting up the Rinks. Even The Buxton Advertiser carried an article on the merits of roller-skating.[51] (*See Appendix 3 "Skating on Wheels"*)

Furthermore, in the days when young ladies had to be chaperoned, skating provided an important liberating effect on young people allowing them to go off together unsupervised.

New characters are now introduced in HRP's diary amongst whom is Mr Pettitt who gave lessons to HRP privately at his home and ran a school at Holme Leigh, Corbar Road, where he took on boarders. HRP is also introduced to the violin and takes lessons.

During the course of the diary he refers to "*Kenilworth*"and "*Pomeroy*", and these may have been the names given to the first building erected and the subsequent extension respectively.

He plays the organ regularly for the Sunday services and is grateful for the "*curtain*" which shields him from the eyes of the congregation. He is critical, as always, of the various sermons he hears from the visiting preachers.

Between 19th April and 11th May 1876 he returned to Windsor so that he could

---

51 Pamela Horne *Pleasures and Pastimes in Victorian Britain* 1998 Sutton Publishing p.18

attend Stokes Music School in London on a daily basis.

HRP learnt to be a good host at an early age. Returning to Buxton, he takes delight in playing typical Victorian games with the guests who are numbering between 40 and 60 each night. The "*Royalists*", the guests at the Royal, are invited to tea to view the charade put on by H.R.P and the guests at Malvern House. The seeds are being sown here for HRP's enjoyment in entertaining guests and visitors which becomes such a feature of the Buxton Hydro in future years.

There is no evidence as to where HRP continued his education after attending Mr Pettit's premises, but he may well have attended a school in Derby, as this is referred to in Thomas's letter.

Matilda Lomas, Thomas's mother and HRP's grandmother, died on 2nd April 1878. She and her eldest son, John, followed Thomas and family from Windsor to Buxton, where they stayed at Malvern House. John must have had private means to enable him to reside there. He is shown in the 1861 census as a landowner and collector of rent from the Baker estate in Kent, Matilda's maiden name being Baker. During his 17 years at the Hydro undoubtedly John was a great support to his nephew and he won great affection from his fellow visitors by his genial manner. He was a shareholder in the Gardens but otherwise took no part in the Town's affairs. He died on the 19th June 1892 when there was a small obituary in *The Buxton Advertiser*.

Thomas continued to manage Malvern House on behalf of H R P having given up the lease of the Royal and instigated the second of the many extensions. HRP's 21st birthday resulted in an article in *The Buxton Advertiser*, dated 17th April 1880, describing the festivities which were combined with a celebration of the completion of the second extension under the supervision of Mr Gladwin, a local architect.

"Coming of age festivities at Buxton.

Thursday being the day on which Mr H P Lomas, son of Mr T Lomas, of Malvern House, Buxton, attained his majority, a series of entertainments were provided for friends, work people and servants. For some time past extensive additions have been made to this House, under the direction of Mr Gladwin, and those who were working at these extensions were invited to dinner at the Cheshire Cheese, Higher Buxton. Mr and Mrs Boughen provided an excellent meal and 34 of the workmen partook of it. It had been intended that a "rearing supper" should be given by the contractors, but owing to the occasion mentioned the coming-of-age and the rearing were combined, and after dinner the contractors provided the means of spending the remainder of the evening in a jovial manner.

Mr Gladwin occupied the chair, and after proposing the loyal toasts, he proposed the "the health of Mr T Lomas, their employer". He spoke in the highest terms of him as an employer, and informed those present that Mr Lomas was satisfied with the manner in which they had done their work, and also at the manner in which they stuck to it. Mr Lomas in speaking to him had informed him of the pleasure it gave him to see that none of the men engaged on the work were in the habit of turning up work the worse for drink, nor were they in habit of leaving their work for the purpose of obtaining drink. This was a most satisfactory statement for him – Mr Gladwin – to hear, as coming from one of the best employers he had worked for since he began business. The toast was received with cheers and musical honours.

Mr Joseph Harrison then proposed the health of Mr H P Lomas, the young gentleman, he said, in whose honour they were met that evening. From what he knew of Mr Lomas he could say that he was most straight forward, upright and of remarkably good business habits. On that day he reached his majority, and he hoped those present would drink to his health with great heartiness, and with him hope that Mr Lomas's "path in life may be strewn with the flowers of prosperity". The company received a toast in a most enthusiastic manner – cheer after cheer being given, as also musical honours. The demonstration was received with every show of sincerity later on, when Mr H P Lomas, accompanied by some friends entered the room.

On 7th May 1881 *The Buxton Advertiser* noted that Mr Herbert Lomas of Malvern House was to be gazetted Lieutenant of the Buxton section of the Derbyshire volunteers. The volunteers were raised in 1794 throughout the country as additional forces in support of the militia and were the forerunners of the Territorial Army.

HRP's stepmother, Julia, died on 20th December 1881, aged 54. Her will, made on 3rd March 1863, unusually refers to Thomas being the husband of her deceased sister

HRP aged 21

HRP gazetted Lieutenant of the Buxton section of the Derbyshire Volunteers 1881

and to the marriage to Thomas *"in accordance with the rites of the Protestant Church of Neufchatel, Switzerland"*.

She was a good mother to HRP but one cannot help feeling that her marriage to Thomas was more of a duty to her sister and it may not have been an entirely happy marriage. Indeed, Thomas married Caroline Symonds, spinster, in Southport on 31st March 1883 at which H.R.P was one of the witnesses. This was shortly after Julia's death and the handing over of the reins of Malvern House to HRP in accordance, although a little earlier than stipulated, with Shore's will.

HRP must have shown good business sense at that early age, and in any event no doubt Thomas wanted to start a new life away from Buxton, although he continued to show a keen interest in the Hydro and held shares when it was floated as a company in 1899.

Thomas Lomas 1906

Thomas and Caroline then moved to Sussex and thence to the spa town of Vevey in Switzerland where they lived together until 1914 when Thomas died. He was buried with the Reverend James Shore in Bridgetown cemetery, where Julia and Isabella were also buried.

Whilst in Sussex Thomas wrote to HRP on 16th August 1906 describing Julia and Isabella. He also refers to Caroline Symonds, Thomas's third wife, as HRP's mother.

Letter dated 16th August 1906 from Thomas to HRP.

Oakwood,   *16 Aug. 1906.*
Haywards Heath
Sussex

My Dear Herbert,
Thank you for the P.C's. They are interesting as having a description on them of the locality and I think them pretty. I am glad to here that you have at last inspected everything, but sorry that the nice plate is broken. I am sending you, herewith, the hair chain of your late mother; I have tried to wear it but it is so fragile and has again become broken, and therefore I send it to you. I am sure you will like to have it, for she was a good mother to you. I have also another one of Isabella, which I hope will come to you some day. If she had been spared, she would have been a good mother to you. She was taller than the others and

superior and of a commanding character, which was shown in the household. Your mother is now much better, but still in her room. The weather showers and much colder.

With love,
Your affectionate father,
Thomas Lomas."

CHAPTER 7

DEVELOPMENT OF THE HYDRO
FROM 1866 TO 1898

Five years after building the original Malvern House in 1866, James Shore erected the first of many extensions. In all the subsequent extensions the original houses were always to be seen in the current building as all the extensions were added on around, above or behind it.

After Shore's death Thomas Lomas, as trustee of his estate, built still further accommodation together with new and improved bedrooms.

In 1883 HRP, who was then 24 and in charge of the Hydro, erected a magnificent dining saloon, along with additional bedrooms, affording dining accommodation for

Buxton Hydro 1885. Illustrated supplement from the Buxton Advertiser
Local Studies Library, Matlock

Hydro Entrance 1883

Hydro Ballroom 1887

Buxton Museum

200 persons, and bedrooms to sleep 110. Buckley's *Modern Buxton* (1886) from whom the above was taken states *"it is hardly too much to say that so important an establishment, fitted as it is with the best and most artistic appointments, helps to give character and importance to Buxton as a favourite and desirable health resort"*.

In 1887 the much heralded Ball Room was constructed, the architect being WR Bryden. Bryden, an important architect in Buxton and responsible for many of the town's projects,was employed as architect for the majority of the building works carried out by HRP.

In the same year, further enlargement was carried out as reported in *The Buxton Advertiser:*

"Enlargement of Malvern House. In this age of progression, keeping pace with the times is one of the first desiderata with all classes and in all businesses, and perhaps no one in Buxton follows the specially applicable axiom of "Success attends where comfort is provided" more closely than Mr HRP Lomas, proprietor of the great hydropathic establishment in Hartington Road. In the beginning of last winter alterations were commenced on the south east side of the building, and by dint of perseverance, but not without the greatest consideration for those staying in the house whilst the work was being proceeded with, a new wing has already been added and completed. Opening from, and as an annexe to the large hall, is an extra dining or recreation room, 30 ft by 30 ft, and 19 ft-high in the centre. The woodwork is of pitch pine, the floors being beautifully polished for dancing. The fireplace is constructed of Derbyshire and black marble, with tiled front. Over the centre of the room is a large stained glass dome light, the glass being of the same kind as in other parts of the house, and supplied by Swain Bourne, of Birmingham. In each of the four divisions of the roof is a window with patent racket ventilators, and so situated that the whole of the inside of the room is lighted in the same degree. The door - way is fitted with nine- feet swinging doors, so that when they open two or three couples may, when the occasion is dancing, pass to and fro without the common inconvenience of waiting for each other to pass, or, what is worse, elbowing. The room is in every way adapted to the requirements of large or small assemblages, and the furnishing is of the most modern and elegant design. The enlargement also consists of a gentlemen's lavatory, 26 ft by 14 ft, the floor of which is of Italian marble; the work has been done by Italian workmen on the premises. Heavy marble tip- up basins, together with patent automatic flushing arrangements and all that the mind of the modern panegyric could devise is supplied even though it is a lavatory. Messrs Jennings, of London, have executed the work, and exceedingly well has it been done. The new smoke-room is 25 ft long and 14 ft wide, and is arranged on the best method and splendidly furnished. The new billiard-room which, when furnished, will be 34 ft by 22 ft by 20 ft and contain two tables, will adjoin. On the first floor six extra bed - rooms, each 12 ft by 14 ft by 10 ft, are arranged, three on either side of the spacious passage. Neat little fire-places with marble chimney pieces are

Hydro Lounge 1898
Buxton Museum

provided to each. Four servants' rooms, 12 ft square, and a dormitory 30 ft by 15 ft are on the second floor. The new wing is approached by a tastefully decorated corridor 60 ft long and 10 ft wide. In all the public rooms the electric light will be fitted as soon as possible, but this undertaking, though it was to have been carried out last year, could not be successfully completed until the work of extension was finished. The proprietor has spared neither trouble nor expense as regards the effectual performance of the work of extension, and the new additions may be said to add repletion to an establishment already embracing every possible requirement of a first class hydropathic".

The billiard room in Hydropathics was also generally the smoking room. It was recognised that smoking was in most cases antagonistic to cures by hydropathy; yet it appeared to be an absolute impossibility to do without a smoking room of some sort. It was to be arranged so that no possible smell of tobacco penetrated beyond the room where indulgence in the habit was permitted. The billiard room was also wholly indispensable, and should be *"large, well arranged, well tabled, and withal a comfortably furnished apartment."*

In 1890 HRP carried out further improvements by adding new types of baths. *The Buxton Advertiser* reported under the heading:

"The Buxton Hydropathic. Extension of the baths.

During the present season Mr HRP Lomas has again been improving his well-known establishment by erecting a new addition to the many improved Hydropathic arrangements which are to be found in this summer and winter residence. The gentlemen's Baths have undergone a complete change. A new spray or needle bath has been so constructed that either the top or bottom sprays can be put in operation by the simple turning of a handle, or the whole force of the bath can be concentrated on to the patient by one operation. There has also been added an improved flowing sitz and mustard bath, with ascending jets, back sprays, and wave specially arranged to Mr Lomas' own design. The next bath to mention is the outcome of considerable experience on the part of those entrusted with the erection of the baths, and is exclusively for spine treatment, this bath is arranged so as to give a local needle bath to the spine, and is of gun-metal secured by fancy clips to the wall. There is also a moveable wave for this same treatment.

In the corner adjoining is a Russian, or vapour bath, with local sprays and douches for hot, cold, or tepid applications, as well as local steam sprays and douches. The whole of these baths are controlled by a set of mixing arrange - ments with thermometer to register temperature, similar to those noticed by us some two years ago, but to all appearance larger, the outcome, probably, of the experience gained by the Engineer. The room is very carefully ventilated, and the design is decidedly handsome, the floor being laid in mosaic, the walls of Minton tiles with coloured dado, finished with a moulded tile in art colour. In the private bathrooms there are improved Roman- shaped baths in one piece of porcelain, similar to those designed by his late Royal Highness Prince Albert, but a decided advance in formation of these baths has taken place, a bold Roman bead, replacing the unfinished edge then noticed, so that these baths are a decided sanitary improvement over the old fashioned ones, which had always to be cased in wood. They stand alone on a set of feet provided to receive them clear of the floor, and being glazed over the roll, are very clean and handsome in appearance. The supply of water is unlimited, and is arranged by an inlet about two-and-half inches in diameter, so that the baths can be filled in a few seconds. The heating apparatus has been extended, and we can safely say Mr Lomas' establishment is at least the equal of any other establishment of the description in comfort and luxury of bath appliances.

The water used is the town water, of which there is a plentiful supply at all times guaranteed by the official reserve on the premises; but although these baths are used in conjunction with the mineral baths, there is no mineral-water used, as the only places where the mineral thermal water baths can be had direct from the springs on the hot and natural baths in the crescent. The whole of the bathing arrangements have been fitted up by Mr John Smeaton of London, the well-known sanitary and hydropathic engineer, the foreman of works being Mr A McKay; the decorations by Harwood, Manchester under the supervision of

Mr Holland; the tiles and mosaic by Mr J H Paterson, Manchester.
Buxton Hydropathic with its 200 beds, is even yet not large enough, and Mr
Lomas is now erecting a west wing, which will contain 20 additional bedrooms.
Mr Lomas has also given an order to the American Elevator Company for one
of the latest improved passenger lifts, which will be fixed during next winter."
R O Allsop in *"The Hydropathic establishment"* stated that:

"the principle in arranging the bathing accommodation is a concentration of
the baths into one group, placed in as accessible position as possible for the
visitors at the establishment. This principle of concentration of bathing
accommodation obtains at Smedley's and has been adopted at Lomas's hydro -
pathic at Buxton – "Malvern House". The inhabitants of the hydropathic
should be able to approach the baths with exactly the same degree of comfort
as they will pass from dining room to the drawing room. Draughty passages and
chilly corridors must be avoided, or where we cure we make ill again. Such
attentions and considerations the majority of patients require; and as for the
vigorous treatment and the spartan living that best suit the plethoric, hot-
blooded, and overfed, it is perhaps, comprised in the regular application of the
two inch cold douche. In many hydropathic establishments we find that the
baths are treated in almost a shamefaced manner, being hidden away as much
as possible. We find them cramped and huddled away in dark basements,
approached by undignified passages and staircases. This is quite the wrong
principle. The baths are necessary; without them there will be no hydropathic
establishment. All things are, in a measure, subordinate to the baths; they must
therefore be recognised as a feature of features to be treated, as regards plan,
design and appearance in as respectful a manner as their importance warrants.
Instead of hiding them away they must be brought forward, and designed as
something in which we take a just pride. Their approaches must be dignified,
their position on the plan an honoured one, and their scope of a size
calculated to produce a sense of respect. If these facts be borne in mind, it may
prevent the designer falling into error and treating the baths as a wholly
secondary matter, to accommodate themselves to the plan, and fill up any of
space that may become available. Allsop goes on "Simple wet massage, at the
hydropathic establishment, may be economically performed in the shampooing
room of the Turkish bath. In a special room, for this treatment, there should be
water fittings, comprising hot and cold supply, basin, hand-bowl, and a rose or
spray. One of the most elaborate massage baths ever arranged was erected
some little time ago at the Malvern House Hydropathic establishment, at
Buxton. By an ingenious arrangement of pedals etc. the masseur can throw jets
of water over the patient and this without for a moment neglecting the process
of massage."

HRP loved all things Italian. He was fluent in the language, in addition to French,

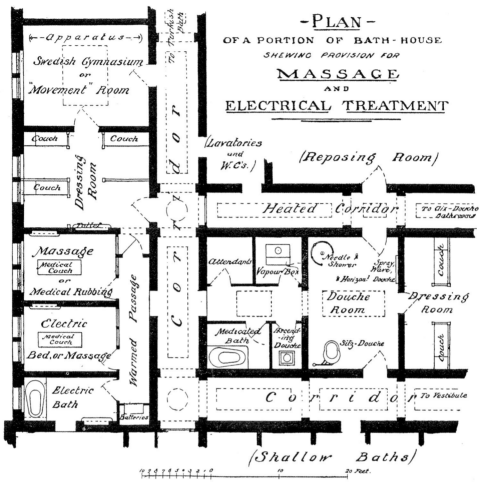

Suite of Rooms for Massage and Electrical Treatment.

Plan showing typical layout of baths

and he incorporated many of the designs in the Hydro which showed an Italian influence. He also employed many Italians as staff and visited Italy on holiday most years.

In 1890 he purchased the Eagle Hotel which was used as an overspill from the Hydro. In later years, as the Hydro did not have a licence to sell intoxicating liquer on the premises, those guests at the Hydro requiring a drink asked one of the staff to purchase the necessary beveridge from the Eagle to avoid breaking the licensing laws.

In March 1891 *The Buxton Advertiser* described the Easter Festivities and the enlarged drawing room:

"In past winters the magnificent Dining Hall, the complete suite of Baths, the elegant Ball and Entertainment room, together with innumerable other public

and private rooms have been added, all of which improvements have made the drawing room too small for the accommodation required, and like the Entrance Hall, it appeared of insufficient size and height for so spacious an establish-ment. To remedy these defects Mr Lomas set himself to work immediately the Christmas festival – a great season of reunion at Buxton Hydro – was over, and within the short space of two months wonderful progress has been made. By building out an octagon on the south side of the centre portion of the Drawing Room, and by carrying this portion to the height of another floor, the size of the room has been materially increased and its ventilation perfected. In the octagon are four windows 16 ft.in height, and in the top circular lights are some exquisite bits of stained glass by Swaine Bourne of Birmingham, illustrative of Scenes in Shakespeare. Though actually one grand apartment the Drawing Room is virtually three rooms, the centre portion being separated from the wings by two handsome portieres. The ceiling of the central portion is very handsome, being set out in panels with rich mouldings in fibrous plaster. It is the work of Harward, of Manchester. In the course of a few weeks the Drawing Room will be entirely furnished by Maple and Co of London. A new wing, containing 30 bedrooms, an American elevator on the most approved principle, and the raising of the ceiling of the Entrance Hall will all be completed before Whitsuntide, and will then call for further notice.

On Thursday covers were laid in the dining room for 180 guests, and this number will be materially increased for the weekend. The Easter amusements commenced with a dance on Thursday. A sacred concert was given last evening, the programme of which was as follows; Solo Organ... Dr Venables Williams. Etc

There will be a dance tonight, sacred concert tomorrow evening, and on Monday the annual Easter Ball will be given, when about 200 guests are expected"

The architect for this project was the well-known Manchester architect, William Davies, who won the contract as a result of an architectural competition.

On October 17th 1891 *The Buxton Advertiser* reported:

"Mr. HRP Lomas the proprietor of the celebrated Buxton hydropathic, has recently resorted to the use of the divining rod to ascertain whether there is water under the land adjoining his establishment. Mr Mullins, the well-known genius of the rod in question, a Yorkshireman, well known in this district, was called in to try his skill, and having armed himself with a small forked branch of a thorn, he walked the land on the Eagle Street side of the premises, and just in front of the old High Peak News Printing Office the little twig was power-fully affected, leading Mr Mullins to declare there was a powerful spring of water at a depth of 70 to 80 feet. A shaft has already been sunk some 40 ft and operations are still going on, the blasting being felt by the neighbours all round.

The boring is very difficult an account of the flinty nature of the rock."

Having its own supply of water available would be useful for the proposed Hydro laundry.

In 1893 there were yet more bedrooms added and improvements made including an overhead covered passageway built from the Hydro to 2 Penzance Villa, later to become the new Malvern House occupied by HRP.

In 1894 electric baths, douche and massage were added.

Allsop advises *"Electricity may be applied to the body, for therapeutic purposes, in several different ways, either in a bath of warm water, or on a bed or couch, and either from dynamos or batteries. A bath for electrical purposes is best formed of enamelled earthenware; the bather is immersed in water of a*

John Mullins – water diviner

considerable temperature, and has copper plates etc., so arranged to pass a current through his body. An electrical bed consists of an ordinary medical couch, upon which the patient reclines. One of the most pleasant and, doubtless most effective, methods of receiving electric treatment is in the hot rooms of the Turkish bath, where specially constructed canvas-seated, easy chairs, with copper plates and connections with batteries are employed. (See Appendix 4 if the reader is curious to know what "other pleasant treatments" were available at Hydros!)

In April 1898, the ballroom was enlarged.

In that year HRP also acquired the tenancy of the nearby Burlington Hotel (later the Savoy) which could be used as a further overspill if there was insufficient room in Hydro.

In the same year he purchased 1, 2 and 3 Stanley Villas, Broad Walk leading the Buxton Advertiser to state that HRP was fast becoming the largest owner of houses in the place. There was only the Duke of Devonshire above him at the time.

In 1899 HRP purchased the whole of the houses in Fountain Street. *The Buxton Advertiser* reported in the edition on 7th July 1899:

"Mr HRP Lomas, proprietor of the Buxton Hydro, has recently purchased the whole of the houses in Fountain Street, which are to be added to the Hydro. In order to accomplish this, the premises are now being gutted preparatory to reconstruction. The entire block, including Mr Lomas' present residence, will provide an extremely handsome drawing room on the ground floor. It will be

Hydro Ballroom 1898
Caterer and Hotel Proprietors Gazette

Savoy
National Monuments Record

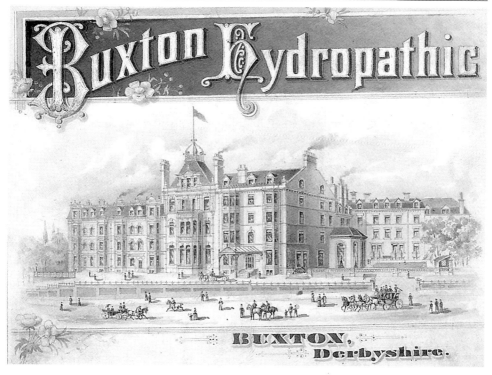

Hydro postcard 1892

Hydro 1892
Courtesy of Buxton Museum and www.picturethepast.org.uk

Hydro extension 1899
Local Studies Library, Matlock

about 70 ft in length by 55 feet in width and the height 18 feet. Immediately over there will be three floors of fine, spacious bedrooms. In the same building there is to be a new central staircase and a passenger lift supplied by the American Elevator Company. The whole of the new block will be fitted with the electric light and warmed with hot-water radiators. Considerable alterations will likewise be made to the main building, for it is intended to provide a very fine entrance hall and lounge, the latter on the continental system. The electric lighting which has been in course of installation during the last eight months, is well forward in the main building and is expected to be complete by Easter. It will be seen from these particulars that very considerable additions and alterations will be made in order to cope with the ever increasing number of visitors to this Hydro."

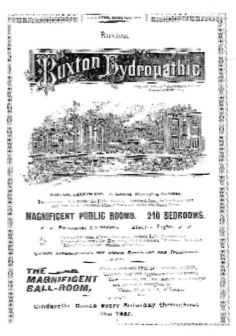

Hydro advertisement in ABC Hotel Guide 1904
Bodleian Library, Oxford

It must not be forgotten that every time an extension was built HRP had to submit the plans for approval to the Duke of Devonshire.

CHAPTER 8

THE YEAR OF FLOTATION AS A LIMITED COMPANY TO REQUISITION – 1899 TO 1917

In view of the substantial development in such a short period of time, not surprisingly, HRP took the opportunity to float the business as a Limited Company.

The prospectus was issued on 3rd May 1899 and was published in *The Times* inviting applications for 55,000 ordinary shares and 55,000 5% preference shares in Buxton Hydropathic Ltd at £1 each.

There was also a debenture to be raised for £50,000 at 4% per annum repayable at 105% after 1914 at the option of the company on six months' previous notice or on the voluntary liquidation of the company.

H.R.P was to take 5000 preference shares, 5000 ordinary shares and 6000 debenture stock in part payment of the purchase price.

HRP 1899 – aged 40

The trustees of the debenture stock were William Poulsom, chartered accountant, and the local banker Isaac Walton. The directors were HRP, Alfred Lomas, and William Armstrong.

Alfred Lomas had always remained on friendly terms with his cousin ever since the early days when he was mentioned in HRP' first diary and they obviously trusted each other.

William Armstrong was the visiting doctor at the Hydro. It was not unusual for doctors to be shareholders and directors of Hydropathic establishments leading to certain allegations of conflict of interest. Nevertheless it lent a certain amount of credibility to the business to have a Doctor as one of its directors. He was a director of the Hydro from its incorporation to 1924. He also wrote two books about Buxton and its waters.

Mr GW Bosworth was company

the LIST of APPLICATIONS will OPEN THIS DAY (WEDNESDAY), the 3rd of MAY, and CLOSE on SATURDAY, the 6th of MAY, 1899.

BUXTON HYDROPATHIC, LIMITED.

INCORPORATED UNDER THE COMPANIES ACTS, 1862 TO 1898.

SHARE CAPITAL £110,000,

Divided into

55,000 FIVE PER CENT. CUMULATIVE PREFERENCE SHARES OF £1 EACH
and
55,000 ORDINARY SHARES OF £1 EACH.

Also £50,000 of Four per Cent. First Mortgage Debenture Stock, redeemable at £105 per cent. after 1914, at the option of the Company, on six months' previous notice. The Stock will also be repayable at £105 per cent. on the voluntary liquidation of this Company and in the other events mentioned at the foot of this prospectus. The Stock will be registered in the Company's books, and will be transferable in multiples of £1.

Issue of 55,000 Cumulative Five per Cent. Preference Shares of £1 each, and 45,000 Ordinary Shares of £1 each at par, and £50,000 Four per Cent. First Mortgage Debenture Stock at par.

The vendor will take 5,000 Preference Shares, and £6,000 Debenture Stock in part payment of the purchase money, and the remainder of the present issues is now offered for subscription.

The Debenture Stock will be secured by a deed of trust by which the entire freehold property will be conveyed to the Trustees for the Debenture Stock holders, and will be further secured by a floating charge upon the undertaking and other property, present and future, of the Company.

The interest on the Debenture Stock will be paid half-yearly, on the 1st of September and the 1st of March in each year, and the dividends on the Preference Shares will fall due on the same dates. The first payments will be made on the 1st of September, 1899, and will be for the amount of interest and dividends accrued from the dates of payment of the several instalments.

The Preference shares are entitled to a Cumulative Preference Dividend at the rate of 5 per cent. per annum, and will rank, both for capital and dividend, preferentially before the Ordinary Shares.

Power is reserved under the trust deed to issue from time to time further Debenture Stock up to £20,000, ranking pari passu with the present issue, but this further issue will only be made for the purchase of additional properties that may be required from time to time, and which will be mortgaged to the Trustees.

The Shares and Debenture Stock are payable as follows :—

	PREFERENCE SHARES.	ORDINARY SHARES.	DEBENTURE STOCK.
On Application	2s. 6d. per Share.	2s. 6d. per Share.	£10 per cent.
On Allotment	7s. 6d. per Share.	7s. 6d. per Share.	£40 per cent.
On the 31st day of July	10s. 0d. per Share.	10s. 0d. per Share.	£50 per cent.

TRUSTEES FOR DEBENTURE STOCKHOLDERS.
WILLIAM POULSOM, Esq., J.P., Broreo-hill, Bootle, Lancashire.
ISAAC WALTON, Esq., Buxton, Derbyshire.

DIRECTORS.
*HERBERT REGINALD POMEROY LOMAS, Esq., Buxton, Chairman and Managing Director.
ALFRED LOMAS, Esq., Tuddenham, Mildenhall, Suffolk.
WILLIAM ARMSTRONG, Esq., J.P., Pictor-hall, Derbyshire.
*Will join the Board after allotment.

BANKERS.
The LONDON and WESTMINSTER BANK, Limited, Lothbury, London, E.C., and Branches.
The SHEFFIELD and ROTHERHAM JOINT-STOCK BANKING COMPANY, Limited, Buxton, Sheffield, and Branches.

SOLICITORS.
GREVILLE, SON, and JARVIS, 2, Staple-inn, Holborn, London, W.C.

BROKERS.
JOHN PRUST and Co., 37, Throgmorton-street, E.C., and London Stock Exchange.
R. A. ARMITAGE and SON, 10, St. Ann's-square, and Stock Exchange, Manchester.

AUDITORS.
JAMES HARRIS, SONS, and Co., 8, Old Jewry, London, E.C.

SECRETARY AND OFFICES.
Mr. G. W. BOSWORTH, Buxton Hydropathic, Buxton.

PROSPECTUS.

The Company is formed for the purpose of acquiring from the Vendor the Freehold of the Buxton Hydropathic, Buxton, Derbyshire, as a going concern, including the plant, machinery, furniture, fixtures, fittings, and consumable stock therein, together with certain other Freehold Properties contiguous thereto and known as Shaftesbury House, Annan Bank, Hornby House, and Malvern House, which are being altered and adapted and will shortly be connected with the Hydropathic.

Buxton has for many years been celebrated as a summer health resort, but it is only during the past few years that it has come into prominence as a winter residence, during which period the average number of winter guests at the Hydropathic has more than doubled.

The baths are a very important and lucrative feature of the establishment. The Buxton Hydropathic is the chief English centre for the "Nauheim" treatment of heart disease. The electric installation, which is believed to be the most complete for medical purposes in England, comprises the several varieties of electric baths and the various forms of dry electricity. All the latest hydropathic methods are largely employed. The "Greville" electrical hot-air treatment, which has so rapidly come to the front, is given here. The baths are largely used by outside visitors as well as by those staying in the establishment. Large numbers of people, however, prefer to stay in the house where the baths are given, thus making them independent of varying weather and other discomforts. A continually increasing number of visitors come for treatment during the late autumn, winter, and early spring, and thus form an additional source of revenue during the least busy periods of the year.

The Buxton Hydropathic has been the property of Mr. Lomas, the vendor, for the past 25 years, and during that period there has been a steady growth in the business, which has necessitated several enlargements. So largely has the business of the Hydropathic increased of late years that the vendor some few months since decided upon further materially increasing the accommodation, and for that purpose acquired the adjoining properties, known as Shaftesbury House, Hornby House, Annan Bank, and Malvern House. The full extent of the additions and improvements will be as follows :—Large entrance hall and smoking lounge, second lift, large drawing room, 45 bed rooms, and domestic offices. These additions and improvements are now in the course of being carried out, and the vendor undertakes to finish the same and to completely furnish the new premises next year without further cost to the Company. Such confidence has the vendor in the undertaking that he has stipulated to take 10,000 shares and to hold the same for a period of not less than seven years from the registration of the Company, and has further agreed to act as managing director for the same period.

Arrangements have been made for the continuance of the valuable services of Miss Thomas, the manageress, who has been connected with the Hydropathic for many years. The Directors have also arranged to retain the present staff.

The property has been valued by the well-known firm of Debenham, Tewson, Farmer, and Bridgewater, and the following is a copy of their report :—

To H. R. P. LOMAS, Esq., Buxton Hydropathic, Derbyshire.

50, Cheapside, London, E.C., February 3, 1899.

We have carefully surveyed the whole of the premises in which this establishment is conducted.

We have prepared and send herewith a complete plan of the whole of the properties, which are situate on high ground with important frontages of about 324 feet to Hartington-road and of about 164 feet to Fountain-street, unquestionably occupying one of the best positions in the place for such an establishment, commanding fine distant views and particularly beautiful home views over the Buxton Gardens.

The Hydro is a substantial stone building expressly erected and particularly well adapted for the purposes of such an establishment. It contains upwards of 140 bed rooms, a spacious entrance hall, vestibule, and inner hall, with corridors, reading room, billiard room, ball room with two galleries, drawing room, dining hall, coffee room, breakfast room, visitors' servants' dining room, dining room for staff, passenger lift from ground floor to the upper floors, numerous bath rooms, lavatories, and all the necessary adjuncts to a large establishment of this description, with commodious kitchens, pantries, larders, store rooms, cellarage and other offices.

There is also a detached laundry, with outbuildings and greenhouses.

The whole property is in good substantial and decorative repair.

The Hydro has an installation for electric light, the completion of which is now progressing, and we understand and assume it will be finished at the cost of the vendor.

The Hydro is thoroughly well and completely furnished throughout.

We are informed and assume that the whole of the properties are freehold.

The vendor has recently purchased the several freehold houses adjacent to the southern end of the Hydro known respectively as Shaftesbury House, Annan Bank, Hornby House, and Malvern House, and is proceeding to rebuild, alter, adapt, and connect the same with the Hydro proper.

These additions will be of great importance and value to the establishment, and will provide an extra large drawing room, ladies' lavatories, and 45 bed rooms. It is proposed that they shall be connected with the Hydro by means of an ornamental glazed corridor.

We are of opinion that before these alterations and additions were commenced the fair marketable value as between a willing buyer and a willing seller of the whole of the properties as a going concern, including the furniture, fixtures, fittings, machinery, and other effects (but excluding the value of the goodwill) was eighty-eight thousand three hundred and sixty-five pounds ... £88,365

The estimated cost of these additions and alterations (including decorating and furnishing and equipping the whole of the rooms) is £15,000.

We understand that the vendor will undertake to complete the same at a cost of not less than that sum, which must, there-

---

Hydro Prospectus 1899. Page 1

The Times

to ... ...to the amount of our valuation 15,000

Making a total of £103,365
One hundred and three thousand three hundred and sixty-five pounds.

DEBENHAM, TEWSON, FARMER, and BRIDGEWATER.

Messrs. James Harris, Sons, and Co., of 8, Old Jewry, London, E.C., Chartered Accountants, have recently examined the books of the Hydropathic, and the following is a copy of their certificate:—

London, 8, Old Jewry, E.C., 10th March, 1899.

Messrs. Greville, Son, and Jarvis, Solicitors, 2, Staple-inn, London, W.C.

Re the Buxton Hydropathic.

Dear Sirs,—We beg to inform you that we have investigated the accounts of the Buxton Hydropathic for the three years ended 31st January, 1899, for the purpose of ascertaining the annual net profit during that period, and we certify it to be as follows :—

For the year ended 31st January, 1897 .. .. £7,338 9 4
For the year ended 31st January, 1898 .. .. 8,512 7 0
For the year ended 31st January, 1899 .. .. 9,521 17 2

Total for the three years £25,372 13 6

Annual average £8,457 11 2

In arriving at the net profit no charge has been made in respect of interest on capital, income-tax under Schedule D, and management by the proprietor, but full provision has been made for depreciation and wear and tear.—We remain, dear Sirs, yours faithfully,

JAMES HARRIS, SONS, and Co., Chartered Accountants.

It will be seen from the above Certificate that the profits have steadily increased during the last three years, and that the average profit for the same period has been £8,457 per annum. If we deduct from this sum £1,000 for the salaries of the Managing Director and Secretary, and the remuneration of the Board of Directors, there is left a net annual income of £7,457

The net interest per annum on the £50,000 Debentures will be £2,000
And the dividend on the 35,000 Preference Shares 1,750
                                                                     3,750

Leaving a sum of £3,707

which is more than sufficient to pay a dividend of 6 per cent. upon the whole of the Ordinary Share capital now to be issued.

From a careful calculation, based upon the amount of business which has had to be declined for want of accommodation, the vendor estimates that the additional premises will, when in full working order, add a net less sum than £1,350 to the net profits of the Company, which will be sufficient to pay a further dividend of 3 per cent. on the Ordinary Shares.

The price to be paid by the Company has been fixed by the Vendor at £130,000, payable as follows :—£5,000 in Preference Shares, £5,000 in Ordinary Shares, £6,000 in Debentures, and the balance of £114,000 in cash, or partly in cash and partly in shares or debentures, at the option of the Directors, and is made up as follows :—

Valuation by Messrs. Debenham, Tewson, Farmer, and Bridgewater, as set out in their report £88,365
Additions and improvements as also mentioned therein.. 15,000
Goodwill.. 26,635
                                                                     £130,000

The business will be taken over as a going concern from the 1st March, 1899, the Company receiving the profits from that date. The vendor undertakes to pay all the expenses of the formation of the Company up to and including allotment, except the ad valorem duty payable by the Company as purchasers and mortgagors of the property, and no promotion money has been or will be paid, nor have any agreements been entered into for underwriting the whole or any portion of the capital of the Company.

The following is the only contract entered into, viz. :—An agreement dated the 24th day of April, 1899, between Herbert Reginald Pomeroy Lomas (the vendor) of the one part, and Alexander Friend, Trustee on behalf of the Company, of the other part, being the agreement for the sale and purchase, and under which Mr. Lomas agrees to act as Managing Director for at least seven years, at a salary of £600 per annum, and to complete the said additions and improvements next year, and to expend thereon out of his own moneys a sum of at least £15,000.

There may be other contracts, verbal or in writing, relating to the business of the Hydropathic, to none of which the Company is a party. Applicants for shares will be deemed to have had notice of the contents of such contracts, and to have agreed to waive any claims they may have on the ground that the law, whether by virtue of section 38 of the Companies Act, 1867, or otherwise, has not been more fully complied with, and every allotment of shares will be made on this condition.

A Stock Exchange settlement and quotation of the Debenture Stock, Preference and Ordinary Shares will be applied for in due course.

Copies of the above-mentioned contract for purchase, the report and valuation of Messrs. Debenham, Tewson, Farmer, and Bridgewater, the certificate of Messrs. James Harris, Sons, and Co. chartered accountants, together with a draft of the trust deed for securing the Debenture Stock, and the memorandum and articles of association can be inspected at the office of the solicitors of the Company, 2, Staple-inn, Holborn, London, W.C.

Applications for shares and Debenture Stock may be made on the accompanying form, and forwarded to the bankers with a remittance for the amount of the application money.

If no allotment is made the application money will be returned in full, and where the amount allotted is less than that applied for the balance will be credited towards the amount due on allotment, and any excess returned to the applicant.

Prospectuses and forms of application can be obtained at the offices of the Company and from the Bankers, Brokers, and Solicitors.

The Debenture Stock will also be repayable in the event of the security created by the trust deed becoming enforceable as provided by the following clauses of the deed.

Clause 14. The security hereby constituted shall (subject to clause 15 hereof) become enforceable in each and every of the events following (that is to say) :—

(1) If the Company shall make default in the payment of any principal moneys or interest which ought to paid in accordance with these presents.

(2) If an order shall be made or an effective resolution passed for winding up of the Company.

(3) If a receiver of the Company's undertaking or any part thereof shall be appointed, and such appointment shall, in the opinion of the trustees or trustee, be prejudicial to the security hereby constituted.

(4) If a distress or execution be levied or enforced upon or against any of the chattels or property of the Company.

(5) If any execution, extent, or other process of any court or authority is sued out against the mortgaged premises or any part thereof for any sum whatever.

(6) If default shall be made by the Company in the performance or observance of any covenant, condition, or obligation binding on the Company under these presents.

(7) If the Company shall, without the assent in writing of the Trustees or Trustee, cease to carry on its business.

Clause 15. Section 20 of the Conveyancing and Law Property Act, 1881, shall not apply hereto, but before making any such entry or taking possession as aforesaid, or any sale, calling in, collection, or conversion under the aforesaid trusts in that behalf (hereinafter referred to as " the primary trust for conversion "), the Trustees or Trustee shall, except when they or he shall certify that in their or his opinion further delay would imperil the interests of the Debenture Stockholders, and except in the case of such order or resolution as aforesaid having been made or passed, give written notice of their or his intention to the Company, and shall not enter upon the mortgaged premises or execute the primary trust for conversion if in the case of such trust arising by reason of any default in payment of any principal moneys or interest the Directors shall prove to the trustees or trustee payment of the principal or interest so in arrear within three calendar months next after such notice shall have been given to them, or if in the case of such trust arising by reason of any distress, execution, extent, or other process or by reason of any breach of obligation as aforesaid, the Company shall, with all reasonable despatch, upon such notice as aforesaid being given, pay out, discharge, or satisfy such distress, execution, extent, or other process or fully perform or make good such breach of obligation to the satisfaction of the trustees or trustee.

Buxton, 24th April, 1899.

THIS FORM CAN BE USED.

BUXTON HYDROPATHIC, LIMITED.

FORM OF APPLICATION FOR PREFERENCE AND ORDINARY SHARES AND DEBENTURE STOCK.

TO THE DIRECTORS OF BUXTON HYDROPATHIC, LIMITED.

Gentlemen,—Having paid to the Bankers of the Company the sum of £................., being a deposit on application as follows :—

2s. 6d. per share on .... 5 per Cent. Cumulative Preference Shares of £1 each .. £
2s. 6d. per share on .... Ordinary Shares of £1 .. .. £
10 per cent. on £ .... 4 per Cent. First Mortgage Debenture Stock.. .. .. £

of the Buxton Hydropathic, Limited, I request you to allot me that number of shares or amount of stock upon the terms of the prospectus, dated the 24th day of April, 1899, and I agree to accept the same or any smaller number or amount that may be allotted to me, and I request you to place my name on the register of members in respect of the shares or stock to be allotted.

Name (in full) ....

Please write   Address (in full) ....
these particulars
clearly.   Description ....

                            Signature ....

                            Date.................... 1899.

Separate Cheques must accompany each application.

Hydro Prospectus 1899. Page 2
The Times

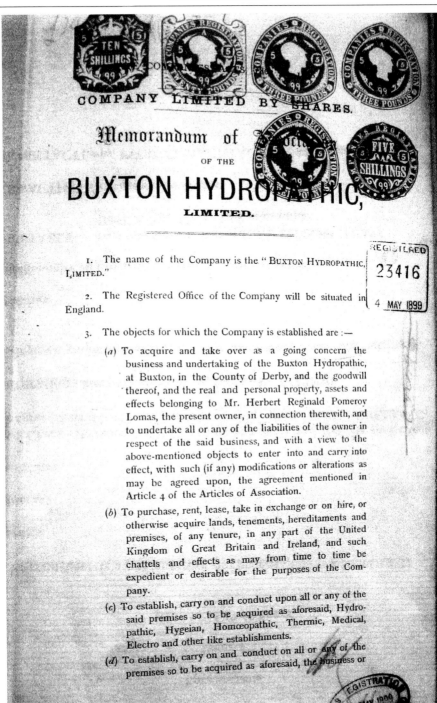

COMPANY LIMITED BY SHARES.

Memorandum of

OF THE

BUXTON HYDROPATHIC,

LIMITED.

REGISTERED

23416

4 MAY 1899

1. The name of the Company is the "BUXTON HYDROPATHIC, LIMITED."

2. The Registered Office of the Company will be situated in England.

3. The objects for which the Company is established are :—

(a) To acquire and take over as a going concern the business and undertaking of the Buxton Hydropathic, at Buxton, in the County of Derby, and the goodwill thereof, and the real and personal property, assets and effects belonging to Mr. Herbert Reginald Pomeroy Lomas, the present owner, in connection therewith, and to undertake all or any of the liabilities of the owner in respect of the said business, and with a view to the above-mentioned objects to enter into and carry into effect, with such (if any) modifications or alterations as may be agreed upon, the agreement mentioned in Article 4 of the Articles of Association.

(b) To purchase, rent, lease, take in exchange or on hire, or otherwise acquire lands, tenements, hereditaments and premises, of any tenure, in any part of the United Kingdom of Great Britain and Ireland, and such chattels and effects as may from time to time be expedient or desirable for the purposes of the Company.

(c) To establish, carry on and conduct upon all or any of the said premises so to be acquired as aforesaid, Hydropathic, Hygeian, Homœopathic, Thermic, Medical, Electro and other like establishments.

(d) To establish, carry on and conduct on all or any of the premises so to be acquired as aforesaid, the business or

Memorandum and Articles of Association of Buxton Hydropathic Ltd
National Record Office

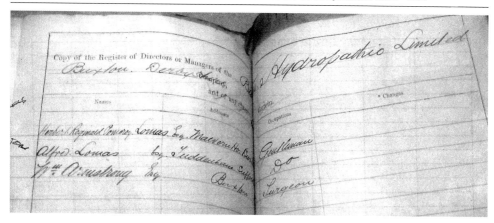

Register of First Directors of Buxton Hyfropathic Ltd
National Record Office

secretary. He was also the hard-working manager of the Hydro to whom HRP was able to delegate much of the running of the Establishment.

The prospectus was as follows:

"The company is formed for the purpose of acquiring from the Vendor the free - hold of the Buxton Hydropathic Buxton Derbyshire as a going concern including the plant machinery, furniture, fixtures, fittings and consumable stock therein, together with certain other freehold properties contiguous thereto and known as Shaftsbury House, Annan Bank, Hornby House, and Malvern House, which are being altered and adapted and will shortly be connected with the Hydropathic.

Buxton has for many years been celebrated as a summer health resort, but it is only during the past few years that it has come into prominence as a winter residence, during which period the average number of winter guests at the Hydropathic has more than doubled.

The baths are a very important and lucrative feature of the Establishment. The Buxton Hydropathic is the chief English centre for the "Nueheim" treatment of heart disease. The electric installation, which is believed to be the most complete for medical purposes in England, comprises the several varieties of electric baths and various forms of dry electricity. All the latest hydropathic methods are largely employed. The "Greville" electrical hot air treatment, which has so rapidly come to the front, is given here. The baths are largely used by outside visitors as well as by those staying in the establishment. Large numbers of people, however, prefer to stay in the house where the baths are given, thus making them independent of varying weather and other discomforts. The continually increasing number of visitors come for treatment during the late autumn, winter, and early spring, and thus form an additional source of revenue during the least busy periods of the year.

The Buxton Hydropathic has been the property of Mr Lomas, the Vendor, for the past 25 years, and during that period there has been a steady growth in the business, which has necessitated several enlargements. So largely has the business of hydropathy increased of late years that the Vendor some few months since decided upon materially increasing the accommodation, and for that purpose acquired the adjoining properties, known as ShaftesburyHouse, Annan Bank, Hornby House and Malvern House. The full extent of the additions and improvements will be as follows: – large entrance hall and smoking lounge, second lift, large drawing room, 45 bedrooms, and domestic offices. Those additions and improvements are now in the course of being carried out and the vendor undertakes to finish the same and to completly furnish the new premises next year without further cost to the company. Such confidence has the Vendor in the undertaking that he has stipulated to take 10,000 shares and hold the same for a period of not less than seven years from the registration of the company, and has further agreed to act as managing director for the same period.

Arrangements have been made for the continuance of the valuable services of Miss Thomas, the manageress, who has been connected with the Hydropathic for many years. The directors have also arranged to retain the present staff."

The property was valued by Debenham Tewson Farmer and Bridgwater and the following is a copy of their report:

"To HRP Lomas Esquire Buxton Hydropathic Derbyshire
We have carefully surveyed the whole of the premises in which this establish - ment is conducted.
We have prepared and send herewith a complete plan of the whole of the properties, which are situated on high ground with important frontages of about 324 ft to Hartington Road, and of about 164 ft to Fountain Street, unquestion - ably occupying one of the best positions in the place for such an establishment, commanding fine distant views and particularly beautiful home views over the Buxton Gardens.
The Hydro is a substantial stone building expressly erected and particularly well adapted for the purposes of such an establishment. It contains upwards of 140 bedrooms, a spacious entrance hall, vestibule, and inner hall, with corridors, reading room, billiard room, Ball room with two galleries, drawing room, dining hall, coffee room, breakfast room, visitors' servants' dining room, dining room for staff, passenger lift from ground floor to the upper floors, numerous bath rooms, lavatories, and all the necessary adjuncts to a large establishment of this description, with commodious kitchens, pantries, larders, storerooms, cellarage and other offices.
There is also a detached laundry, with outbuildings and greenhouses.
The whole property is in good substantial and decorative repair.
The Hydro has an installation for electric light, the completion which is now

progressing, and we understand and assume it will be finished at the cost of the Vendor.

The Hydro is thoroughly well and completely furnished throughout.

We are informed and assume that the whole of the properties are freeheld.

The Vendor has recently purchased the several Freehold houses adjacent to the southern end of the Hydro known respectively as Shaftsbury House, Annan Bank, Hornby House and Malvern House, and is proceeding to rebuild, alter, adapt and connect the same with the Hydro proper.

These additions will be of great importance and value to the establishment, and will provide an extra large drawing Room, Ladies' lavatories, and 45 bed - rooms. It is proposed that they shall be connected with Hydro by means of an ornamental glazed corridor.

We are of opinion that before these alterations and additions were commenced the fair marketable value as between a willing buyer and a willing seller of the whole of the properties as a going concern, including the furniture, fixtures, fittings, machinery, and other effects, (but excluding the value of the goodwill) was £80,355"

Interestingly, a cellarage was shown in the valuation. A full licence to sell intoxicating liquor on the premises was not obtained until 15th February 1930!

The later valuation of the Hydro under the *"The Lloyd George"* 1910 Finance Act (an Act requiring a valuation of all freeholds throughout the country) described the property less glowingly:

"Finance Act 1910
Valuation of Buxton Hydro Co. Ltd.

Occupier   The Buxton Hydro Co. Ltd.
Owner   do.
Interest of Owner   Freehold

Particulars, description, and notes made on inspection.
Stone built slated Hydropathic establishment overlooking the Buxton Gardens.

The Buxton Hydro contains;
covered terrace, drawing room, smoking room, billiard room, living room, restaurant room, all room with spring floor, 36 ft by 38 ft radium room, and selling rooms, managers room, office and rooms in basement used as stores. Linen room, servants room, pantries, coal and slick cellars,shel room, kitchen, storerooms, larders, staff room, bedroom, grocery store, and out to hall, four cellars 12 ft square, usual domestic offices, 2 ft Waygood-Otis passenger lifts. Ladies and gents spray douche vapour and hot air baths. Ladies and gents lavatories, 177 bedrooms (note 28 of these are inferior bedrooms i e bedrooms

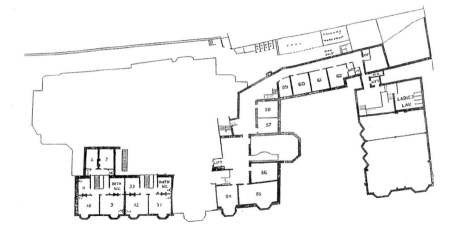

FIRST FLOOR.

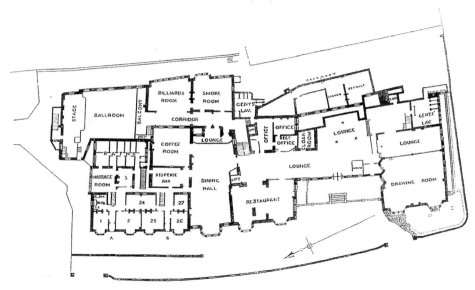

GROUND FLOOR.

Plan of Ground and First floors of Hydro
National Monuments Record

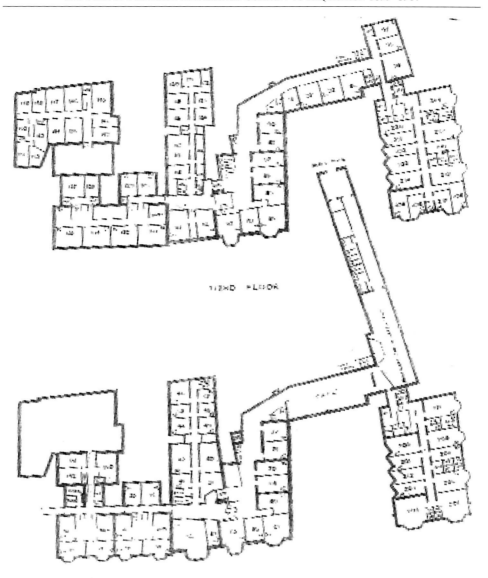

Plan of Second and Third floors of Hydro
National Monuments Record

with obstructed views and bad outlooks). Extensions and additions have been made to the building at various times so that the premises have not been arranged to the best advantage. There are six different staircases consequently a great amount of valuable space is taken up with landings. The external condition of the premises is good. The internal decorations are in very fair condition. They there are no grounds and gardens to the Hydro. Market value as personally agreed with John Berry. T.G.F. £46280."

and the Savoy as:-

"Valuation of Savoy Hotel.

Occupier   *Lomas Herbert Reginald Pomeroy.*
Owner   *Duke of Devonshire.*
Interest of Owner   *Freehold*

Particulars, description, and notes made on inspection.

Fourth-floor : four bedrooms (staff) and box room, 1 bedroom and wine room up other staircase.
Third floor: 11 bedrooms (1 staff 10 visitors)
Second floor: 2 bedrooms, linen room, bathroom, H. M. closet, lavatory. 10 bedrooms. W.C.
First floor: Wash house, outside coals boots and yard, wine room, manager's sitting room, kitchen scullery, larder, waitresses' pantry, dining room, lounge, gents lav. and W.C. Drawing room, small dining room. 1 bedroom.
Ground floor: smoke room, lav.urinal and W.C. Bar, wine store, hall, office, wine cellar, bottled cellar, beer cellar, small smoke room, bar and vault, W.C.
Licensee.   Mr H H Kirk (Manager for Mr Lomas)
Licence duty £158. Comp. levy   £20 this year formerly £40.
About 4 barrels a week average, two and a half gallons a week spirits, 4 dozen half-pints bottled beer, turnover between £4000 and £5000. Free house.
Valuation   Market Value of Fee Simple in possession of whole property in its present condition.

Net annual take say 8% on £4500   £360
          Y.P.   22
          £8100
   Comp. Levy £20 x14Y.P. 280
          £7820"

This was a large turnover of alcohol for the Savoy, being a very small hotel! Returning to the prospectus, the chartered accountants, James Harris sons and Co stipulated the annual net profits for the Hydro for the years ended 31st January 1899 as follows:

For the year ended 31st January 1897...	£7,003.	9	4
For the year ended 31st to January 1898...	£8,512.	7	0
For the year ending 31st January, 1899...	£9,521.	17	2
Yearly average	£8,457.	11	2

In today's terms £8,457 equates to about £581,754. The Accountants go on to say that there should be ample profits available to pay a dividend of eight per cent and a further three per cent once the improvements had been made.

HRP was to receive £130,000 from the sale made up of 5000 preference shares; 5,000 ordinary shares and 5,000 debenture stock and the balance of £114,000 in cash, in today's terms approximately £7,844,808.

The first list of shareholders included people from all over the country some of whom had obviously stayed at the Hydro and were sufficiently impressed to invest money in the venture. There were also a number of local people and permanent residents at the Hydro who invested in the company.

Thomas Lomas, HRP's father, purchased 2000 shares and his new wife, Caroline, 900. In later years a number of the Bulteels became investors. Even the opposition hoteliers, such as Chas. Smilter, proprietor of the Crescent Hotel, were not above investing in the company, although that may have been because they wanted to keep an eye on how the Hydro was progessing. In total there were 303 shareholders and the application was oversubscribed.

The Buxton Advertiser in its edition of 6th May 1899 noted:

> *"The first directors are Herbert Reginald Pomeroy Lomas (who will join the board after allotment), Mr Alfred Lomas of Tuddenham Mildenhall, Suffolk (a cousin of the first named) and Mr William Armstrong J P, Pictor Hall, Derbyshire. Mr Herbert Reginald Pomeroy Lomas has shown himself so able a manager of the establishment in years past that he needs no help in that direction. His cousin will no doubt render requisite assistance, and Mr Armstrong, as medical officer, so to speak, of the Hydro, will show that it is perfectly compatible to do his duty at once to patients and shareholders."*

The timing of the flotation was impeccable.

The well-known catering company, Spiers and Pond Ltd, announced in 1898 that they had arranged to build a hotel in Buxton "*which is to eclipse any establishment of the kind now existing there.... no difficulty is anticipated as to obtaining a full licence, it being a matter of notoriety that such a hotel as now contemplated is urgently required to satisfactorily meet the requirements of the town.*"

HRP was wise to float the Hydro before the future Empire Hotel was built.

It was on 24th May 1899 that Queen Victoria visited Buxton, two years after her Diamond Jubilee. At this time Buxton was in its heyday, leading the country as a fashionable resort with its 15 quality hotels and increasing numbers of visitors.

Although the company documents, now held at the National Archives, do not show the accounts of the company until 1907, at no stage subsequent to that date were the net profits to exceed £6,400. The net profits from 1907 until 1917 were:

1907... 4636
1908... 5210
1909... 4636
1910... 5210
1911... 6490
1912... 5421
1913... 5378
1914... 4914
1915... 5429
1916... 5622
1917... 5233

Dividends of five per cent for the ordinary shareholders were regularly paid during this period, even 8% in 1901. Fairly steady, but not showing the great promise of earlier years.

The Caterer and Hotel-keepers Gazette announced on 15th June 1900:

"The first years' working of the Buxton Hydropathic as a limited company proved entirely satisfactory for its shareholders not only received an 8% dividend but in addition a goodly sum was carried forward to next year's accounts, and some £1,300 written off as to depreciation. The popularity of this favourite Hydropathic seems to be moving by leaps and bounds, and the want of increased accommodation for winters has been met by the directors (Mr HRP Lomas as their able and most practical chairman and managing director) by the addition of a new wing, which is now complete, and will bring the capacity of the Hydropathic for visitors up to 350. In the new wing will be found, in addition to some 40 large and well furnished and ventilated bedrooms,

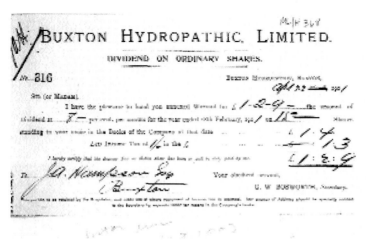

Dividend Warrant of Buxton Hydropathic Ltd
Buxton Museum

lavatories etc, a large dining saloon (making in all four at this establishment) and a handsome new drawing room. Other features of this fine Hydro are an attractive lounge, new electric lift by Waygood and company and the entire lighting of the building by electricity. The whole of the furnishings and cabinet work are by Messrs. Maple and company. Mr Lomas is ably assisted in the management by Miss Thomas and Mr Alex Friend."

In 1905 a dividend of four per cent was declared and £1,100 carried forward and £300 placed to the credit of the new laundry which was added the previous year.

The *Caterer and Hotel-keepers Gazette* gave details of the new Hydro laundry:

"The practice is growing for large hotels and Hydros to clean their soiled linen and that of their guests at their own a private laundries. The proprietors of the Buxton Hydro have gone a step further and, having recently added a model laundry to their already greatly enlarged premises, have announced that they are prepared to receive outside work from private families. The new laundry is lofty, well lighted, and well ventilated. Soiled linen and other fabrics are received at the door on the ground floor, and after undergoing the various processes of cleansing, ironing,airing, etc are passed on for delivery from a higher landing, so that the soiled and finished articles never come into contact. The washing machines and hydro extractors, supplied by the Liddell Engineering Company, of Kingston on Thames, are on the ground floor, while on the first floor the drying, ironing and calendering take place. Here there is in use the Blackman Drying System, which consists of a square wooden structure in which the articles are placed and through which a constant current of fresh-air is created by powerful fans, the moist air being drawn out by other fans at the top and discharged through ventilators, the clothes thus receiving the advantages of natural open-air drying. There are machines specially constructed for every class of work, such, for instance, as goffering. The hand irons are all heated by gas, consequently there is no waste of time in changing heaters. There is a special department for curtain and blanket cleaning. An interesting feature of the new laundry is that distilled water is used through - out".

In August 1906 the valuations in the Buxton and District Share List was 10/3 for the £1 ordinary shares, 16/6 for the £1 cum.pref.shares and 85 for 100 4% Debenture stock.

Still the improvements continued and in April 1912 *The Caterer and Hotel-keep - ers Gazette* noted:

"The Buxton Hydropathic at Buxton, one of the largest and most up-to-date establishments of the kind in the kingdom, has recently installed one of Messrs McDowell, Steven and Co's large centre ranges in its commodious kitchen. The range is of a special type, 12 ft long by 5 ft wide, with descending flues taken

below the floor level into a vertical chimney. It is fitted with six large ovens and three fires, and is capable of doing a very large amount of cooking. The range has rounded corners with O.G moulding, bright guard-rail all round, strong plate rack, and the hobs are framed and panelled, and are 2 in. thick by 2 1/2 in. thick over the fires. Above is fixed a large galvanised iron hood, connected with a brick flue, its object being to carry away the fumes given off during cooking operations. A new double potato and vegetable steamer, supplied by the same firm of London engineers, has also been added. This has two separate chambers, and each is capable of steaming 3cwt.of potatoes at one time, or 6cwt. in all. With these additions to the kitchen equipment, no difficulty should be experienced in catering for the large number of visitors who continually resort to the Buxton Hydro, which is ably managed by our subscriber, Mr G W Bosworth."

In September 1914 *The Gazette* tried to encourage the hotels and Hydros in the spa towns of England to capitalise on the closing of the German spas to British visitors in view of the commencement of the First World War; *"The virtual closing of the German spas to visitors of British nationality has offered an excellent opportunity to our own inland watering places such as Harrogate, Buxton, Strathpeffer or, Llandrindod Wells, etc.which, so far as the efficacy of their curative waters and variety of "treatments" are concerned, yield not a jot to such overrated spas as Homburg, Nauheim, Wiesbaden, and Karlsbad. In some of these diabetic clinics on the continental plan are sure to be installed, and particulars of one such are to hand from the Buxton Hydro Hotel, where a separate wing is devoted to the clinic rooms. There is a long list of dietaries, the meals being prepared in a special kitchen controlled by a cook thoroughly trained for diabetic work. An inclusive charge is made to patients, which embraces the free use of the Buxton waters, strongly "activated" with added radium, the radio-oxygen treatment, and the baths, electrical and otherwise, the only extras being medical fees, medicines, and wines and spirits. We have no doubt the Hydro, so well managed by our old subscriber Mr G W Bosworth, will find due reward for its enterprise."*

In November 1914 the Empire Hotel in Buxton, which was erected in 1901, was commandeered for the purpose of the billeting of Canadian troops. It was built of imported Bath stone and lavishly decorated with glass and marble and attracted a wealthy clientele of European diplomats.

But the success of the Empire was to be short-lived and it was used as a hotel for only 11 years. The Buxton climate proved too severe for the stone which began to erode and the economic climate and changing fashions also took their toll.

Spiers and Pond Ltd who owned the Empire Group of hotels, including the Empire at Bath and the Granville Hotel at Ramsgate, suffered from declining profits in 1913 and eventually a Receiver was appointed in 1916. The company did however recover and the Granville Hotel reopened in April 1920.

There was now some indication of the impending upheaval for the Hydro. On 2nd

Empire Hotel
Courtesy of Derby Museums and Art Gallery and www.picturethe past.org.uk

October, 1917 HRP was informed that the Hydro, described as a hotel by GW Bosworth, company secretary in the notice to the shareholders, was to be taken over by the government for the purpose of a Canadian hospital.

The effects on the Hydro lasted for a number of years as it was closed for three years breaking the continuity of the business.

CHAPTER 9

OCCUPATION BY THE GRANVILLE CANADIAN SPECIAL HOSPITAL

The final straw for Lieutenant Colonel J T Clarke, the commanding officer of the Granville Canadian Special Hospital in Ramsgate, came on 22nd August 1917at 10.45 a.m. Four bombs from 10 enemy aircraft were dropped in the grounds of the annexe resulting in two men being killed and several patients and personnel being injured. 198 patients were temporarily evacuated to the Canadian Convalescent Hospital, Epsom and 229 patients to Lord Derby's War Hospital in Warrington.[52]

The War Office had taken over the Granville Hotel at Ramsgate in September 19th, 1915 as a hospital for the Canadian wounded. The Spiers and Pond Group of hotels purchased the hotel in 1899 but it had been closed since January 1915. It was in a poor

Granville Hotel, Ramsgate

---

52 Canadian War Diaries www.collectionscanada.ca

state of repair and required a great deal of remedial work. Electric and hydrotherapy had been a feature of the hotel.

The original idea of it being purely a convalescent hospital was changed and on November 20th it became known as the Granville Canadian Special Hospital for the treatment of shell-shock, nerve diseases and lesions, and injuries of bones and joints. Chatham House was also taken over as an annexe in March 1916. This was formerly a boys' school. It contained various kinds of workshops and a large gymnasium.

An article in *The Times* of October 11th, 1916 gave an idea of what a patient could expect when he was admitted to the hospital:

"The Canadian Special Hospital. Patients curing themselves. Anyone who knew a certain hotel on the coast before the war should visit it in its new guise of Special Hospital of the greatest importance for Canadian soldiers. Cases likely to make a slow recovery are, if possible, sent to it before they become chronic, for it is much easier to loosen an elbow joint made stiff by a rifle bullet, if the adhesions are recent, than if they have been allowed to become old and firm.

On arrival the patient is seen by the board, who prescribe his treatment. In the examining room there is a "shrine" with votive offerings of crutches, splints, and spectacles, with which the patients arrive and without which they depart. The moral effect of this sight probably begins the cure. The treatment may be heat, light, electricity, or massage. The really special feature of the hospital is that it is very largely self-contained and that the patients are made to cure them - selves. The commanding officer has been wounded, and most of the unusually small permanent staff are disabled men. Work and Play. When a man arrives he is a full patient, he wears hospital blue, is allowed to do no work, and has very little leave; he is made to feel that he is a patient rather than a man. His ambition is to "get his khaki", when he at once becomes primarily a man and only incidentally a patient. Khaki men have such electrical or other treatment as they may want, and go for re-education to the gymnasium, where there are many ingenious devices for bringing the various damaged groups of muscles gradually into play. All the men who go to the gymnasium are expected to play some game so as to learn to use their damaged muscles naturally and spontaneously. All khaki men are on light duty daily for a few hours, for the benefit of the hospital. Some are cooks, some do clerical work or are in charge of the recreation room, and some are dining-room attendants. A stiff shoulder, which receives treatment half-an-hour every day, is not regarded as a reason for neglect either of work or play. The khaki men knock off work at 4p.m., and have plenty of passes in contrast to the men in blue, who have few. There is great competition to get into khaki.

The hospital does its own work by the help of its khaki men. All the splints are made on the spot. A blacksmith made deaf by the guns forges those of the "Thomas" variety. Flat metal splints are much in use, and some inventive genius has commandeered the tin boxes in which the tea arrives and welded them into excellent arm splints. Men on light duty make hospital lockers and run the electric plant. Victims of shell-shock paint furniture, do light gardening, or look after fouls. The doctors bear emphatic testimony to the value of light work in cheerful surroundings for the cure of shell-shock, many cases of which are sent to the hospital.

Of those who enter the hospital 60 per cent return to full duty and 16 per cent to light duty, and of the rest, those who have received to the full all that time and medical science can accomplish are with regret discharged. Some are transferred to hospitals more suitable for the treatment of acute illness. The patients are so well and usefully employed that the usual hospital atmosphere is quite absent. The small wards into which the hotel bedrooms have been converted are a great advantage. The hospital, with its two annexes, has beds for a thousand patients."

Ramsgate was in a vulnerable position and became England's most bombed town during the war. It had been attacked by a Zeppelin in May 1915 when the town appeared to revel in the novelty but this did not last long as more raids followed between 1916 and 1918. The 1917 raid year was particularly terrible when Ramsgate was terrorised day and night by all types of aircraft. On 17th June 1917 a Zeppelin dropped a torpedo near the harbour which hit an ammunition dump in the original fish market causing a number of explosions. The organised Gotha fleet's attack on Thanet in general and Ramsgate in particular took place on the morning of 22nd August 1917. The fleet consisted of 10 huge bombing Gothas probably comprising a section of the third German bombing squadron from the St. Dennis Westren, Goutrode and Mariakerke aerodromes in Belgium. An eye-witness described the scene; *"The machines appeared in battle formation from the eastward. They were formidable-looking craft of immense and uniform size, moving forward deliberately and slowly as if on display for the benefit of the public. From doorways and roofs crowds witnessed the aerial battle. The invaders appeared like silvery dragon flies glistening in sunlight. They dodged in and out of the white and black puffs of smoke which appeared just before them"*.[53]

In view of the bombing the commanding officer deemed it advisable to find a safer position for the hospital. He had to move quickly and found an ideal situation in the middle of England where the hospital could remain unmolested by bombs. To the end of replanting the Granville in Buxton the authorities took the two largest and most palatial hotels in the town, the Buxton Hydro and the Palace Hotel. The Hydro was considered ideal for the main hospital with a bed capacity of 700 especially as it already had a number of baths and equipment which would help to heal the patients. The Palace Hotel had a bed capacity of 650. The following auxiliary buildings, as compliments to the hospital, were also taken – the Devonshire Hotel, for quartering

---

53   Chas A F Austen *Ramsgate Raid Records 1915-1918* The Addiston Publicity Bureau

THE ILLUSTRATED LONDON NEWS, Sept. 1, 1917.— 237

THE AIR-FIGHT NEAR MARGATE: "GOTHAS" FALLING.

DRAWN BY S. BEGG FROM A SKETCH BY AN EYE-WITNESS.

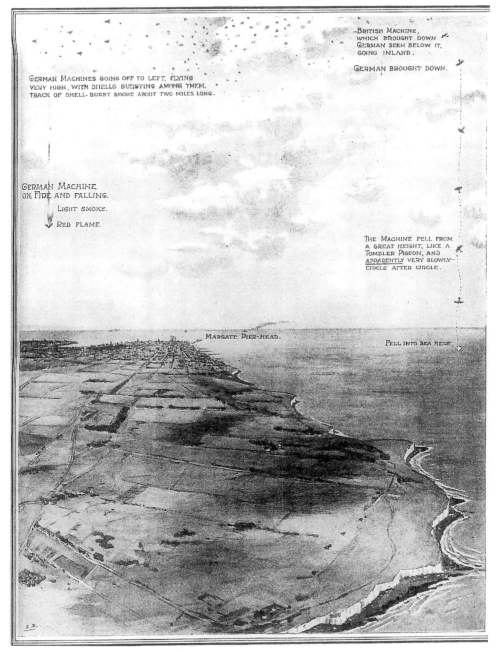

Bombing near Margate, 1st September 1917

Illustrated London News

93

AIR RAIDS.

To enjoy immunity from the dangers of Hostile Aircraft
and the worries of housekeeping,
visit

The EMPIRE HOTEL, BUXTON,

OR

The EMPIRE HOTEL, BATH.

In both of these Establishments the acme
of luxurious comfort may be obtained.

Empire Advertisement
The Times

the personnel; the Grosvener Hotel, along with 1 and 5 Rochester Terrace, for the accommodation of the nursing sisters; the Pavilion Hotel for the officers; the Kensington Hotel, for the Pathological Department, Dental Surgery, and Red Cross stores; Salt's ironworks for the housing of the Arts and Crafts; the Oddfellows Hall along with the Torr Street gymnasium, for the gymnasium department.

The Peak Hydro was also later used by the Canadians.

The Empire Hotel was used for the billeting of Canadian soldiers. The hotel had previously advertised visitors to come to the Empire in Buxton and Bath to escape the air-raids!

In February 1917 *The Caterer and Hotel-keepers Gazette* complained of the wholesale commandeering by the government of hotels, and in a lesser degree of club-houses, naturally causing considerable perturbation in catering circles, and it was felt to be somewhat unjust, and in some cases unnecessary. It continued:

"It is happily described by The Times as "the passion for great establishments."
It would almost appear that hotels are the only suitable buildings for accommodating the great bureaucracy which has been called into existence by war conditions. But there are big office blocks and wholesale warehouses, as well as temporally disused museums in London, which might be used to satisfy the office mania of newly created government departments, the heads of which must apparently have nothing less than an entire hotel, club house, or great private mansion for the luxurious accommodation of themselves and their army of subordinates.
It is urged that hotels can be quickly cleared, but no consideration is given to the hardship and inconvenience caused to permanent and temporary residents evicted at the shortest notice. Then, again, most of the hotels are large

company undertakings with thousands of shareholders, who see with much in quietude their properties impounded and their flourishing businesses brought to a dead stop. It is true that compensation is promised by the state, but even fixed on the most liberal basis, the ultimate loss must be considerable, for that intangible but very important asset, "goodwill", will have been largely destroyed. We must, of course, all suffer in these critical and exacting times for the good of the state, but it is scarcely fair that one industry should bear more than its proportionate burden of sacrifice."

In October *The Gazette* carried an article entitled:

"Buxton hotels commandeered. The great Derbyshire spa, whose marketplace is said to be the highest in England, will have its public accommodation seriously curtailed by the closure of five establishments which are to be devoted to the requirements of wounded Canadians. It is unfortunate for the respective proprietors that their successful businesses should be closed down and a little hard that the mountain spa is to be deprived pro tem. of five establishments, while other well-known resorts not far away escape scot free. The fact that Buxton was already the Canadian discharge depot no doubt influenced the War Office authorities in their action, and we can only hope that the question of compensation to shareholders and proprietors, when it comes up for settlement, will be dealt with fairly and generously.
From a wider point of view, the selection of Buxton as a recuperative resort for the wounded is irreproachable, for its high altitude, fine air, salutary springs, and admirable curative arrangements render it an ideal sanatorium".

The Canadian war diaries from 18th September to 31st October 1917 set the scene for the journey from Ramsgate to Buxton. They do not give such a comprehensive picture of the state of the Hydro when taken over as that for the Granville hotel as the move had to be carried out with great speed.

They contain a short write-up of the daily events and a monthly report from the various departments to the commanding officer. Examples of the YMCA reports giving details of the arrangements being made for the entertainment of the patients are annexed. Extracts from the war diaries also include news of the armistice and peace having been signed. Examples are also shown of the treatment records, quartermaster reports and the very important Arts and Crafts department.

It was obviously not just a hospital but published its own newspaper, made artificial joints and was as self-sufficient as it could be.

The Hydro was certainly *"fit for the purpose"*. The glass domed coffee room was used as an operating theatre providing ample light for the surgeons; the ball room could be used for shows, films, concerts and services on Sundays. The baths were used to help the patients exercise their limbs again and of course there were plenty of bed-rooms for the patients.

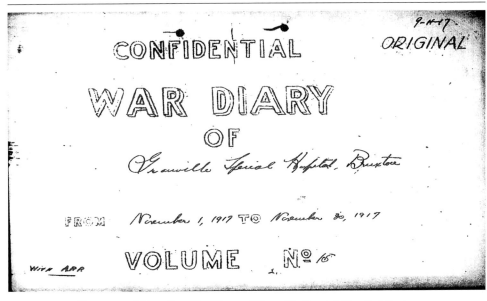

First page of Canadian War Diary of Granville Special Hospital Buxton
Canadian Records Office

WAR DIARY. Continued. G.C.S.H. Sept. 1917.

Sept. 18th. 10.00.a.m. Lecture to Officers, "Remedial Gymnastics", Capt. W.C. Lowry.
2.30. p.m.   "   "   "   "X-Ray Routine", Major J.D. Morgan.

Sept. 19th. 10.00 a.m. Lecture to Officers "Results in the Treatment Department", Capt. W.F. Kenney
2.30 p.m.   "   "   "   "Medical Corps Work at the Front", Major W.G. Turner. MC.

Sept. 20th. Officer Commanding returned from leave.
10.00.a.m. Lecture to Officers "The writing up of Documents for Patients", Capt. N.G. Cooper.
2 .30.p.m. "Orderly Room" Lecture to Officers, Major Steyner Ellis.

Sept. 21st. 10.00.a.m. Lecture to Officers "Medical Corps Work at the Front", Major W.G. Turner, M.C.
2.30. p.m. Staff Meeting.

Sept. 22nd. Routine.

Sept. 23rd. Stand to, Air-Raid warning 12.30. a.m. to 1.15. a.m.

Sept. 24th. Officer Commanding proceeded on tour of Inspection to various Hospitals.
Stand-to Air-Raid warning 9.20.p.m. to 10.15.p.m. Enemy machines in neighbourhood. Local guns were fired
No. casualties or damage.

Sept. 25th. Stand-to Air-Raid warning 7:10. p.m. to 10.30.p.m. Enemy machines in neighbourhood. Naval guns were
fired, no local casualties or damage.

Sept. 26th. Officer Commanding proceeded to Buxton from Eastbourne to look over new Hospital sites.

Sept. 27th. Stand-to Air-Raid warning 7.30. to 10.35.p.m. Nothing in this neighbourhood.

Sept. 28th. Stand to Air Raid warning, 7.30. to 10.50.a.m Enemy machines in this neighbourhood. Local guns were
fired. No casualties or damage.

Sept. 29th. All Officers, N.C.O's and Men proceeded to different Hospitals for duty with the exception of
5 officers and 51 other ranks.
Stand to Air-Raid Warning 6.30. p.m. to 10.50.p.m. Heavy firing took place at intervals.

Sept. 30th. Officer Commanding returned from Buxton.
Stand-to Air-Raid warning 6.45.p.m. to 10.50.p.m. Heavy firing at intervals.

O.C. Granville Canadian
Special Hospital, Ramsgate.

War Diary September 1917
Canadian Records Office

Granville Canadian Special Hospital,
(Treatment Department)
Buxton Derby.

B

December 1st.1917.

To:
Officer Commanding,
Granville Canadian Special Hospital,
Buxton.

Sir;

The following is a summary of the work done by the various departments devoted entirely to treatments, for the month ending November 30th.1917.

On November 9th, this department commenced treatment, all apparatus being in good working order, with the exception of Radiant Heat apparatus and Electric water baths, the wiring of which had not been completed.

TREATMENT STAFF.

O   October 20th.Mr.J.McRay, civilian masseur, was taken on the strength of this department.
October 21st.25177 Pte.Bailey B.masseur, was admitted to hospital and was transferred to C.A.M.C.Depot November 11th.
Nov.7th.Capt.E.P.Tammy posted as M.O.i/c Treatment Dept.
Nov.7th.Capt.J.C.R.Stone posted to Treatment Dept.
Nov.14.Capt.E.P.Tammy cease to be M.O.i/c Treatment Dept.on transfer to No.16.Canadian General Hospital, Brawshott.
Nov.15th.Capt.J.C.R.Stone posted as M.O.i/c Treatment Dept.
Nov.22nd.M/S.E.T.McDowelI reported for duty as instructor in massage.On same date M/S.Tomlinson,M/S Wade and M/S Hall reported for instruction.

ELECTRO-THERAPEUTIC APPLIANCES.

All this apparatus is in good condition and working satisfactorily, with the exception of Electric Water Baths, wiring of which is not yet completed.
Sept.31st.received from A.E.Dean and Co.one resistance coil for Inductive Wall Plate, renewal.
Nov.9th.Received from A.E.Dean & Co.six spring contacts for Faradic Throbber and two secondary interrupter coils.The six spring contacts sent back to A.E.Dean & Co.Nov.21st.to be fitted with platinum points.
Nov.19th.Received from A.E.Man & Co.Spare Wilson Modulator in faulty condition (wiring of rheostat broken)and was sent to Arts and Crafts Dept.of this hospital for repair.

RADIANT HEAT APPARATUS.

This apparatus is working very satisfactorily.One large bell lamp was taken over from the Buxton Hydropathic Hotel in good condition.

Static apparatus and Nose Bath were taken over from Buxton Hydropathic Hotel for use in this department.

DRY CARBONIC BATHS.

Through lack of accomodation all these baths were not installed.Those in use have been re-enamelled and are giving good results.

Page 1 Report of Treatment Department 1st December 1917
Canadian Records Office

From Capt.C.V.Scott
Officer i/c Arts & Crafts.

To Officer Commanding,
C.C.S.H.

Arts & Crafts Dept.,
Granville Canadian
Special Hospital,
Buxton,Derbyshire.
1st.January 1919.

Sir,
I have the honour to submit the following report on Arts & Crafts for the month of December 1918.

In general the results have been satisfactory both in the work turned out and the attendance of patients.

The total number of two-hourly treatments given during the month was 1491, a decrease of 350 from November bringing the average down to 62.12 attendances daily.The number of two-hourly treatments given in the different departments are as follows:-

Mechanical Dept."	114	Artificial Limb Dept.	197
Electrical "	131	Fretwork Dept.	166
Painting "	47	Signwriting Dept.	95
Carpentry "	145	Sheet Metal "	251
Tailoring "	105	Wood Carving "	111
Printing "	53	Blacksmith "	19
Saddlery "	57		

The daily summary registered on the last day of the month as follows:-

Total Capacity.   164
Total at Present.   63
Total Vacancies.   101

The work accomplished in the various departments is described below:-

MECHANICAL DEPT: This department has been kept very busy,and during the month the work of turning out Metal Massage Tables,Special Orthopaedic Appliances,and the various Hospital Repairs,has been done in a very creditable manner. A Special Hook has also been completed and fitted to an arm amputation case,with the result that he has been enabled to do a certain amount of brush and crayon work in the Signwriting Dept. The patients all show a marked improvement both in their work and disabilities.

SHEET METAL DEPT: In this department,the work entailed by hospital repairs has not been quite as heavy,but the demand for splints has been about the same as the month previous.A large number of stock appliances which we had on hand have been overhauled and are being packed up to send to the Central Medical Stores. The patients employed in this dept.,all like the work and a marked improvement has been noted in their condition.

PRINTING DEPT: During the month this dept.,has been working to capacity. A large number of Hospital Forms have been printed,as well as the Menus for the Patients Xmas Dinner. The patients have shown unusual interest in the work,with the result that there has been a fair attendance and considerable improvement in their condition.

TAILORING DEPT: During the month several Arm-Chairs have been re-covered and upholstered,owing to them being badly worn,as they have been in daily use in the recreation rooms at the Hydro for over a year. This has furnished good material for the patients to work on,and the usual amount of interest has been taken in this work,as well as their ordinary routine and taken on the whole this department has had a very successful month.

SIGNWRITING & PAINTING DEPTS. These depts.,have been exceptionally busy this month.Crutches,Massage Plinths,Splints,Poison Cupboards, and all the minor repair work,have had to be attended to,as well as Xmas Signs and Hospital Card work. There has been a good attendance of patients here ,with very good results.

SADDLERY DEPT: The work has been,as usual,very heavy in this department. A large number of Orthopaedic Appliances have had to be leather covered,as well as an order for 24 Drop Foot Appliances,which are entirely of leather. Owing to this department being very small,only a few patients can be employed here,but the results derived by them,have been very good.

PEG LEG & ARTIFICIAL LIMB DEPT. This department is without a doubt our busiest one,and the work has been turned out in a very workmanlike manner. There has been a large turnout of Peg Legs,and also a good showing from the patients.

CARPENTRY DEPT: The work of repairs to the hospital,and the making of some Hand Looms for our own hospital,as well as some poison cupboards, a Plaster Bandage Box,and new Crutches,has kept this dept.,going steady for the month,and,as the different jobs supply ample interesting work for the patients,they have shown a marked improvement in their disabilities.

Report of Arts and Crafts Department 1st January 1919
Canadian Records Office

Granville Canadian
Special Hospital,
Buxton: Yorkshire.

June 2nd, 1919.

Y.M.C.A. WAR DIARY REPORT - May. 1919.

To:-
The Officer Commanding,
G.C.S.H., Buxton, Derbys.

Sir:-

I beg to submit the following report of the work of the Canadian Y.M.C.A. in the Granville Canadian Special Hospital, (Buxton Hydro), and Peak Annexe, for the month of May, 1919.

ENTERTAINMENTS Owing to the exceptionally fine weather, it was found inadvisable to continue the usual concerts in the Recreation Hall, as the attendance did not merit the expense. The weekly London concerts, held in the Hippodrome for O.D.R. men, also our own patients, have, however, been continued right through the month, and have been well attended.
On May 21st, through your kindness in engaging all the ground floor seats in the Opera House, about 400 patients were able to attend the matinee of "My Pigeon Post", which was generally very much appreciated, especially by the very bad cases, for whom special arrangements were made to attend.
A concert was given by local talent in the largest ward in "A" Section on Thursday, May 29th, where bad cases were brought from other wards. This was much appreciated by men confined to their beds.
O.D.R.Band concerts have been given weekly, and just lately, during the hot weather, it has been arranged for these to be held under the verandah in front of the hospital, instead of in the Recreation Hall, which answers admirably.

CINEMA
ENTERTAINMENTS Have been given 3 times each week, but again, owing to the very fine weather and patients being allowed to remain out somewhat later, the attendances have fallen off so much, that it is thought advisable to reduce the number of performances to one or two, instead of three weekly.

MAGAZINES,
WRITING PAPER
& LOCAL
STATIONERY. These have been freely distributed at both places, and made good use of.

LIBRARY At both places is made fair use of.

SUNDAY NIGHT
UNITED SERVICE. This was discontinued early in May by Captain Armour, owing to small attendance, and a big United Service being held in the Picture House.

OUTDOOR
SPORTS The 6 tennis courts and 2 croquet lawns have been put into good order and are being freely used. Often at night time there are 50 or 60 patients, Nursing Sisters, and Personnel on the ground. The great difficulty at the present time is in getting equipment, for the Y.M.C.A. of Canada is easing up with supplies of Sports goods. We are sadly in need of more tennis racquets and particularly of tennis balls.

Believe me, Sir, to remain,

Yours respectfully,

Hon. Captain,
Officer in Charge,
Can. Y.M.C.A.

YMCA Report May 1919
Canadian Records Office

The number of Canadians had a considerable impact on the social scene in Buxton. The war diaries show that special performances were laid on at the Buxton Opera House. In the afternoon of 12th November 1918 a performance of "David Garrick" by the Forbes-Knowles company took place. On returning from the Opera House the patients were given a special supper and the evening wound up with a dance at the Hydro.

A Hospital Concert Party and orchestra was organised for the purpose of entertaining the patients. Concert parties were brought from London, Liverpool and Manchester and local artists were generous in their efforts to entertain the patients. On Sunday afternoons the Boots orchestra was engaged for regular recitals.

A baseball club was formed, and two teams from the Granville played in a local league. The six tennis courts and two croquet lawns were put into good order and were being freely used. Often there were at night times 50 or 60 patients, nursing sisters, and personnel on the ground. The great difficulty was in getting equipment as the YMCA in Canada were easing up with supplies of sports goods. They were sadly in need of more tennis racquets and particularly of tennis balls.

The stark and sobering entry for June 3rd 1919 read:

"Hospital visited by Colonel E.C.Hart, A.D.M.B., Canadians, Liverpool
2543 Amputation Cases discharged from Hospital from 1915 to May 31st, 1919.
17,000 patients passed through Hospital. The amputation cases are divided as follows:-
Arm Amputations   718
Leg Amputations   1825
Total: -   2543"

On 20th June 1919 the Hydro was evacuated ready to hand back to HRP who no doubt had the unenviable task of turning it back into a hotel again.

James Shore may well have approved of the new use for the Hydro, although not obviously the reasons the patients were there, but HRP's main purpose for the building was as a hotel and a business proposition. This was severely restricted during and immediately after the war. What happened to the 60 or so permanent residents and living in staff is a matter for conjecture, but presumably they found alternative accommodation.

Another difficulty was that in April 1911 out of the 9 waiters living in at the Hydro, 8 were from Germany or Austria. Many foreigners came to work in the catering trade in the nineteenth century to learn English or escape political or religious persecution. Europe was not seen as such a safe place as England. They came from countries that regarded hotel work as an honourable occupation and were used by the Hotel owners to raise the standards of their hotels. The palatial highland hotels upheld their status by employing continentals "typically a French chef, German waiters and Italian or Swiss managers."[53]

---

53 *The Golden Age of British Hotels* Derek Taylor and David Bush Northwood Publications 1974

Buxton Hydro, Granville Canadian Special Hospital

Canadian patients at Hydro entrance

Courtesy of Buxton Museum and www.picturethepast.org.uk

In 1880 the Globe commenting on the improvement in British hotels said "the guest comfort is enhanced by service in public rooms being performed in great measure by foreigners. English staff are not as good."

The looming problems in Europe meant that there would have been a strained atmosphere in the Hydro. Could this have been the cause of the waiters' one day strike? (*See post Chapter 15*)

HRP then had a long battle claiming rent for the loss of the use of the building and a claim for dilapidations. The hearing was scheduled for 30th May 1919.

The government had tried to argue that compensation was an ex-gratia payment not a payment as of right, but in the De Keysar's hotel case it was decided that although public benefit may require interference with the rights of individual subjects, yet public benefit did not require that the value of the subject's right should be confiscated. The case was decided in the summer of 1920. HRP was not alone in having to issue proceedings against the government. Spear and Pond Ltd who owned both the Empire and the old Granville hotel in Ramsgate, had to take proceedings under the Defence Act 1842. Their case was also stood over until the result of the De Keysar's hotel case had been heard.[54]

54 *The Times* 25th June 1920

CHAPTER 10

DECLINE OF THE HYDRO 1920-1945

HRP could not wait until settlement of the Hydro's claim against the government had been finalised as it may have taken many years, so he took the opportunity of carrying out further improvements to the hotel as well as converting many of the bedrooms to en-suite.

On August 7th, 1920 the Hydro placed an advertisement in *The Buxton Advertiser* that it was now open for business as usual.

Not quite as usual because over the ensuing years, habits of the general public changed and no longer did they stay for a number of weeks but only a few days, and this was to be one of the reasons why things began to go downhill. From all intents and purposes the Hydro carried on as before the war, the entertainment and balls were as lavish as ever. However, the balance sheet showed a different story.

The directors' report of 12th August 1922 reads:

1920 advertisement in Buxton Advertiser concerning reopening of Hydro

"The directors in submitting the accounts for the year ended the 28th February 1922 desire again to point out in explanation of the figures shown below that the company is still without a settlement of the claim against the government for reinstate - ment of the hotel after the military occupation and for rent during the period of reinstatement etc. It is impossible to say when the claim will be settled but every effort has been made to obtain an early and satis - factory settlement.

The number of visitors does not compare favourably with former years, and the falling off of business can only be attributed to the connection having been so completely broken during the war years the hotel was closed, owing to military occupation."

Notice concerning commandeering of Hydro

The report for 1924 and 1926 was similar except that the 1926 report stated:

"The Award has now been declared, and as soon as the Directors can ascertain the debits against it such as income tax etc. they propose to make a payment on account of the arrears of dividend due to the Preference Shareholders.

The Directors wish to place on record their high appreciation of the patience shown by the shareholders during the trying time of waiting for the War Compensation Award.

Your Board are gratified to report the successful opening up of the fine front vista, overlooking Buxton Gardens and the hills beyond, made possible by the removal of houses on the Broad Walk and laying down a hard tennis court on the site, which considerably increases the amenities of the Hotel for guests, and is a valuable improvement. The property has been transferred and handed over to the shareholders free of all cost to the company by Mr HRP Lomas".

In an attempt to provide further impetus to the business HRP used his own money to demolish the houses in front of the hotel, which he owned, and laid down hard tennis courts.

The balance sheet during the history of the Hydro showed splendid years leading up to its incorporation, averaging £8,457 per annum net profit for the first three years

Hydro tennis courts
Courtesy of the Board Collection and www.picturethepast.org.uk

to 1899.

There were no accounts for 1918 and 1920 although compensation was shown for each of those years. The 1922 and 1924 reports of the directors blamed the poor figures on the military occupation and the 1920 report on the General Strike and the high cost of fuel.

Thereafter between 1920 and 1930 the profits were flat at £5,000 per annum. The really serious reduction in profit was between 1931 and 1937, even showing a trading loss in 1937.

Inflation had been rising since the war and the compensation paid for dilapidations by the government did not take this into account.

In 1899 to help to raise finance for the purchase of the Hydro by the company it issued a debenture by way of first mortgage on the freehold of the company amounting to £50,000. There was also a floating charge given in favour of the debenture holders. Interest had to be paid to them as well as the preference share-holders.

HRP was trying to borrow himself out of trouble. In December 1926, as the profits were subdued after the First World War, and the compensation was not adequate to cover the cost of reinstatement, HRP took out a £3,000 mortgage on the Eagle Hotel which he had purchased from the Duke of Devonshire in 1890. This now belonged to the company. A further mortgage on the Eagle was raised on 13th April 1928 for an additional £3,000. He had previously borrowed £2,000 on the security of The Link, 2 Hartington Road.

In the October 1931 the second annual conference of members of The Hotel and Restaurant Association took place at the Palace Hotel Buxton and AWH Lomas was on the conference committee. HRP also attended the conference and put forward a resolution recommending the formation of a publicity committee.

HRP was still trying hard to bring visitors to Buxton!

In November of that year he wrote to *The Caterer and Hotel-keepers' Gazette:*

"Buxton and winter sports. Our very old subscriber, Mr HRP Lomas, managing director of the Spa Hotel, Buxton informs us that given a reasonable fall of snow, Buxton will enjoy a very excellent winter sports season this year.
"The Buxton and District Skiing Club is being formed and an expert has been down from London giving the club organisers advice, and says that in his opinion, given a reasonable fall of snow, there is no district in Great Britain better suited to skiing and winter sports.
"Arrangements for a new and excellent toboggan run are in process and also arrangements for curling and skating. The whole matter depends upon the weather, and there is more than a sporting chance that we may have a good winter with some very suitable snow, when Buxton in general – and Buxton hotels in particular – will do all in their power to show visitors that Buxton compares very favourably with Switzerland".

Despite his endeavours, in 1933 he had to sell the Eagle to Ind Coope and, as the hotel's licence had been used to provide the Hydro with intoxicating liquor, the need for the Hydro to have its own licence was imperative. This was obtained in February 1930, the Directors' Report for 1930 stating that they were pleased to inform the shareholders that they had been successful in obtaining a full excise licence for the Hydro which became operative on 15th May 1930. They went on to state that this should prove a great convenience to visitors and was essential to the prosperity of the hotel.

In 1931 the company changed the name of the Hydro to the Spa Hotel, HRP being upbeat about the future of the Spa and Buxton in the article in *The Buxton Advertiser* proclaiming:

"The Hydro is dead. Long Live the Spa!
Why a hotel changed its name.
"Hydros are invalids' homes", said Mr H R P Lomas. "The number of invalids we get here is small in proportion to the number of healthy visitors. Women nowadays are out playing games and trying to imitate men; they have no time to be ill".
Mr Lomas is the managing director of the biggest hotel in Buxton, which had it its name changed from, "Buxton Hydro Hotel" to "Spa Hotel" on New Year's Day. He was replying to a "High Peak News" reporter who asked him the

SPA HOTEL

(Formerly Buxton Hydro Hotel).

A. A.   Fully Licensed.   R. A. C.

"VERY COMFORTABLE": that is the special reputation that we have won at the SPA HOTEL. It has arisen among our guests, simply because it expressed what they honestly felt about us.

The truth is that while we can claim splendid situation, hot and cold water and radiators in most of the bedrooms, electric lifts, everything that a hotel ought to have, we have never felt that these were enough in themselves. The comfort that we study lies more in a little human consideration, in taking a **personal** interest in your wants, in having a helpful, willing, thoughtful staff.

In studying good honest human creature comfort of this sort, we have had a long experience. Come any time—alone, or with your family. We mean to go on earning that phrase—" very comfortable."

PLEASE ADDRESS YOUR

You'll find the Hotel, with its 240 rooms, is placed just off the main road, with lovely views across the undulating country, yet central for shops and entertainments. Right opposite are the Buxton Gardens—sheltered and very sunny, where are numerous Tennis and Croquet Courts, Bowling and Putting Greens. Our own Tennis Court is just in front of the Hotel. The station is a five minutes' walk.

Notice how as many of the bedroom windows as possible are set at sun-catching angles. In the majority of bedrooms hot and cold water is laid on, as well as radiators or gas fires which you yourself control. There are also suites of rooms with private bath and toilet.

We offer much reduced residential terms for business and professional men.

ENQUIRIES TO THE MANAGER.

Front of Spa Hotel brochure

reason for the change.

"For a long time we have been more of a hotel than a hydropathic establish - ment", added Mr Lomas.

"But you still provide hydropathic treatment?" he was asked.

"Since the Corporation have had the baths we have reduced ours. Now we have no water treatments at all, but only electrical treatments, which are still administered under the qualified supervision of Miss Rigby, B P A."

"I suppose you have to cater for a different type of guest nowadays".

"Yes. People don't come to Buxton now to stay for three weeks or a month. Usually they come in motor cars and are "here today and gone tomorrow". That is why, since last May we have been a fully licensed hotel."

"Should you say that there has been a falling off in the number of visitors to Buxton?"

"No; in fairly normal times the numbers are probably greater than they used to be. Just at present, of course, we are hard hit, like everybody else. Owing to the *depression in trade, we are not getting our usual number of visitors from Lancashire and Yorkshire.*

"Do you think that the Buxton will regain its old prosperity?"

"As soon as we get a definite revival of trade, Buxton will come into its own quite as quickly as other places, if not more quickly; because it is a beautifully managed, clean town, with wonderful air, wonderful waters and surrounding scenery as fine as any in England".

"What led you to select the name, "Spa"?"

"For one thing, we thought the name would be good for the town. Every advertisement we pay for will draw people's attention to the fact that Buxton is a spa. But it took us nearly a year to decide. We had many other names under consideration, but we felt that high-sounding names like "Majestic" didn't suggest comfort. This has always been a home from home, a place where you are known as an individual not as "No. 75"

As a desperate measure, on the retirement of the long-serving Bosworths in 1930, HRP brought in his recently trained second cousin, AWH Lomas, to try and turn the Hydro around. All to no avail, AWH Lomas married, and perhaps seeing that there was no hope for saving the Hydro he bought the smaller and more manageable Royal George Hotel in Perth, Scotland in 1936. F J Aymes was appointed manager in his place. HRP was 75 at the time and would have been too old to take an active part in the day-to-day running of the Hydro.

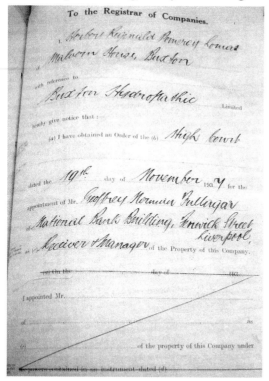

Notification of appointment of Receiver of Buxton Hydropathic Ltd
National Archives

To the dismay of the company's shareholders, on 19th May 1937 HRP obtained an order from the court to appoint Geoffrey Norman Fullagar Receiver and Manager of the property of the Buxton Hydropathic Company Limited. It could not carry on its business any longer and pay the interest of the debenture holders, which was considerably in arrears.

The first public indication that all was not well surfaced in the *Buxton Advertiser* on the 19th August 1937 when it was reported that there were rumours that the Spa was about to close down and that HRP would neither confirm or deny that this was true.

Further similar rumours were reported on the 13th November 1937 and on the 27th November it was reported that a Receiver was now in charge of the Spa.

As Receiver, Mr Fullager would attempt to carry on the business with a view to paying its debts and he would try his best to keep the business going. With this in view, and to keep the hotel in the ownership of the company, he found a prospective tenant, Griffin Hotel Company Ltd and entered into a lease of 21 years on 26th February 1938. The hotel was closed for a short while until Griffin took over but the bar remained open and the Buxton and Devonshire Laundry (part of the Hydro) continued. The number of staff had, of course, to be reduced.

The Griffin Hotel was one of the largest and best known hotels in Leeds and they had applied for a new licence and permission for a comprehensive scheme of improvements.

Griffin Hotels had plans for the newly named Spa Plaza which included wrestling and boxing matches in the ball room – quite a difference from the old days of fancy-dress balls and other similar functions previously held at the Hydro. Unfortunately Griffin's stay at the Spa Plaza was short lived. They too had issued a debenture to assist with the purchase of the fixtures and fittings, and improvements and lease of the Spa. They were unable to make the payments on the debenture and on 7th December 1938 a writ was issued by the debenture holders. An order was made for the winding-up of the company on 15th March 1939.

One wonders why proper inquiries were not made by Mr Fullagar as to the soundness of the tenant – perhaps taking guarantees from directors as would be the case nowadays. Obviously, trading conditions were hard at the time and he was grateful for any prospective tenant.

Nevertheless, the licence was transferred to Mr E Wilks in April 1939 and the search was again on for another tenant or, better still, a purchaser for the hotel.

It was to be a whole year before a purchaser was found during which period the hotel stood empty.

The history of the Buxton Hydro mirrored the history of Hydropathics generally. Before World War Two it can be divided into four periods: the pioneers of 1843-1863; the boom of 1864-1882; the bust followed by years of consolidation between 1883 and 1914; and finally, the Great War and decline from 1914.[55] The boom was the product of the promise of profits and was followed by a crisis due to over-expansion. A combination of the Companies Act and John Smedley's made the development of Hydropathic institutions much more rapid. The supply ran away with demand and it is not surprising that in the years up to World War One no further Hydros were established and their fortunes were mixed. Nevertheless, the period following the crisis was one of consolidation. Most survived. Some faced severe setbacks.

The 1880s saw the bankruptcy of many Hydros due to increased competition.

Where the medical attention at the Hydros meant something, they survived much

---

55   Bradley p.429

better, particularly as more was being learnt all the time about the methods of treatment which were most effective. Inventors came up with a new type of bath almost as regularly as the annual Paris fashions. At the Imperial Hydro Blackpool in 1885 there were 10 different varieties; Turkish, Russian, spitz, needle, spray, rain, plunge, warm, cold or sea water. The Hydros were a world where there was room for the genuine healer and the quack, the professional and the amateur, but like a casino, the majority of the players lost.[56]

Many of the Hydros were able to pay their shareholders in the 1890s between 7 and 12 $\frac{1}{2}$ per cent. per annum.[57]

In 1889 there were 104 Hydros in the UK;[58] one in Ireland, 18 in Scotland, 4 in North Wales, and 68 in the North of England, and seven in the Midlands and south. "The town of Hydros", Matlock, had 19.

This picture continued until World War One when many were commandeered for military or naval hospitals. For those that escaped there was a bonanza after the end of the First World War. When the armistice was finally signed a great spending spree started which helped the hotels already in operation, but came too early for those which had been commandeered. Compensation for damage which would have covered the cost of putting their properties back in order at pre-war levels was inadequate due to the level of inflation.

Most of the Hydros managed to stagger, more or less effectively, through the cycle of depression and recovery that characterised the inter war years.

Though often burdened by debt, hotels did recover in the early twenties. Little by little the situation improved as real wages increased and world trade expanded but unhappily it was not to last, and the Wall Street crash finally killed off many hotels for good.

The outbreak of World War Two again saw the majority of the Hydros requisitioned for military purposes which further thinned their ranks when peace returned.

No doubt HRP could not have faced another upheaval similar to that in the First World War

On the 22nd February 1940 the Norwich Union Life Insurance Society, having appointed a nominee in the contract so as not to disclose its identity to Mr Fullagar, entered into the conveyance to complete the contract. The debenture was discharged and no doubt there were many disappointed shareholders who went empty-handed.

The hotel had been closed since the beginning of the second-world-war with only the bar remaining open and the Norwich Union were to spend the next five years at the Spa, Buxton yet again providing a safe refuge in time of war.

The Society produced a brochure describing their move to Buxton as follows:

"The exigencies of war have changed to some extent the lives and habits of

---

56 Taylor p.94
57 Bradley p.434
58 p.39

practically everyone, and not least those of the small section of the Head Office Staffs of the Life and Fire Offices who now find themselves amongst the Derbyshire hills.

The spreading of risks has always been an essential feature of a successful insurance business, and it is therefore not surprising that when the tempo of war was suddenly speeded up in the early summer, the management decided to decentralise certain portions of the business normally conducted at head office. Tentative plans had, of course, been in existence for some time, but owing to the demands of the Services they had to be modified somewhat. However, in June, the Life Society purchased the Spa Plaza Hotel at Hartington Road Buxton and as soon as certain portions of it had been made ready for occupation sections of the Mortgage, Investment, Annuity, Estates, Surrender Values and Claims departments from the Life Office, including most of the "advance guard" who had temporally been at Birmingham, moved to Buxton. As further sections of the hotel were made ready, the Home Accounts and Renewal Issue departments of the Fire Society, together with their valuable machinery and equipment, were transported to the same destination.

Naturally this immediately caused a crop of rumours, especially in Norwich, to the effect that "Norwich Union are evacuating" but that this is quite untrue will be obvious from the fact that the total staff (Life and Fire) now in Buxton only amounts to 120, or only about one sixth of the total personnel at head office.

In selecting Buxton the management made a happy choice from every point of view as work can be carried on without interruption and the town itself is a pleasant a place as an exile could hope to find in the present circumstances.

The building acquired by the Society is well situated on steeply rising ground near the centre of the town and overlooking the Pavilion Gardens. As it had been unoccupied for some 18 months prior to our taking over, a considerable amount of cleaning, redecoration and restoration was necessary to make it habitable. Indeed work is still in progress and advantage is being taken of the opportunity to provide additional bathrooms and other improvements.

As may be imagined a great deal of organisation was necessary to ensure the smooth and efficient conduct of the Office work and the maintenance of the personnel and Mr Day, who undertook this task, has been tireless and completely successful in his efforts. Everything within reason has been done to ensure the comfort and welfare of the residents and whilst it is something of a wrench for most people to leave their homes for an indefinite period, the arrangements at Buxton had been so well planned and executed that everyone is in excellent spirits.

The departments of the Life Office occupied what was originally the large entrance lounge, whilst smaller rooms leading off the lounge are used by Mr Hines (secretary), Mr Meiklem (assistant manager), and Mr Day (Investment secretary). "The Law" is represented by one of the Life Society's assistant solicitors, Mr Stuart.

Spa ballroom occupied by Norwich Union staff

The fire departments are under the charge of Mr Eric Williamson (assistant manager), the very fine ball room on the first-floor housing the machines (Accounting, Addressall and Comptometers), the clerical staff being in an adjoining room. Mr Davies (Home Accountant) is close by, whilst accommoda - tion is also provided for the necessary stocks of stationery etc.

In addition to the offices, the building is used for residential purposes by the life office staff and their families and also by a number of the Fire Office ladies, whilst lunches are also provided for the male section of the Fire staff who are living in the town.

The catering side of the hotel is in the very capable hands of Mr D Walsh Howarth, whose services were most fortunately available owing to the fact that the hotels of which he is managing director have been requisitioned. Needless to say his hotel experience has been of the utmost value.

Amongst the facilities provided may be mentioned the comfortable lounge with plenty of easy chairs and a piano, the games room with facilities for table tennis and other games, a large drawing room, another smaller lounge on the first floor for quiet reading and writing, and, by no means the least important, a spacious and lofty dining room.

Our building has its own ARP organisation and a series of lectures on first aid has been given by Mr Riches of Norwich, who is an authority on the subject. An office section of the Home Guard has been formed under the command of Mr

Eric F Williamson and keen interest has been maintained, whilst a large number of the staff have also become members of the Auxiliary Fire Service.

A branch of the Athletic Association has also been started and bowls and tennis are going particularly strong.

The hotel was erected just over 40 years ago and during the first 30 years of its life was known as the "Buxton Hydro" specialising in therapeutic and other treatment in addition to its functions as a hotel. It is a substantial and imposing building of the later Victorian style, one feature being the "saw tooth" design which gives many of the principal bedrooms of the south wing a splendid view of the gardens opposite and the surrounding hills.

The hotel was twice modernised, the name being changed successively to the Spa Hotel and then to the Spa Plaza.

The features in Buxton have gone a long way towards minimising the natural regret of those in Buxton at the necessity of leaving home, but all have realised the wisdom of the directors' action and wholeheartedly co-operated in efforts to make conditions at the hotel and contact with head office run as smoothly as possible. There is, of course, a feeling of annoyance that "that wicked man" should have made it necessary to leave home but, the necessity having arisen, everyone realises and appreciates that the Office could not have chosen a better place than Buxton and cannot have done more than has been done in these last few months to make the staff contented and comfortable. We trust that the return of happier times will not be long delayed, so that the head office staffs may again be united at Norwich."[59]

There were also extracts in the Society's in-house magazine;

"First arrivals at the Spa Hotel found a deplorable state of affairs. Beds had not been made since the previous residents had last occupied them over a year previously. The ball room floor was covered with refuse, and the balcony was littered with monkey nut shells.

Under the supervision of Mr C F Day (Investment Secretary) members of staff set to work and soon cleared the portions required for office use sufficiently to allow desks and cabinets to be placed in position.

Unfortunately the weight of the accounting machinery proved too much for the ball room and steel girders had to be used for reinforcement – or the whole department would probably have been deposited in the kitchens below.

It was some weeks before the rest of the hotel could be made habitable for members of staff and their families, and as a temporary measure some were accommodated in nearby private hotels whilst others were billeted in private homes.

Staff found life in the hotel an unnatural kind of existence. It was alright for a holiday, but communal living had its drawbacks, not the least of which was the

---

59 Norwich Union Magazine Michelmas 1940

absence of privacy of home life.

Also, it was impossible to cater for the likes and dislikes of the individual so far as food was concerned and this took a long time to get accustomed to

Those living outside the hotel had the ordeal of reaching the office after very heavy snowfalls. Snow sometimes reached above "wellingtons" and when the thaw set in there was the water of the same depth to wade through!

Against this there was the big advantage of being free from the air raids which Norwich suffered, and we were fortunate to miss such ordeals.

Two families at Buxton lost the whole of their homes in Norwich.

It was a relief that a series of daily bulletins was sent from Norwich and exhibited on the hotel notice boards giving an outline of the previous night's happenings and enabled us to keep in touch with affairs at home.

The restriction of trunk telephone calls to only 6 minutes duration meant that every communiqué to Head Office had to be typed out, handed to the switch - board operator who read the message to the HQ operator, who wrote it down and passed it down to the department. The same procedure was used for the reply. "This system proved very successful" wrote one contributor, "although it was sometimes wise to obtain verification of the message delivered!"

The winter months were long and trying, and it was mainly the efforts of the various committees which were formed which made life bearable.

A "Men's room" for the benefit of the older male members of staff has been comfortably furnished and here they can sit by the fire, smoke their pipes and enjoy a game of snooker when they feel so disposed in the evenings.

Another room was fitted up as a wireless room."[60]

Meanwhile HRP was still living at Malvern House and on 25th July 1941 he died, having appointed his second cousin A W H Lomas, A W Bulteel and WG Bulteel as his executors and trustees (*see post*).

60   Norwich Union Magazine Michelmas 1945

CHAPTER 11

FROM HYDRO TO HOTEL

James Shore's reason for coming to Buxton was to open up an establishment on strict hydropathic lines similar to Smedley's at Matlock. Shore's was one of the first hydros in Buxton. He wanted to provide a place where invalids could take the baths with a background of religion and with his interest in homeopathy this would assist the patients to recover. The patients' families could stay at the Hydro if they wished but there would be very little entertainment and certainly no alcohol.

With Shore's personality Malvern House quickly expanded and he soon gained a reputation both in the town and with the visitors.

Whether he was the great man of business that some saw him is doubtful, although he was quick to spot Buxton's potential.

Religion played a very important part at Malvern House with two services on Sundays open to all. He founded the Free Church of England in Buxton and continued to subscribe to that organisation.[61]

Visiting preachers gave sermons on Sundays. Religion was therefore very much part of *"the cure"* and Shore was just the man to provide that aspect. Having suffered a great deal already in his earlier life and with his own rheumatism he would be sympathetic to the patient's problems.

After Shore's death the services continued with the 16 year-old HRP playing the organ *"behind the curtain"*. From Thomas's letter to Emily, Thomas appeared to take the services, although it is not known for how long this lasted. Certainly, on Sunday 23rd January 1876 HRP states in his diary that there were *"few to service"*, although on the 30th January there was a *"good evening congregation"*. Attendances therefore varied.

By 1881 there was a resident chaplain to take the services.

The first brochure gives details of the hours when the baths could be taken. It emphasises that the town's water only was used in the baths at the Hydro; the natural mineral water could be obtained at the Duke's baths.

Shore would employ *"experienced medical rubbers"* to massage away the aches and pains of the patients.

After Shore's death Thomas built an extension comprising new and improved bed-rooms. In 1883 HRP built a new dining room providing accommodation for 200 persons. The emphasis must surely now be shifting towards a hotel, and particularly

---

61 Free Church of England Magazine

when the ball room was built in 1887. The accommodation was also becoming more luxurious.

It is only in 1890 that HRP turns his attention to improving the baths. He obviously feels it is still an important adjunct to the hotel business and *The Buxton Advertiser* described them in its report of the opening. (*see ante*)

In the 1899 brochure rules and regulations of the bathing department are given. The diseases which claimed to have been successfully treated by the various baths are many and some of the electrical arrangements would make today's electricians shudder!

The brochure emphasises the "*Naheim saline baths*" with the "*Schott exercises*" referred to in Appendix 4.

The 1916 brochure has one page only relating to the bathing arrangements and particular mention is made of the "*recent installation of the four cell electric Schnee baths*" and the "*static wave treatment*" which had also been introduced.

The 1929 Spa of Blue Water advertisement barely mentions the baths and the latest 1930s brochure did not mention them at all.

The brochures indicated that there was no resident medical attendant, although W Armstrong was a director and shareholder. As already mentioned Medical men were often appointed as such to lend credibility to the business.

This could lead to accusations of conflict of interest and in 1905 there were several weeks of correspondence in *The Buxton Advertiser* between Dr Lorimer and the Buxton Hydro.

The natural mineral waters had been taken over from the Duke of Devonshire by the Buxton Corporation in 1904 and Dr Lorimer, a local doctor, had written to the Buxton Urban District Council complaining that the Hydro, in its prospectus when floated in 1899, gave the impression that the Hydro used the natural spring waters in their baths.

The reply from Mr Bosworth on behalf of the Hydro was sent to *The Buxton Advertiser*:

"To the editor
Sir, – enclosed please find a copy of a letter sent to the chairman of the Buxton Urban District Council, in reply to the communication "The Buxton hydro - pathic and the Buxton waters" from Dr Lorimer read at the last council meeting. I shall be obliged if you will insert in your next issue, – yours, etc, G W Bosworth, secretary.
Mr Councillor Brown,

Dear Sir, – my attention has been drawn to a letter sent to you by Dr Lorimer, respecting the Buxton Natural Mineral waters and the Buxton Hydropathic Ltd in which he makes statements which are untrue and misleading. The paragraph he quotes as appearing in the prospectus of the Buxton Hydropathic Ltd he mutilates in a manner that distinctly alters the meaning. The original paragraph is as follows, the words in italics having been omitted by Dr Lorimer:

The baths are a very important and lucrative feature of the establishment. The Buxton hydropathic is the chief English Centre for the "nauheim" treatment of heart disease. The electric installation which is believed to be the most complete **"for medical purposes"** *in England,* **"comprises the several varieties of electric baths and the various uses of dry electricity. All the latest hydro - pathic methods are largely employed. The "Greville" electrical hot air treatment, which has so rapidly come to the front, is given here".** *The baths are largely used by outside visitors as well as by those staying in the establish - ment. Large numbers of people, however, prefer to stay in the house where the baths are given, thus making them independent of varying weather and other discomforts.* **"A continually increasing number of visitors come for treatment during the late autumn, winter, and early spring, and thus form an additional source of revenue during the least busy periods of the year."**

These are the identical treatments which Dr Lorimar on behalf of the Buxton Medical Society in his recent interview with the Baths committee laid stress upon, as being absolutely necessary for the welfare of the town and the installation of which he urged. I consider that the action of Mr Lomas, the then proprietor of the Buxton hydropathic, should be commended rather than condemned, as those methods were introduced into this establishment many years ago, and have been the means of bringing large numbers of people to the town.

I challenge Dr Lorimer to bring forward a single case where an official of the Buxton Hydro has informed anyone that the Buxton natural mineral waters are to be obtained in this establishment. On the contrary, the following paragraphs, which have appeared in our official tarif booklet for the past 12 or 14 years, prove in themselves that we have systematically brought before the public and advertised the mineral waters and baths as being the property of the Duke of Devonshire:

"Buxton Hydropathic, Buxton, Derbyshire. Many invalids and convalescents have their attention directed to the necessity or value of treatment by mineral waters, and, having only the continental springs in mind, dismiss the thought with regret, from considerations of time, distance, or expense. They should know, however, that at Buxton there are springs which compare favourably with the best, and can be reached quickly, cheaply, and easily. Buxton is situated at an elevation of 1000 ft on the limestone rocks, which, whether in Colorado, or elsewhere, are the prime cause of dry, exhilarating air, and it has been long famous for its mineral waters. In bygone generations these waters had all the merit derived from experience, so far as it was possible to communicate it, but now they have an absolute and scientific value (capable of test by any medical man) manifested in the result of careful analysis stated in the following table:

One gallon of water taken from	contains cubic inches of carbonate		
	Nitrogen	Oxygen	Acid
Gastein, Austria...	4.0	3.6	-
Wildbad.Wurtenburg	4.7	1.0	44.3
Buxton, Derbyshire	6.1	-	4.1

The numbers visiting the town for the purpose of taking a course of baths and drinking the waters are constantly on the increase, and, of course, it is impossible to state the number of cures. One test can however be supplied. The Devonshire Hospital accommodates or treats a large number of patients (about 3000 on an average during the year) of whom probably 90 per cent are suffering from diseases of rheumatic or gouty character. Of these 60 per cent have been permanently cured, and in incurable cases a great alleviation is secured. This is undeniable proof at the efficacy of the Buxton waters when used under medical advice, and the result is in accord with the results of the chemical examination of the waters with the fact that at Buxton, more than at any other springs, in the agitation of the waters in bathing, the liberation of nitrogen is more energetic, the chemical result more intense, and the whole combination of influence to which the patient is subjected more "capable of acting on the human organisation".

The springs are the property of the Duke of Devonshire. They are offered to the Public for drinking and bathing on fixed advertised terms, and can be utilised only in the proper building set apart for the purpose.

Bathing department – To invalids suffering from rheumatism or gout, " The Buxton Hydropathic" is attractive on account of its proximity to the pump room and the mineral baths, whose reputation for the cure of these diseases is world - wide"

Copies of this letter are being sent to the Buxton Advertiser and Herald offices for insertion in their next issues – Yours truly, G W Bosworth, secretary Buxton Hydropathic Ltd."

The reply on April 29th was:

"To the editor. Sir, – I observe from your issue of the 22nd inst. that my letter to the chairman of the Buxton District Council about the baths, has elicited from the Buxton Hydropathic Company Ltd a discursive letter, containing a personal attack upon myself beneath notice. The letter is a mere piece of audacious bluff, and therefore requires little comment, the question at issue having been disguised and evaded by its rambling irrelevancy.

It matters not whether the quotation from the equivocal paragraph of the Hydropathic prospectus is condensed, or italicised, or amplified. The equivocal wording is not altered, neither is its ambiguity removed. The paragraphs extracted from the "official tariff booklets" have nothing whatever to do with the question. Does the hydropathic Company really mean to imply, that they were so scrupulously conscientious in preserving the public from deception that, along with each copy of their prospectus, was also issued a copy of the "official tariff booklet" as an antidote? Was the prospectus to be studied by the aid of this illuminating key to the right interpretation of its doubtful passages? The simple practical question, however, which requires a straight answer is this: what impression would be conveyed to the unbiased mind of the plain man, living at a distance from Buxton, knowing nothing about its baths, by reading the paragraph referred to in the Hydropathic prospectus? What meaning would be attached to it? Would it not be that Buxton baths and treatment could be obtained in the Hydropathic? I leave the answer to the common sense and judgment of the impartial reader.

Referring to my former letter. The question at issue has not been touched. My statements remain unassailable and, I venture to add unassailable. I therefore reaffirm: 1) That there is an impression abroad among patients from a distance, that the Buxton baths and those in hydropathics are identical. 2) That as their doctors are generally cited for this misleading information, it is possible, that interested medical shareholders in the hydropathic companies, or those who have perused their prospectuses, may directly or indirectly have been concerned in diffusing the impression. 3) That a paragraph in the prospectus of the Buxton Hydropathic Company about its baths are ambiguous and deceptive; while the Peak Hydropathic professes to have a thermal spring, similar to the Buxton mineral water, if not identical. This spring, so far as known to me, has never been analysed. 4) That there has been a loss of revenue to the Buxton baths from these erroneous ideas. 5) That in the interests of the town and its ratepayers, it is desirable that the council, having acquired the baths should take such steps as they think fit to protect themselves against loss of money from these competing interests. Yours etc. G Lorimer Buxton April 28th 1905."

On the 6th May the Hydro replied:

"Sir, – In reply to Dr Lorimer's letter appearing in your issue of the 29th ult. Dr Lorimer, while evaiding two plain issues – one , my challenge to give the name of anyone connected with the Buxton Hydropathic who has ever claimed that the Buxton Natural Minal Water is used in our baths; the other, the definite statement in the prospectus that the baths given in the Buxton Hydropathic are only those special ones which the then proprietor of the Natural Baths refused to put in, which by the way, Dr Lorimer now asks the council to adopt – falls back upon the insinuation that there are a considerable number of medical shareholders in the Buxton Hydropathic who are spreading amongst their patients the fiction that the Mineral Baths are to be obtained under this roof.

Would Dr Lorimer suggest that, because he is and has been for years a share - holder in and a director of a certain hotel in Buxton, he would use his medical influence for the benefit of that establishment and to the detriment of patients? As a matter of fact, there are very few medical shareholders in the company. The prospectus was issued six years ago to a limited number of persons, nearly all of whom were former customers of the Buxton Hydropathic. On the other hand, over 15,000 copies of the official tariff booklet have been distributed during those six years, and in each one the following paragraphs have appeared:

"The springs are the property of the Duke of Devonshire. They are offered to the Public for drinking and bathing on fixed advertised terms, and can be utilised only in the proper buildings set apart for the purpose.

To invalids suffering from rheumatism or gout "The Buxton Hydropathic" is attractive on account of its proximity to the pump room and the mineral baths, whose reputation for the cure of these diseases is worldwide." which I think will prove to any broad-minded person our good faith. Yours etc. G W Bosworth, Secretary."

The final reply on 20th May 1905 was:

"Sir, – It is scarcely necessary for me to take notice of the letter of the Buxton Hydropathic Company, who have no better explanation and defence to offer the public having been deceived through their baths than by pointing to the fact, that I hold shares in the Lee Wood Hotel, in which, however, there are neither baths nor hydropathic appliances.

1) That visitors from a distance are deceived as to the difference between Buxton Baths and hydropathic baths; 2) That this error has originated in and spread from the hydropathics and has received currency through their prospectuses; 3) That money has been lost to the Buxton Baths in consequence, are indisputable facts which they have not attempted to deny. Neither can these facts be disproved by the artifice of raising a dust on irrelevant issues, and then proclaiming innocence and "good faith to broad-minded persons."

Two points may perhaps require notice before finally disposing of them.

1) In regard to the equivocal paragraph of the prospectus, the Company say that they have made "a definite statement, viz., that the only baths given in the hydropathic are those specified in the prospectus".

This interpretation is untenable. As a matter of fact, it is incorrect, and is contradicted by the long list of baths which appears in your weekly advertising columns, with the whole stock-in-trade set forth to the public.

The baths specified in the prospectus are specified, not because they comprise the only baths given, but because they hold out to the investor the specially high remunerative return which will result from them; therefore, to back out, under the shelter of a limited and restricted reference, is altogether inadmissible.

2) The second is: what in the language of bluff is called their "challenge to name any one of their servants who has said that their baths contain the natural water?" I do not number hydropathic servants among my associates; it is, therefore, absurd to expect that I have learned from a direct expression of their sentiments upon the subject of baths. If there servants have been sufficiently subtle and careful not to commit the Company by saying that their baths contain the natural water, or even if they have been candid enough to say that their baths do not contain the natural water, all this is nothing to the point, and would not prove the absolution of the hydropathic from the error in question and show that it has not originated and spread from it.

Error creeps in insidiously, till "a little leaven leaveneth the whole lump" and the history of the rise and spread has been this:

A stranger arrives at the Hydropathic – he is medically examined, and is informed that the natural mineral water Baths are powerful remedial agents, so powerful that they are positively dangerous, even deadly: In order that the system may be properly prepared for them he must first undergo a preliminary course of milder baths in the Hydropathic to render him fit for the more formidable ordeal.

How long it takes to prepare systems, how many systems are incapable of preparation, and never reach the natural water, or how many systems succumb to the preparation, I know not, neither do I know what portion of intelligences are capable of clearly comprehending the difference between degree and kind of bath, assuming that these distinctions had been duly explained. The result is, that in process of time, the differences between kind and degree of bath are confused, lost, and pass into oblivion, and finally so permeate and pervade the public mind being transmitted by rumour – that the identity of hydropathic baths and Buxton Baths has now become fixed and unquestionable.

What about the official tariff booklets? Enquiry leads me to express a doubt whether this instructive and orthodox literature is so well known as represented: but, allowing that there is such document, and that its circulation has been even in millions of copies – its statements are in perfect harmony with the teaching in the Hydropathic – and it is therefore absolutely useless for clearly enlightening the public, and refuting error, which has entered by another door, and spread and propagated itself in another direction.

Before concluding, I wish to express pleasure in learning that the number of medical shareholders is small, and that the very generally prevalent rumour, that the Buxton Hydropathic had done a splendid stroke of business by having nearly all its shares taken up by doctors – is not correct, but even this pleasing intelligence must be received with reserve, for, on account of medico ethical reasons, shares may be registered in other names, or the medical title or qualification may be omitted altogether – a subterfuge by which the letter of the medical ethical principle is observed, while the spirit is violated – medical shareholders may be more numerous than appear. Referring to the same prospectus, I observe that the medical director has set a precedent by adopting the latter method, viz.: suppressing the medical title, though it is possible that in deference to the exigencies of the company promoting his name should appear on the company prospectus with all semblance of the glamour of a county magnate of a baronial chateau.

The Buxton Hydropathic Company think that "thanks and commendation" are due to their former proprietor for erecting baths, rather than "condemnation". Surely the injury of the reputation of the Buxton Baths is no ground for commendation and gratitude – they might as well expect a public vote of thanks for his having disfigured the district by erecting a chimney for his washing business.

So far as I am concerned this subject is at an end. In the interests of the town and its ratepayers, the attention of the Council has been directed to what, doubtless has been a very serious loss of revenue, and if I have succeeded in convincing them – and from the numerous letters and expressions of thanks received I trust I have not been altogether unsuccessful – my object has been attained. – Yours etc. G Lorimer. Buxton May 18th 1905.

There the matter ended.

Temperance at the Hydro?

Whilst there is no evidence that Shore permitted alcohol it is most unlikely as he wanted to keep to strict hydropathic rules.

Indeed on 28th January 1874 HRP writes that *"Marston had been drinking and was sent away"*.

As far as Thomas and HRP are concerned, HRP refers in his diary to having a brandy and soda at the Pavilion Gardens, he had previously politely refused the beer offered whilst visiting Windsor Castle.

On February 1876 the Rev. Chapman stayed at Malvern House and asked for a pint of Bass's pale ale! He was either asking *'tongue-in-cheek'* or he was testing the system to observe whether alcohol would be served.

HRP also had a glass of sherry in London when attending Stokes School and a brandy and hot water at the Cat and Fiddle, near Buxton. On holiday in 1905 and 1906 he made references to purchasing beer on the odd occasion, so he definitely was not teetotal.

The problem was that to be a strict hydropathic establishment no alcohol should be sold on the premises.

As the entertainment grew so it was expected by the visitors that they could drink alcohol either with their meals or at the various functions. To get round the problem HRP purchased the nearby Eagle Hotel, he already had a lease on the Burlington Hotel (later the Savoy), so that the accommodation provided by the hotels could be used as an overspill for the Hydro, and the Eagle's alcohol licence could be brought into play so that the guests at the Hydro could order their drink and the waiters would then go over to the Eagle to obtain it – rather a long-winded process! An occasional licence was applied for when there was a ball or other function.

In February 1930 HRP applied for a full on licence for the Hydro, opposition to the application coming from the Palace, St.Anne's, the Crescent, the Old Hall, the Savoy and Grove Hotels and the Buxton branch of the British Women's Total Abstinence Union. The usual arguments from the opposition hotels were that there were sufficient hotels that had licences and there was no need for any more. HRP's barrister stated the present application was being made due to the changing habits of visitors, the directors of the Hydro considering it essential in order to carry on the business successfully in the future.

As things stood at that moment visitors had to buy their drinks in advance and then by the bottle, the bottle and glass being taken over from the Eagle which meant that the guests would have to wait some time for their drinks.

The 1910 Valuation gave details of the alcohol sold at the Eagle which would obviously include the orders taken from the Hydro. The barrister stated that visitors no longer came to stay three weeks but since the advent of the motor car they only stayed two or three days, and if they wanted a drink they wanted a single glass not whole bottles. He continued that as of recent years Buxton had become a centre for conferences and a great percentage of the delegates wished to go to licensed premises. HRP stated that he gave up a career as a medical student 50 years ago to take on the management of the Hydro started by his grandfather. He estimated that the turnover with the Eagle for drinks in advance was £2,000 per annum.

HRP confirmed that the hotel had never previously had a full licence and that he did not take alcohol himself! That might have been true then but it is clear from HRP's

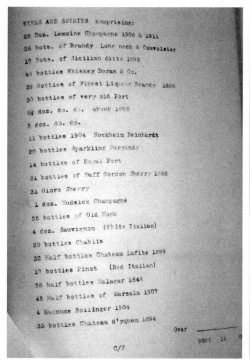

Page 1 Malvern House cellar inventory   Page 2 Malvern House cellar inventory

diary that he used to consume alcohol and indeed in a valuation for insurance purposes in 1918 of the contents of Malvern House there was a wine cellar which was by no means empty, although the drinks could have been used to entertain his personal friends.

The opposing barrister asked HRP whether the Hydro was founded on good old-fashioned hydropathic lines like Smedleys. HRP replied that it was. The barrister stated that as the Hydro had prospered so well without a licence in the past there was therefore no need for a licence now. HRP was asked if he was satisfied with the way the Hydro had been run and he replied that he was never satisfied with anything.

HRP was then cross-examined regarding the present treatments supplied at the Hydro. *"You have derived your present prosperous position from those who have patronised your Hydropathic establishment? – No, I don't agree with you there. About 15 years ago it was called Buxton Hydro and we took the name of the hotel because the Hydro was then going out. I would like to mention one thing in particular: there was a lot of treatment given then in the house on the same lines as Smedleys. Since the Corporation bought the baths we have shut down all treatments as we did not wish to be in competition with the corporation. We now only give three special electrical treatments.*

Buxton is a place to which people come for Hydropathic treatment and it is essential to have a good and well-equipped Hydro establishment? – No, not at all. Hydropathic establishments are things of the past.

You intend to become an hotel and cease to become a Hydro? – Yes.

I suppose Buxton does not get so many visitors as in the past – We get perhaps more people but they do not stay as long.

I suggest that the hotel accommodation is more than adequate? – I do not think it is.

The figures put forward by learned counsel show that hotel accommodation is distinctly decreasing- a large hotel like the "Empire" has gone out of action – There were very good reasons in each case.

The demand for hotel accommodation in Buxton is unfortunately, not what it used to be? – I don't agree. For conferences which are a new thing since the war, there is a lamentable shortage of accommodation; in fact, it is almost a farce to advertise Buxton as a conference town when there are so few bedrooms in the town. Harrogate is a great rival, and we have to bear Harrogate in mind.

I suppose you were aware that in this town and in all parts of the country there is a strong body of people who hold temperate views. Teetotallers often do not want to go to licensed premises. I am suggesting that your house, not being licenced, would prove a very great attraction to this type of people? – That is a matter of opinion.

You give some treatment at the Hydro? – Only electrical."

At the end of the hearing the licence was granted.

HRP's description of the Hydro treatments showed that when the corporation took over the mineral baths the treatments at the Hydro decreased and that in 1930 they only gave three special electrical treatments.

It is arguable that HRP should have applied for a full licence at an earlier stage but in those days he may not have wanted to offend those visitors who genuinely wanted to stay in an alcohol free establishment. There were many who came from Yorkshire and Lancashire who held temperate views. In addition there were restrictive covenants in the title deeds of the Hydro against the sale of intoxicating liquor on the premises. These were subsequently varied.

The emphasis on entertainment, not really part of the Hydro ideals, began, as is shown in HRP's diaries, in 1876 and this indeed was the way HRP wanted it to continue. So the change from hydro to hotel gradually took place from that date to 1934. The change from hydro to hotel was finally declared in the article in *The Buxton Advertiser* entitled "*The Hydro is dead, long live the Spa*" (*see ante*)

Chapter 12

HYDROPATHIC IDEALS

In 1891 R.O.Allsop described The Hydropathic Establishment as:

"an institution seriously hydropathic, and yet one from a stay within whose walls even the sound and robust visitor may derive rational enjoyment.

The most desirable type of building for our present purpose would be rurally situated, large, and provided with a very complete bathing department. It would not be a mere hotel, but would seek to uphold its reputation as an honest Hydropathic sanatorium. In such an establishment, severe and hopeless disease would be absent; but the invalid and the temporarily broken down should be able to benefit from the cheerful association of health and vigour. Nothing in its management should interfere with the ease of the sound and hearty; while at the same time the weak and ailing must be protected from the thoughtlessness of health and strength. In a word, it should not be a hospital, but a sanatorium and a home of Hygeia, such as one may hope will, in the not distant future, exist in numbers near every great city, and increase and multiply in country districts."

"Large cities are not the proper places for hydropathic establishments, although even in such positions they often prove successful and the very greatest boon to suffering humanity. It is in the country that the hydropathic is at home. Pure air, bright sunshine, peaceful surroundings, and facilities for exercise in the open, form an essential part of the treatment of the hydropathist. Therefore the site chosen should be such as is bracing and always salubrious. High standing grounds are in accordance with the creed of the hydropathist: "Man muss Gebirge haben"[62] "A true hydropathic establishment grows from small beginnings. It earns a gradually-increasing reputation – not for its gay, boarding-house attractions, but for the cures effected therein, the comfort of its every arrangement, and the care and attention bestowed on visitors and patients".

Luke states in his 1919 handbook:

"Hydropathic establishments of any pretensions should admit friends as well as invalids". "There should be a call for institutions for a better class of people, all under one roof so they do not catch cold going from the baths to the

---

62 Priessnitz

accommodation, especially in winter". "They are not nursing homes for those are too often depressing and more for acute cases, but large establishments preferably in pleasant, healthy, country places, or resorts where observations of every kind can be carried out and all forms of treatment as indicated" "Hydropathics are but a halfway house". "A Hydro is a high-class hotel pension, generally situated in some quiet, breezy place, surrounded by lovely scenery, which tempts the inmates to solitary walks on hillsides and down valleys in pure air".

The Continent too had strayed from the strict dictates of Priessnitz's hydropathy. Nerves, indigestion, sometimes plain obesity, due to too many meals and too little exercise, generally ended the season. Then the cure at a foreign spa became a necessity, and London society was compelled to visit such places as Homburg, Marienbad, or Wiesbaden. The taking of baths, the drinking of large quantities of spa water, a restricted diet and plenty of walks in the surrounding countryside were part of the routine. In the view of a German commentator, *"Idleness without boredom"* was an essential ingredient of a successful cure.

There was of course more to taking a cure than a rigid regime of dieting, bathing and taking the water. Wealthy socialites were able to meet and exchange news and gossip, as well as display their smartest clothes, attend concerts and make excursions into the countryside. The Countess of Fingall, who visited Bad Schwalbach in 1897 with a friend, remembered meals eaten out of doors among flowers, and although they were supposed to be *"doing the cure"* the food was delicious: *"When anybody wanted to pay you a compliment, as a gallant friend of mine did, they offered you a rose bath. For this, the petals would have been picked from hundreds of roses and strewn on top of glutinous water. You lay in your bath with roses up to your chin and presently a tray was laid across the bath on which was placed a cup of delicious chocolate and "brioches" for your enjoyment."*[63]

The Caterer and Hotel Proprietors' Gazette took a rather cynical view of the "upstart" Hydropathics. The Hydros felt themselves to be superior to the ordinary hotel and *The Gazette* at first did not want to recognise the hydropathic establishments as hotels at all. However, in December 1884 they introduced news of the Hydros under the heading *"Hydropathic Jottings"*.

In March 1885 they reported that a fine smoking room had recently been added to Smedley's Hydropathic establishment at a cost of £200. *"This is rather an innovation"* stated *The Gazette, "as the use of tobacco, if not interdicted, is at least discouraged in the majority of Hydropathics"*.

In June 1887 *The Gazette* published an article:

"Invalid hotels. A project for the establishment of invalid hotels in different centres and health resorts has at various times been brought before the notice

---

63 Pamela Horn pp.147-148

of the trade, and has recently been again ventilated. For ourselves, we cannot look upon the scheme favourably as an investment for men of business to enter into. In the first place there is, and would be, the uncertainty of obtaining a constant supply of invalid guests, whilst the hotels could do nothing more than what is done already by various sanatoriums, hydropathic establishments, various invalid homes, and the extension of hospitals for private paying patients already under the guidance of skilled medical men, who necessarily can exercise more control over fractious or irritable patients than any man of business could do. Invalids are necessarily troublesome, fanciful, and irritable, and they cannot be catered for in the ordinary table d'hote, or uniform system, as the ordinary guests of an hotel can; besides that unceasing source of expense and annoyance, a tradesman who undertakes to cater and take charge of even one invalid, let alone two or three dozen, would incur grave moral, if not legal, responsibility. He would have the antagonism of the whole of the medical profession, and this is not a light thing to encounter. Then, again, how would an unprofessional Caterer know the exact line with moral responsibility of his patients begins or ends in the case of mental aberration? In the event of the slightest mistake being made he will be proceeded against by the Council of the Medical Registration Association, who have the command of a long purse. On the whole, therefore, we would strongly advise non-professional men to leave invalids alone. The risk, trouble, and responsibility is at all times great, and the pay, as a rule, incommensurate."

The Gazette had shortly prior to this article carried a feature praising the Buxton Hydro!

However the tone continued in November 1901:

"Hydros. The hydropathic establishment, though founded on an unstable element, is a fixed institution in this favoured land. Though its existence has been comparatively short, hardly dating back for a generation, and being little older than the discovery of the non-poisonous nature of soap, it has developed wonderfully already. The establishment, original style, was a very different place from its successor. It was essentially hydropathic – harshly and severely so. You went there because you were ill, and you went to be cured, and there was no nonsense about the cure. The bleeding, blistering, and bolusing era of medicine had scarcely then passed away, and the apostles of the new medical religion agreed remarkably with those of the old in requiring physical torture as a basis of recovery. There sprung up like lightning a variety of new torments which would have delighted the heart of grand old Philip himself. You were boiled to a pulp, you were currycombed to a steak, you were shot at with water arrows like another St. Sebastian, you were tied up tight in a pudding cloth and steamed, and swelled, with nobody to cut the string, and you had solid lead poured on your devoted head till your brain was in a whirl, and you lost consciousness of everything earthly except your wife's temper. Each hydro vied

with the other as to which should have the most unpleasant treatment: and the man who could advertise the latest ingenuity in torment was the master of the situation. The man invented the liver pack which should bring out all the liquor you had drunk since boyhood held the belt, till a greater than he invented the upshot squirt, which should carry you 10 ft in the air and keep you there. But a change has come over the spirit, if not the water, of the dream. Not only has Dr Wild given place to Dr Mild there, as elsewhere, but hydros are no longer to be taken au grand serieux. Recreation rules instead of maceration. Those cunning hydro managers have found out that there exists a very large class of people who will only take a holiday when their "health requires it"; with whom illness is the only flag under which they will enlist for a "high old time". For such do they cater. By saying you are going to a hydro you kill in the minds of suspicious relatives and friends all light thoughts of your abandoning business for mere pleasure. When you are once there, you can, of course, make a pipe light of your lists of baths without any one saying you nay, and you may eat three thoroughly full meals a day without anybody being surprised. Yet all the time there is that pleasant halo of being somewhat of an invalid around you, and when you write home after enjoying a day's rollicking excursion with some kindred invalids, you inform your anxious friends that you are a trifle better, and that the "treatment" suits you.

The "treatment," as has been hinted above, has not necessarily much to do with hydropathics. You may have water to drink if you like, of course, but you are not obliged to. It consists in the first place of an abundance of fresh air and pleasant scenery, for the men who go to prospect for hydros have something of the older monkish eye for site. Another important feature of the treatment is the square meal. Each patient may expect his neighbours at table to eat little, being invalids, but he himself has no notion of stinting, and consequently there is a run on the more succulent dishes, and a filling up with solid slices, which makes the inexperienced spectator pause aghast. That lady over there looks pale; she is no doubt a great sufferer; but the way flitches disappear before her at break - fast, with eggs to follow, shows that there is vitality left in her somewhere. The man who sits next to you seems fidgety before dinner, and says little; he has no doubt tried every doctor in England, and failed to be cured, and is only here as a last resource; and after you have seen him put away soup, fish, two legs of fowl, three slices of roast beef, and half an apple tart, you wonder what he really does eat when he is well. The "treatment" also includes early hours, thus keeping well up that moral tone which is one of the graces of the hydro. Early to bed and early to rise is the motto. You are awakened early, and breakfast is early, dinner is early, and the subsequent cup of tea or coffee is both small and early; and there is no exciting literature to be had, so that by 11 o'clock you feel resigned to bed. But there the hydro is highly moral in this respect, there are concessions to the flesh, loopholes for those hardened sinners who would rather leave than submit themselves to the treatment. They have only to pay a little *extra, to have breakfast at any time they like, and they have only to get into the confidence of one of the established visitors of the house in order to be smuggled into some snug corner of the building where the cheerful glass and the friendly pipe may be enjoyed till cockcrow. The "treatment" also includes music in the drawing room. Now "a little music in the evening" is a horror to a good many people in ordinary life, and the death rate from it stands some - where between scarlet fever and lobster sauce in the official returns; but such is this sphere of the hydro that it seems quite divested of its fatal properties, and its hearers are endowed with a charmed life. The guests, as a rule, really seemed pleased to hear playing and singing. What life at the place must have been when you had both the old scourging treatment in the morning and music in evening besides, one cannot imagine without a gasp; but that is all changed. Perhaps the music is a substitute for the water treatment; and it certainly reproduces for us with wonderful accuracy the shudderings down the spine, the swimmings in the head, the creepings of the flesh, and the spasms of the muscles which it was the delight of Doctor Wild to inflict.*

But the best part of the hydro "treatment" is, after all, the congenial society. So well known is the society of these establishments for its congeniality, that the congeniality actually forms a line "in the bills," and is especially advertised; and when you write for a prospectus you will be sure to find the "congenial society" well to the fore among the attractions. The society is very varied, but it is all congenial. There is the young lady from thirty to forty, who is a great feature at the hydro. She may be skittish, or she may be demure; she may be sentimental to the verge of tears or smart to the borderline of agnosticism; but in all cases she is congenial. The hydro makes a speciality of this young lady, and has some sweet things to show in that department. They are safe there, because papa knows the proprietor very well, and mamma thinks a little change is good for them. Then, of course, there are the widows, whose society is a treatment in itself; and there are the frisky married ladies. It seems a strange irony of fate which brings the latter to such sedate establishments, but the mystery is revealed when we remember that they have husbands. Your frisky wife always has a grave husband. He may not be naturally grave to begin with – far from it; but her friskiness speedily sobers him. As he finds that his gaiety is not in it with hers, and as, besides, in the language of the stage, he does not like to "queer her pitch," he always subsides into a rather melancholy individual. The frisky wife, then, comes to the hydro because her husband wishes to be quiet, but she takes it out in extra friskiness, arch looks, slang, anecdotes, and side-splitting comments on your neighbour. On you, too, of course, as soon as your back is turned. She it is who gets up the charades and the tableaux vivants and the excursion parties. She it is who tells everybody who everybody else is, and is the Dod, Post Office Directory, and Trade Protection circular of the hydro rolled into one. Then there are the married men who are away from home and their wives, with whom the hydro is usually well stocked.

They are all congenial in their way, and the study of their little tricks and manners is part of the treatment too; but this is a subject which would require a volume to itself, so remark - able are their phases. Besides these objects of interest, there are the regular hydro trotters, the people who spend most of their days in wandering from hydro to hydro all over the country, with an occasional dissipation in a boarding-house by way of change. These are the deposi - taries of the true hydro legend, and from them you can hear, and shudder as you hear, the history of the dark days of oatmeal porridge, stewed apples, and compulsory pack. But they also are congenial."

Front page of music for "Hydropathic Treatment'
British Library

It was not only *The Gazette* that held a cynical view of the hydros. In 1883 The Graphic had satirised the visit of the writer Edmund Goss to one of these establishments in a cartoon entitled "*A Hydropathic Legend*" and in 1904 J Foden Williams poked fun at the hydros by writing the words to a humorous song entitled "*The Hydropathic Treatment*". No doubt this was sung at many a party at the various hydros throughout the country, though not apparently at Theatres and Music Halls!

"THE HYDROPATHIC TREATMENT.

1

Not so very long ago, Oi was fee!in' very ill,
Sure, my appetite was goin' very quick;
So Oi went to see my docthor; and asked him for a pill
That would shtop mise1f from afther feelin'sick.
Sez he, "My little man. It isn't pills you want,
"But the Hydropathic Tratement, if you please,
"And for a month or so to a Hydro you must go;
'Where you'll find a certain cure for your disease."

Hy-dro-pathic? Tratement Hydropathic?
Now whativer does the crazy docthor mean?
Is it something for to eat? Is it rubbed into your feet?
For the loikes of it Oi've never really seen!

131

A Hydropathic legend

Hy-dro-pathic? Tratement Hydropathic?
Faith Oi couldn't undershtand the docthor's statement:
But to miself sez Oi, "Well, if Oi have got to die,
Sure Oi'll die by the Hydropathic Tratementl"

2

When Oi got into the place what is called a Hy-der-o,
Oh! Oi wondered what the folks were doin' there!
For a healthier set of patients Oi wouldn't wish to know,
And wid smokin' they were poisonin' the air!
The medicme they had, it didn't look so bad,
So Oi thought Oi'd take the Tratement loike the rest;
And very soon Oi found, that Oi'd got to "stand" my "round"
Of some Hydropathic Tratement for the chest!

Hy-dro-pathic Tratement Hydropathic!
Sure, Oi'd loike to be an invalid for good!
For the medicine's a treat: you can take it mixed or neat,
And it's just the stuff you want for makin' blood!
Hy- dro-pathic! Tratement Hydropathic
Oi could take it day and night without abatement!
And when them gintlemen asked me what Oi'd have again,
Oi would call for-"some Hydropathic Tratement!"

3

Well, Oi'd been there for a week, but no doctkor had Oi met!
Still, Oi felt a great improvement in my health;
So Oi simply went on takin' all the "pathic" Oi could get,
And kept sendin' home for extry bits of wealth.
We'd a Hydropathic dance, and when we got the chance
We had Hydropathic spooning in the hall:
Oi'd a Hydropathic kiss from a Hydropathic miss,
And it wasn't half bad takin' sure at all!

Hy-dro-pathic! Tratement Hydropathic!
Sure Oi shan't forget that Hydropathic kissl
"Oh!"sez Oi "now this'll cure me, for it seems to go right through me,
Oi can shtand a lot of medicine loike this!
Hy-dro-pathic! Tratement Hydropathic!
It is now Oi undershtand the docthor's statement
What Oi wanted all my life was a dacent lovin' wife,
Which Oi got by the Hydropathic Tratement!"

Finally, in September 1910:

"The Hydro habit. We have heard a good deal in recent years about "the restaurant habit," but this is quite different from the "hydro habit," according to the picturesque explanation of the latter in the Daily News.

The hydro habit is the habit of visiting, for pleasure only, the same hydro for the same holidays of each year. Essentially, it has nothing to do with hydropathy.

Between holiday seasons hydros are devoted, more or less, to their legitimate function of removing half the ills the flesh is heir to; during the holiday seasons, more particularly Easter, Whitsun, and Christmas, they become no more than big playgrounds, from which the bona fide patients appear to have been spirited away.

Everybody knows this, but what is known only to the hydro habitue is the extent to which all well-established hydros collect each holiday, not a miscellaneous party of pleasure-seekers, but a circle of old friends who meet year by year with all the enthusiasm of a family reunion. Thus, the newcomer in search of sociability often starves in the midst of plenty until he gradually becomes one of the family himself, and the period of this novitiate will depend quite as much upon the hydro as upon himself, since the families of some hydros are comparatively variable and correspondingly easy of access, whereas others are hedged round with an exclusiveness beside which the Royal Yacht Club would seem familiar and inviting.

It follows that, whilst the debutant who may have suffered a cold douche or two under the ingenious impression that they were a necessary justification of his presence, the coldest douche he is likely to get is the contrast between his own polite reception and the reception of one of the older members of the hydro family. The manager, in making his announcements for the day, will gravely inform the company that "Mr Bings arrives by the 2.3," and when Bings stands in the entrance hall wiping his perspiring forehead, there is barely room for him. His hand is shaken until his arm aches, his back is probably red with smacks, his eyes weep with laughter, and everyone looks as if he were a fortune unexpectedly bequeathed to them. His immediate bodyguard will be a circle of children (who never forget); beyond them a crowd of chuckling friends who want to know "who called "solo" and got "misery"? or"who won the winking competition"? and make sundry other references to dark mysteries which surround Mr Bings.

Should you feel a twinge of jealousy, you must remember that Bings has been coming here every Easter, Whitsun or Christmas, or all three, for twenty years, and is proud to produce banquet menus for every year to prove it. Without him the big family would be incomplete. Nobody but Mr Bings could be imagined at the head of table No.3. Nobody else could reply to the toast to "The visitors" on the banquet night.

But the debutant may take courage. At his first meal someone is sure to ask him to pass the salt, and by seizing the opportunity smartly he may dazzle the salt -

less individual by a sparkling epigram on the weather. Or, if he is fortunate, he may spill something or nearly knock someone down by rising incautiously, and then the whole table will love him. The luckiest newcomer I remember saw a waitress drop an egg from her tray into his cup. It was a small cup and a tight fit, but the egg fell with a clean "plunk" that spouted the scalding coffee a yard high. The laughter landed him into the bosom of the family on the instant, and he never looked back. But such a rapid and showy entry into the family circle is not for many.

The hydro habit takes a firm grip after the second or third visit, and the more it grips you the more delightful it becomes. Moreover, it is surprisingly inexpensive, apart from the expense in entertaining which it saves at holiday times. At the more fashionable hydros you may revel in such luxuries as Turkish, Russian, spray, and needle baths, mustard sheets, liver packs etc., free of charge, but if you want erasing your masseur will cost you two or three shillings per hour. Other sports you get free of charge in the house or grounds, although your golf tickets usually cost two shillings per day.

Some energetic hydros, deploring the paucity of general holidays, arrange "special weekends" from time to time. This brings the family of habitues together again from Saturday to Monday, and the charge rarely exceeds a guinea.

When making a first visit to a centre such as Matlock or Malvern, you can assure yourself of finding a congenial hydro by putting your case before the first hydro habitue you can buttonhole, for although he never swerves from allegiance to his particular establishment, he is invariably a descriptive directory of every other hydro in the neighbourhood. Tell him who and what you are, whether you prefer your company young or old, whether you are sporty or studious, whether you play bridge or whist, what outdoor sports you favour, whether married or single, and, if the latter, whether you wish to be the former, and he will choose a hydro for you that fits your case like a plug."

CHAPTER 13

PUBLICITY AND MARKETING
OF THE HYDRO

HRP was alive to the use of marketing tools from a very early age, especially the power of the press.

Although the other hotels had reporters commenting on the various social events, invariably the reports of "*the goings on*" at the Hydro were written up favourably and each year "*records*" were broken for attendances at the Christmas and New Year events.

In the early days toasts were given and "*the gentlemen of the Press*" were never forgotten.

An example of HRP's "*editorial propaganda*" is shown in the article in *The Caterer and Hotel Proprietor's Gazette* for August 15th 1888 when one of its journalists visited the Hydro. It was the practice at that time to publish an article in the trade magazine about selected hotels and their proprietors. There was a drawing of the Hydro and HRP and there followed a three page article entitled "*A Derbyshire Hydropathic.*" It began by extolling the merits of Buxton as a health resort and followed on with:

1888 Drawing of Hydro
Hotel and Caterers Gazette

1888 Drawing of HRP
Hotel and Caterers Gazette

"Buxton, however, apart from its attractions as a spa, is now gaining a fame which promises soon to become a lasting and leading feature of the town, viz., as a winter residence for the debilitated, and a pleasure rendezvous for their "sisters, cousins, aunts," and gentlemen relatives and friends on the look-out for the former during the summer months and holiday seasons. This social development of Buxton has been chiefly brought about by the erection of numerous elegant hotels and catering resorts designed to meet the demands of the fashionable reunions which take place, more especially at this time of year, and are in a large degree due to the energy displayed by the proprietor of the house which we have chosen as a suitable subject for review in our present issue. We submit the following sketch (taken on the spot by our special correspondent) to the notice of our readers with the hope that they may be able to gather there-from some items of practical interest and value in the conduct of public catering.
The Buxton Hydropathic Establishment and winter residence, formerly known as Malvern House, is the oldest, as it now is one of the best, institutions of its kind in north Derbyshire".

There followed a fulsome and extensive description of how the Buxton Hydro came into existance and of the characters involved and continued:

"Upon coming of age, Mr Lomas (whose portrait we here present) took over the entire management, and by dint of perseverance, a strong belief in the necessity for strict personal supervision, even down to matters of detail, super - added to that natural charm of manner which always marks the inborn gentle - man, he has succeeded even beyond his most sanguine expectations, and made the Buxton Hydropathic far more than an ordinaryhotel, a veritable home from home, where the numerous guests, often numbering considerably over 200, join together in their meals and social recreations more as one large family than as so many groups of strangers. We came upon them in the midst of their festivities, when the house was almost crowded out, as it always is during the months of August and September. An informal dance was going on for those who cared to join in it, music in the spacious drawing-rooms, billiards and other games in other parts of the house. We had just missed some striking tableaux vivants, but were in time the next day for a tennis tournament in the beautiful public gardens facing the building. Concerts and theatrical performances vary the round of amusements from time to time in the large recreation hall of the establishment, and thus keep the guests pleasurably engaged during the whole of their stay.
There are at present over 130 bedrooms, a large billiard room with two tables, a well ventilated smoking room, drawing rooms, dining hall, reading and music rooms, besides every accommodation for private servants on the most liberal scale imaginable. The house is furnished and fitted with the very best of every -

thing, and great praise is due to Mr Lomas for the excellent sanitary arrange - ments of the building (which is carefully warmed by means of hot water pipes from a low pressure boiler), in as much as he has hitherto been his own architect. The kitchen is in the proximity to one end of the dining hall, and all the meals can be thus served almost out of the pots and pans into the plates of the guests at table. The fare is excellent, varied, and always cooked to perfection. The cordon bleu of the institution, Mrs Conley by name, has been in her present situation for 15 years, and has never been known to serve a dish to which exception could be taken. We are inclined to believe that faithful and well-tried servants speak more for the high reputation of an establishment of this kind than any testimonial, however eulogistic, from without its walls; and Mr Lomas can boast that, of the 30 to 50 servants on his staff, over 15 have been in constant employment for periods ranging from 12 to 22 years.

The feature par excellence, however, which distinguishes the Buxton Hydropathic from all others of its class in this country, is that, in addition to the usual hot and cold, needle, shower, spray, wave, douche, sitz, steam, mustard pack, liver pack, and other forms of bath common to establishments of this kind, it possesses by far the finest massage treatment apparatus in England, while but few of those on the Continent, as at Aix-les-Bains, Baden-Baden, Eisenach, Alexandersbad, etc. can compare with it. This unique apparatus, and, indeed, all the other appliances in these celebrated baths, are the work of the well-known expert sanitary engineer, Mr John Smeaton of 56 Great Queen Street, London W C, who also designed and fitted the Duke of Devonshire's new massage baths at Buxton, and the Leamington Spa Corporation Baths.

The special room devoted to this treatment of which more anon, is neatly tiled all over, and furnished with a couple of dressing chamber's somewhat similar to those of a Turkish bath. The room is of small dimensions; since the several appliances have to be used quickly one after the other; and the patient should not therefore be allowed to make too long a detour from one to the other. In one corner is placed the fixed thermal vapour bath, provided with a number of local douches for cooling the temperature of the body at any desired spot, and these can be made to strike the patient either in jets or sprays, and can be worked at will by the bather or attendant with the utmost ease. The inner lining of this box is of tinned copper, and the steam in rising from beneath is made to pass through a trellised seat; and besides the various sprays and jets, a local steam douche is attached, which can be directed to any chosen part by the masseur or masseuse (male or female operator). Now comes the principal feature of the treatment: the patient is placed upon a central tray-like bath, about 6 ft long, by 2 ft 9 in. wide, and 8 in.deep, made of strong hammered copper, thickly lined with tin. On each side of the bath run longitudinal perforated copper tubes, which can be operated by the masseur (in case a gentleman is undergoing the treatment), so as to throw a spray of water over any desired section of the body. The head of the patient meanwhile rests upon a suitably disposed air-pillow.

The water-supply for the basin of the bath is conducted thereto by means of a two-inch inlet pipe, the temperature being previously regulated to an unvarying nicety by means of a special mixer, provided with a delicate thermometer (a speciality of Mr Smeaton's), and thus the desired temperature of the sprays, etc. can all be exactly secured. The masseur must be fairly well up in human anatomy to perform the various movements of Petri-sage, effleurage, and tapotement, as laid down by Metzger for the treatment of rheumatism, intestinal sluggishness, tic douloureux, tendency to gout etc. These consist in complicated manipulations of sets of muscles, or each muscle separately, stroking them continuously along the direction of their fibres, picking them up in certain parts, and subjecting the portion to firm pressure, and so on, for fuller details of which we must refer the reader to special papers upon the subject.

Now, it so happens that Mr Lomas has managed to secure both accomplished masseurs and masseuses for his baths, so that gentlemen and ladies can now avail themselves of a course of treatment which is rapidly gaining ground, as a sure method for the relief and reduction of all forms of a nervous disorders, and even of severe inflammation due to accidents; indeed, so efficacious is the treatment, that the highest medical authorities of the day now insist upon it as an essential branch of hospital and general medical education."

A further example of HRP capitalising on opportunities as they arose was in the report of the Christmas party in 1895 when, once again, records were broken. During Christmas and the New Year there had been from 250-300 visitors staying at the Hydro, including a party of 100 from Sheffield. This was one of the first fruits of the Dore and Chinley Railway, and 100 'wandering' advertisements of Buxton and the Hydro ensured a large crop of Yorkshire people during that year. HRP had used the new railway branch to entice 100 guests from Sheffield to come to his Hydro. He also had Manchester in his sights and knowing that the Belle Vue Zoological Gardens was one of the biggest attractions in the North West of England he advertised in their brochures, the Dore and Chinley new line making Manchester more accessible to Buxton.

In the August 1912 edition of *The Hotel and Caterer's Gazette* the Buxton Hydro was described: "*as the largest establishment of the kind near and far. Sumptuously appointed on quite modern lines, it boasts of 260 rooms; the cuisine is excellent, and the Telegraph address "comfortable" amply justified. Mr G W Bosworth, the manager, has an orchestra permanently engaged; there are amusements each evening, concert artistes grace the platform on Sundays, and a dance takes place every Saturday*". The journalists who wrote the piece stated that he had met vocalists and elocutionists who spoke in terms of high praise concerning their frequent appearances at the Buxton Hydro. This was just another example of HRP making sure that the Hydro was kept in the media.

The first advertisement of Malvern House, in *The Buxton Advertiser* for the 5th October 1870, was a fairly modest affair by later standards and shows Mrs T Lomas

Advertisement for Malvern House and Royal Hotel 1870
Buxton Advertiser, Colindale

as the Lady Superintendent for Malvern House and Miss Atkins as matron of the Royal.

Divine service took place on Sundays both in the morning and evening, quite in accordance with strict hydropathic principles!

Thomas had taken to advertising in Murray's Travellers Handbooks to various countries, which included such diverse titles as "Russia, Poland and Finland", "The Mediterranean", and "The Bengal Presidency", in which he placed an advertisement in 1881 *"Buxton. The Hydropathic and Boarding Establishment. Malvern House. A comfortable Summer and Winter Residence for patients and visitors. Overlooking the public gardens. Resident Chaplain.[64] For particulars apply to Lady Superintendent. NB. Entirely new Bath Rooms, with all the modern improvements, have been added."*

When HRP took over, the wording in the advertisements was much more informative and enticing, as for example in Buckley's *"Modern Buxton"* 1886.

Advertisement for Buxton Hydro
Buckley's Modern Buxton

(copy) The Hydro had changed its name to the Buxton Hydropathic Establishment and Winter Residence but was still using "Malvern House" in order to retain its goodwill. Here again is an example of HRP using the press to get his message across. The quotes he gives are very upbeat, but they also show that he identifies himself with Buxton just as much as his hydro. Again he emphasises the personal nature of the Hydro.

HRP started to use words such as "the best", "most advanced", and other extremes. He was not afraid to blow his own trumpet!

Emphasis was also laid on "winter residence" as he wanted to expand the season from spring and summer only to include the winter months.

By now HRP was not just using the local paper for his advertisements but also the guides for Buxton and in 1890 he advertised in the *"Handbook to the Mediterranean: its Cities, Coasts and Islands"* a far cry form Buxton, but people reading this guide would also be potential customers for the Hydro. As Buxton was such an important

---

64 The resident chaplain appears from the 1881 census to be R J McGhee.

BUXTON'S
HEALING SPRINGS

NO place in Great Britain surpasses Buxton in its rich endowments of Nature. Not only is it "hill-girt" amid magnificent scenery and bracing air, but from "the depths under the earth" there bubbles up a seemingly inexhaustible supply of healing waters impregnated with radium and other mineral properties.

These wonderful waters come direct from the rock at an actual temperature of 82 deg. F. They are dispensed at the St. Ann's Well, where is situated a palatial and comfortable Pump Room, and unlike the somewhat nauseous draughts at other Spas they are odourless and not unpleasant to the taste. Sufferers from Sciatica, Rheumatism, Gout, and kindred ailments gain great relief and subsequent immunity from torturing pains by the special treatments to be obtained at the fine Thermal Baths of the Buxton Corporation. Here are "cures" applicable to the state, constitution, and condition of those who seek relief.

The Buxton Corporation have, and are, spending thousands of pounds to make Buxton's Thermal Baths not only the foremost in Great Britain, but in the World, for the wonderful healing springs have brought relief and happiness to many from far-off lands, who now bless the opportunity they were afforded while visiting England of undergoing a "cure" in Buxton.

To secure first choice of accommodation for your holiday write now to J. M. Scott (Dept. A), Information Bureau, Buxton, for Official Guide, giving list of Hotels and Apartments available. Application may also be made to the various offices of Messrs. Thos. Cook & Son.

THE WORLD'S GRANDEST SCENERY IN MINIATURE

BUXTON HYDRO HOTEL, BUXTON.

Official Hotel to the R.A.C., A.A. & M.U., and A.C.U.

260 ROOMS.   **OVERLOOKING PUBLIC GARDENS.**
INCLUSIVE WINTER TERMS FROM 4½ GUINEAS PER WEEK.
Near Mineral Baths, Wells, and Opera House.
Golf Links within 5 minutes of Hotel (Sunday Golf).
Complete Suite of Hydropathic and Electric Baths.
AMUSEMENTS. DANCING. ORCHESTRA.

Telephone: 211 & 212.   Telegrams: "Comfortable."   G. W. BOSWORTH, Manager.

Advertisement for Buxton and the Buxton Hydro 1920's
The Times

spa town many guidebooks were written, as well as other guides on hotels and hydropathic establishments in the UK. More often than not the Buxton Hydro appeared in them with a report by the editor

So far as the national papers were concerned, advertisements ran monthly in *The Times* from 1920-1931 in conjunction with articles extolling the merits of the spa towns. The advertisements merely had a drawing of the Hydro with basic details but in later years they had to try a little harder. In April 1927 a "sample weekend" was advertised whereby if you stayed a week-end and were not "comfortable" you would not be charged.

In 1931 the sample weekend continued under the Spa's name.

Advertisements were also occasionally run in medical magazines such as *"The Prescriber".*

Buckley's Modern Buxton has already been referred to and others included;

Buxton as a health resort – Dr JC Thresh. 1883.

Parrott's guide to all the hydropathic establishments of Great Britain – 1889 described Malvern House Hydropathic Establishment as *"This celebrated establishment is pleasantly situated, and replete with every modern improvement. It overlooks the pavilion and public gardens, in which are numerous tennis courts, bowling greens etc; and also is quite close to the renowned mineral wells. .....*

W H Robertson's *"Buxton and the peak"* (published by Ward Lock – 1897) struck a similar note with added information relating to the cost of a stay…"

Pension: 9/- to 15/- per day, or 63/- to105/- per week" which Mates Illustrated Guide to Buxton, 1905, as being moderate charges.

In 1903 *"The Peak Thorough Guide"* is less than complementary about the chimneys serving the laundries at the Palace Hotel and the Hydro: *"two factory-like chimneys belonging respectively to the Palace Hotel and the Buxton Hydro are the reverse of an adornment to the town, and constitute an architectural breach of the peace."*

"The Spa of Blue Water" 1929 contains a large description of the Hydro. The drawings certainly give the impression of the building being grander than it really was, especially if one looks at the photographs just before it was demolished in 1971. A certain amount of artistic licence was undeniably used!

In the *Michelin Guide* to Great Britain 11th Edition. 1930, the Hydro was classified under the code*"large and luxuriously appointed, palace hotels where every*

Let's be Sane

How apt hotel proprietors are to indulge in vain repetitions —"premier," "leading," "exclusive," "ideal," and the rest of them. In these battles of the superlative, we ourselves have been guilty enough in the past.

It seems better to say simply that the Buxton Hydro Hotel is just a very comfortable place, and leave it at that. Comfortable—now that means something, something we can substantiate.

If you care to come along for a week-end, and you can honestly say you have not been comfortable, we shall simply refuse to charge you. We aren't going to endanger our 50 years' reputation.

There is no room to tell you here about our 260 bedrooms, our hydropathic and electric baths, our dances and other amusements, or our special week-end scheme for 30 -. May we send you our booklet "A study in comfort"? Let us know.

BUXTON HYDRO HOTEL

Buxton is in the heart of the Derbyshire Peak. It is our good fortune to have many natural advantages round us. We hope to make it yours, too.

Advertisement for Buxton Hydro Hotel 1927
The Times

BUXTON HYDROPATHIC LIMITED. PROPRIETORS.

ALL
COMMUNICA-
TIONS TO BE
ADDRESSED TO
THE MANAGER.

BUXTON HYDRO HOTEL,

BUXTON.

DERBYSHIRE.

September
Twentysecond
1922.

Dear Sir

We have much pleasure in stating that a refined
Official Souvenir, Handbook and Tariff for Buxton Hydro
Hotel is now being prepared.

The design is unusual, the Illustrations
will include delightful pencil drawings, and no expense
is being spared to make it the finest book of its kind.

The book will be placed into the hands of
thousands of well-to-do people, who contemplate visiting
Buxton; Guests will constantly receive copies for use
whilst in Buxton, and it will be sent to all enquirers for
bookings.

Special copies will be bound in velvet suede
leather for presentation to distinguished Visitors. Members
of big Corporations, leading Rotarians, also Harley Street
Specialists, and leading Medical men will receive copies.

A definitely limited number of pages have
been reserved for approved Advertisements of high-class
businesses, offering an exellent means of securing the
attention of influential people.

Messrs. Cross-Courtenay Limited are responsible
for the work, and have arranged to design the layout, each
advertisement page in good style, and to act in all matters
relating to the handbook.

We feel sure you will be glad to take
practical advantage of this well-considered scheme

Yours faithfully,

Manager.

Hydro letter heading 1922

Colour postcards of Buxton Hydro and Lounge 1899

SPA HOTEL
BUXTON - DERBYSHIRE.

Telegrams - "Comfortable, Buxt
Telephones - 211 - 212 Buxton.

Postcards of Buxton Hydro and Spa
Buxton Museum

BUXTON HYDRO HOTEL.
BUXTON - DERBYSHIRE.

Telegrams - "Comfortable, Buxton
Telephones - 211 - 212 Buxton.

comfort can be served" and came top of the list of Hotels featured, even though unlicensed.

Hydro luggage label
Buxton Museum

There is very little available on Malvern House in the way of brochures but as can be expected HRP went to town on producing the first brochure in 1899 for the Buxton Hydro. He used the original drawing of the Hydro, which again shows the artistic licence some-times used by the Victorians. The Telegraph address is *"Comfortable, Buxton"*. The words "comfortable" and "comfort" are used time and time again in newspaper reports and future brochures and are words which HRP wanted to be associated with the Hydro. The brochure begins by emphasising the benefits of Buxton as a spa town, the spring water being the property of the Duke of Devonshire and obtainable in separate buildings and explaining that the spring water could not be taken at the Hydro. This was to become an important point raised in later years when the spring waters were taken over by the corporation and correspondence arose in *The Buxton Advertiser* that the Hydro was informing visitors that they could be taken at the Hydro. (*See ante*). There was accommodation for the private servants of visitors.

The second brochure in 1916 refers to the Buxton Hydro (Hotel) and there was less emphasis on the baths. HRP used quotations such as

"The Beauty of the House is order; The Blessing of the House is contentment; The Glory of the House is hospitality." and *"when friends are at your hearthside met, Sweet courtesy has done its most. If you have made each guest forget that he himself is not the host"*. This sounds somewhat over-sentimental these days.

Other Buxton businesses were advertising in the Hydro brochures, including Milligan's, the well known haberdashery, and Hargreaves and Stotts, both of which were businesses in which HRP had a stake.

The letter heading for The Hydro, dated 30th April 1909, has the original drawing used showing horses and carriages from the original print. At a later date the same drawing was used in a postcard but with slight differences, in particular, a motor car in the foreground.

The 22nd September 1922 letter heading has the same drawing but without people, carriages, or cars! The same letter seeks local businesses to advertise in the Hydro brochure. A similar letter in 1925 shows a different drawing altogether.

The later cards gave a colour perspective to the Hydro. The Hydro luggage label shows the omnipresent *"comfortable"* shown on it.

CHAPTER 14

ENTERTAINMENT AT THE HYDRO

Right from the beginning HRP wanted his guests to be entertained (*see diary entry –*
charades) and his lifelong interest in music had a bearing on the entertainment
provided by the Hydro.

One of the first entertainments took place on 11ᵗʰ August 1883 when Aptommas,
the famous English harpist, gave a concert at Malvern House an account of which was
in *The Buxton Advertiser*.

> *"Aptommas at the Hydropath Malvern House.*
> *Aptommas, a name familiar to those who delight in skilled expositions of*
> *classical as well as romantic and national musical selections upon the harp*
> *gave a performance on Thursday evening in the capacious new dining hall of*
> *this splendidly appointed institution. The room is capable of seating between*
> *300 and 400 persons for a concert, and this was the first public entertainment*
> *given in the room, which was well attended, and we need hardly say,*
> *thoroughly enjoyed by enthusiastic admirers of the harp. The acoustic*
> *properties of the room are decidedly good, and we understand that visitors have*
> *expressed much satisfaction. As a special feature to be introduced by Mr*
> *Aptommas, the idea was conceived of permitting the audience to select a*
> *programme from the repertoire presented by the performer to his listeners*
> *during the past 20 years of public performance. Thirty pieces in all were*
> *submitted, and each member of the audience made a selection upon slips of*
> *paper supplied for that purpose. In the first and second groups a majority of*
> *votes was secured for Scottish melodies, consisting of airs, reels, and strath*
> *pays, and songs without words (duet and spring songs), Mendelssohn. The*
> *selection in part second was the "Harmonious Blacksmith", Handel; "Home,*
> *Sweet Home", with variations, which was finely rendered; the "Greek Pirates*
> *Chorus", (Alvars), gave scope for illustrating the really marvellous power*
> *which the performer possesses in handing the instrument. There was*
> *considerable applause at the conclusion of the selection.*

There is a "plug" in the paper for the new telephone system linking Malvern House
with the Shakespeare Stables. HRP is beginning to appreciate the use of the media.

It is probable that HRP, now 25, had some idea as to how he wanted to run the
business.

In August 1883 Malvern House was still being used as the title and the list of

Page 1 Appotomas Programme 1883
Buxton Museum

Page 2 Appotomas Programme 1883
Buxton Museum

visitors shows 84 guests, a great improvement on the number of guests previously staying.

Amongst the visitors were Harry Bulteel and Mrs H and G Shore,

In January 1884 the first of the many staff New Year Balls was given by HRP, an account of which was in *The BuxtonAdvertiser.*

"New year's Ball at the Buxton Hydropathic Establishment.
On Tuesday last, New Year's Day, Mr HRP Lomas, the proprietor of the above establishment gave a ball to his servants and their friends, in the large dining hall at Malvern House. The party to the number of 45 assembled at 8 o'clock, and dancing was kept up with spirit until 11 when a most recherche supper was served in the Servants' Hall. The three tables literally groaned with Christmas fare. The visitors in the house were scarcely behind Mr Lomas in their anxiety that the servants should enjoy themselves. All assembled in the dining hall either to join in the dance or to watch the merry party, and when supper was announced the younger portion acted as waiters and waitresses, and ministered to the comforts of those who daily so diligently wait upon them. Supper over, the visitors withdrew, and Mr Durandeau, chairman, asked the company to drink that toast which, as loyal Englishmen, they were always proud to honour, viz., "the health of Her Majesty the Queen, and the Royal Family" (cheers)
The toast having been duly honoured,
Mr Joseph Gladwin rose to propose the next toast – the toast of the evening – "the health of their host and employer, HRP Lomas, Esquire. (loud and contin - ued cheering) He admired Mr Lomas as an Englishman and as a good friend to the town. He was always kind and considerate to his servants and showed his good feeling by giving them a rare treat like the present. They had all spent a most pleasant evening this New Year's Day. (Hear, hear) He had known Mr Lomas now some four or five years, and had always found him prompt and fair in business, and in fact a real Englishman. (Cheers). He asked them to drink health, long life, and a happy new year to Mr Lomas.

This is the first time the Buxton Hydro is mentioned. The staff were waited on by the visitors (topsyturvydom), a feature which was to continue at the New Year Staff Balls and was much appreciated by all concerned.

The entertainment laid on for the visitors included a trip to Manchester by railway to see the pantomime.

The scene is now set for the unique atmosphere of the Buxton Hydro, a place where guests were made to feel at home with plenty of entertainment to encourage them to visit at all times of the year, especially at Christmas and the New Year where previously Buxton's season had been limited in view of the inclement weather during the winter.

By January 1891 *The Buxton Advertiser* was expanding its account of Christmas at Hydro. Mr Fred Goddard still conducted the Pavilion Band and descriptions of the dances and menu were given. Mr Walton proposed the toast to HRP. He said that the Hydro had a good man at the head of it and HRP superintended the minutest details himself. A toast to "the press" was also given by Mr Walton, no doubt in the hope that the Hydro's celebrations would get a good review in *The Buxton Advertiser.*

He also stated that: *'He could speak of it from its very commencement and it had been a great pleasure to see it grow with the growth of Buxton and always keeping well to the front. All the latest improvements had been incorporated in the building, and no establishment in England could boast of better baths, pleasanter room, or more home comforts – things which those visitors who came year after year and time after time knew how to appreciate, and only left the Hydro filled with a longing to come again (applause). He thought one great secret of the success of the Buxton Hydro had been the continuity in manage - ment and working staff. Many of those he saw around him had been servants for years, and visitors liked nothing better than to see year after year the same faces to welcome and wait upon them, though of course some of them would get married (laughter). He thought they might be assured that the success of the Buxton Hydropathic would continue for years to come. They had a good man at the head of it, and he need not tell them that it mattered not how complete was the establishment if there was no one to take charge of the machinery, and keeping it (applause). Mr Lomas superintended the minutest details himself, and it was that, seconded their willing service, commanded success (appluase).* Certainly the menu, which was printed in the newspaper, was a feast for the working class Hyrdro staff.

Menu
Boned turkey. Sirloin of beef and horseradish sauce.
Round of beef.
Boiled chicken. Roast chicken.
Veal and ham pies.
Hand – tongue.

Plum puddings. Mince pies.
Chocolate puddings. Lemon cheesecakes.
Rhubarb tarts. Custards.
German tarts. Coconut sandwich.
Orange jelly. Rock jelly.
Italian cream. Pineapple cream.
Charlotte Rouse. Stewed fruit. Trifle.
Dessert.

The article went on to describe other Christmas entertainments at Buxton Hydro:

Friday December 26th. Theatricals, programme as follows;
Ruth's Romance:
A summer's evening sketch, in two acts
To be followed by one original sketch entitled:-
Yellow Roses.
Wednesday night, Theatricals- programme
Bubbles.
To be followed by a Dance"

The entertainment expanded to other times of the year to include Whit weekend, Easter and even "a tennis week" which was now being held in Buxton. In August, the Hydro having been extended yet again, 250 visitors were entertained during the week and music, tableaux vivant and dancing were described in the Buxton Advertiser on the 7th August 1891;

"Tennis week at the Buxton Hydropathic.
The Buxton Hydropathic has this week well kept up its reputation for pleasant and lively evening entertainment. In a large company of visitors, numbering about 250, were found an amount of ability to entertain rarely met with. Music, represented by the pianoforte, violins, guitars, mandolin banjos, etc; singing by ladies and gentlemen whose well-trained and efficient voices gave general satisfaction; recitations, which moved to mirth and touched the more tender feelings; tableaux, in which scenes for beauty and perfection of arrangement are seldom met with in amateur circles; and dancing, which was kept up with spirit and vivacity, served to wile away the time each evening after tea, and send the visitors to bed well pleased and satisfied, and even night itself was with many made fretful with dreams and reminisces of the pleasures of the past. On Monday and Wednesday there was a dance. On Tuesday there were some very striking tableaux vivants. The first represented a sculptor's studio, with statues etc. including one of Truth, a fisher boy, a bust, and that of a monk, to which latter the sculptor was putting a few finishing touches, turning with well satisfied and admiring gaze on the lovely statue of Truth. The figures, which were all of the purest white, were well shown up by the rich crimson drapery of the studio. Another beautiful group was that of the four seasons, with winter ushering in the New Year. Four scenes from the " story of Cinderella"; one from the "Merry Wives of Windsor", Act 3 scene 3: "The story of Blue Beard", including the chamber of horrors and the sad fate of Fatima, and the grand finale with magnesium light effects, brought the evening's entertainment to a happy conclusion. On Thursday there was a programme consisting of recitations and instrumental music. On Friday a concert was given, and the week's amusements will be bought a close this evening with another dance."

The 1892 Annual Ball was once again described at length in *The Buxton Advertiser.*

Mr J Gladwin, "*contractor for all the recent additions in the mammoth establishment*", proposed a toast to HRP. He said "*the large number of visitors then in the house from all parts of the world, and the fact that they came year after year, was in itself sufficient proof of the popularity of the Hydro, over which Mr Lomas ruled in a manner which excited the praise of all.*" HRP was gaining a loyal band of followers for his Hydro.

In 1897 Whitsun was now celebrated at the Hydro, the entertainments ranging from dancing and concerts to gymkana, the arrangements being similar to those fashionable in India (HRP visited India for one month in the following year):

"*Whitsuntide at Buxton Hydro.*
The Whitsuntide festivities at Mr Lomas popular Hydro have been exceptionally varied and attractive. On Saturday night there was the usual weekly Cinderella, and on Sunday a sacred concert in the ballroom. The programme was long and varied, and gave every satisfaction. The vocalists were Misses Ella Sears, Nellie Shipman, Hahn, Hebelthwaite, Shipman, Whitaker, and Messrs Edgar Jones, Bowner; violins and mandola, Miss Whiston, Miss Threlfall, and Mr George Shipman. The Buxton Hydro Glee Party sang some choice pieces. Mrs Hesketh presided at the piano. On Monday morning a gymkana was held in the garden attached to the Hydro, the arrange-ments being similar to those in vogue in India. The principal events were as follows; Slow cycle race, Miss Manning; three-legged race, Misses Jones and Mead; needle and thread race, Miss Manning; potato race (gentlemen), Mr

Cricket Match
Courtesy of Buxton Advertiser and www.picturethepast.org.uk

153

Stratton; fast cycle race, Miss Whittaker; potato race on cycles, Mr Stratton; potato race (ladies), Miss Shipman; cycle race, with umbrellas, Mr Stratton. Handsome prizes were awarded the winners and distributed by Mrs Cooke. The success of the gymkana is very largely due to the untiring energies of Mr J H Cooke, who acted as secretary. Mr Stratton was the starter. A cricket match, Ladies v. Gentlemen, was held in a field near the college in the afternoon, but the ladies were singularly unfortunate, only scoring 11 compared with 34 by their opponents. In the evening the annual Whitsuntide ball was held, when there was a large attendance. Music was supplied by members of the Pavilion Band, under the conductorship of Mr F Goddard. Refreshments were supplied in the buffet in the large entrance hall, and dancing was kept up with spirit until a later hour. On Tuesday night a large party went to the Pavilion Theatre to witness the performance by the Chatsworth House Party. The list of visitors at the Hydro will be found in another column."

The season at the Hydro was now spread out over the year and in view of its success in 1899 H.R.P floated the Hydro as a limited company (see ante)

In the 1890's Buxton was so dedicated to serving the wealthy that one inhabitant in seven was in domestic service.

The Hydro went from strength to strength.

The increasing popularity of Buxton went hand in hand with that of the Hydro. In 1905 King Edward VII stayed at the Empire Hotel and polite Manchester society turned up in droves.

The January 1913 Peak Hunt Ball was described thus *"A brilliant function. Of the multitudious social events which are included in Buxton's winter season programme it can at once be said that none appeal to the hearts of Peakland hunting men and women in the same degree as the hunt ball. Indeed it may not inappropriatly be described as the chief social function in that broad expanse of real stone-wall country which has been so well hunted by Mr R W M Nesfield, Colonel Robertson-Aikman, and the present highly popular master and splendid sportsman, Mr Walter C Tinsley.*

During the season in Buxton there were at least four orchestras: the Hydro, the Empire, the Opera House and the Pavillion Orchestra itself. Sometimes they all joined together, as they did at "a special war matinee" on 26th August 1914. "The small spa burst with music carried on the rarefied air from open windows and across the fragrant gardens: in the bathing rooms the visitors could accurately say with Shakespeare's Ferdinand "This music crept by me upon the waters…with its sweet air."[65]

The First World War had already begun, and the 2nd January 1915 edition of the *Buxton Advertiser* in their editorial wrote about the first of the patriotic "thrills" when the town's gallant young men, with their seniors, left for training and service. The paper continued *"What more striking object lesson could be given than by the thousands of soldiers in the making – marching and drilling in all weathers – who*

---

65   Kenneth Young *Music's Great days in the Spas and Watering places* MacMillan 1968

have made of Buxton a military town for the time being! Most pleasant has it been from our office windows to watch them drill for weeks, and as we write, hundreds of them go bravely by, their band playing patriotic airs which stir the blood this wintry day opening the New Year. Most welcome has been the coming of the soldiers here and elsewhere, and their presence has continuously and forcibly pressed home the great Resolution for the New Year – urging others to go and do likewise, to sight their duty, and instantly answer their Country's call'.

The message sounded slightly incongruous against the usual upbeat reports of the Christmas festivities. *"BUXTON HYDRO HOTEL. Memorable always are the great Christmas gatherings at Buxton Hydro Hotel, and that of last week was no exception to the long rule. The merry party was over 300 in number, the general arrangements for the comfort, happiness and entertainment of everybody worked on just the same magnificent scale, an honest and hearty welcome greeted old friends and new, but there was just a little something missing from the merry picture, and it was those who are upholding all that is dear to us – those but for whom there would have been a no merry Christmas in Old England. There was, however, consolation in the fact that everything that lay in the power of human beings to do for absent relatives and friends had been done. From beneath the holly and mistletoe many a good wish came from the heart of absent ones"*

Easter 1915 showed another record for that season and there were those in residence who *"could claim a quarter of a century's visit at Easter; there were scores who have united under the same happy auspices for a dozen and more years. They were indeed happy in the fact that they could if only for a few days, leave dull care in a measure behind, and have the "change" that is so necessary, beneficial, and restorative to the health that has been impaired or broken by war's or other worries. In no place could that "change" be found in more perfect framing than at Buxton Hydro Hotel, situated in the centre of the most healthy and invigorating county in England. Recreation and entertainment were on the same prodigal scale that always pertains. Indeed, the variety and attractiveness of the daily programme are a panacea that never fails."*

The entertainment continued without flagging until 1917 when the Hydro was commandeered for the Canadian Army Hospital (The Granville Hospital) ending in 1919. (see ante). Undoubtedly this was a big blow to HRP and the shareholders of the Hydro.

The December 1921 *Buxton Advertiser* account for the Christmas festivities did not seem to be all that different from previous years. The first of the Pierrot Balls was mentioned and friends of HRP are shown dressed in appropriate costume.

In the 1870s many of the seaside resorts had band concerts and performances by itinerant musicians, including the Christy Minstrels with their faces blackened by burnt cork.[66]

---

66 Pamela Horn p.138

Pierrots at fancy-dress ball, Buxton Hydro 1921

During the 1890s the minstrels faced a challenge from Pierrots, introduced from France in 1891. More refined and carefully dressed than their minstrel counterparts, with faces whitened by oxide of zinc, they were immediately successful; hence the popularity of the pierrot balls at the Hydro.

Some commentators of the time expressed certain distaste for the "swinging" London atmosphere of the early twenties angrily contrasting the loss of the million war time dead with those who survived to make merry. Richard Aldington wrote *"To the sound of 10,000 jazz bands, with the ominous tom-tom undertone beating on the nerves, those sinister years shuffled and shimmied their dance of death. When evening twighlight sank with heart- shaking sadness over the million silent graves, already the taxis and cars crowded the streets, hurrying to restaurants and parties; all night the restless feet slid and stamped, and the niggers grinned over the drums, and the joyless rejoiced without joy; and at dawn, when the wind breathed an immense sigh over the cross marred desolated fields, the feet still stamped and voices still shouted for more drink, and paler cheeks more plainly showed the smear of reddened lips. A happy time. You could almost hear the rattle of the bones in this macabre pageant, dulling thought and feeling like a villainous drug, which had always to be renewed in larger and longer doses."*[67]

Despite these opinions, once again, in January 1925 the account of the Christmas festivities seems to show that the war had had very little effect on the prosperity of the Hydro:

"The Buxton Hydro Hotel.
The word "record" is probably more frequently used by journalists at holiday periods than any other. Record scenes at railway stations; record postal mails; record weather (rarely seasonable, mark you!); and record numbers at hotels. Last year was, of course, a record of the Buxton Hydro Hotel. This year was "the" record. And we have this on the no less authority than of Mr H R P Lomas (the managing director), who certainly is the one person in Buxton who is best qualified to speak on past Christmas seasons, seeing that this is the 42nd Christmas he has witnessed at the Hydro, commencing with the days when there were comparatively modest numbers at Malvern House (the original beginning of the Buxton Hydro Hotel) until this year, when there were over 440 actually staying in the Hotel, 500 sitting down to dinner on Christmas and Boxing Day, and yet another 700 who were turned away from sheer lack of accommodation. We are sorry about those 700, not only because they missed a wonderful time, but from a purely selfish point of view, because it meant 700 people less in Buxton, and every additional visitor to the town means increased benefit to everyone.
The proceedings began on Tuesday, December 23rd, for the benefit of the early comers, with military whist.

---

67   Richard Adlington *Soft Answers* Penguin 1949

Fancy-dress balls at Buxton Hydro 1921, 1924 and 1925

Fancy-dress ball at Buxton Hydro 1926

HRP at Fancy-dress ball 1921

HRP at Fancy-dress ball 1922

On Wednesday, the 24th, the great influx began. If you would like to know the definition of the words "great influx", we would suggest that you should exchange places with Edwin, the head porter, or Miss Hall at the reception office another year, and you will then get a good insight into what it means when 400 guests arrive on one day, 800 or more pieces of luggage, and a thousand-and-one innumerable questions to be answered. A great influx. Poor Edwin! Poor Miss Hall!

The The Dansant and Cinderella dance in the evening broke the ice. Introductions were made, old acquaintances met, and to Miss Dundas, the dance hostess, we will remove our hats in great respect for the skilful way in which she solved the problem of introducing practically everyone in the ballroom at one fell swoop.

The Paul Jones dance, which is so popular in

When guests arrived by sleigh

Guests arriving by sleigh
Buxton Advertiser – Jean Askew GCSE project

Canada and in America, is the only feasible way of getting everyone known to each other, and so well was it received that at one period there was some doubt whether those parties participating would ever allow it to finish. The way Miss Dundas eventually ingeniously piloted everyone out of the ballroom was a masterpiece.

On Christmas Day, in addition to the usual The Dansant, "a book tea" was held in which 60 took part and Mrs A G Law won the prize.

Of the excellent Christmas dinner, words fail us. As mentioned above, 500 people not only sat down to dinner, but got their dinner without undue delay, and credit must be given to the head waiter and his battalion of waiters and waitresses who worked hard, willingly, and, more important still, kept their heads.

To all the ladies, beautiful ostrich feather fans were distributed, and to every - one caps and novelties. After dinner, dancing continued until midnight.

Boxing Day at the Buxton Hydro Hotel is always associated with the fancy dress ball. To Mr S Turner (a regular visitor to the Hydro) and his committee, congratulations are to be offered on the wise manner in which they made their decisions for such artistic and original costumes, judging was exceedingly difficult. Certainly there were far more people in fancy dress costumes than in previous years.

Yet another record!

The list of prize-winners was as follows; Juveniles: 1 Miss O Stuart-Smith, "wet winter":2 Miss "cowboy"etc. Ladies: 1 Mrs Masters "newsboy"; 2 Miss and Mrs. Lane "wooden soldiers" etc. Gentlemn 1 Baron Bertouch-Lehn "Capt. Hussars" 2 Mr Flude "Widow Twanky" etc.

Mrs Griffiths Hughes calmly distributed the prizes, and was cordially thanked on behalf of those present by Mr Turner, in an excellent and witty speech.

On Saturday more dancing, and yet more dancing, and Mr and Mrs Bosworth, the managers, with the same skill as conjurors produce rabbits from a hat, distributed favours and yet more favours, which seemed to be more excellent and original as each succeed another.

The effect of the favours from Paris, plus the coloured limelights and decorations at the Saturday-night dance, will long be remembered.

On Sunday there was a guessing competition during tea, Miss Harrison Jones proving an easy winner.

The concert in the evening, which has always been such a recognised feature of the Buxton Hydro Hotel, was particularly excellent, Captain J A Coughlan making a very good chairman. The programme is appended; Selection, orchestra, "Samson and Delilah"; song, Miss Smith, "Down in the Garden"etc.

On Monday the annual pierrot ball was held and once again Mr and Mrs Bosworth produced surprises in the shape of more original favours. It always has been a mystery to us as to exactly what Mr and Mrs Bosworth did when they went on their continental holiday last year.

Now we know. It was to ransack the Continent for the favours for this year's Christmas festivities. Complementary remarks respecting these surprises were general, and it would be difficult another year to establish any further record in this respect.

Wednesday night being New Year's Eve, there were special festivities which were enjoyed by a very large number, both by those staying in the hotel, and many prominent residents of Buxton and neighbourhood.

As usual, just previous to the midnight hour the whole gathering assembled in the lounge and joined in singing "Auld Lang Syne" and in the customary manner the old year passed during a momentary period of darkness and the New Year was ushered in with a blaze of light.

Apart from the general proceedings of each day, there have been many indoor amusements which were particularly popular owing to the unseasonable weather prevailing outside. Ping-pong tournaments, golf putting tournaments, billiards, and a successful gymkhana lasting two days.

On Christmas Eve Mr R Gardner and Miss Dundas lead a farondale and several cotillion figures.

Last but not least let us not forget the Orchestra of seven, who rendered excellent music, were lavish with encores, and never grew apparently wearied.

With dancing playing such a prominent part, much depends on an enthusiastic and willing orchestra and those who have enjoyed the dancing cannot say "thank-you" enough for all the pleasure the orchestra gave."

Miss Lillian Dundas was hired by HRP to assist with the entertainments. She was a dancing teacher from London who went on to become a successful organiser and was liked by the guests.

The Jan 1927 account of the Christmas festivities makes mention of a very special guest:

DANCING.

Miss Lilian Dundas

HAS NOW RETURNED FROM LONDON WITH ALL THE

Latest Dances,

AND IS GIVING LESSONS AND CLASSES DAILY AT THE

Buxton Hydro Hotel.

Operatic Creek. Ballroom Dancing.

Students Trained. Schools Visited.

Number Dance Club.

Advertisement for Lilian Dundas
Buxton Advertiser

"Princess at Hydro.

Septuagenarians do the Charleston

As usual, every available inch of space had to be utilised to find accommoda - tion for the visitors anxious to spend a right royal time at the Hydro Hotel. Many requests for rooms had, in fact, to be refused, and in order not to dis- appoint patrons Mr Bosworth obtained all the available accommodation in Broad Walk, Hartington Road and Bath Road. It was quite the best Christmas in the history of the Hydro, the applications for rooms being easily a record.

A distinguished visitor on Monday night was the Princess Manorama of Indore. She was the guest of Alderman and Mrs Blanchard, a former Lord Mayor and Lady Mayoress of Sheffield, and enjoyed herself immensely. The Princess, on the advice of Professor Patrick Geddes, is undergoing tuition with Mrs Albert Law at the Modern School Matlock.

The programme of attractions was very diverse, but a great feature was made of dancing. The Dansants were especially popular, and so great was the demand for tables that many of them had to be placed on the balcony and even in the corridors leading to the bedrooms.

By 1930 the accounts of the various festivities were beginning to wane. In an attempt to reverse the Hydro's fortunes its name was changed to the Spa Hotel (*see ante*) and Mr. AWH Lomas, HRP's second cousin, was appointed as manager.

In the November of 1937, despite its apparent success, a Receiver was appointed to take over the affairs of the Hydro as it was unable to pay its debts!

Although the entertainments were always well supported throughout HRP's running of the Hydro the problem was the lack of people staying throughout the rest of the year. It was not just the Hydro that suffered in this way, it was the whole of Buxton as is shown by the attached table the contents of which were taken from the List of Visitors – every picture tells a story! The decline in numbers starts sharply after the First World War.

Spas fell out of favour between the two world wars. The Edwardian upper middle classes who had been the mainstay of the spas and hydros were now a thing of the past. The new affluent class holidayed with package tours to seaside resorts. The boom years were a thing of the past.

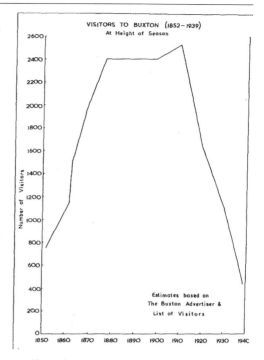

Chart showing visitors to Buxton 1852–1939

Trevor Marchington theses

CHAPTER 15

STAFF

Like many Victorian employers HRP appreciated his employees and, as we are told by management gurus today, recognised that his staff were the business's greatest asset and as such were treated properly.

One of his greatest innovations was the annual staff ball where the guests waited on the staff. This was introduced in 1883 and continued during the whole of H R P's management of the Hydro. *The Caterer and Hotel-keepers Gazette* referred to "*topsy-turveydom*," as it was known, being "*the reversal of the roles of guests and servants, the staff dining in unaccustomed state, waited upon by those they are in the habit of serving, and the affair producing any amount of mirth and jollity. The custom, too, had its useful as well as entertaining side, since it brought home to casual unthinking guests of big establishments what a lot of skill, ability, and training was necessary for the comforts of life which they were accustomed to accept very often without recognising their full merit.*"

On 8th January 1927 *The Buxton Advertiser* states of the 44th annual staff ball:

"Tennyson said that "The path of duty was the way of glory", and on Thursday night the staff of the Buxton Hydro Hotel were fitted with halos to proclaim their – perhaps to them not always – glorious year's duty excellently accomplished. No matter how crinkly the Treasury notes or how new the silver coins in an employee's wage envelope, they only get to the pocket, whereas such a mark of appreciation as a night wherein the management and visitors of the hotel say, "Your work's well done; you deserve a rest, and "turn to" and make the rest night the most enjoyable time possible," reaches straight to the heart and fortifies the body for future exertions. Such is the spirit of the Buxton Hydro Hotel staff ball, which grows in popularity amongst both visitors and staff alike. On Thursday night, when the 44th Annual Ball was held, about 450 of the Hydro's staff and their friends assembled in the lounge of the hotel to enjoy an assured pleasant evening. Led by a piper and the management, the assemblage trooped through the lounge and upstairs into the ball room, where after a parade, hands were crossed for "Auld Lang Syne" which gave place to waltz music, and the ball had started.

Supper was a delightful meal, served by the visitors themselves, and the excellence of the repast can be envisaged when one remembers that visitors to the Buxton Hydro "know what's good".

Even before the First Annual Christmas ball, at HRP's coming of age festivities, *"the servants at Malvern House were treated to an excellent repast, after which they were allowed the use of a large new room in which to dance. They and their friends enjoyed this and other pastimes, and spent a most enjoyable evening"*.

In June 1887 HRP organised a treat for his staff in celebration of Queen Victoria's Jubilee. Over a period of three days they were all taken to Manchester by rail to visit

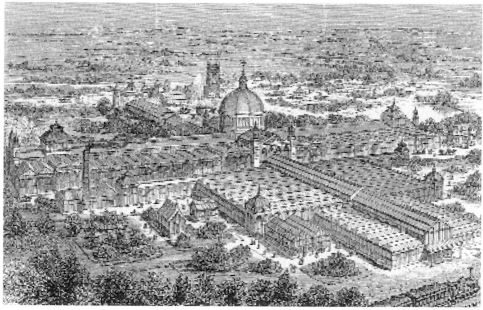

Manchester Jubilee Exhibition
Illustrated London News

the Manchester Exhibition as reported by *The Buxton Advertiser*, "*Buxton Hydropathic Establishment. Jubilee Treat. Scarcely will there be any single section of the community which will not be prompted by a loyal feeling to in some way celebrate her Majesty's Jubilee, or have reason for remembering demonstrations inaugurated by others. Mr HRP Lomas, proprietor of the above-named far-famed Hydropathic establishment, has, with his wonted considerateness, initiated what may serve as an act worthy to be followed by employers of the same class of labour. As a jubilee treat to his numerous servants, he has conceded a day's holiday and given them the opportunity of visiting the Manchester Exhibition, all expenses incurred being defrayed by himself. Not only has he thus taken into consideration his servants' well-being, but he has most generously presented each one with a tangible reminder of the occasion. The first contingent visited the exhibition on Tuesday, the second on Thursday, and the last section will do so today. Such action will strike more deeply than the simple giving of a dinner, which seems to have been universally hit upon as a Jubilee reminder. The servants duly appreciate the kindness of their employer*".

In 1888 about half of the staff of 30 - 50 had worked for HRP for between 12 and 22 years.

In December 1928 a representative of *The Caterer and Hotel Keepers' Gazette* paid a visit to the Hydro meeting HRP and Mr Bosworth, the manager. On the day of his visit HRP and Mr Bosworth had been attending the funeral of the hotel's head "boots", Mr J T Butlin,who had been engaged at the Hydro for the long period of 36 years. He was informed that the present chef, Mr E Harris, had about 30 years' service, and the head hall porter, Edwin Aslin, about the same length of service.[68] Mr and Mrs Bosworth would have been at the Hydro for 30 years in the February, and a few years back the former was elected a director of the Hydro.

The journalist noticed, when looking over a copy of "*Buxton Beautiful and Romantic*" published by Buxton's Bureau of information, the following unusual testimony to an hotel chef's capabilities and adaptabilities; "*Our chef is one of those people who take their calling very seriously. He tells us he is an artist. Well, that may not interest you – but the results of his artistry probably will. Two rare points about him are certainly these: that he seems to inspire all his staff with his own high standard, and that he can be simple as he was elaborate. He knows what you feel like after a few hours in the "Peak" air. You'll find that a Lancashire hot-pot, or a round of beef, are managed with the same understanding as his dainty French dishes. (The chef alluded to is Mr E Harris, who has so long controlled the kitchens of the Buxton Hydro Hotel)*." The journalist went on to describe the Eagle Hotel as a busy commercial and family establishment in Buxton's Market Square. He found that there had been both structural improvements and great business development during the period that had elapsed since his last visit. The hotel was also under the control of Mr Lomas, of the Buxton Hydro, and was fully licensed with a separate restaurant and cafe, and other rooms for special functions.

---

68   Mr Harris lived at Leyland Cottage on Hardwick Square and Edwin Aslin at ? It is believed that HRP bought three houses for staff accommodation

Hydro staff 1908
Courtesy of Buxton Museum and www.picturethepast.org.uk

However, all was not always plain sailing so far as the staff were concerned. In May 1913 the waiters at the Hydro held a "one-meal" strike. It fizzled out very quickly because some of the guests came to the rescue and served their fellow guests at dinner. Other waiters were quickly installed and the matter passed without further incident. *The Buxton Advertiser* recorded the waiters' action.

"One-meal strike at Buxton Hydro Hotel. Dinner was ready to be served at Buxton Hydro Hotel on Saturday night to 250 visitors when a representative (who was not a member of the staff) of 10 of the permanent waiters went to Mr G W Bosworth, the manager, and said they demanded an increase of wages of two and sixpence a week, a whole day or two half days holiday a week, and an undertaking that they must not be dismissed under two months.

As the wages demanded were above the standard, and as it was impossible to comply with the other portions of the demand, the request was refused, and the waiters struck. They were then – our representative was informed by Mr Bosworth – ordered to leave the premises within half-an-hour. The waiters took their departure in due course.

Naturally some concern was caused amongst the 250 visitors, who did not see the usual response to the clanging of the dinner gong. The situation was explained by Mr Bosworth, and at once a number of gentlemen offered their services. They were accepted and the dinner was served, the amateur waiters filling the gaps splendidly.

Dinner over the strike may almost be said to have ended. Other waiters were installed. Some the same night, others next morning. "Everything went as usual at Sunday morning's breakfast", stated the manager. In reply to a question as to what was the length of service of the strikers Mr Bosworth said "Some of them have been here two years and others less".

Asked what were the waiters' hours Mr Bosworth informed us that they worked about five hours a day. "There are four meals a day, breakfast, lunch, tea, and dinner, and they go out after each meal."

The gentlemen who filled the vacancies were not only thanked by the manage - ment and their fellow guests for the manner in which they performed their self- imposed new duties, but congratulated upon relieving what might have been proved a more awkward situation".

In April 1905 *The Buxton Advertiser* reported the "*Sad suicide of a coachman*". George Wells, aged 48, had been a coachman to HRP for 18 years but:

"On Saturday morning he abruptly closed a career in which he had made him - self very popular with all classes, visitors and residents alike.

He went to the stables, off Torr Street, about ten a.m, and as he did not return home his wife sent a boy to see where he was. The boy found the yard door locked, and scaling the wall, saw, upon entering the stable, the body hanging. He was at once cut down, but life had been extinct for an hour or two. The deceased went about his last act in as methodical manner as was characteristic of his general work. He went out and bought a length of line, and fixed it as to length of drop etc on one of the top rungs of a ladder leading to the hay chamber. Then he dressed his horses in their best clothing, cleaned everything, even to the shovel, and when all was spick-and-span, he doubtless locked the gate and committed his last act.

Why he should have done it is a perplexing question. He was healthy and strong and steady, and had the confidence of his employer and everybody else. But a week ago he was told by Mr Lomas that it was his intention to give up keeping horses, and should have them shot. This appears to have preyed upon his mind. He had, further, asked a Higher Buxton livery stable proprietor if he would find him a job, and was at once offered one, being told that he could start at Easter. But he was not even under notice from Mr Lomas.

George Wells was the last man in the world Buxton people thought would have done such a thing."

HRP then gave evidence and described him as one of the best coachmen he had ever come across and he was very fond of all animals and very fond of the dogs.

Due to the coming of age of the motor car in 1900 many horses must have been surplus to requirements and destroyed. A correspondent to *The Hotel and Caterer's Gazette* in 1907 noted "*The vogue of the coach horse is doomed. At Eltham last week*

I saw a hansom cab, minus its shafts and wheels, made to do duty for a commodious garden seat".

It may seem that HRP was callous about the horses, but he was an animal lover noting in his diary written while on holiday in India in 1892:

"Thursday March 17th.
Chota Haziri[69] at 7.30. Started in carriage at 8 o'clock which I got Abdul to get as I considered hotel charges very high. Heard noise, Abdul said my carriage had arrived but hotel manager had beaten horse about head etc. and man and sent them off premises. He then came to my room and asked why had not taken one of their carriages. I told him, he then offered one at half price and begged hard but gave him a bit of my mind and refused to have it. When I was ready I sent Abdul to bring man to door but manager would not let him on premises and said I must walk out to it. I was very vexed, went out to garden, beckoned driver in and stood and watched so that the man was not touched. The poor horse was trembling all over with fright.

Friday March 18th.
Chota Haziri at 6.30 o'clock. Got things put together. Had same man to take things to station as I had yesterday. Before leaving sent for manager and pitched it into him right well. Told him amongst other things that he was not fit for anything but a servant's place, as he was unable to keep order. At station met other man who beat the horse. Gave it him also, told him he was nothing more than a low, mean, coward."

In December 1921 there was a long article in the Buxton Advertiser about a confidence trickster who stayed at the Hydro and stole jewellery and other belongings of guests, many of the staff giving evidence at the Court.

---

69   Small breakfast

CHAPTER 16

SOME INDIVIDUAL MEMBERS OF STAFF

Miss Anne Atkins was matron when Shore was running the Royal in 1870 and in the 1871 census she was shown as having been born in Leicester and aged 40.

After Shore's death, Thomas Lomas wrote to Emily Bulteel stating that he thought highly of Miss Atkins and wanted her to stay on as matron. There is no mention of her in the 1881 census and presumably she had moved on.

Advertisement showing Miss Atkins as matron
Buxton Advertiser

In HRP's diary written in 1876 he surmises that Miss Atkins is *"after"* a Dr Webster, one of the visitors, as one of the first questions she asked him was whether there was a *"Mrs Webster"*. It is not known when she left Malvern House but perhaps she became Mrs Webster!

The Reverend W Bailey headed the Royal after Shore's death and was asked to *"supply the pulpit"* as mentioned in Thomas's letter to Emily. HRP declared in his diary that he thought he preached well – no mean praise as HRP was highly critical of many of the sermons he heard!

The Rev. Bailey was also referred to in HRP's diary when he leads the *"Royalists"* on their visit to Malvern House to watch HRP's charades.

He preached a special sermon in the Malvern House Church on the death of Shore.

In the 1881 census Miss Eliza Thomas was described as a head waitress, aged 25. She is referred to again in 1887 in *The Buxton Advertiser* account of the 4th annual staff ball when a toast was given *"to the book-keeper Eliza Thomas"*. In the 1891 census she was referred to as a book-keeper and so had officially been promoted to this post. At the 1892 and 1895 staff balls the health of Miss Thomas was again proposed and in the August 1898 fancy dress ball *"HRP was simply indefatigable in making sure everybody enjoyed themselves ably seconded by Miss Thomas."*

A further promotion followed for Miss Thomas. By August 9th 1899 she had been made the manageress. On August 9th, 1899 there was an article in *The Buxton Herald and Visitors' Gazette* which although describing a ball at the Hydro made reference to her as the manageress. She seems to have been a woman of many talents, according to an article in the Buxton Herald and Visitors' Gazette which describes her as someone who:

> .... *so tempers the wind to all the shorn lambs, that feed 30 sheep without partners; Miss Thomas, who can beat the champion sprinter of the universe in getting people together for theatrical parties; Miss Thomas, who (to use a French expression) makes "la pluie et le beau temps" at the Buxton Hydro – under the commanding aegis of Mr Lomas; Miss Thomas, who rings the bell at progressive whist, and says, in a would-be stern voice "silence, please" several times repeated; Miss Thomas, who waves the light fantastic toe in the mazy dance with the best of them; Miss Thomas, the ubiquitous and Protean like, that springs upon you either in the deep and darkening vaults near the linen room presided over by sturdy Mrs Murray and nimble-fingered Agnes; or Miss Thomas, as she is wafted up on angel's wings (first time I heard a hydraulic lift called that way, Ed.) to yon under the flagstaff, and says in a small-sized voice," May I come in," and inquires as if the whole future of the Hydro depended on it, whether the you have got rid of that "Mother, come and kiss your boy before he dies" kind of feeling; Miss Thomas who – Miss Thomas that - Miss Thomas where, here, there, everywhere – ah well, if her godmother and godfather had only called her Eliza, as a fitting co-regent of the great Eliza that ruled the waves (for does she not rule the waves of the bath and massage department well?) – she would have been complete. Now, read in plain English what I've talking about.*

Buxton Hydro Ball and Presentation.

During the progress of the ball, a presentation was made to the indefatigable and obliging manageress – Miss Thomas, in the shape of a silver bead purse containing 25 guineas subscribed by the visitors in commemoration of her birthday, which only became known to them after dinner on Sunday evening. – a committee of five was formed consisting of Messrs Albery, and Jowett, Millar, Jacobs and Barker – and in about 12 hours £26 was collected, owing to the hearty spontaneity with which all the visitors contributed for such a meritorious purpose – Mr Albery, as the oldest visitor to the establishment, was selected to make the presentation. – Mr Jowett, who acted as treasurer, handed the purse with its contents to the chairman who in a few well-chosen and heart - felt words, paid tribute to the ceaseless and unsefish efforts of Miss Thomas on behalf of the visitors and then presented her with the purse – Dr Londini, another old and honoured guest at the Hydro, acknowledged in very neat and appropriate words the present on behalf of Miss Thomas who was deeply moved. General applause, together with musical honours and repeated cheering for Miss Thomas by all the visitors, closed these highly successful proceedings.

The following is a little presentation ode all by my lonesome:-

Who puts each notice on the board?

And when at whist you've briefly scored,

Who complements you like a lord?
Miss Thomas.

Who darts about with eagle-eye?
And coaxes entertainers shy... (who say, they like to sing so much, only they
haven't brought their music, and yet, if you are wise in the ways that the world,
you will know that they – have got a whole box full upstairs)
Why
Miss Thomas
Who ministers to all our ills
And guides our good or evil wills,
And sees we duly get our bills,
Miss Thomas

The 1899 shareholders register when the Hydro was floated reveals Miss Thomas as holding 50 ordinary shares in the company.

In a revealing article in *The Buxton Advertiser* in 1949 entitled "*Golden era of can - dles and crinoline*" (*see post*) she was referred to as "*a tall grey figure, who, inter alia, had the interests and welfare of over a hundred maids under her control*".

She retired in 1905 through ill-health having been connected with the Hydro for 30 years *The Buxton Advertiser reporting*:

"*Farewell to Miss Thomas. This has truly been a record week of gaiety at the Buxton Hydro, though with a strong note of sadness running through. From far and near old friends gathered to say farewell to Miss Thomas who, to the deep regret of all who know and appreciate her unfailing kindness, is obliged to resign the post she has held for so many years as manageress.*

Last Wednesday she gave a dance to the staff, in which many of the visitors took part. Mr R Goddard's band kindly gave their services. Needless to say, the music was first-rate and all thoroughly enjoyed the evening; not the least interesting part being the presentation by the staff to Miss Thomas of a hand - some clock and illuminated address, as a token of respect and regret at her departure; and also to Mr A Friend, who is resigning, was presented a valuable gold ring and address, testifying to the esteem and regard in which he has been held by all...

We understand old friends and visitors to the Hydro have collected a testimonial, as a token of esteem and affection. It has amounted to a goodly sum, and will, no doubt, be a source of gratification to her for many years to come."

In the same edition of *The Buxton Advertiser* a regular guest from Liverpool wrote:

"*Sir, – As one of the oldest, if not the oldest visitor of the Buxton Hydro, I consider it almost a duty to give public expression to my feelings of regret, which, I am sure, are shared by many old visitors, at the retirement of Miss Thomas. She stands as a prominent figure in the history of that establishment, in whose growth and development she took a most important part and active interest. The disappearance of her familiar figure will create a great void, and she will be sadly missed by hundreds of visitors who will remember her many good qualities and her conscientious desire to please. To me, personally, she has ever been a much valued and kind friend, always ready to minister to my comforts and to cheer me in times of illness, for all of which I owe her my ever - lasting gratitude. She may rest assured that she carries with her the good wishes of many hearts for her happiness and welfare, and also the enduring remembrance and staunch friendship of many of us. – Yours etc Liverpool. E. Londini March 15th 1905."*

After Miss Thomas retired Mr. F.W. Wehrhahn was appointed general manager. He was for fourteen years manager of the Hotel de l'Europe, Hamburg, and for two years prior to the Hydro director of the Queen's and High Cliffe Hotels, Margate. This was not a "home grown" appointment and was not a success, Mr. Bosworth was therefore appointed in his place in 1908.

In the 1901 census George William Bosworth was shown as secretary, his wife,

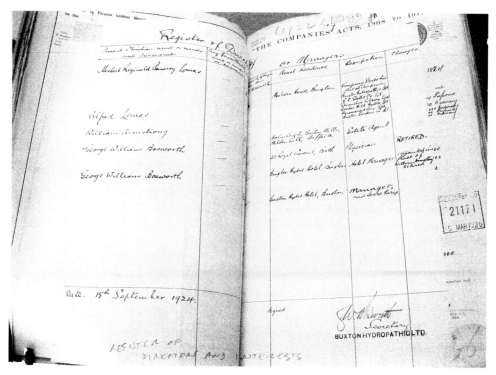

Register of directors interests 1925
National Records

Helen Bosworth, being under manageress. When the Hydro was floated as a company all the Hydro company documents were signed by him as company secretary. He was 37 and was to become HRP's trusted hard-working manager in 1907, holding that post for 32 years as well as continuing to be company secretary.

HRP was able to delegate most of the functions of running the Hydro to him and one could be forgiven for believing him to be "*the man in charge*". He certainly appeared to be "*the front man*". His name was at the end of all the Hydro brochures and advertisements. He signed most correspondence and answered the allegations contained in Dr Lorimer's letters to *The Buxton Advertiser* (*see ante*) albeit probably in conjunction with HRP.

He held 50 shares in the company and eventually became a company director on the retirement of Dr Armstrong in 1925.

Naturally, the Bosworths played an important part at the various balls at the Hydro including "*ransacking*" the Continent for the various favours handed out at the functions.

In January 1930 Mr and Mrs Bosworth retired at the 47th annual staff ball and their retirement was duly recorded in *The Buxton Advertiser*:

> "*Buxton Hydro Hotel. Staff gifts to Mr and Mrs Bosworth.*
> *Over 250 guests assembled in the lounge of the Buxton Hydro Hotel at 8:45pm last Friday for the 47th annual staff ball when Mrs Bosworth and Mr HRP Lomas led the procession in a stately march into the ball room. When tradition had been thus honoured, the orchestra struck up a popular foxtrot and dancing began in earnest.*
> *The great event was yet to come. Mr Wilks having obtained silence with his never-failing gong, then expressed his pleasure in calling on Mr. Edwin Aslin, the oldest member of the staff, to bestow on Mr and Mrs Bosworth, the manager and manageress, a small token of the affection in which they are held by one and all. Mr Aslin then made the presentation of two handsome motor rugs to the accompaniment of vociferous applause. Both Mr and Mrs Bosworth expressed their surprise and delight at this unexpected gift, and in their turn thanked the staff must cordially for their kindness and loyal help at all times, and especially during this arduous Christmas season.*
> *Mr HRP Lomas, the chairman of the company, who was loudly cheered, then referred to his warm personal regard for Mr and Mrs Bosworth, and confidently foretold brighter times for Buxton.*
> *The presentation was followed by a further one of a table scarf from the staff of the Eagle Hotel, the ceremony being prettily performed by Master Graham Smith. With songs and cheers the guests and visitors adjourned to the ballroom where dancing was continued until the early hours of the morning.*"

Mr Bosworth was 67 when he and his wife retired and was indeed a "*true and faith - ful servant*" of the Hydro.

As the social functions at the Hydro were so important, in 1922 HRP hired a dancing instructress to organise the balls and give dancing lessons. Miss Violet Dundas was a dancer from the Haymarket in London and had performed in Calcutta, Bombay and Singapore. She was a small elf-like figure and was evidently a great success. In the Christmas festivities in 1924 *The Buxton Advertiser* noted "*The Paul Jones dance, which is so popular in Canada and in America, is the only feasible way of getting everyone known to each other, and so well was it received that at one period there were some doubt whether those participating would ever allow it to finish. The way Miss Dundas eventually ingeniously piloted everyone out of the ball room was a masterpiece.*"

In the festivities of 1927 *The Buxton Advertiser* records "*The Charleston was in great demand. Those who did not know it were eager to learn, and Miss Dundas had as avid pupils a lady and gentleman of 70 years of age! She was heard to remark that never at any previous season at the Hydro had she had so many pupils*".

She had rather a tragic end. She was a great friend of Miss Brock, one of the "leading" permanent residents at the Hydro for many years. In March 1929 Miss Brock died. It was a double blow for Miss Dundas who had also lost a relative in the same year, she became very depressed and on 18th September, 1929, she jumped from the hotel roof and killed herself. *The Buxton Herald* takes up the story:

The tragic story of how a well-known local dancing instructress became "so tired of life" that she jumped from the roof of the Buxton Hydro Hotel, was told to Mr Sidney Taylor (coroner for the High Peak) at an inquest on Thursday morning of last week, concerning the death of Miss Lilian Violet Dundas, which occured the previous day at the Buxton and District Hospital.

Miss Dundas had resided at the Buxton Hydro Hotel for about seven years as a teacher of dancing, and was a popular figure in the social life of the town. It appears that following the death of a relative, and later of her friend, Miss Brock, she became very depressed. Sidney William Dundas, of 13 Stradella Road, Herne Hill, London identified the body as that of his sister, who, he said was 32 years of age. The last time he saw her was in November 1925.

Edwin Aslin, hall porter at the Buxton Hydro Hotel, who resides at 2 Leyland Cottages, Hardwick Square, Buxton said that Miss Dundas had resided at the Hydro for about seven years. On 11th June this year, at about 9 o'clock in the morning, he had occasion to go outside in front of the hotel, and there saw a lady lying on the gravel. He went up to her and found that it was Miss Dundas. She seemed to be badly hurt and was groaning. When he attempted to pick her up she said "O leave me alone. Let me die".

The coroner: Do you think she was quite conscious?

The witness: Yes, quite.

What did you do? I knocked on the side door and sent for Mr Bosworth and Dr Harburn.

Judging from the position she was in, what opinion did you form as to where

175

she had come from?
From one of the bedroom windows or the roof.
What height would the roof be from the ground?
About 40 feet.
Is that anywhere near her bedroom?
No, her bedroom is on the other side.
Were there any windows open?
I didn't notice.
I suppose you have seen a good deal of her. Has she ever seemed peculiar in her manner?
She seemed very depressed recently after the death of Miss Brock. Miss Brock was a great friend of hers."

Edwin Aslin was another long-serving member of staff who, in the 1901 census, was shown, aged 20, to be the gardener.

By 1925 he had progressed to head porter and is referred to in the 3rd January 1925 edition of *The Buxton Advertiser* as having to deal with "*a great influx*" of visitors, 400 guests on one day, 800 or more pieces of luggage, and a 1001 innumerable questions to be answered.

In 1930, when the Bosworths retired, as the oldest member of the staff at the Hydro he made the presentation of "*two handsome motor rugs*".

He is another example of a member of staff who rose up through the ranks of the Hydro.

Around 1920 Ernest Wilks started working at the Hydro as assistant manager, residing with his family in Penzance Villa. At the Bosworth's farewell party he used his "*never failing*" gong to obtain silence. He always made speeches at the staff balls.

As his family were strict Methodists and he was teetotal, he was not altogether pleased when the Hydro obtained its licence. He hated having to be at the Hydro while locals were having a drink at the bar.

Spa brochure showing Edwin Aslin
opening a motor vehicle door
Buxton Museum

Spa brochure showing E. Wilks
on reception
Buxton Museum

AWH Lomas top left – Claridges, Paris

He was told that on the Bosworth's retirement he would be promoted to manager, but unfortunately for him, HRP's second cousin and son of Alfred Lomas, A W H Lomas, was appointed manager.

However, he was made company secretary and signed all the various documents when a receiver was appointed in 1938. Shortly afterwards he retired.

HRP had paid for the schooling and training of his second cousin as a hotelier. He had started his career in the kitchens at Claridges on the Champs-Elyses, Paris, and then became a waiter at Monte Carlo and Office Manager at the Savoy in London. His first management position was at the Royal British Hotel, Edinburgh and HRP, as a last ditch effort to save the Hydro, appointed him as manager in 1931. It was all to no avail and AWH Lomas, anticipating the hotel problems and having married Kitty Grocott, whose father was accountant to the Buxton Corporation, he left to take over the Royal George Hotel in Perth on 19th April 1936. F J Aymes was appointed manager in his place.

The domestic employees were as vital to the smooth-running of The Hydro as the managers and HRP appreciated this fact.

Alexander Friend was HRP's personal secretary in 1901and held 50 shares in the company. He was also the "*buyer in*" of provisions for the Hydro.

Mr Turner was his butler, valet and friend between 1921 and 1941. He attended HRP's funeral in 1941.

Mrs Pakeman was a maid for HRP and worked under Marion Britain, who was his housekeeper. She is now dead but her daughter remembers she had a great admiration for HRP, describing him as a "*gentle gentleman.*" When she got married HRP gave her a tea set which was passed on to her daughter. Her mother thought he was a wonderful man but a bit of a loner and very reserved. He kept his staff for long periods and was not hard on them. He treated them as equals. If they broke anything, he would

AJ Turner

have it repaired without comment. She remembers a lot of visitors at the Hydro, in particular, mothers with daughters hoping that HRP would "*cast an eye*" on them as they knew he was very wealthy.

Perhaps the best way of seeing life as it really was for a domestic servant is through the eyes of a worker. A 15 year old Buxton schoolgirl carried out a project for her GCSE exam when The Spa was about to be demolished and she interviewed Alice Godwin:

"Alice Godwin started work at the Hydro the week before it opened after the First World War.[70] The furniture was stored at Burbidge Institute and each bit had a label on, as to which room it went in, but it never seemed to end up in the right place. She started work at seven in the morning and worked 13 hours a day until eight at night. Sometimes she went on till 10 and then she would have two hours off the following day. She earned five shillings a week and food. Her breakfast was the only meal she had at home, and she had half-an-hour to rush home and get it, and rush back. Dinner in the hotel was always stew and she told me she had not eaten stew since. She had several jobs at the Hydro and one was as the lift girl. Once she had to take the Duchess of Devonshire and another lady up in the lift. The Duchess was wearing a dress with a train. All was all right until the Duchess tried to get out of the lift. Twice she tried but she could only move forward a few inches and then she was stuck. Then Alice noticed that she was standing on the train. Quickly she moved it and this time the Duchess shot out of the lift.

She worked at the hotel during the time HRP had it. He had stained glass windows put in at the back of the hotel. This was expensive at the time but it meant the windows never had to be curtained. The drawing room curtains were from Alton Towers, along with some gilt mirrors. The curtains were pink brocade with a gold crest. Underneath the drawing room was a store room for basket chairs that were used in the drawing room and for underneath the veranda. When Alice first worked at the Hydro there was no licence and they had to send boys out to fetch the dinner wine.

70 i.e. after Hydro had been requisitioned for the Granville Canadian Hospital

Different areas of the Hydro were given different names. The four houses where the Reverend Shore had begun were now called A and B Houses. In the winter these were closed off along with the coffee room and dining room. The dining room was occasionally used for big banquets. When the dining room was closed the restaurant was used instead.

The hotel also had about 60 residents. In room 52 was Miss Brock and in the adjoining room, her friend Miss Dundas, the resident dancing teacher and entertainer (for guests). Miss Brock was a big person who always dressed in tweeds. She had a chauffeur called Ellis. Her car was a Rolls Royce and she would never go out in it if she thought it was going to rain. A man used to come up to check her car every year from Derby and he used to say that car was in better condition than when it left the factory. When she was going out, she liked someone to accompany her to the car. Alice sometimes had to do this and then tuck a rug around her when she was in the car. When it was cold out she would say in a loud voice (so that other people could hear) that there was no need for the servant to go out with her but they knew if they didn't then in the lounge that night Miss Brock would be saying how a certain person would not accompany her to the car that afternoon.

Another resident was a lady called Mrs Kinlock Wylie. She only went out once a year and that was to communion on Christmas morning. She had two sons, Malcolm and Alastair. One year they bought their mother an expensive fur coat. One breakfast Malcolm happened to ask her mother where her new coat was and was horrified to learn she had left it in the ladies' cloakroom. Alice was quickly sent to get it back.

There was a back entrance to the hotel that was used for any coffins and this got called the coffin entrance. There was a flat roof to the hotel where visitors could walk and after Miss Brock died her friend Miss Dundas committed suicide by jumping from it. Another suicide happened a few years later when a German member of the staff hung himself.

Another thing Alice sometimes did was to work in the bar. Sometimes people would buy her a drink. About the cheapest drink was 2/6 or 12 1/2 p. She had an arrangement that instead of having a drink she would have the 2/- or 10 p and the hotel kept the rest. The same worked when she was serving sweets.

One day near Christmas she was serving sweets when someone brought a 9d or 3 1/2p bag of sweets. She gave these to Alice as a present. Later when Alice was going down to the kitchens she noticed a little girl who worked there and gave her the sweets instead. Later when she came back the little girl said "you did mean me to have them, didn't you?", and she found a 10/- note or 50 p in the sweets. Alice of course had to say yes.

She also got gifts of handkerchiefs from the gentlemen who stayed there. They were in the cotton trade and would go off to Manchester and other places.

HRP owned Milton House and sometimes the Duke of Devonshire stayed there. When he did the staff of the Hydro used to like to see him set off in his car. They nicknamed the car "rabbit" because the Duke would sit jogging in it and then it would suddenly set off at a fast speed.

The hotel used the town's electricity supply but it could make its own. The hotel also had a joiner shop where the central yard is now. They made their own ice cream and had cold storage in Manchester. This meant if they got grouse out of season they could keep it till it came into season and they sometimes kept it for just under a year. They would have someone come every so often from Bradleys Furrier to remodel the ladies' furs and also sell more. The porters ran a betting book for Lamford although it was illegal.

Miss Bennett was one of the linen keepers. The linen room was on the way up to the laundry. The housekeeper was Miss Rigby and she was scared to go on to the top floor of the hotel. Whenever she had to go up she would ask someone to go with her. Edwin Aslin was the head porter and he was there through the First World War and at the Spa bar in the second.

The staff was made up as follows:
Manager and wife.
1 under manager.
2 joiners.
5 engine house staff.
2 linen keepers.
4 plate pantry keepers.
1 head waiter.
2 wine waiters.
1 book-keeper.
1 receptionist.
16 chambermaids.
16 waiters.
3 in central office.
1 hall porter.
1 under hall porter.
3 luggage porters.
3 daily workers.
4 lift girls.
4 still room staff.
2 kitchen porters.
1 billiard marker.
2 carvers.
2 in orchestra in week. 5 at the weekend.
1 entertainer.
1 head chef.
1 pastry chef.
2 apprentice chefs.

1 regular chef.
2 people in out house peeling vegetables.
2 masseurs.
A total of 90 staff a lot of which lived in at the hotel. There were also 2 night watchmen." [71]

Barbara Sharpe (nee Brunt) tells the story of when she was a girl she was asked to deliver a birthday cake to a Major Brown who lived in a suite of rooms at the Hydro with his valet. Her instructions were to take it to his room, knock on the door and give it to his valet. This would have been quite straightforward were it not for the revolving door at the entrance to the Hydro. She entered into the door and as it started to turn she slipped and sat on the floor, still carefully holding the cake in her hands. She was then stuck and could not get up easily because of the cake. She also ended up going round and round in the door as people came in and out of the hotel. One of the porters, Sid Dawson, was aware of her plight but thought it quite funny although he eventually rescued her and the cake was safely delivered!

---

71   Jean Askew (nee Skidmore) *Spa Hotel* 1973

CHAPTER 17

PERMANENT RESIDENTS
AND NOTABLE VISITORS

The foremost of the 60 or so permanent residents were Mrs Brock and her daughter Miss Winifred Brock.

Mrs E B Brock first came to live at the Hydro in 1899 and stayed there till her death in 1932 aged 80, her husband, Dr John Brock, of Hove having died some time previously. HRP would bring gifts back for Mrs Brock which he purchased on holiday.

Her daughter also resided at the Hydro until she died on 4th March 1929 aged 45.

HRP occasionally went on holiday with Mrs Brock's son, W O Brock, also a resident of the Hydro. He died in July 1933 at Rhyl aged 55. In his will and codicil he left his mother's Rolls Royce to her chauffeur, Harry Ellis of 22 Torr Street and several legacies to HRP, his staff and other permanent residents.

Winifred was the leading light of the permanent residents. She was an accomplished musician and was extremely popular with the other residents, visitors and staff at the Hydro. She took a great interest in the entertainments given at the Hydro and was described as "*the General*" at the 1926 Christmas ball. She was called upon to make a speech and replied that she could not give a speech, and declared that "*the general*" would have been in a pretty pickle without the assistance of all the visitors in the room. Miss Brock had to listen through her blushes to the thunderous rendering of "*For she's a Jolly Good Fellow*".

On Boxing Day in 1921 she appeared as "*prehistoric man*" in the fancy-dress ball.

In the 1923 Boxing Day fancy-dress ball she and her helpers were praised for "*the able way in which they accomplished the difficult task of judging, and the admirable decisions arrived at.*"

She was also involved in the social life of the town, being a member of the Cavendish Golf Club.

A week after her death *The Buxton Advertiser* noted:

"writing of her regret at hearing of the passing of Miss Winifred Brock, whose death at the Hydro Hotel was reported in our issue of last week, and recalling the many deeds of kindness the deceased lady made, a lady has penned the following; "I always admired the generous way she sang for the Tommies during the war. I was at one concert, given as a sending off to men who were

going to France next day, and they would not let her stop singing, though her accompanist could not stay.

She said she would go on singing if someone would play for her, so a person volunteered, went up on the platform and "vamped" horribly, while she delighted the men by singing as willingly and as well as ever. Not many people with such a splendid voice would have done that, and I always thought it so good of her".

Mrs Brock did not have such a high profile, but would be called upon to present the "*handsome*" prizes to the winners of the fancy-dress balls.

The music for the early social events was mostly provided by Fred Goddard and the Pavilion Band. By 1899 the Hydro had its own, albeit, small orchestra which was augmented from time to time by traditional orchestras as and when necessary. Some of these were the Wyoma Jazz orchestra, Dick Richards band, Sammy Greenwood, and Tommy Kinsman and his band.

HRP met many eminent and influential people, some of whom he entertained in the magnificent library at Malvern House. The Hydro had a long succession of distinguished visitors amongst them were W S Gilbert, D H Lawrence, Dr Mary Scharleib, Charles Garvice, the novelist, and the pioneer suffragette Emily Pankhurst. She stayed at the Hydro in July 1909 and gave an address to 250 people from around the country in the lounge at the Hydro. In addition Ottoline Morrell visited the Hydro in 1915 when Bertrand Russell was also staying.[72] She was a pre-eminent literary and political hostess in London society and the Bloomsbury Group and had amongst her acquaintances Henry James, D.H.Lawrence and Siegfried Sassoon. She suffered from severe headaches and other illnesses travelling to many spas and resorts around Europe seeking treatment.

Dame Margaret Lloyd George stayed at the Hydro in 1904, writing to her husband in May stating that she was disappointed "*not to have had a letter from him*".[73]

Vera Brittain also attended various functions at the Hydro.

HRP must also have known many members of the aristocracy and royalty who attended the various balls.

He was a friend of Baron Bertouch-Lehn who was a frequent visitor to Buxton and was honorary attache to the Danish legation in London from 1913 to his death in Buxton on 17th August 1936, having held similar appointments in Vienna in 1910 and Rome in 1912. It was in Rome that he met HRP, and ever since coming to England he had visited Buxton as the guest of HRP usually about twice a year at Christmas and Easter. The baron liked the air of Buxton, which he said did him more good than that of anywhere else. He was the 12th Baron in succession. He was a bachelor, and had a brother who was also engaged to the diplomatic service in Tokyo. In a letter from him to his brother he talked of meeting the Queen of Denmark in London and attending a

---

72 Ottoline Morrell *Early Memoirs of Ottoline Morell* Faber and Faber 1963
73 House and land records. The Lloyd George papers. Personal correspondence and papers L9/1/1/43

party with the UK Royal Family. He was taken ill on the night of his death whilst having dinner at Malvern House with HRP. *The Buxton Advertiser* stated that his death was a great blow to HRP. He died in a nursing home in Buxton of cirrhosis of the liver and alcoholism. His funeral was held in Denmark.

J Bertouch-Lehn

CHAPTER 18

HRP

HRP's first diary provides some idea of how his character was going to develop.

Losing his mother at such an early age meant that he was particularly close to his father.

Julia's marriage to Thomas was no doubt a duty to her deceased sister to look after her child. Moreover, he was an only child and was probably spoilt both by Thomas, Julia and his grandfather, James Shore. HRP makes no mention of him in his diary but he was obviously desperate to return to Buxton. It would be interesting to know whether there was any mention of Shore in the missing pages.

He was a promising pupil but his schooling seems to have been mixed; firstly Julia taught him Greek and other subjects, then he was sent to boarding school in Cheshire whilst Thomas and Julia assisted Shore in Buxton, then on to Clifton for a very short while, Mr Pettit in Buxton

HRP 1892

and finally studies at Derby. Apart from Greek he was also taught Latin, French and the usual subjects. He also showed early promise as a musician learning the piano, organ, and violin and in later life a teacher used to visit the Hydro from London to give HRP piano lessons. He owned a Steinway piano in 1911. Playing the piano in Victorian times was mostly a female accomplishment but even males were assured in 1895 that "for an educated man to seat himself at the piano is no longer thought effeminate".

He was a sociable child enjoying meeting the guests at Malvern House and arranging charades, organising trips to the countryside and visiting the roller-skating rink at the Pavilion Gardens.

He was obviously a "*people person*" and this comes through in his dealings with the staff, treating them on an equal footing. He was popular with his staff, many of whom were brought up through the ranks and stayed at the Hydro for many years. He trusted his staff and felt able to delegate much of the running of the Hydro to them.

As in many middle-class Victorian homes religion was very important to the family, the young HRP attending church twice on Sundays, and on one occasion three times, but from the later diaries religion did not seem to have played such an important part during his adulthood.

He was a strong royalist as can be seen from his first diary and his trips to see Queen Victoria at Windsor. He went to the Coronation of George V on June 22nd 1910 staying at the Constitutional Club in London. The Club has been described as:

"A bastion of the Conservative party, the armed services, and chauvinism. Ladies were admitted to the dining-rooms, but only through the back entrance, after threading their way through assorted garbage cans and climbing an unusually steep staircase, though there may have been a dilapidated lift. The heating arrangements were non-existent. The lower rooms were supposed to be warmed by coal fires and the bedrooms by electric heaters, into which one put shilling pieces with alarming frequency."[74]

HRP was handed Malvern House at twenty four years of age and expansion of the business was swift. He was a great publicist of the Hydro, advertising heavily in the local and national papers, and ensuring that the Hydro had a high profile. Guidebooks and the local press mostly had good things to say about the Hydro and he ensured that that the Hotel and Caterers Gazette knew about the development at the Hydro.

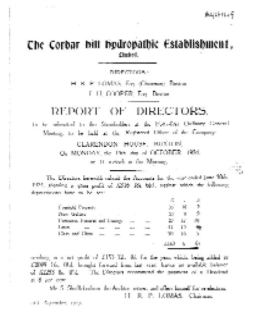

Report of directors of the Corbar Hill Hydropathic Establishment 1924

He had great business acumen and kept a close eye on the finances. His diary in India shows just how meticulous he was about the cost of services and goods. He was also pedantic and to begin with was very much *"hands-on"*.

He was typical of the Victorian benevolent businessman. He was also a good administrator.

The Canadian occupation of the Hydro during the First World War hit him hard but with hindsight he may have expanded too quickly.

HRP was not just a hydro and hotel owner but had many other business interests. His other directorships included The Lee Wood Hotel Company, Corbar Hill Hydropathic Ltd.,

74 *Closely Guarded: a life in Canadian Security and Intelligence* John Starnes 1998 University of Toronto

Milton Hotel
Courtesy of the Board Collection and www.picturethepast.org.uk

E C Stott & Co Ltd. (a removal and warehouse company), Devonshire Library Ltd., New Radium Ltd. and Hargreaves and Son Ltd. He also owned the Milton Hotel, a small hotel opposite the Hydro, used for overspill purposes.

HRP or James Shore at one time owned or occupied The Eagle Hotel, The Royal, The Buxton Hydropathic, The Grosvener Private Hotel, Leewood Hotel, Corbar Hill Hydropathic and the Burlington all shown in the attached Illustrated Supplement and Visitor's Guide from *The Buxton Advertiser* dated September 1885.

Although HRP did not take a big part in public life of Buxton, he was on the board of directors of the Buxton Gardens Company which ran the Pavilion Gardens complex. In February 1899 *The Buxton Advertiser* in their editorial column stated: *"There is a vacancy on the board of directors of Buxton Gardens Company consequent upon the resignation of Mr James Brown, who has been a director ever since the company was formed. If we might suggest a name, we would say Mr HRP Lomas, of the Buxton Hydropathic, would make an excellent director. By the management of his own business he has proved himself a prince of organisers and an up-to-date Caterer for public want. Moreover, he is thoroughly independent, and in every way would be an addition to the strength of the directorate."* The newspaper continued on 4th March 1899 *"To fill the vacancy caused by the retirement of Mr James Brown, the directors of the Gardens Company have appointed Mr HRP Lomas of Buxton Hydro. This is exactly in accordance with a suggestion made in this column a short time ago. The appointment will have to be ratified by the shareholders at the Annual Meeting. Mr Lomas will make an excellent director and there is no doubt he can "put a lot of*

Supplement to Buxton Advertiser showing hotels in Buxton 1885
Local Studies Library, Matlock

traffic on the line." He was on the Board of Directors from 1899 to 1926 when the Borough of Buxton took over the Company. He was a Director when the Company issued 4% Debenture Stock for £25,000 to fund the building of the Opera House in 1902. Later on, he allowed the opera group the use of the ballroom at the Hydro for rehearsals.

As the Hydro overlooked the Gardens, it would have been useful for him to have a say in any possible development.

In addition he owned many properties in Buxton. It was stated in December 1898 that HRP was fast becoming the largest owner of houses in the place and there was only the Duke of Devonshire above him at that time.

Samuel Gladwin designed investment property for him which included Rochester Terrace a block of four-storey town houses with Italianate features to the first floor and four cottages in Torr Street.[75]

In June 1921 *The Buxton Advertiser* contained an article entitled *"Grosvener Mansions."* It continued:

"When domestics cease from troubling and the tenants are at rest. Our text, taken from the writings of the man of patience, needed a little adaptation before being applicable to the subject. The troubles of those connected with housing schemes in any form are manifold, and in order that residents may be attracted to Buxton it is necessary that accommodation should be available for those who wish to enjoy our air and all the great advantages Buxton possesses above other residential towns. Thus the more people are attracted to Buxton to settle down, the more likely are we to reduce our rates. To build cottages costing from £800 to £1,000 is a very grave risk, for when they are built we doubt if they can be occupied by those for whom they are erected, at a paying rental, even when the State aid is taken into consideration. Fashions and methods of business change with the times, and in bygone days of exceptional prosperity the townsmen of Buxton were wont to build huge private and company houses, many of which have served their purpose and have now become a thing of the past – out of date.

There is no need to particularise in this direction. It is obvious there are many buildings which are not earning one penny in rates which could be adapted by go-ahead capitalists into flats and let at such a figure as to show a good profit. Perhaps it is one of the many involved questions which would have to be answered by the Ministry of Health; but would it not be possible for the borough council to acquire some of these properties and turn them to good account as flats before building any more expensive cottages? At least the scheme might be gone into, possibilities discussed, and prices obtained. Tenants need not enter into the question. There are occupants for flats at all rents. People who nowadays are scared of taking a house because of the difficulties,

---

75   Mike Langham *Buxton A People's History* Carnegie Publishing 2001, p.180

would be glad to take a flat where domestic labour is reduced to a minimum. A practical objection or impediment might be urged against such a scheme, but nothing very serious occurs to us at the moment. Old Buildings. It may be that the expert or alleged expert will put forward the argument that old buildings cannot be satisfactory adapted to the new idea. This is disposed of immediately by the instant success which has attended Mr HRP Lomas in his scheme of conversion of what was Kensington House and the Grosvenor Private Hotel into 12 flats. The town owes a debt of gratitude to Mr Lomas for his initiative, for instead of empty property bringing in nothing to the local exchequer we have now 12 new ratepayers on the books paying their share towards a common burden. Grosvenor Mansions. By the kind permission of Mr HRP Lomas and the courtesy of the tenants we were allowed to view the new homes and surprise is a very mild expression of our feelings. Mansions in miniature, they certainly are. All flats face the Broad Walk and take in one of the most glorious views in Buxton. A complete vista of the fine gardens is obtained from every drawing room window and many of the bedrooms, and it appears as though one were residing in a huge park of well cropped lawns and varied with beds of flowers; guarded by the beautiful trees clad in the full verdure of June: a gorgeous sight. Construction. As we stated the two houses have been apportioned into 12 flats; four of eight rooms, four of six rooms, and four of five rooms, including bathroom and kitchen. These are entirely self-contained and are so planned that domestic work is reduced to a minimum. A continuous hot water supply has been installed and all the apartments are centrally heated. No lead pipes have been used for conveying the water. All are of copper, and everything used evidences the careful thought of the trained, cultured mind. Expense has not been spared in the conversion, and the result is a pattern worthy of the widest imitation. Only 12 tenants were needed, and Mr Lomas had between two and three hundred applications. If any serious attempt is made to construct from other almost derelict buildings similar accommodation, Mr Lomas will be pleased to give the names and addresses of people whose wishes could not be complied with. It is a big question for the town. More residents means less rates, and the more businessmen from the surrounding towns that are induced to settle down here, the more likely are we to receive better attention from the railway companies. Grosvenor Mansions are ideal.”

His properties also included Street Farm at Pomeroy where he built several cottages for the workers on the farm. The village was named after him and he was invited to open the Memorial hall in 1921 as recorded by *The Buxton Advertiser.*

“The Reverend TJ Pearce, the president of the movement set up to build the hall, stated that the hall which had been erected to the memory of the fallen, and those who had returned, would be non-sectarian, and would be used for

Signs showing Pomeroy Cottages and Memorial Hall

pleasure and enjoyment, and also probably for educational purposes. He was going to ask a gentleman to open the hall, who was known through-out the whole district. That was Mr. HRP Lomas, who was the means of the name of Pomeroy being instituted in that neighbourhood.

At a very pleasing little ceremony a presentation of a key of the building was made to Mr HRP Lomas, by Mr T C Bailey. He asked Mr Lomas to accept the key, and keep it as a memento, and also as a useful article, for if at any time he was in that district he should come in and inspect the Hall.

Mr Lomas said it gave him great pleasure, and it was a considerable honour to open the memorial that day. This Memorial Hall could be used as a school in the winter time, and might be the means of saving the lives of many little ones. (Applause) He thanked them most sincerely for the key, which he would certainly never part with. The property he (the speaker) bought up there, he bought without seeing, and it was a strange coincidence that it was the same spot where his grandfather had a seizure on 12th of August 1874. He had no idea the population of this community was so wholehearted, and the good feeling existed which enabled them to carry out that wonderful work in such a wonderful manner. He thanked them all for the honour they had done him, and hoped they would all live many years to have the use of that building (applause.)"

Would Shore have approved of HRP's emphasis on the business side of the Hydro? The answer is probably yes, despite the departure from the original purpose of Malvern House. After cessation ministers very often poured their energy into industry and business. Shore was becoming something of a businessman himself and would have been very proud of the successful way in which his grandson developed the business.

HRP in addition to his business acumen was a cultured man. He had extremely good taste and took the lead in much of the interior design of his buildings. He also had a considerable collection of paintings. Malvern House where he lived at the end of his life was not the original Malvern House as that had been incorporated into the Hydro in 1899. He built Penzance Villas half of which eventually became Malvern

House linked to the Hydro by a corridor bridge.

As the insurance of his valuable paintings was prohibitive he built the first floor of Malvern House out of concrete to protect them. In Victorian times the first floor was usually made of wood.

He imported much of the labour from Italy to lay the marble floors in his buildings.

He was an expert in antique furniture and an authority on glassware, giving lectures at the Art Section of the Literary Society. Various glass, china and other objects were placed with the Buxton Museum for exhibition, amongst which is a charming oil painting of Buxton and the Crescent painted in 1837 by J Smith (shown on back cover). The museum still has some of the items.

In November 1918 he instructed Maple and Co Ltd from London to carry out a valuation of the contents of Malvern for insurance purposes which shows, amongst other things, the books in his library and the wines in the wine cellar. His library contained 1053 books, in addition to which he owned the complete works of Sir Walter Scott in a separate book case. The wine cellar was well stocked as can be seen from the extract from the inventory (*ante*). There were 530 pieces of glass and china in his collection.

HRP was a great linguist being fluent in Italian and took many holidays in Italy and Europe. He was particularly fond of Venice, staying there for one month on one occasion. He met many of the Anglo-American colony of authors and historians who lived out there including Horatio Brown, EF Benson and Constance Fletcher, whose pen name was George Fleming.

On 4th November 1922 he visited the Theatro Nuovo in Verona whilst on holiday the entry in his diary being: "*Morning visited churches and Theatro Romano. There are many Fasisti or (Black Shirts) here. Today is anniversary of Italian armistice. Saw half hour procession, many Facisti who were much cheered. Lunch Restaurant, after dinner Theatro Nuovo, opera Strauss. Theatro very full, about 80 officers, many soldiers and Fasisti. 7 of them took possession of a large box. Patriotic tunes were played, everyone standing, the Fasisti demanding several, the officers standing when played. The Fasisti are rebels, and the whole thing is like a comic opera. Show finished 12.15. Fine evening.*"

Despite being such a traveller he was not too happy with the proposals made by commercial companies in 1882 for "*joining England to the Continent of Europe by a Railroad under the Channel*". HRP added his signature to a Protest against such a Railroad the Protesters "*feeling convinced that (notwithstanding any precautions against risk suggested by the projectors) such a Railroad would involve this country in military dangers and liabilities from which, as an island, it has hitherto been happily free – hereby record their emphatic protest against the sanction or execution of any such work.*" [76] HRP's childhood hero, Sir Garnet Wolseley, was one of the main protagonists and wrote an article in the pamphlet which may have influenced HRP to attach his name to the list!

---

76 *The Channel Tunnel and Public Opinion* 1882

In his early days HRP must have had considerable energy to expand the business so fast. He was clearly a man of vision. He was seen as fair but firm by his staff who showed him great loyalty all being proud to work at the Hydro. He was charming and an excellent host. He knew how to look after the gentlemen of the press so they give gave him good reports in their magazines and newspapers.

In later life he was described by one of the staff as a "*gentle gentleman*". If a maid dropped a piece of china off the mantelpiece in one of his rooms, he would say nothing and replace it surreptitiously so that there was no "*awkwardness*".

At this stage he was seen as a "*bit of a loner*", quiet and reserved.

As he was a bachelor and had no immediate family he must have been rather a lonely figure. He had been on good terms with his cousin Alfred from very early on and Alfred had been on the board of directors of the Hydro for many years. HRP visited him in Suffolk on many occasions where he lived with his four daughters and one son, A W H Lomas, who HRP helped to become an hotelier and who was also one of the executors and beneficiaries under his will.

He was Buxton through and through and was always ready to take the opportunity to promote the town.

HRP's obituary in *The Buxton Advertiser* of 1ˢᵗ February 1941 read:

"*Mr HRP Lomas. Dies at 81. Controlled Spa Hotel for over half a century. Mr Herbert Reginald Pomeroy Lomas, controller of one of Buxton's largest hotels for over 50 years and the owner of much property in the town and district, died at his home, Malvern House, Hartington Road, on Thursday morning at the age of 81, after four weeks' illness.*

By his passing the town loses one of its best-known and most picturesque figures, slender, with distinguished features, he gave the impression of having stepped out of the 18ᵗʰ century. His last illness was also his first; until last Christmas he had never, since childhood, spent a day in bed. During the early part of this winter he was frequently out and about, walking with a step and carriage that would have done credit to a much younger man. A bachelor and an individualist, he took little part in public life, but helped many good causes unostentatiously. (There then followed a summary of his time in Buxton)

The funeral is arranged to take place on Tuesday next at Totnes, Devonshire which was the home of Mr Lomas's grandfather and where his mother is buried."

Chapter 19

THE FINAL YEARS

On 2nd August 1945 the Norwich Union Society placed the Spa in the hands of Jackson Stops and Staff for sale by auction

The auctioneer's particulars described the Spa as *"built like the rock of ages overlooking the finest views for miles"*.

On the copy particulars held by the National Monuments Record notes have been scribbled by a prospective purchaser working out the possibility of converting the Spa into flats. Unfortunately for the Spa he did not continue with the purchase. Instead Freehouse Ltd purchased the property on 23rd September 1945.

Between 1945 and 1948 the Spa struggled on until it closed again in January 1948.

In May of that year a correspondent of *The Buxton Advertiser* took a nostalgic look at the Hydro and Empire Hotels:

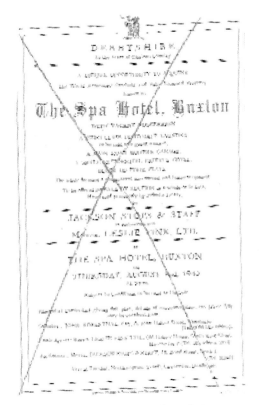

Page 1 auction particulars 1945
National Monuments Record

*"Golden Era of Candles and Crinolines. Empire and Spa Hotel. Memories.
The other day I finished reading "Buxton under the Dukes of Devonshire", and one realises that here is that indefinable something that lives in the hearts of all old Buxtonians. It has an atmosphere that is not too far away in time, but is just near enough to get right under the skin, and as I laid the book down I became quite wistful at the golden memories of a Buxtonian era of candles and crinolines, of Pompadour lace and lavender.
Right from the beginning one realises that here is a local history that not only arouses the nostalgia of all over 60, but is also a valuable index to the changes*

LOT 1

THE SPA HOTEL

WITH VACANT POSSESSION ON COMPLETION

Fully furnished and fitted throughout with the most up-to-date Appliances (the Purchaser shall have the option to take over at Valuation the Furniture and Fittings, etc.)

The property is substantially built in stone, and stands in an unrivalled position, and equipped with modern lighting, heating, plumbing, sanitary and service installations.

The Accommodation comprises, briefly:—

Ten Public Rooms, including Dining Room, Ballroom with Balcony, Billiards Room, Lounges, Drawing Rooms, Rest Rooms, etc., 107 Bedrooms, the majority with wash-hand basins and many with Private Bathrooms, 43 Public and Private Bathrooms, 25 w.c.'s, Three Toilet Rooms, 10 Offices and Staff Rooms, Storerooms, and excellent Kitchens and Still Rooms

THE FAMOUS SPA COCKTAIL BAR

Central heating, Two Waygood Otis Passenger Lifts, and one Service Lift. Hard Tennis Court

MAIN SERVICES INSTALLED

THE BUXTON & DEVONSHIRE LAUNDRY

WITH VACANT POSSESSION

At the moment doing a large and profitable business as a Public Laundry, and is also capable of dealing with the requirements of the Hotel. The property is built in stone and comprises a LAUNDRY BUILDING, fully equipped with excellent machinery, Laundry GARAGE, etc., the whole of the Machinery, Fixtures, and Fittings, Motor Vans, etc., can be taken over at Valuation.

LOT 2

THE MAGNIFICENTLY-PLACED MAIN ROAD BUILDING

known as

THE SPA GARAGE

MARKET PLACE, BUXTON

A modern building with internal floor area of over 900 square feet, containing:—

Large Central Garage, Offices, and Workshop, Nine Lock-up Garages to hold Fifteen Cars, and Men's Rooms, Petrol Pumps and Storage Tanks capable of holding a total of 2,000 gallons.

Let on a quarterly tenancy at a nett rental of £304 per annum.

LOT 3

THE IDEALLY SITUATED

MILTON HOUSE PRIVATE HOTEL

BROAD WALK, BUXTON

Facing the Pavilion Gardens and comprising:—

Two Dining Rooms, Smoke Room, Private Sitting Rooms, Two Kitchens, Fifteen Bedrooms, with hot and cold water in all. Three Bathrooms. Boxroom.

Main water and electricity

Let on a five years' lease from June, 1941, at a net Rental of £163 4s. 0d. per annum.

LOT 4

A SMALL BLOCK OF FOUR FLATS

IN HARTINGTON ROAD, BUXTON

... convenient to the Hotel, and forming a first-class investment.

Page 2 auction particulars 1945

National Monuments Record

in taste and habit of nearly 300 years of Buxton life.

I wonder what the characters of those times would think of the glittering modernity that Buxton enjoys today? To mention only two items – the grandiose cinema, and the miracle of radio.

After an absence of a few decades one wonders after even so short a time, let alone 300 years, whether the experiment of visiting the old town would be a painful one. To discover in every familiar nook and corner only phantoms, to find the old magic, the old human charm was gone. One thinks of certain events relating particularly to its large hotels that have happened during the last decade.

It would certainly give me an awful ache to stand in the stubble and rank growth of nettles and weeds, and gaze at the gaunt and defunct Empire Hotel. What a phantasmagoric picture, and what a ghostly mockery it must appear to the Buxtonians who knew it in its heyday.

Looked on in wonder.

How values have changed and so quickly! How regal in the old days, and in what a grand situation was the old Empire Hotel, especially when seen in the distance from the crest of Solomon's Temple. Set in a vast soaring landscape, it looked quite imposing and was rivalled only by the superb position of the Palace Hotel.

It will now be some 55 years ago when Pettit's school had their football ground where the Empire now stands, and I remember they gave we Hardwick Square School boys many a good game on that playing pitch. In those days there was no Carlisle Road, and it would be about seven years later when Buxtonians looked on in wonder at the rapid growth of the huge modern caravanserai, another link in the great chain of Empire Hotels forged by Spears and Ponds of London.

I can still picture their house flag at the mast head proudly waving in the blue over the Park and musing upon it I think of the hotel's old opulence, its expensive furnishings, the never-ending ascent and descent of its elevators, its volatile messenger boys in pillbox hat and buttons, its busy telephones and Continental air. What a lambent palace it was in the dusk of the evening.

Huge staff.

One thinks of its palatial rooms, where wealthy guests dined to the music of artistes in uniform and its huge staff of liveried servants that functioned so efficiently, all scattered to the four winds. What a pregnant story for an Arnold Bennett, or even an Edgar Poe, for it has its grim side. The story of the Empire Hotel has indeed a touch of Stevenson's "New Arabian nights", something of Prince Florizel of Bohemia about it.

One minute this vast and intricate organisation was in full swing, and the next minute up come the expensive floor coverings, down come the rich furnishings, out go its profusion of exotic flowering shrubs, and the long line of furniture vans roll away, leaving behind the deserted stage and props of a gorgeous broken show. A sum of £150,000 – that is what the building cost; the same job today would cost a quarter of a million – practically going down the drain. It seems incredible!

How strange to realise at this moment it is just a bleak shell of frouzy smelling rooms and empty echoing corridors invaded by a homeless band of people called "squatters" who with their sticks of furniture have dug themselves in. One can imagine, in the darkness, their dim lights like glow worms, and a strange furtive atmosphere of watching and listening at doors, and of figures hovering unexpectedly in gloomy galleries.

Shattering!

One can fancy the stir and flutter there would be amongst these apparitions if, deep in the stillness of the night, there suddenly came with shattering reverberations through the musty vicinity, the ghostly boom! boom! of the old dinner gong.

It is rather odd, but the old Empire Hotel, had, for me, a feeling of something transient. I remember watching it rise from the turf in the park, floor by floor, like some huge mushroom growth. I recall the army of strange workmen who appeared on the scene. The very stone with which the building is faced came mysteriously in huge blocks by rail from distant parts, and was not the hard endurable gritstone of the peak. It was stuff you cut; in fact the workmen did cut it to size with saws, like cutting wood. They called it Bath stone, and Buxtonians declared it would never stand up to the climate. In a phrase the Empire Hotel was in Buxton but not of it.

The Spa Hotel – or the old Buxton Hydro as I knew it – was entirely different. It had grown up with the town, one had seen it rise from a boarding house – the Malvern – throwing out over the years a wing here, a bay there, finally reaching the sprawling proportions of today, it was indeed Buxton! It had a freshness and easiness that was all its own; it was bourgeois.

It was nothing out of place to see performing in a spacious foyer at certain hours of the day, a group of pierrots in full regalia. You could often hear amongst the seated guests the plonk! plonk! of the banjo and the castanet of the bones from the nigger minstrels, the guests unconsciously tapping their feet to the lilt of "Lu-Lu" or "Little Dolly Day Dream".

Here too, you would hear the reedy squeaking voice of Harry Bailey's Royal Punch and Judy, and the gorgeous procession of the travelling circus often entered the drive to pass by its extensive portals.

I think also of the summer evening when we members of the Buxton Band, under the baton of Sid Boughen entertained the guests out on the loggia after dinner. As a boy in the employee of the doyen of booksellers – Mr J E Clare [77] – I looked

---

77 The daughter of ET Wilks remebers "Grandpa Clare", as the children used to call him, giving the children a book every Christmas such as "Wind in the Willows". He was a kindly white-haired gentleman who was very cultured and owned a bookshop in the town

after a little newspaper stall in the old Hydro and happy memories come deep and fast.

One sees once again that tall grey figure of that efficient hostess Miss Thomas, who, inter alia, had the interests and welfare of over 100 maids under her control.

Porters recalled.

Like the characters of some old play, the figures I saw with the eyes of a boy pass before me – old Woolley, Shotter, Britton and Teddy Powell – the hall porters in their cinnamon garb and gold lace, their glittering fobs and key chains; the tall military figure of Claude Williams, the czar of the dining room; the podgy figure of Mr Friend, the "buyer in" of provisions, a powerful commissariat carefully watched and ministered by Buxton shopkeepers; and down below in the depths the prespiring kitchen staff.

Bailey's Punch and Judy Show
Courtesy of Buxton Museum and www.picturethepast.org.uk

What a hive was that steaming greasy basement, heavy with the pervading smell of food, the chefs, for ever cooking in tall hats and dress of white linen. How clever were these disciples of Lucullus at dressing plates with viands, like expert milliners dressing hats, they even matched the colours, a touch here, a touch there, and hundreds of plates waiting on dinner wagons would be decked out in no time.

At salads they were a joy to watch. A fat thumb would race along the spine of a cucumber and, chasing it with the rapid precision of a machine, would come the flashing knife, leaving a trail of thin luscious wafers. Right through from soup to the dessert and coffee it was an art in culinary juggling, nothing went wrong and there were no excuses, the fish and potatoes cooked by steam would be hauled out of the steel chambers done to a turn.

Spicy Gossip.

In thinking of those odorous basements of the Buxton Hydro, I wonder where the army of scullions, many of them foreigners, are today? I particularly think of that little band who cleaned and polished the boots and shoes of the guests. Oh, their spicy gossip! Of the 400 or more guests they knew everyone.

In the early hours 400 pairs of boots and shoes would come down to them in large hampers, upon the soles of every pair was chalked the number of the bed -

room from which they had come, and during the process of cleaning and polishing the stories they tossed to and fro about many of the owners were remarkable.

They were a veritable school for scandal, they made free with reputations with - out the slightest provocation, and many of their stories – like those told by anglers – lost nothing in the telling. What a huge staff the old Hydro had in its day. They had their own chef and dining hall in the basement, and it was interesting to note, prominent upon the walls of this room, the singular notice "Maids are not allowed to sit with the men".

The Night-Watch.

What a strange feeling came over one, after the fierce bustle of the day, to wander round these basements in the silence of the night-watch and realise that upon several floors somewhere above were close on a thousand people all horizontally recumbent in all stages of slumber. The only people on the move would be the trio of night-watchmen under the eye of old Shelmerdine prowling silently like cats along the mute corridors and deserted, dimly lit, hall and lounges.

How strangely restful and cosy, in the dead hours of night, appeared those carpeted bays with their palms, their luxurious chairs, and the faint lingering scent of perfumes, so contrasting to the basement, where, throughout the night, there was always something doing, maybe the man with his bucket of insect powder carefully dusting behind the warm pipes of troughs in the kitchens in his nightly war with the cockroaches, or the plumber and the electrician giving the electric baths and water pipes "the once over", or occasionally, after a late duty genial "Monty" of the billiard- rooms would come down to the pantry and help himself to a chicken leg.

Enjoyed to "Tootle"

Looking back, I think of the many guests who turned up year after year at the Hydro, prominent amongst them old Stowell, a keen disciple of Izaak Walton, and Attenborough, the big London pawnbroker, and his wife and daughters, whose hobby was playing the cornet, and every morning when the coaches drew up he would go out, and after a chat with the drivers and buglers, would enjoy a good tootle on the coach horns.

A great annual event, I remember, was the staff ball, an occasion when the whole order would be reversed, the guests in the main dining hall waiting upon the staff, a procedure which provided many hilarious moments.

This was followed by a general exodus to the ball room, where, till the early hours of the morning guests and staff danced upon an equal footing. Another great event was the High Peak Hunt Ball, when the elite the Peak would drive up in costly turn-outs.

The monarch who ruled over all this was a rather lonely and slender figure – the great HRP Lomas – keen and pedantic, but strictly just. He built the place up from a small boarding house, "The Malvern".

Dear old hotels and Hydros of Buxton town; their story was both gay and tragic, and what a fine muster they made during the golden days of the Devonshires before the world began to wobble".

It appeared that things were looking up when a new Purchaser was found on 30th August 1949 being Spa Hotels (Buxton) Ltd and the Spa was reopened in 1951. Geoffrey Hewlett, the owner of the Palace Hotel, formed the new company. At the AGM of Buxton Palace Hotel Ltd on 7th May 1951 Mr Hewlett stated *"our acquisition of the Spa Hotel is a help to the business and the hotel will be a great asset when national conditions improve"*. The freehold was transferred to the Prudential

Auction particulars 1964
National Monuments Record

Auction site plan of the Spa
National Monuments Record

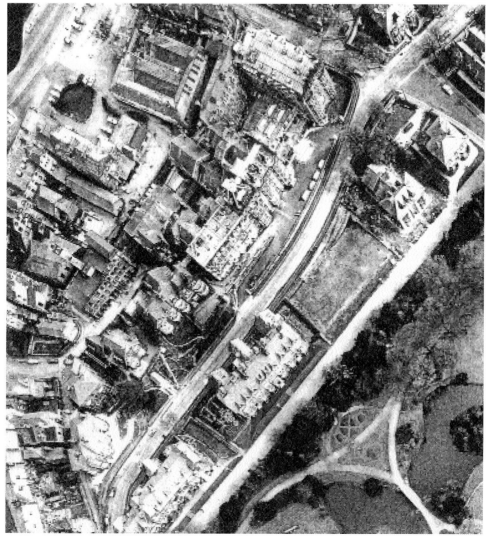

Aerial photograph of Spa 1965
National Monuments Record

Assurance Company Ltd in 1952 with a lease back to Spa Hotel (Buxton) Ltd. There had been some considerable rivalry in the past between The Hydro and the Palace and no doubt Mr Hewlett took great delight in taking over the Spa.

Still conditions did not improve and in 1964 the Spa was again put up for auction by the Prudential but was sold privately.

In 1965 aerial photographs were taken of much of Buxton including the Spa which provides good photographic evidence of the hotel before it was finally demolished.

In 1966 the Spa was now owned by Heddon Hotels. This too was short-lived and the bailiffs were sent in to shut the hotel in January 1967. The Spa was finally sold to Mr and Mrs S Brigham in October 1967

There it remained until 1973 when it was compulsorily purchased by the High Peak Borough Council. Between 1967 and 1973 the Spa was in its death throes. Vandals started to desecrate the hotel, and squatters took over.

Naturally councillors voiced their concern about the fires at the Spa and its possibly becoming "*another Empire Hotel*".

In 1922 the Empire at Buxton had been put up for auction but did not reach the reserve price. In the Second World War it was used for the billeting of British troops and suffered a similar fate to the Hydro as was mentioned in *The Times* for December 8th 1949:

"*Squatters evicted from hotel. About a dozen bailiffs and 60 policemen arrived at the Empire Hotel Buxton yesterday with coaches to take away 15 families of squatters, and furniture vans to take their belongings to store. The squatters, who had barricaded themselves inside the building, were evicted under the authority of a writ of possession order granted by the High Court.*
Seven men were arrested, and appeared at a special court at Buxton last night. They were remanded until Saturday, three of them in custody."

A final decision on the Spa's future was made on the 4th May 1973. Some of the borough councillors were in favour of demolishing and rebuilding it as mixed housing with a bias towards providing flats for the elderly whilst others were suggesting the scheme be delayed whilst further investigation was made into an offer

Empire Hotel before demolition
Courtesy of Derbyshire Local Studies and www.picturethepast.org.uk

Demolition of Empire Hotel
Courtesy of Buxton Advertiser and www.picturethepast.org.uk

Demolition of the Spa Hotel
Norwich Union cirular

to erect on the site a new three-star hotel with conference and tourist facilities.

Arguments were put forward that there were already enough hotels in the town trying to make a living for yet another one. The Spa was one of 14 hotels that had closed down in the last 20 years. The arguments raged on and eventually the council granted themselves permission to demolish the Spa and erect a block of retirement flats on the Spa site.

As in all cases there were arguments on both sides as to the efficacy of the decision. On the one hand there is nothing worse than having a large building empty for years attracting vandals and squatters, the building deteriorating all the time through want of repair. In particular this is not pleasant for neighbours. On the other hand here was a building, which, although it may not have been of great architectural merit (it was not listed in Pevsner's *Derbyshire)*, had many architectural features which were of importance and perhaps the council could have granted itself permission for retirement flats, but retained the main features of the Spa. The building was itself structurally sound, but it is likely that the cost of converting the Spa into retirement flats would have been greater than the cost of demolishing and starting from scratch.

Nevertheless, there were some in Buxton who mourned the passing of this former grand hotel. *The Buxton Advertiser* in its occasional notes column on 4th May 1973 opined:

> *"The Spa Hotel. Although no one could possibly describe Buxton Spa Hotel as a pretty sight now, there was a time when its portals welcomed many guests, when its dining room was full, and its ball room and bars thronged with merry-makers. It is always sad to think of such places falling into neglect and disrepair until they reach the point where they have to go.*
> *The Reverend James Shore, when he decided to set up in the catering business in Buxton, could not have realised how much impact the venture would subsequently have on Buxton. He could not have visualised the great success he would have when he bought his first guesthouse, which eventually led to the building of the Spa Hotel."*

The fifteen year old schoolgirl from Buxton in her GCSE report gave a graphic description of her trip round the empty Spa with the borough surveyor:[78]

> *"My visit to the Spa Hotel happened on the 12th February 1973.*
> *Outside, today, the Spa Hotel looks a mess, but there are still signs of what it must have looked like in its heyday. It used to have a veranda and visitors could sit there when it was sunny.*
> *We entered through a revolving door into the reception/lounge where the head porter and page boys used to meet the visitors.*
> *We went off to the right to the billiard room and a billiard table was still there.*

---

78 Jean Askew

This billiard room used to be upstairs. Above the fireplace was a beautiful, decorated mirror with a painting above it.

We proceeded up the stairs of the new wing or south wing to see some of the bedrooms. The new wing is the section near Hartington Road, and some of the guest rooms in this wing have bathrooms attached. We moved along a back corridor looking in the rooms and went up a staircase labelled TOWER. We walked along and went to see some of the staff rooms, one of which was labelled "chef". The staff rooms were quite big but the floorboards were rotten. We walked back a little way and went into one of the linen rooms. In here there were still a few pillowcases on the table and the walls were lined with cupboards still marked for sheets etc., and in the corner was a spin dryer. We then walked care - fully down the remains of a burnt staircase to a gallery which overlooked the reception hall/lounge. The main stairs used to be where the gallery is now. They were moved when people kept falling down them because of the glare of the big room below.

As we had come to a dead end we had to go back up the burnt staircase. Our guide told us as the hotel had no proper floor-level, but split levels it was very hard to find their way around. At this moment our guide from the town hall had to admit that he was lost and he told us he had lost his deputy in the building. Next we went into a strange room, it was a bedroom at the front and close to the window were several wooden archways in pale green which gave no indication as to what they were for. We found a staircase to take us down but unfortunately the door was blocked and so we went to a staircase exactly the same and climbed through some barbed wire to get down to the ground floor. Our guide told us that when the hotel was closed a lot of the doorways were blocked up.

We climbed up four flights of stairs to get to the attics. At the end of the passage of attics was a big room which was used as the staff dormitory. We went back down the four flights of stairs and paddled in a few inches of water along a dark passage to the kitchens. Although the kitchens are really on the ground floor they are underground at the back. We came up another passage back into the reception hall/lounge. Here we had a look at the reception desk and the manager's office. In reception was a numbered board for the room keys which went from 41-275 although not all the numbers were mentioned. Across the hall we peered in through the broken glass to see a cocktail bar. This room and the one before it used to be all one room that made up the hotel's restaurant. In the reception hall/lounge there was the lift with the ropes still there. There were three lifts in the building, this one, one in the south wing, and a service lift in the kitchens. Next we went into the dining room, looking down on this was an observation balcony whose windows could be opened or closed. The dining room was originally built as a chapel. Beyond the dining room was a coffee room with a glass dome. We went up to the back of the balcony in the dining room by a sodden wet stair carpet. There were two rooms along here. One was a bar with a white grand piano. Another could have been a sitting out room or for serving refreshments to the ball room. Earlier in the hotel's history there was a billiard room and the one with the piano in, a smoke room. For gentleman would never smoke in the drawing room then, but had their own special room for it.

The ball room was at the end of the corridor. This corridor used to have big mirrors along it. The ball room also had mirrors along one wall, and there was also a stage with wings at the far end. There was a balcony over the door with a velvet balcony rail. In this balcony, HRP used to have his own pipe organ, but this was later sold to one of the chapels that needed an organ. The ball room was well known for its spring floor. Some ball rooms just had springs under the middle area but the Spa had springs all over.

As we walked out I couldn't help noticing the lovely mosaic floor of the reception hall/lounge. HRP brought Italian craftsmen to Buxton to lay it and others. It's sad to think it is all gone".

The Buxton Advertiser continued the theme "*A bedroom lampshade swings silently in the gentle breeze which floats in through a gaping, glassless window fifty feet above the ground, smoke blackened plaster glimpsed through the stone window frames testifies to recent fires; huge heaps of ripped out floorboards where elegant feet once trod now litter the ground, interspersed with fragments of wrought iron railing. Broken glass lies everywhere. The Spa Hotel, at one time a gracious, well-upholstered and tastefully appointed play-ground for the well-to-do meets a long and painful death, and somehow one wonders if Buxton will ever be the same again.*"

Whilst no doubt some could not wait to see the building demolished many people were quite emotional by the parting of this old friend of Buxton.

A letter from a former employee of the Norwich Union in *The Buxton Advertiser* of June 1973 read:

"For the past few weeks, I have been watching with sadness, the demolition of the Spa Hotel, my home and office for five years, and have marvelled at the soundness of the structure, which was built to last, and so different from modern building.

If taken in hand two or three years ago, it could easily have been adapted in exactly the same way as the council now propose with the new building i.e. flats, bed sitters, communal lounge etc.

When we came in July 1940 the Spa was in a very derelict condition having been empty for several years, and it was a year before all the bedrooms were ready for occupation; but when we left all had basins with hot and cold running water, gas rings and fires or central heating – even the top floor, where mine was, and still standing as I write.

Many a supper was cooked for our friends on these gas rings, and I even made some elderberry jam, "pippy" but edible.

So many things happened during our years at the Spa – grave and gay. We worked very hard and for the first year had no half-day holiday, and only a week to go and see our parents in Norwich; and we were very homesick for them and our friends, and worried about their safety.

After a time, when the risk of invasion lessened, which was the reason for a coming to Buxton, we settled better and found outside friends and interests.

The Pavilion Gardens provided a feast of music with its very good resident orchestra, and guest artistes, and Buxton has never lived up to that high-standard since.

The weather, however, is I am sure, better than it was then, as it seemed to rain incessantly and was very cold.

I cycled miles into the surrounding countryside, but there were no maps or sign - posts and nobody would tell me where I was and they were very suspicious of my strong Norfolk accent, but after I joined the local rambling club, I gradually fanned out. I was an ARP warden in the town. I joined W.E.A. classes. All this gave me many more interests and friends.

If I stayed in the hotel in the evenings, I found myself working, as there was so much to do, the trouble when living with one's work. Most of the men were in the Home Guard and went on strenuous exercises.

Life at the Spa was a mixture of a boarding school, a prison, and a hotel. At first the food and service were very good and almost hotel standard, and each after - noon in the office we were served by a handsome young waiter with a dainty afternoon tea with best china and "silver" tea service, which gradually got to thick white cups and no saucers or food, on a tray dumped on the stairs. It was our teas that we missed most, and my lifeline was the Stanley Arms, where they served mammoth teas at a very low price.

The married ladies were the most unhappy, having left their homes in Norwich, and although they had their families, it was a difficult place in which to bring up children. They also felt they could have done far better with our rations, and in the last year our meals seemed to consist mainly of oxtails and bad fish, which became quite a joke.

One man who haunted a local shop was known as "chip chase Charlie".

In June 1945, we returned to Norwich, mostly glad, but with some regrets and unforgettable memories.

Thank you, Spa Hotel, for your safety and shelter during those five wartime years, and your superb view of the hill which I loved so much. You will soon be gone, but not forgotten by yours etc

Ex Norwich Union Insurance Company."

It would be interesting to see whether the council would take the same decision nowadays or whether with all the E.E.C. grants available for preservation of buildings the old Hydro could have been saved.

The headline in *The Buxton Advertiser* (*see ante*) exclaimed "*The Hydro is dead, long live the Spa*", but unfortunately neither the Hydro nor the Spa are now "*living*" despite HRP's exaltation, but hopefully the memories of the Reverend Shore, HRP, the Buxton Hydro and the Spa will continue. So much of HRP's heart and soul went into the building of the Hydro and although the architectural merit of the building may not have been as great as that of St Anne's Crescent, at least Buxton is beginning to value its old buildings with the help of the various grants that are now available and far-sighted developers who are sensitive to old buildings and their past.

We must be thankful that the Crescent with its magnificent architectural beauty is in the process of being converted back to a spa in the natural baths and a hotel which hopefully will again be the pride of the town.

These buildings are part of our heritage and it is a tragedy that so many have been raised to the ground over the years.

JAMES SHORE, MARTYR OR AGITATOR?

Thomas Latimer wrote in The Western Times:

> *"Imprisonment of the Reverend James Shore.*
> *The tyrannical and oppressive conduct of bishop Phillpotts has aroused general indignation. Influential meetings have been held in various parts of London, and the impulse given to the movement, will be felt throughout the kingdom....*
> *Meeting at Whitechapel... Sion chapel, Whitechapel is stated be the largest chapel in London, and according to the report in Tuesday's Daily News a meeting of about 5000 people assembled on Monday night, for the purpose of receiving the report of the deputation appointed to visit the Reverend J Shore a prisoner in the jail of Exeter..."* *"Meeting at Exeter Hall... A public meeting was held this day in the large room of Exeter Hall, with a view to adopt such measures as may lead to the liberation of the Reverend J Shore MA now imprisoned in the jail of St Thomas at Exeter at the suit of the Bishop of Exeter. The meeting was convened for 11 o'clock but long before that hour the body of the hall was pretty well filled by an audience, the larger portion of whom were ladies. The side galleries, which were exclusively set apart for ladies, were also filled some time before the chair was taken..."*
> *"Plymouth. "on Wednesday morning a numerous and respectable meeting, convened by W Burnell Esq. the mayor, was held in the Guildhall of Plymouth, to consider the case of the Reverend James Shore..."*
> *"A meeting has been held at Norfolk, expressing the deep sympathy of the inhabitants in the case of the Reverend James Shore and their detestation of the persecuting spirit of intolerance manifested by the Bishop of Exeter. A committee was appointed to petition Parliament in the matter."*
>
> (March 24 1849)

In further editions there were additional articles;

> *"A moral song.*

> *For a Big and Busy Bishop, by a Little Busy Bee.*
> *How doth the "Apostolic" See*

Improve a Prelate's power
To gather victims every day,
His wrath on them to shower!

How skilfully he spreads his net!
How he doth drag them in!
And labours hard to store a cell
With good men- for their sin!

Go, grasp an "Apostolic" See,
You may be busy too;
Old Harry ever, ever finds
Some dirty work to do.
In empty pomp, in venomed rage,
Have his long years been passed,
Oh! Will he ever dare to give
A true account at last?

London, Doctors' Commons.
Note by the poet. "I would print this in a large type – the size used for children's
books, for Harry is a babe – in grace."
"Public meeting at Devonport. On Wednesday evening a meeting was held in
the town hall of Devonport to take measures for liberating Mr. Shore..."

(31 march 1849)

"Editorial. The Right Hon. the Lord Lieutenant of this county has addressed the
following letter to the Reverend James Shore enclosing the liberal sum of £20
towards his relief – we shall leave the letter to speak for itself. We had
intended to follow the matter up the some general observations, but we shall
refrain from doing so, in the hope that the bishop will respond to this appeal to
his better nature – for that in fact it is – by declaring his determination to
abandon all vindictive proceedings. The Protestant public are beginning to
understand that Mr. Shore might have turned Roman Catholic, as young Mr.
Collyns, and old Mr. Newman did – and no penalty would have been incurred
by him – but he cannot turn Protestant Dissenter without being sent to prison.
Now this law will not do for the 19th century – and the sooner Bishop Phillpotts
washes his hands of it, the better. Clovelly Court, April 2 1849.

Sir, – Understanding that some of the friends of religious liberty, who, at the late
meetings at Exeter and in London, expressed their sympathy for your sufferings,
have followed up that expression with some contributions for your relief, I beg
to add the enclosed for the same object. In doing so, however, I wish not to be
misunderstood. As the legality of the proceedings against you has been affirmed

210

by every court, civil as well as ecclesiastical, to which they have been referred. I cannot impugn, though I may regret, the conduct of those by whom such proceedings were instituted, but I have a right to denounce the inconsistency and injustice of that state of the law under which, as we have so frequently seen of late, clergyman seceding from the Church of England are allowed to under - take the Ministry of the Church of Rome; whilst those who, like yourself, desire to devote their services to a dissenting congregation, subject themselves there - by to prosecutions and costs.

I hope that the just and tolerant spirit of our legislature will soon remove this blot from our statute book, and that all seceders will be protected alike in fol - lowing the dictates of their conscience, and in doing what they consider their duty to God.

I have the honour to be, sir,

  Your obedient servant,

    Fortescue."   (April 7 1840)

"Imprisonment for dissent.

The Patriot taxes the London committee in Mr. Shore's case with the want of business tact, and we have heard the same opinion delivered by parties from the North of England who have visited Exeter. It is to be regretted that a committee has not been organised and armed with power to send competent delegations to everytown in England. The people have been so much mystified with talk about costs, that they hardly realise the fact that by law a clergyman seceding from the established Church is now imprisoned on account of that secession, and that if instead of turning Dissenter he had turned Roman Catholic he would not have been subject to any Episcopal interference whatever that, in fact, he might laugh at all the bishops and all the courts in England.

Mr. Shore continues to be visited by the friends of civil and religious liberty from distant parts of England and the messages of sympathy are sent from many public meetings

At Bradford, in Yorkshire, a large meeting has been held…

The Bristol delegation, who were charged with an address of condolence from the great meeting…

The Nonconformist gives an account of several meetings in various parts of the country on behalf of Mr. Shore…

Colchester… A numerous meeting over which the Mayor presided was held in the guildhall, Newcastle on Tyne…

Bristol. A public meeting for the purpose of addressing a letter of sympathy to Mr. Shore and petitioning Parliament on his behalf was convened on Friday at the Great Room, Broadmead. The room which holds 2000 persons, was filled to overflowing with a respectable and enthusiastic audience and as a proof of the extensive interest which the subject has excited, it might be mentioned, that nearly 2000 persons failed to gain admission after 7 o'clock…

Hull. A meeting of the anti-state Church Association was held in this town on Friday, in the music saloon of the Mechanics Institute, which was crowded by one of the largest audiences ever assembled in Hull...

Mr. Ralph Barnes's eyes have been watering over all this sympathy for the Reverend James Shore. As so much true love bade fair to end in a subscription to pay the costs and thus help him out with an important item on the bill. But we hear that the London committee have very wisely confined their appeal for subscriptions to the object of aiding Mr. Shore's family and the strait to which the Episcopal "attachment" and preceding love manifestations have placed them. It appears to be the determination not to pay the costs till payment of costs will free the Reverend Gentleman. At present, if costs of suit No. 1 be paid, Mr. Barnes will walk in with costs for suit number 2, and if number 2 be duly discharged then there is the grand object of all, the imprisonment for preaching to be carried out.

Therefore the London committee do well not to collect for the bishops costs, but for the solace of Mr. Shore's family, for it be observed, the bishop has never come forward and declared that when the costs shall have been paid, he will forgo all revengeful feelings and let his Reverend brother out of jail. To pay the costs, whilst the law stands as it does, would not relieve Mr. Shore from jail, as all proceedings necessary to keep him in for contempt of court in having preached, have been taken. His liberty is now in the hands of bishop Phillpotts...

Letter in Western Times:

My Dear Sir Curling, I have just learned that you are to be the chairman of a meeting, having for its object the reformation of such laws as that by which Mr. Shore has been imprisoned.

May I request you to signify to that meeting my hearty concurrence with such a proposed Reformation.

I have had no sympathy with Mr. Shore in his secession from the Church of England, nor did I, by any expression of sympathy or otherwise, help to put him in prison.

Being there, I feel a very decided, a very just, and a very unbiased indignation at his imprisonment.

There are some people who seem to feel Mr. Shore's imprisonment as if it had happened a 1000 years ago, or as if it had happened in the moon, or in a distant planet. There are those who seem to think it a thing as unavoidable and irremediable, as a hailstorm or a thunderstorm. There are others who lay the blame of Mr. Shore's imprisonment merely on the subordinate agents, acquitting the principal author of it, as if he had been ignorant of it, or could not help it. There are others who deliberately justify this imprisonment.

But this imprisonment, when all is said and done, is a thing that cannot be justified, being as contrary to the plain principles and precepts of Christianity, as darkness is contrary to light. Woe unto them that call evil good, and good evil.

Believe me, yours most sincerely, H E Head...

Shore's reply to address the deputation in London was:

My Dear Friends, I received with the most lively satisfaction and deepest feelings of gratification, the address which you have now presented to me. An honour so great I never could have anticipated, as an address of sympathy and kindness emanating from a meeting so vast, influential, and intelligent, and conveyed to me in a manner so truly gratifying to my feelings. Such important advocacy of the principles of religious freedom far more than compensates for any little personal inconvenience I may have experienced, and will tend to cheer me as long as I may continue my present confinement. I especially value this demonstration as a token for good to my country. The simple fact of my imprisonment is itself a matter of little moment, it is only when viewed in connection with the acting out of the principles which brought me here, that it emerges into importance, and I rejoice in this expression of the goodwill of so many of my countryman as showing that they are not disposed to acquiesce in those so-called principles of Puseysm which are now threatening to deluge the land. While, however, I cannot but repudiate laws which fetter the preaching of the gospel, I truly compassionate those who, by carrying them into execution, have brought me into my present position. To the members of this deputation and to those through whose kindness you have been commissioned to visit me in my prison, I have no words to express my deep feeling of thankfulness, and I can only pray that Divine Being may reward you a thousand fold into your bosoms, who has taught us that one characteristic of His approval at the final day of decision will be, "I was sick and in prison, and ye came unto me"

April 7 1849

What the Bristol men have done.
We fulfilled, on Friday last, the mission devolved on us by the great meeting at Broad Mead by visiting Mr. Shore, in his prison cell. To the address of condolence with which we were charged, Mr. Shore returned the accompanying reply. Greatly were we struck with the calm and Christian bearing of this victim of episcopal oppression. If we esteemed him before we now entertain for him sentiments of love and veneration, for we are satisfied, that, in his harassing and protracted struggle with the Bishop of Exeter, he has been moved by no mere frivolous or obstinate resistance to ecclesiastical authority, but solely by a conscientious regard to right. His, under another form, is the same battle fought by confessors for Christ in the olden time. Our conviction is, that Mr. Shore's fate, as also the fate of the Clergy Relief Bill, depends very largely on the energetic demonstration of public opinion, and we, therefore, trust that

213

in every town throughout the land, such demonstration will be made, and made at once. We found in Mr. Shore's prison cell, Mr. Alderman Forbes of Bradford in Yorkshire who with great Christian kindness had for some days been administering to this brother in bonds. Such generous thoughtfulness will not be forgotten when the true bishop of the flock shall say, "I was in prison and ye visited me". Mr. Shore's expenses, arising from the episcopal tyranny of which he is the victim, have been, and still are very large, almost ruinously so. We are sure this need only be known to call forth the responses of liberal aid. We think that with ease a hundred pounds may be forwarded from Bristol. We shall, either of us, be happy to be the receivers of such contributions. We pledge our - selves that not one farthing should go to the bishops costs, that the whole shall be concentrated to the Christian service of ministering to the comfort of our imprisoned brother, and his afflicted family. Solomon Leonard, George Henry Davies, William Gregory, Henry Isaac Roper.

Bristol 19th April 1849

(Reply from Shore in response to Bristol address similar to previous)
Western Times April 14 1849

Exeter: Saturday, April 14 1849. County meeting on Mr. Shore's case. In accordance with the resolution of the public meeting at the Subscription Rooms, a requisition for a county meeting is in course of signature. It has already received 686 signatures. It is signed by two baronets, several county justices, admirals, captains RN, the mayors of Plymouth, Barnstaple, Okehampton, Southampton Torrington, etc.etc. and by churchwardens in their official capacity. The requisition on the whole has been very respectably signed, and it is still proceeding, the people are in earnest.

Bishop Phillpotts has written another pamphlet (addressed to the Archbishop of Canterbury) in defence of his conduct in persecuting the Reverend James Shore. But that is not all. He has bamboozled the Times with an early copy of the brochure, and beguiled our great contemporary of some of his best thunder. As we gather from our contemporary's leader, which is Phillpotic in its remarkable deviation from the facts, the Bishop relies upon the old misrepresentations which so signally failed at the Devon Spring Assizes, in the memorable year of Grace 1848.
We must however, wait till we see the pamphlet itself.

St Thomas's jail, Exeter April 13th, 1849.

Dear Sir, I write you a hasty line, just as your paper is going to the press, to tell you that I have this morning received a pamphlet, written by the Bishop of Exeter, on my case.
I am glad that the Bishop of Exeter has taken this step. We shall now be able to test his statement by the facts, when it will be seen that the bishop's letter

greatly damages his own case as it regard myself. He begins by admitting that the law ought to be altered, and yet he has been enforcing against me a law which he now condemns by that admission.

The bishop has endeavored to make out his case with his usual ingenuity, but ingenuity is badly exercised, if it be not accompanied by candour. The bishop has mutilated my correspondence, leaving out parts of the most important, and entirely misrepresenting the matter throughout as it regards myself.

What his Lordship states, on the authority of a memorandum from Mr. Cousins, is entirely a fabrication, so far as I am concerned, from beginning to end.

I reserve myself for a full answer to these misrepresentations. I am etc. James Shore. Western Times April 14ᵗʰ, 1849.

"Release of Mr. Shore.

The London committee having seen that Mr. Ralph Barnes was determined not to abide by his letter to the editor of the Times, of the 10th March, sent down the money for payment of costs in the Court of Arches suit, and on Wednesday morning Mr. Shore was let out of custody. The Reverend Gentleman returned to Totnes by the evening train, having taken a cordial leave of the worthy governor of the prison, Mr. T. Burch, and his family, from whom he had received the kindest of attentions throughout his confinement of three months. This release is a relief for the bishop who has to thank the London Committee for the costs he has received, and also for a relief from that sense of degradation to which he must have been subject, in reflecting that he had made a solitary exception in this case, and forcing the law against a man with whom he had had a personal quarrel. The old gentleman has case-hardened, as we all know: nevertheless, he began to feel a little uneasy at Mr. Shore's obstinacy, for Churchman did not like the imprisonment, and the bishop's ingenious candour and appolistic disclaimers did not entirely satisfy them. Of all the men who have seceded from the Church, Mr. Shore was the only one who had been punished, and bishop Phillpotts was the only bishop who had enforce the law home to punishment, and bishop Phillpotts had had a personal quarrel, and Bishop Phillpotts had professed to deal very candidly and very considerately towards his victim, yet, notwithstanding all this candour, the Bridgetown snare was laid for his ruin, and here we have the result.

Well, what will our right reverend friend do next? He in fact has done nothing yet. Ralph Barnes, the secretary, a fond man over a moneybag, "hath enforced costs, that's all". But the costs were the consequence of an interdict against preaching. That interdict has been disregarded, and will be again. Mr. Shore will preach on Sunday; will Bishop Phillpotts proceed further? If "no" why did he begin to proceed? To make a bill for Ralph? A senseless supposition that, which we never will believe, for they do not share the spoil. Ralph is a fond man over a moneybag, and knows his rights, "and knowing, dares maintain" as the patriotic poet sings.

If "yes", then have the committee done right in taking a course that will draw on our right reverend friend to the high and open ground of spiritual authority, and the people of England will see what that is. But if he do proceed further, what will the right reverend father in God, my Lord of London, do with the Rev. Baptist Noel?

Henry dare not proceed further; Ralph, the secretaryhath deposited the money in the savings bank and there the matter ends.

The Bishop's donkey won the first prize at the Torquay races in 1846. We chronicled the fact at the time. There will be no episcopal donkey race in 1849."

Western Times June 2 1849.

The Reverend Shore.

This gentleman having been released from the jail at St Thomas's (as stated last week) after payment of the costs incurred in the Arches' Court, and before the judicial committee of Privy Council, did not feel it right to obey the "monition" by which he is prohibited from preaching. Accordingly he preached again to his faithful and attached congregation at Bridgetown on Sunday morning last at risk of a second imprisonment, from which he could only be freed by a revolution in the law, an interposition of royal authority, or a promise never to preach again, which promise, as a conscientious teacher, conceiving himself solemnly pledged to the work of the Christian ministry, Mr. Shore could never make. Bishop Phillpotts, then, has it in his power still to incarcerate Mr. Shore for life, as the law at present stands. Much speculation was raised among those who did not know the consistent quiet firmness of Mr. Shore's character, as to whether he would, so soon after escaping from a tedious durance, has had his liberty and placed his personal comfort and health at the mercy of the exasperated prelate. The people of Totnes, we were told, were not generally apprised of his intention to preach on Sunday, and the assembly, though tolerably numerous, was not much larger than usual. All was conducted in the accustomed manner, there was no excitement, no parade, but the affectionate glances cast from pew and gallery towards the pulpit, and the attentive interest of the people, showed how much joy they felt, that their esteemed Minister had been delivered from his painful imprisonment, and had returned to his home, to the spot long hallowed by domestic and social endearments.

The reverend gentleman forbore to make the slightest direct allusion, in his sermon, to his own trials, but the subject chosen was appropriate to recent events. The text was the 1st. Chapter of St Paul's 2nd epistle to the Corinthians 2nd... The discourse was entirely of a practical nature, its aim being to present the consolations of religion as the means of sustaining the mind in adversities and trials... In the course of the prayer offered previous to the sermon, Mr. Shore expressly returned thanks that this congregation were permitted again, with him, to assemble for worship as they had been accustomed to do.

Whilst the *Exeter Flying Post* took the Bishop's side with:

The "Martyr" and his friends.

With a pertinacity which smacks more of pluck them honesty, the partisans of the dreadfully persecuted Mr. Shore continued to insist that he is imprisoned for "preaching the gospel." It is no joke for a man to be confined in prison; but it is a joke, and a good one too, to witness the efforts of a few Sir Sapients who are ineffectually exerting themselves to make the world believe that black is white. In the very teeth of a statement which is not controverted, because it cannot be, we find one or two of the newspapers in this district reiterating the nonsense that the bishop has persecuted Mr. Shore, even to prison, and that Mr. S now lies "incarcerated in a dungeon for conscience sake." It may suit that worthy man's purpose very well to keep such a story afloat: before you can get up a tolerable amount of sympathetic steam, it is necessary that there should be a little excitement, and that will never be raised by stating the fact that the man is in prison for non-payment of costs, incurred by his own proceedings, vexatiously taken, and still more vexatiously prosecuted. People, nowadays, do not feel inclined to "sympathise" with every thoughtless mortal who, actuated by chagrin, seeks to annoy those with whom he is engaged in a legal contest by rushing headlong into most unjustifiable appeals and trusting entirely to accident for a decision in his favour. Something more than obstinacy is requisite to enable a man to ingratiate himself into popular favour; and there - fore, it is that Mr. Shore and his truth loving friends would fain blink the real state of the case, and make it appear that he is imprisoned, not for costs, but for "preaching the gospel" The editor of a Devonport paper, who writes sensibly enough upon almost every other question, has altogether forgotten himself in this instance, which is evident from the following extract be: It is true that the reverend gentleman is nominally imprisoned for the bishop's Law Costs: but for what were those costs incurred, to prevent Mr. Shore from preaching the gospel." Now, there is not a word of truth in all this. We don't exactly under - stand what he means by Mr. Shore's being nominally imprisoned: but we do understand that the other part of the clause is pure invention: the bishop's costs have nothing at all to do with the matter: as we stated last week, we repeat again, and it is necessary to use repetitions when men are so willfully obtuse, that they will not comprehend plain facts; Mr. Shore for an offence against the ecclesiastical law, is cited in the Court of Arches: during the progress of the case he applies to the Court of Queen's Bench to stop the proceedings: the decision is adverse to him: and the Court of Arches ultimately pronounced sentence against him: and admonished him as to his future conduct. From that sentence Mr. Shore actuated by that amiable and christian spirit which has ever distinguished him from his fellow mortals, appealed to a judicial Committee of the Privy Council. On that appeal the sentence was confirmed, and the case remitted with all its incidents, save the costs incurred in the Appeal, to the Court of Arches: and further, Mr. Shore was condemned in the costs incurred on behalf of Mr.Barnes in the appeal. Mr. Shore, (having glorious and beneficial effects of martyrdom ever before his eyes) refused to pay such costs: and a writ of attachment was issued against him, upon which he has since been apprehended.

The foregoing are the literal facts: and anyone putting upon them the construction which the Devonport editor has done, implies a state of mind which no honest man will envy.

Without wasting any more words upon our Devonport contemporary, we come at once to another of Mr. Shore's defenders, the editor of the Western Times, a very valiant man, who made a snatch at martyrdom and missed it, who, this time 12 months ago, was an unsuccessful candidate for incarceration, and sympathy, but too, accidentally was deprived of the honour of one, and the pleasure of the other. He, too, willfully persists that Mr. Shore was imprisoned for "preaching the gospel". He then gives a long history of the SHORE case from the commencement, with the view, no doubt, of throwing dust in the eyes of the public deceiving them as to the exact position in which the recusant is now placed. That he is liable to imprisonment for contempt of an order from Court of Arches, does not contravene the fact that he is now in prison for Mr. Barnes' costs. Supposing that there were a score of legal documents hanging over his head, each one involving his personal liberty unless it complies with certain conditions, how could they in the least degree affect the case in question? If the man chooses rashly to enter upon proceedings which involve him in costs, he must abide by the consequences; and it is rather too bad, indeed it is not honest, to blame others for the trouble which he has brought upon him - self. Let the present question be settled upon its own merits, and those alone; Let not the public mind be confused by mixing it up with matters which are separate and distinct; let him pay the costs which are justly due, and we shall be quite prepared to deal with the other portions of his case when they come legitimately before the public; but we decline being tempted into discussion upon a matter with which at present we have nothing whatever to do.

There is one part of this martyrdom business which we look upon with lively satisfaction; and we look to it for the purpose of congratulating the members of the Church of England upon the fact, that Mr. Shore's conduct is rightly appreciated by all sound Churchman. It is true that there is to be found one here and there of the members of the Establishment, men who, like Mr. Shore, are fond of agitation and love the notoriety which arises out of it; and like him seem to care less for the religion which they profess to teach, than they do the indulgence of their own vain gloriousness, who have taken part in the movement originated by the dissenters; but they are few, very few indeed; and they are just that class of men who so far as the welfare of the Church is concerned, were better out of the pale of the establishment than in it. The great body of Mr. Shore's sympathisers are the members of the "Evangelical

Alliance" or in other words the anti-state Church party. Men who preach up toleration, whilst at the same time they are amongst the most intolerant of the earth; whose only notion of religious liberty is just that which they would dictate, and nothing more; who are most violent in their declamation, furious in their opposition; who are as inconsistent as the winds, arbitrary, tyrannical, dogmatical, claiming for themselves the freedom of thought and action, whilst, they deny it to others; and seeking the overthrow of the Church in order to promote their own personal aggrandisement. Such men who have now taken Mr. Shore by the hand, such are the men with whom the editor of The Western Times and other similar journalists are in league; and it is these men who are now agitating the community to sympathise with their hearts, and relieve by their purses, the mild, and amiable, and Christian man, who at the instance of his own folly, is in an inmate of the ward in St Thomas; holding his levees, and playing off some of those amusing vagaries which are expected from "martyrs". The other day we find that he gave an audience to Sir Culling Eardley, the very man be it remembered who was kicked out of the West Riding for his extreme intolerance and bigotry.

Connected with this there is a nice little bit of by-play on the part of our friend of the Western Times: with all his professions of veneration for the person and character of Mr. Shore, he is evidently jealous of him, being one of those selfish mortals who can bear no rival near his throne, is determined, if possible, that the public shall not lose sight of what he has gone through; so every now and then in his attempted defence of Mr. Shore, we find some very pointed allusions to his own case, nicely dovetailed, to avoid perchance, the imputation of egotism; not content with saying his say about Mr. Shore, not content, further, with endeavouring to place friend's position in a wrong light, he must needs spin a yarn about himself fancying, probably, on the recurrence of the March assizes, that he is yet the "observed of all observers". The delusion, however, is a simple one, it cannot result in harm, people smile at his weakness and walk on. That is just what we feel disposed to do; and, therefore, wishing him a cup brimful of pleasure, we take our leave, with the sincerest aspirations for his mental and bodily comfort.

Exeter Flying Post 22 March 1849

Mr. Shore.

It is with the most lively feelings of satisfaction that we have to announce a partial recovery of this illustrious "martyr" from his recent indisposition. With the feelings of a "man and a brother" we all sympathise deeply with those who labour under bodily suffering; and in a far higher degree is our sympathetic nature worked upon when we find a fellow creature, temporally though it may be, deprived of his liberty, and the privilege of "taking the fresh-air" to renovate his shattered frame. To see one, the brilliancy of whose intellect was the admiration of thousands, and for the expense of which the wide range of unlimited space hardly afforded ample room and verge enough, "cribbed, cabin'd and confined," like a caged eagle, within four walls of a melancholy dungeon, for the simple act of "preaching the gospel" were, indeed, a sight to make the angels weep. "Chesterfield", we understand, did weep; and his tears fell so profusely whilst indicting an epistle to his talented London contemporary, that he was compelled to throw the original aside, and, amid sobs and deep- heaved sighs, dictate to his amanuensis a very incomplete (because underrated), account of the dear "martyrs" sufferings.

Now, however, all is joy and gladness; Mr. Shore has not only recovered from his bodily indisposition, but his mind, also, very fortunately for society, is restored: reason has again taken her seat, the hallucination under which he laboured has been dissipated, and having thus become both physically and mentally convalescent, there is every possibility of his being speedily restored to the bosom of his family, and of his again enjoying the society of the highly cultivated and profoundly metaphysical and classical would- be- martyr of Fore street Hill. If this be not a source of congratulation to the whole world, we shall be at a loss to know what is.

Some ill-natured people have propagated a rumour to the prejudice of the amiable Mr. Shore: happily, however, the rumour carries a lie on the face of it, and, therefore, will be at once denounced. We allude to the statement that the pious Divine is bartering his conscience for liberty. We don't believe it. It is true that some of his impetuous friends, for a purpose which they understood, but which of course Mr. Shore knew nothing of, stated that he went to prison for conscience sake: the principal actor in the business thought he was nab'd for costs, incurred by his own act of indiscretion, and which at the time he was unable to pay. "All staff" says the excellent man, who boasts that the bishop has "feathered his nest," "leave that to me. You're in prison for conscience sake, if we don't make a good thing out of this and ensure your popularity, I'm not the Honourable Member of St.Petrock's, that's all". And away he sets to work, seeking to establish the delusion; but not succeeding, he leaves his victim really to act according to conscience; and that estimable gentleman at once pays a portion of his debt, and awaits for a remittance of the remainder, arriving at the very just conclusion that a stroll over the green fields, along the banks of purling streams, with beautiful landscape for a prospect, and the winged songsters for companions, is far more agreeable, to say nothing of conscience, than self incarceration, which might, probably, eventuate in self-murder.

We heartily rejoice that this change has taken place; Mr. Shore will be better for it, his family will be none the worse; and we only hope that should he ever again get into difficulties, he would take our opinion upon the matter in preference to that of the editor of The Western Times, to whom he owes an eternal debt of gratitude for the great blessings which he has experienced during the last few months.

The martyrdom farce is nearly played out: two actors only remain upon the stage; and it is just possible they may continue to furnish us with a little further amusement before the curtain drops forever upon their folly. "Certain Christian gentlemen" have through christian Latimer, paid the costs which the "good man" himself incurred; and the latter "Christian" trusts that as Mr. Barnes "hopes to be saved hereafter", he will give the contumacious Divine a receipt in full of all demands. We should suppose that Mr. Barnes does not entertain the slightest apprehension upon the subject. If all creditors jeopardise their soul's salvation, by seeking legitimately to obtain that which is justly due to them, we fear that that there are many rogues in the world who will come off scot free, and continue to plunder society with impunity. Mr. Shore or "certain Christian gentlemen", have only to fork out £124.1s.10d.: that is to say a just debt must be paid, and the prison doors will be opened.

Exeter Flying Post 31st May 1849

Mr. Shore.

The ex Martyr has not treated us with that respect to we consider ourselves entitled: he slunk away from his prison on Wednesday morning, without apprising us of the circumstance. This was rather too bad: we have invariably felt a deep interest in his welfare; and our readers will recollect how rejoiced we were last week at the prospect of his being speedily restored to liberty. We are aware that the "would–be–but–the–jury–would–not–let–him–be Martyr had a stronger claim upon Mr. Shore's regard than our humble selves, who have never been in the slightest degree ambitious of figuring at the stake or luxuriating in a dungeon; and we think that Mr. S selected a fit and proper man in the person of the "modern Chesterfield" to send an insulting letter to a gentleman, enclosing the first cheque in part discharge of a debt legally due. He could not have acted differently: Mr. Shore, we are told is a Christian and possesses before share of that noblest of Christian virtues - Charity, which "suffereth long and his kind:" he could not, therefore, do otherwise than select his fellow – Christian on Fore-street-Hill to be his fellow locum tenens. All this was right and proper; but Mr. Shore was wrong in not apprising us of his intended departure from the ward of St Thomas. We knew very well that the act of "certain Christian gentlemen", in paying the Piper and obtaining his release, would play havoc with Mr. Shore's conscience, that in short he would suffer a double "martyrdom". His conscience told him he was right in going to prison, or even to death, for "preaching the gospel;" and his conscience, also told him he was right in submitting to incarceration for not paying costs incurred by himself: so that his conscience sent him to prison, and his conscience kept him there, till the before-mentioned "Christian gentlemen" treated his conscience with contempt, paid the money, and left the sheriff no alternative, but forcibly to eject the "good man" from his lonely dungeon. This was cruel; we have Mr. Shore's oft-repeated declaration that since his imprisonment he had experienced greater degrees of comfort, and received more blessings, then he ever enjoyed his life before; and, therefore, to bundle him out of his elysium, against his conscience, was an act of unkindness which his bitterest foes – supposing, for a moment, such an excellent man to possess any – would never have dreamt of.

We are informed that the parting scene, enacted by Mr. Shore and his portly jailer, was most affecting. Mr. Shore gave Mr. Burch his blessing; and the latter gentleman was so overcome at witnessing the pious resignation of "the martyr", whilst passing through the trying ordeal of a compulsory violation of conscience, that he was obliged to seek relief in a copious flood of tears.

Mr. Latimer, we are told, was in attendance with a cab; and when Mrs. Shore's harp was brought to the door, he eyed it wonderingly for a short time, and then said to that lady, "I'll take care of your fiddle;" thus showing his perfect acquaintance with musical instruments.

The Western Times announced that Mr. Shore was to preach in Bridgetown chapel on Sunday. Whether he did, or not, we have not been at the trouble to enquire, - feeling confident that very few people indeed care anything at all about it.

Exeter Flying Post 7th June 1849

Likewise *The Times* took up the cause on behalf of the bishop asserting that Phillpotts would be in dereliction of duty if he had not taken legal action and that it was the law that should be repealed. Correspondence continued between Shore and the Bishop and his secretary in *The Times*:

The Times April 12th 1849.

The Bishop of Exeter has published a letter to the Primate containing a simple documentary statement of Mr Shore's case. That everybody will be undeceived by this letter is more than we expect, because it is not everybody that will read it. Mr Shore has been exhorted to the honours of martyrdom, and hawked about the country to the infinite delight of that numerous class which, next to a sea serpent, or a dwarf, a calf with six legs, and an Indian chief, delight in beholding a real live Martyr. With that class this gentleman has become an object of pious veneration, and we fear we should unsettle their faith altogether if we attempted to disenchant them of Mr Shore. There are, however, persons in this country who know already there is such a thing as apocryphal martyrdom, and that many a " Martyr" deserved most richly what he got. There are also persons who know that no religious community, no association, no club, can be constructed without rules, or carried on without enforcing them. To such persons we think the bishop's letter will be an efficacious appeal. We do not expect them to think, – we do not think it ourselves, – that the bishop has acted throughout the whole of this trying affair, – viz, from August, 1832, to the present time, – with an infallible judgement and unruffled temper; but we do not see why a man is to be put out of court simply because he is too sensitively alive to the responsibilities of his office. Once admit such a precedent, and we shall establish a rule not only for driving every man of susceptible temper from his post, but also for destroying every law and institution not administered by infallible agents. We make these observations, not an account of anything in the letter, but simply because some people think a sharp controversialist fair game for any sort of usage.

(There then followed the facts of the case)

This is not the case of a conscientious Dissenter, or a Dissenter at all, prosecuted for his dissent. It is the case of a clergyman, who declares he is no dissenter, publicly officiating without, and in defiance of the diocesan authority, and doing this in a building which had been built and licensed for the services of the Church, and which its builder and his patron had expressly engaged should never be applied to any other purpose than those services. It is the case of an attempt to employ the "prestige" of a church, and the "prestige" of a clergyman, against the Church and its authorities. If clergyman and their patrons may conduct themselves in this manner, playing fast and loose, declaring their devotion to the church one week, snapping their fingers in the bishop's face the next, and using the same building, at pleasure, for a church or a meeting- house, of course it is a farce to talk of discipline. Honest dissent is another thing. There are scores of a dissenting preachers who have renounced Episcopal ordination and who derive no little influence from the fact that they were once church ministers; but no one ever molests them, – no, not even Henry Exeter, though there are some in his diocese. We are not aware of a single instance of deprivation or penalties for simple dissent. Clergyman and layman are equally unmolested. Mr Shore's "persecution" is a sheer imposture. The danger against which the Bill before the Commons is levelled is a ridiculous bugbear, though, as the Bill does no harm, it may as well pass. As for the legal proceedings, Mr Shore left the bishop no alternative but to institute them. It was he who dragged the bishop from court to court, in the face of all warning and remonstrance, till the climax of his persecution is, that having appealed to the law, he now finds the law is against him, and, like other obstinate and unfortunate suitors, he has the costs to pay. We are sorry for him, because he seems to have a certain amount of good intentions, and is evidently a favourite with his congregation; but as for his "martyrdom", that is all fudge. Of course, the Duke, who pushed him into the scrape, has franked him through the courts. If anybody is a martyr, it is the Bishop, who has not the Duke of Somerset's purse to draw upon, and who has probably paid hundreds to Mr Shore's tens in this stupid affair.

Editorial.

We yesterday inserted a rather angry letter from Sir Culling Eardey in reply to our observations upon the case of his friend, the pseudo-martyr, Mr. Shore. The

particular passage the worthy baronet undertakes to refute was as follows:-
"this is not the case of a conscientious dissenter, or dissenter at all, persecuted
for his dissent. It is the case of a clergyman who declares he is no dissenter,
publicly officiating without, and in defiance of, the diocesan authority, and
doing this in a building which had been licensed for the services of the
Church". Sir Culling asserts that this is false, inasmuch as Mr. Shore had
declared himself a dissenter previous to the performance of the service for
which he had been prosecuted. Had Sir Culling stopped there, we should not
have thought it necessary to add another word on the subject. Such of our
readers as put faith in Sir Culling would have taken his unsupported
affirmation. Others would not. He went on, however to produce what he
considers a proof of his statement – viz, a letter from Mr. Shore to the bishop's
secretary, written before the particular service which formed the legal ground
of the subsequent proceedings. But nothing can be less of a proof than the
letter in question. It says not a word about dissent. It is written by a man who
must be presumed to know what he was saying, as he and his patron had been
fencing with the bishop for 12 years in praiseworthy attempt to establish a
church position near Totnes, insulated as much as possible from the diocesan
authority. Mr. Shore, thus versed and practised in ante episcopal warfare,
confined himself to these guarded expressions – "I no longer regard myself as
a minister of the Establishment. When I found it impossible any longer to
submit to the discipline of the Church as administered by the Bishop, I felt it my
duty to withdraw from his Lordship's jurisdiction." This is all he said on the
point. He did not withdraw from the Church of England. He did not say a
syllable about it. He was only dissatisfied with Dr. Philpott's mode of
administering its discipline; and under that feeling, which he had freely
expressed ever since he came to Totnes, he withdrew, not from the Church, but
from Dr. Philpott's jurisdiction.

Mr. Shore had a warm but not very reverential attachment to the church, and a
general opinion of its soundness. He was also attached to his chapel, to his
congregation; to his patron and to the family Heaven had gathered round his
hearth in the period of his ministry. He wished to stay and tried hard to stay. He
preferred to do so with a licence from the Bishop. He was, however,
unfortunately situated. The Duke and the dissenters of Totnes together put him
into a false position, and made his name to the banner of a schismatical
agitation. He found eventually that he could not continue to officiate with the
bishop's licence, so he resolved to officiate without. He did not dissent. He never
pretended to do so. He merely said that he no longer considered himself a
member of the establishment, and that he had withdrawn from Dr. Phillpotts'
jurisdiction. A man who acts thus may be a martyr to the difficulties of his
position, a martyr to his patron, a martyr to his friends, a martyr to his family,
a martyr to his irresolution, a martyr even to his amiable feelings; but he is not
a martyr to the rules of the Church. We deeply regret Mr. Shore's case. If we are

to trust his expressions of attachment to the church, we regret that he was not allowed to continue at Bridgetown on his original footing. But we cannot call him either a dissenter or a martyr.

The Times 18th April 1849

The Reverend Mr. Shore.

We subjoin a letter which Sir C E Eardley, apparently in a state of the most alarming excitement has sent us, on the subject of his unfortunate friend, Mr. Shore. It will be observed that he charges us with "misquotation" and to the best of our remembrance, the eccentric Baronet has never yet either written a letter or made a speech which did not contain one or more charges of this sort against somebody or other...

Sir; – I am thunderstruck at your misquotation of a communication which I made to you three days ago.

I sent you a letter from Mr. Shore to the Bishop of Exeter, in proof of my assertion that Mr. Shore declared himself a dissenter before he was prosecuted. Of that letter you say in today's paper "it says nothing of dissent". You add, "Mr. Shore, thus versed and practised in ante-episcopal warfare, confined him - self to these guarded expressions – "I no longer regard myself as a minister of the Establishment. When I found it impossible any longer to submit to the discipline of the Church as administered by the bishop, I felt it my duty to with - draw from his Lordship's jurisdiction". This is all he said on the point. He did not withdraw from the Church of England. He did not say a syllable about it." Sir, you have suppressed a portion of that letter which chiefly bears on the point. Mr. Shore, in the close of his letter, after referring to the steps he had taken, adds, "I have made particular inquiries, and I find that this has been received as a sufficient declaration of secession from the establishment in other cases which have occurred in this diocese; but if more is required in my case, I shall be obliged by learning what is necessary".

With this letter lying before you, you have told your readers that Mr. Shore "did not say a syllable about withdrawing from the Church of England." A man expresses his belief that he had done all that was necessary "to secession from the establishment", but if more was requisite in order to do so, he waited to be told; and you say that this person has not declared himself a Dissenter!

I venture to request, sir, that if you comment on this letter, you will allow the letter and the comment to appear in the same number, that your readers may judge of the fairness of your quotations.

Your obedient servant, C E Eardley. Torquay 18th April.

The Times 20th April 1849

Rev. James Shore.

At a meeting of the committee, held Monday May 28th 1849 it was resolved;

that in a meeting for the final settlement of the costs in the case of the Rev. James Shore, the committee, though yielding to the moral arising out of Mr. Shore's health ill-health, to terminate his imprisonment as speedily as possible, and to other considerations, do most solemnly protest not only against the exaction of these costs, but against the whole coercive measures adopted by the Bishop of Exeter in Mr. Shore's case, as utterly inconsistent with the bishop's profession as a minister of the Gospel of Jesus Christ, at variance with the sound recognised principles of religious liberty, and founded only on a fiction of ecclesiastical law, that a clergyman dissenting from the Church of England remains, not withstanding the provisions of the Toleration Act, under episcopal jurisdiction, and still liable to punishment by the canon law.

That, in giving a final order for the payment of costs incurred in the Court of Arches, this committee wait, with some anxiety, to see if the Bishop of Exeter will, in the face of the strong expression of public opinion against his whole course, proceed to execute upon Mr. Shore the impending writ de contumace capiendo, for preaching the gospel contrary to his monition; to obtain which writ all the previous expensive proceedings in the ecclesiastical courts, have been adopted and which will, contrary to the avowed spirit and intention of statute law, deprive a British subject and a Christian minister of his personal liberty for an act of non-conformity in a matter of the religious conviction.

The following subscriptions have been received in addition to those previously announced; For the costs... For the support of Mr. Shore's family...

Edward Craig. Robert Ainslie Hon. Secs.

The Times 30th May 1849

The *Illustrated London News* took the middle line:

The Reverend Mr. Shore.

The case of Mr. Shore is receiving a far greater share of public notice than either he or his friends anticipated. Large public meetings in different parts of the country, and deputations visiting in prison, are a kind of honour which the former Minister of Bridgetown did not expect. And there is little doubt that the proceedings which have been instituted against him will accelerate the passing of a law to remove all pains, penalties, and a disabilities from such of the clergy of the Church of England who may wish to quit her communion. The course and the manner of Mr. Shore secession differ from every other case which has come within our knowledge. He says that he now entertains opinions differing from those of the church by whose doctrine and discipline he remained bound for upwards of 15 years, and is therefore compelled by his conscience no longer to continue either a minister or a member of it.

By his secession, Mr. Shore has done no more than has been done by many other persons against whom no ecclesiastical proceedings have been instituted. Some clergyman of the Church have, we know, joined the Church of Rome, and have been ordained among its ministers, and bishops have remain silent. Others have become dissenting ministers, and no notice has been taken of them. Some few have altogether laid aside their clerical functions and have embarked in trade. Against the latter, indeed, no penal steps can be taken, as they are beyond the reach of ecclesiastical authority. The law is singular: a clergyman may cease from performing the duties peculiar to him, become, in all outward respects, a layman; may turn merchant, shopkeeper, be a lawyer, an officer in the army or navy if he can, and no bishop can interfere to prevent him. But if, after leaving the church, he continues to read prayers and to preach the gospel, the episcopal power may immediately be brought against him, and he may be punished, because at present, by the law of the land, once being a priest he must ever remain one. Holy orders are, at present, indelible, and all the decisions in the case of Mr. Shore are founded upon this. The law will no doubt be altered during the present session, and so it ought to be. It is singular that such a legal restriction should exist in a Protestant community, whose peculiar boast is liberty of conscience in spiritual matters, and who separated from the Church of Rome on that very ground. Let the law pass, and the Church of England will receive no damage. Some few clergymen perhaps, will take advantage of it, and far better they should, than remain unwilling preachers of doctrines to which they do not give their assent, and reluctantly submissive to a discipline against which they would fain rebel, and the scriptural foundation of which they deny. If the present law does not make hypocrites, it certainly may be said to have a tendency to foster hypocrisy; and the Church of England wants none in her ranks but the sincere adherents to her belief, and the cheerful supporters of her discipline. Let all others have full liberty to depart.

The case of Mr. Shore is briefly this…

With the various motives assigned to the different actors in this unhappy scene we have nothing to do. We have to enable our readers to form their own opinion, simply stating the facts of the case. The law under which Mr. Shore suffers still exists; before the present session closes, it will, in all probability, be either modified or repealed, and there will be no longer a cause for the heart burnings and painful feelings which have been so powerfully excited.

(Illustration of Shore in prison)

The Deputation.

A deputation, consisting of Sir C E Eardley, Rev. Messrs. Binney, Stoddart, Hinton, Ainslie, and Bean, waited on Mr. Shore in jail. After joining in religious exercises with him, they left him to the solitude of his cell, and came forth to advocate his case.

Illustrated London News 7th April 1849

The church press was also divided as to the merits of the case. *The Christian Times* of 13th April 1849 described meetings held at Liverpool, Ilfracombe Leicester, Finchley, Bristol, Paisley, Bath, Glasgow and Torquay to protest at Shore's imprisonment. On 25th May a letter to the editor was published:

"Mr. Shore's costs.

Sir, From your paper of Friday last we learn that that £100 is still wanting to open the prison doors for the release of God's suffering and persecuted servant. We gladly respond to the invitation by forwarding a small sum of £1 towards the payment of the bishops costs, as a token of deep sympathy with Mr. Shore, and of obedience to that final and gracious redeemer, who has said "in as much as ye have done it to those my brethren, ye have done it to me". Yours respectfully G T.

P.S. While writing this my two dear boys have urged me to let them send two and sixpence each. "For what father" they say, "should we do if you were in prison!" The oldest is 10 years, the other 8 years of age."

In another issue they stated "a serious crisis, most unquestionably is coming to the established Church. That church has hitherto, to use a very humble and undignified simile, become too much like a lobster pot. The way in has been easy enough, anyone can get in. The way out has been absolutely impracticable."

"Mr. Shore's case – The Times and the Chronicle.

The Times and the Chronicle continue to labour at their awkward vocation of vindicating the procedure of the Bishop of Exeter against Mr. Shore. The Times affirms that the bishop was merely a passive impartial administrator of the law of the land. To this, the reply is very short. If so, why does he pass by a higher game? The Reverend Mr. Bulteel, formerly a fellow of Exeter College, and man of ancient family and high connection, has officiated from long time, and does still in Exeter, occasionally. By the union of the canon and the statute of 1813, Mr. Bulteel is as much in the bishop's power as he was at his first out set in non-conformity. Yet the impartial administrator of the law leaves him untouched. The Chronicle asserts, also, that the bishop never contemplated the imprisonment of Mr. Shore, but merely his deposition from orders. Why, then, did he proceed upon the statute of 1813?"

The Christian Times 30th March 1849.

The bishop's costs.

The following letter from Mr. Shore, the bishop's martyr, in Exeter jail, is an acknowledgement of a generous offer by a gentleman in the North of England to pay the bishops costs. The letter appears in the North and South Shields Gazette:-

"The jail, St Thomas's, Exeter. March 17th 1849.

My Dear Sir, I have no words to express my thankfulness for your truly kind and generous offer of effecting my liberation, by the payment of the whole of the bishops costs. My confinement, however, within bare walls and iron grated windows, has not changed, and I am sure will not change, my principles, and should be the same conscientious conviction which brought me, still keeps me here, I cannot help it.

While therefore I have no language to express my grateful sense of your kind - ness, I must add, in justice to myself, that I should be truly sorry if any friend or friends of mine would take from under us our present vantage ground, by making a compromise with the Bishop, by paying his expenses. Indeed, if the costs were paid today, I should still be at the tender mercies of his Lordship. I may be put back into prison again tomorrow for contempt of court, for preaching the gospel.

I should therefore, rather live and die in prison than in any way be a party to the atrocious iniquity and wrong, of putting the civil sword into the hands of ecclesiastics, for the purpose of enabling them to coerce men's consciences in matters of religion, and to inflict civil penalties for the purpose of carrying out spiritual sentences. My principle is this – that in matters of religion, man is responsible to God alone. To my own Master, I stand or fall, and I will not admit any other Lord or head in spiritual concerns, but that Divine Being who knoweth what is in man, and who alone is infallible and consequently is alone worthy to judge the conscience, and exercise irresponsible power.

Were such a compromise effected, I should feel as if I had laboured, and toiled, and endured for the last five years almost in vain. I would, therefore, far rather continue in prison, a standing monument of priestly usurpation, domination, cruelty, tyranny, and wrong, than sanction the payment of costs entirely incurred for preaching the gospel as a Dissenting minister, especially as I should still be liable to imprisonment, and that for life, for simply preaching, even if the whole of the costs are paid.

With the truest regard, believe me, my dear Sir, yours most sincerely in the bonds of the gospel, James Shore."

Supplement to *The Christian Times* 30th March 1849.

"The Rev. Mr. Shore and the Bishop of Exeter.
Last week, a public meeting was held at Sutherland Chapel, Walworth Road, for the purpose of expressing their sympathy towards the Rev. Mr. Shore and to consider the best means to effect his liberation.

The Rev. Dr Reede presided, and said that having a personal knowledge of the Rev. Mr. Shore, whom he had lately seen in prison, he could certify that a more quiet, peaceable, and inoffensive man did not exist, and that his imprisonment arose from the system of persecution that ought not to be allowed to exist in a free country, and was subversive of the liberty and right of opinion which every man was entitled to. He regretted that it had been left to non-conformists to fight the present battle: but as it had been left to them, let them take it up boldly. Why did not the members of the Church come forward and express their opinions? It is a question in which they are concerned. Why imprison Mr. Shore alone? Why did not the Bishop of London proceed against the Hon. Mr. Baptist Noel?

The Christian Times 13th April 1849

"Serious indisposition of Mr. Shore.
We have received the following letter, which has been sent by the Rev. J Shore to a member of his committee in London; The Jail, St. Thomas's Exeter, May 9th 1849.
My Dear Sir, since Saturday last I have been laid on a bed of sickness, with a very severe attack of the old complaint in my side. I am now much freed from pain, but very weak; and consequently I obliged to avail myself of an amanuensis to send you a few lines. I am sure you will be glad to know that I find my double imprisonment of jail walls and sick bed, no unprofitable discipline. I never found the Saviour more precious, his gospel more sweet, or his presence more sustaining; and I look forward with no small delight to that glorious era when, instead of prisons, sickness, sin, and sorrow, the redeemed will fully, entirely, and everlastingly realise harmony, purity, and peace. The more I reflect upon the subject of the payment of the bishops costs, the more I am convinced of the propriety of my former determination in this matter. While, therefore, I cannot sufficiently express my thankfulness for the kindness intended, I can in no way be a party to such payment. Should I be sacrificed by this refusal, I shall at the least, have given a convincing testimony that I value the free and unfettered preaching of that gospel which is man's birthright, which is ordained by its Divine Author to be as free as the air we breathe, and which is "the power of God unto everlasting salvation", far too highly to pay the costs of a professed Protestant bishop, which were incurred in a prosecution against me for declaring to an attached congregation the way to spiritual liberty and eternal life. As I understand that some of my friends are anxious to know whether my views have undergone a change on this subject, I feel it due to them, as well as myself, to make them acquainted with my feelings, and I should be glad if you would take some opportunity of doing so. It was but a short time since, I saw in a newspaper, a copy of a letter which I sent to a friend on the point before us, and one paragraph so exactly expresses my present views that I will conclude with it; "I find that bare walls and iron grated windows, have not, and I am sure, will not change my principles; and should the same conscious conviction which brought me, still keep me here, I cannot help it, for I shall live and die with the unwavering opinion, that, in matters of religion, man is responsible to God alone."
That you may abundantly enjoy that presence and blessing of the Divine Author of our being, which is nowhere more richly to be realised then in a jail, is the heartfelt desire of
My dear Sir, yours very sincerely, in the bonds of the gospel, James Shore.

This letter indicates what we thought was likely to occur – the rise of active inflammation in his particular disease. We do not mean to anticipate doleful results: but we do most deliberately and solemnly ask, if a Minister of the gospel is to be left languishing and declining in a prison, into which he has been thrown in consequence of the bad application and the doubtful interpretation of an absolute law? What would the people of England say, and what will the Bishop of Exeter say, if any untoward event should occur? But we must look to the highest quarters in the land for interference in this most distressing case. It is a matter for government, and we believe that Lord John Russell could not do a more religious and benevolent act, and one more acceptable to the people at large than to terminate the intricacies of this very painful prosecution by opening, authoritatively, the prison door. We call for his Lordship's prompt interference. We entreat that he will give the substance of the letter his attentive consideration; and, seeing the difficulties of the case – the conscientious objection of Mr. Shore to pay the bishops costs, and the conscientious refusal of the bishop to let Mr. Shore free without – that the government would come between them, and remove an objection which may soon be painfully serious."

The Christian Times May 11th 1849.

Liberation of Mr. Shore.

Rev J Shore to Sir C E Oakley, Bart. Bridgetown, Totnes, May 31ˢᵗ 1849 My Dear Sir, – yesterday the jailer opened my prison doors, and I now found myself in my own home, surrounded with every blessing.

I feel deeply grateful for the sympathy and kindness manifested towards me by so many Christian friends. I can only express my heartfelt thanks, but I am sure, my dear sir, that neither you nor they will be forgotten when, in the "Valley of Decision", those thrilling word shall be heard, "inasmuch as ye did it unto one of the least of these my bretheren, ye did unto me." It is true I could not myself have taken the step by which I understand my liberation has been affected. I may err in judgment, but to my mind the principle is the same, whether I am imprisoned for costs incurred by a prosecution against me for simply preaching, or for preaching itself. I know that many, whose opinion I highly value, take a different view of the matter; but I have, for upwards of the last five years, suffered too much from deferring to the judgment of others, in with - drawing my letter to the Bishop of the 11th November, 1843 and signing a declaration to meet his Lordship's requirement, ever again, under any circumstances, to deviate from my own convictions. I have regretted the step I then took but once, and that has been ever since, and I could far rather have died in prison, had the will of God been so, than I could have been a party to the course of effecting my liberation by the payment of the bishops costs. I am not, however, insensible to the kindness shown me, although my liberty may be of short duration; for certain it is, that if the bishop had any conscientious feelings at all in commencing this prosecution against me, he is bound, according to his own profession, to carry out the laws of his church, and I shall very shortly be in prison again for preaching (as I feel in conscience bound to do) contrary to his monition. Indeed, I am already virtually under contempt of court for so doing, and Mr. Barnes is provided with evidence to certify it. How strikingly does such a state of things show the fearful evils resulting from the legalising of priestcraft. That system must be wrong which gives the power to a professed Bishop of the Church to put a minister in jail for simply obeying the express command of the great Shepherd and Bishop of Souls, and preaching his gospel. If, however, it must be so, I would far rather be in prison for preaching the gospel, than I would have my liberty, if I must be silent in the redeemer's cause. Whatever may befall me in this matter, I am happy in the firm conviction that I am in the path of duty. I have hitherto been supported by this conscious - ness, as well as cheered by the sympathy in kindness of my friends. I feel truly grateful to yourself and to the members of the committee, and all my many other kind friends to whom I am so greatly indebted; and praying that the Great Head of the Church may reward you a thousand- fold into your bosoms, with sincere esteem, believe me, my dear Sir, most truly and gratefully yours James Shore. Sir Culling E Eardley, Bart. P.S. - I am thankful to say I am much better in health; but still I am weak, and my side is troublesome. I trust, therefore, that you will excuse my employing an amanuensis. By stooping to write I bend just across my side, which occasions me great inconvenience. J. S.

The Christian Times 8th June 1849

"Biography. The Rev James Shore.
The subject of the present notice has recently occupied a good deal of the pub - lic attention, in consequence of the course pursued towards him by the Bishop of Exeter having terminated in his temporary incarceration. As in all similar cases, public opinion has been divided, both with respect to the character of the individual, and the merits of his controversy... In concluding this sketch, it is not necessary to apologise for its bearing so much on that one point which has brought Mr. Shore so prominently before the public. So far as we can judge from his publications, and from some little personal intercourse, Mr. Shore is a man that would have been content to have found his place and work in the more retired walks of ministerial life. He is a person of fair average ability; one who would himself smile at any attempt to make him out "a genius"; he has good sense, sincere piety; - is thoroughly evangelical, and even, perhaps, a little tending to very marked Calvinism in his doctrines. The portrait that accompanies this notice is remarkably faithful, and gives a perfect idea of his bodily presence. Mr. Shore's publications consist of several sermons, which he has been called to print in the course of his ministry, together with statements of his case – especially his answer to the Bishop of Exeter – which has been rendered necessary by his peculiar circumstances. His style of composition and of thinking seemed to increase in force as his trials deepened; till, at length,

from the jail at Exeter, there occasionally came forth utterances that rose into grandeur and eloquence. The sort of reasoning, too, to which he has been subjected by the bishop and the judge, are believed to have had such an effect on his understanding, that, whatever he might have been when his trials began, however dimly he "saw men as trees walking," he is now most intelligently and strongly a Non-conformist, and almost fancies that the principles of dissent from political establishments of religion, may be seen as plainly as if they were written in the sky in letters of light.

We shall print in our next number, as a curiosity, the bills of costs which were incurred by the bishop in the prosecution of Mr. Shore, and which the latter was condemned to pay in addition to his own. It is not often that such documents see the day; and these, at the lowest estimate, may be regarded as an illustration of the working of the, "corrective discipline of the church".

The Christian Times 13th July 1849.

"Breakfast to the Rev J Shore.

The Rev Mr. Shore having come up to London on matters of private interest, the London committee which had been acting on his behalf, felt it desirable to invite him to a breakfast, at which free conversation might take place on the subject of his recent trials, and an opportunity thus afforded to congratulate him on his deliverance from imprisonment. A large and respectable company assembled, yesterday morning, at Radley's Hotel, at 8 o'clock. Edward Swaine, Esq., occupied the chair, supported by the secretaries and many of the committee. After breakfast, Mr. Swaine, addressed Mr. Shore as follows: Dear Christian brother, we congratulate you on the termination of that imprisonment which you have endured, for no other crime, as we believe, than from preaching the ever - lasting gospel. (Hear, hear). We have rejoiced to behold the Christian spirit which has sustained you under that course which I will not allow myself to characterise; ...

Mr. Shore, who was received with loud cheers, then spoke as follows: Sir, and dear Christian friends, – I am deeply grateful to you for the kindness shown me, and especially am I thankful for the manifestation of feeling, elicited by my case, in favour of religious liberty. As an individual, it is not of much moment whether I am in or out of prison; but as it regards the community generally, it certainly is a matter of very great consequence whether the preaching of the gospel may be followed by imprisonment, and that legally, or whether religion shall be entirely free. (Hear, hear). It is on this ground that I have always endeavoured to fix the attention of the public on the charge against me. It was simply for preaching and praying with my congregation without the consent of the bishop, and after I had done everything which could legally enable me to take the status of a non-conformist minister. (Hear). It was on this charge, and on this alone, whatever may be said on the subject of costs, that I eventually found myself within the four walls of a jail; and it was on this ground that I felt it my duty to be no party to the payment of the costs. I am fully convinced, that all has been done for the best, but so far as principle is concerned I for one can see little difference between imprisonment for costs incurred for preaching, or imprisonment for preaching itself. Certainly, to mind and, if the preaching be right, the costs must be wrong, and consequently, imprisonment for these costs must be wrong also. ("Hear", and cheers.) Besides - and this had great weight with me - I felt that the bishop, by putting me in prison, placed himself in a wrong position, from which I was not inclined to free him. I considered it rather my duty to stand upon my right as a citizen of the kingdom of Zion, and say, let the bishop liberate me freely, or let the system, of which he is the instrument, bear the scandal and offence. ("Hear" and cheers). It may be asked, How is it that you are not in prison, instead of having the pleasure of meeting so many kind friends on this occasion? Every time you preach in the archdiocese of Canterbury you are guilty of contempt of court, for which contempt you are liable to be incarcerated. I think Mr. Binney solved the question when he said – "they feared the people". (Hear, hear). I am perfectly convinced that it is to that alone I owe it that I am not now in prison. But although the mass of the people are with us at present, it does not follow that it will be always so, and therefore, I am anxious that the law on the subject should be altered... Mr. Shore then enumerated the cases of persons, who like himself, had suffered persecution in the diocese of Exeter. As most of these cases are now well known to the public, it is not necessary to enter into minute details. The first was that of the Rev. Mr. Bulteel, who quitted the establishment and preached the riches of Christ under the canopy of heaven. The bishop, hearing of the circumstance, requested the churchwarden of the parish to call a parish meeting, and to levy a church-rate, which rate was to be applied to the purpose of prosecuting Mr. Bulteel for having preached the gospel out of doors, and also a Mr. Harris, a clergyman, for having listened to him. The churchwarden called the meeting, but informed the parishioners that he also had heard Mr. Bulteel's sermon; and that it was an admirable discourse, and that he, for one, could not put his hand in his pocket to prosecute so good a man. (Cheers)... Mr. Shore also mentioned some other cases; but those we have stated are sufficient to give our readers an idea of the condition of religious liberty, or rather of religious tyranny, in the diocese of Exeter. In conclusion, Mr. Shore said: The prison, if you go there with a good conscience and a good cause, is not the worst place in the world. I can truly say that I left it with far greater reluctance than I entered it. (Hear, hear). I realised there, more than I had ever done, the gracious presence of my God, sustaining and comforting me. It has also brought me to feel, that, with regard to the Lord's people, he will mercifully give them grace equal unto their day. (Loud cheers)... The Rev Thomas Binney was called up by the unanimous voice of the meeting. He advised them to obtain copies of the bill of costs in Mr. Shore's case which had been published in the Christian Times, and which were now to be published in a separate form. He assured them that the items were well worth the trouble of perusal. They would serve to illustrate one particular property which, according to St. Paul, a bishop should always possess, and that was vigilance. The Bishop of Exeter was uncommonly vigilant – ("Hear, hear", and laughter) – for he seemed to be watching all the ecclesiastics and people in his diocese, and coming down upon them if they offended. ("Hear, hear" and laughter.) The proceedings terminated about 11 o'clock."

The Christian Times 27th July 1849.

The English Churchman naturally sided with the Bishop;

"It is a good deal the fashion among a certain class of controversialists in the present day, whenever the Bishop of Exeter publishes a pamphlet, or makes a speech which tells, to ascribe its force to his Lordship's command of language, his controversial skill, his sarcasm, and so forth; whereas, without denying his Lordship's high intellectual powers, and polemical talents, we believe that it will be generally found that his strength lies quite as much in his facts as in any - thing else. This is pre-eminently the case in his Lordship's recently published letter to the Archbishop of Canterbury on the case of the Rev. Mr. Shore, to which we alluded last week.

As we then stated, that letter is made up, mainly of actual documents, and the part which the Duke of Somerset appears to have acted, from the first, is any - thing but what we might have expected from an English nobleman:- in fact, as a lay member of the Church, his Grace appears to have acted quite as un-worthily as Mr. Shore has done in his clerical capacity. Were the discipline of the Church in full active force, there can be no doubt that both priest and patron would stand together before their spiritual superiors to receive the censures of the church. As it is, the whole punishment of their joint schismatical acts falls upon the clerical delinquent - i e, the personal punishment; but we presume that, to use the language of the Times, the Duke has had the grace to "frank" Mr. Shore through the various courts in which he has unsuccessfully endeavoured to obtain a legal sanction for his schism and his subterfuges… Of the miserable author of this wholesale schism we have already spoken on several occasions, and it is painful to think or write of him as he deserves. His one object appears to be, "by good words, and fair speeches, to deceive the hearts of the simple". Because a single Priest refuses to nominate him - whereby, like thousands of better man, he is prevented, as a Minister of the Church, from continuing his ministrations in one particular spot – he, with all his solemn vows upon him, marches off to a magistrate, and publicly swears that he dissents from the Church, although there is not a particle of evidence to show that he is conscious of any change whatever in his views and opinions: his evident intention being to evade the law of the Church, and the control of his bishop, in order to retain the same position, and teach the same doctrines, as he did while he was professing to be a faithful minister of the Church! Was there not a most fearful and profane "lie in his right hand," when he went before the magistrate and, by his oath, called God to witness that he "dissented" from the Church of England? The whole question of his assumed dissent rested upon the single circumstance of his being nominated by one parish Priest out of fifteen thousand. If Mr. Cosens would have nominated him, he would have proclaimed himself a staunch churchman, but failing in obtaining the particular nomination, he calls God to witness that he conscientiously dissents from the Church! Within less than a month before taking this oath, he writes to the bishop expressing his regret that he cannot obtain his Lordship's sanction for resuming his duties as a minister of the Church: and in the very same letter he intimates that in consequence he is about to become a dissenter! Can anything more flagrantly

Unconscientious, and unprincipled be imagined? and yet, such is the depth to which Dissent has sunk, that "conscientious" Dissenters welcome such a man to their ranks, and support him as a martyr to their principles; whereas it is quite clear that he would have turned his heel upon them if Mr. Cosens – a "High Churchman" – would have nominated him, and the bishop of Exeter would have licenced him".

The English Churchman 19th April 1849

Shore certainly spent much effort in his campaign to put over his case to the public by visiting many parts of England and Scotland and to that extent he did alert people to his plight. No doubt the Bishop and his friends saw this as '*agitation*'; nevertheless he held a sincere belief in his cause and obviously suffered a great deal as a result.

DIARY OF HRP

"Herbert Lomas
January 20th, 1874.
The college, Clifton.[79]

January the 20ᵗʰ 1874 Tuesday
Went with Allen to get a piano at Smith and got a Collard and Collard for 16/- a month not a bad one. And got a pair of boots at Goodenough's. Coming home saw Mr. Allen in a Hansom who was going to the Suspension Bridge and asked us both to go, but there being not enough room, I did not goAllen came back and also the piano. We had a small dinner at 12 o'clock, then went both to the college with Papa.[80]

After waiting a little we were shown into a room number one. There were about 90 in the room. The exam paper was given out which was very hard and we worked till four it being then about one o'clock. Then we were sent out for an hour, while the masters decided what

HRP aged 14

forms we should go in, I went in and found I was in the lower third form. When Allen came out he was allowed to stay till 9 o'clock. We had, after tea, music and Papa brought out his flute for Alan to hear. He was very pleased. He started off about half past eight for the college.

January 21ˢᵗ 1874 Wednesday
Was at the school for prayers at the chapel, and was accosted once on the road by a boy who wanted to know whether I belonged to the college and also my name.

---

79 Founded in 1862
80 Thomas Lomas

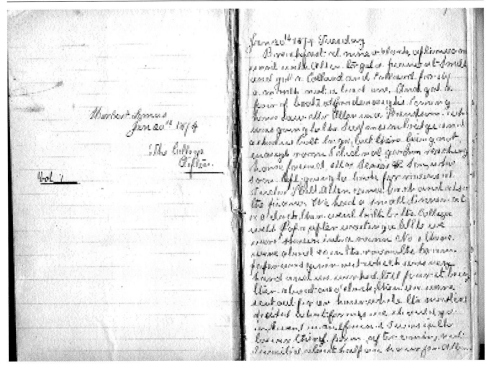

First page of HRP diary 1874

Mr.Percival after prayers gave a small sermon in the pulpit calling the college the most Christian set of boys for the size in the world. After service I was sent with my form to No. 14 room. Did an arith. and geog. paper and were let out at a quarter past one for dinner.

After dinner Allen called for us and we both with Papa went in a carriage to get some college caps, my colour was black with green stripes, Allen's black with white stripes. Went back to school at half past 3 o'clock, went in the same schoolroom. Did a grammar paper and a little Latin prose. Were let out at five. Went to the large schoolroom and had our voices tried whether we were to go to the choir or not. They did not decide. When I got home had tea, learnt lessons and told Mama[81] about Stokes.

22ⁿᵈ January 1874 Thursday

Was at school at 9 o'clock. Found I ought to have been there at a quarter before nine. Went into the same schoolroom and said the lessons we learnt the night before which took us to a quarter to 11. Then we were sent out for a quarter of an hour. Came home, had some biscuits. Went back again. Did some Latin grammar till 12. Then went to another room, one out of the big room, for arithmetic and were let out at one. I walked home with a boy named Jack. He was in my form. Not a bad fellow but awfully ugly.

---

81 Julia Lomas nee Shore

After dinner Allen came to us and we went to big schoolroom for call over at 3 o'clock. After that we saw some of the boys going to play football, the stripes against the plain, but we did not stop but we came away and went with Papa and and Mama up the town. I got some clothes ordered and bought my Diary Book and a jacket book to put down the lessons in. Allen also bought a large writing desk. We left him at our house to go home coming. Got a little work done before tea. More work after tea. Wrote a letter to Georgie. Had some music. I began "La Reigne." Had supper and went to bed.

January 23rd 1874 Friday

Had prayers in large schoolroom, the Litany, we standing all the time in a heap. After prayers had call over. Went to same schoolroom. Said lessons. Went out at a quarter to 11 for half-an-hour. Went in again. Did Latin prose till 12 o'clock. At quarter past 12 went into room number one to be examined in French. Very hard paper and did very badly. Went home. Had dinner. After dinner prepared a lesson. Went down the town with Papa to try on my clothes. The overcoat was too long. It looked like a dressing gown. On coming home found Allen there. We both walked to the college. At 4 o'clock had an hour's arith. from old Bartholomew. Then went to room number 14 for an hour. Did Palestra. Had lessons. Went home, had tea, did lessons. Mama did some Greek. She began the Andesta. Had a very little music, had supper, went to bed.

January 24th 1874 Saturday

Was at school at a quarter to nine. Had prayers, call over and then did an hour's arith.and then an hour's geography with Moberley. We were call out at a quarter to 11 to have our places given us in chapel. After that, went to the Physie. room number 10 and were called over and the book ordered but there was no time to do any lessons. After that went to Moberley for some Greek grammar. Got an order for more books. Went home, had dinner. Went back for call over. Saw Alan and we both went to the Z. We found a great many boys from the college there. Alan was most pleased with the lions and tigers. Not a bad collection of birds. Three golden eagles etc., some very nice parrots but they made an awful noise. Came home, found that Miss Nash had been waiting to see me, and Papa and Mamma would persist in saying that I was tired when I was not. Had tea, did lessons. I wrote a theme on the dirty roads and the crossing sweepers. Had some music. Supper and went to bed.

January 25th 1874 Sunday

Had breakfast at 20 past nine. Allen came to us, we all went to college chapel, no sermon because there was sacrament. After, Allen and I went a walk up to Suspension Bridge, but he being afraid of being too late, left me. Went home and had dinner. Allen came again, went back to school for lessons for an hour, came back through the field. Moberley spoke to me, he is not a bad fellow. I like him, he seems very kind. Had tea, after tea, went with Mama and Papa to Bathesda, had a new man and the room was awfully hot. Spoke to Miss Nash, came home, had supper and went to bed.

January 26th Monday

Had prayers and call over. Went to 14 room and did a scripture lesson and grammar, then went out for a quarter of an hour. Came in, did a Latin lesson. Sanstara, red-headed boy, Moberley told him if he had to speak to him again he would send him down the bottom, not two minutes after that he was sent down bottom. Came home, had dinner, went back to school at 4 o'clock. Did lessons. Sanstara was sent down again, were let out at six. Came home, had tea, I did not feel well, had a headache and cough which hurt. Did lessons and went to bed after supper.

January 27th 1874 Tuesday

Papa called me at 20 past seven. Said it was 20 past eight, I nearly went to sleep. He came in again at half past and said I was to get up. About five minutes after that Mama came in to see how I was. After thinking a little said I was not to go to school but lay there. She came in afterwards and brought me breakfast, and a little after breakfast I got up and was down a little before 10 o'clock. Had some music, and tried "the Duet Marth". Had dinner, after dinner I sorted the music and wrote a letter to the Old Bur(jopham). Had a letter from Georgie.

Allen came and said that it was settled that Mr Percival was going, much to my sorrow. Allen had been playing football and was very tired and had also a pain in his side. Mama went out and bought a bottle of gum.

January 28th 1874 Wednesday

My cold, not being better, did not go to school. A letter came from Buxton to say that Marson had been drinking and was sent away, so we did not know what to do.

January 29th 1874 Thursday.

Did not go to school because of my cold. Papa bought me a paper about some people who tried to go to the moon.

January 30th 1874 Friday

Had a letter from Paddock. Sent him one and Gerard Oakes and Morris.

January 31st 1874 Friday

Papa and I each had a letter from Mama Allen came.He said something about their going to a concert, but did not know much about it. He also said that in the school there was a society called the debating society like the House of Commons, and at that time it was debating whether supernatural power was superstition or not. He did not know how you became a member, but he says that their members have to speak before the assembly and attend meetings, which I should not care to do.

February 2nd 1874 Monday

Papa told me I was not going to college again and that they had almost made up their minds to go to Buxton, then I should have a few lessons from Mr Pettit.

February 3rd 1874 Tuesday

After dinner Mama got ready to go with Mrs. Senior for a drive. The carriage came for Mama first, then went for Mrs. Senior, on passing, it called here again and Mrs. Senior invited me to go, which I was very glad to do. We went first to an old book-shop, and saw a very old and room at the back with beautiful carved wood.

While Mrs. Senior was looking over the books she said we ought to go to St Mary Redcliffe Church as it was a very old one and was near, so we went and Mama was very much pleased with the coloured windows, they were coloured very well. On coming back we saw Mrs. Senior nearly ready. When she was ready we went to another bookshop, Mama bought a Maunder's Treasury of Knowledge, 10 shilling book for two and six, and I bought a very old book printed in the year 1662 for 3d. Afterwards we went to a few more shops. Mrs. Senior bought an old picture for five shillings.

February 4th 1874 Wednesday

Went out to see Miss Church and Miss Nash. Miss Church was not in but had gone out for a few days, Miss Nash was in and was very glad to see us. It was a beautiful house inside, the house is just opposite Betherda, in Great George Street.

February 5th 1874 Thursday

On coming down found a letter from Mr Henderson, he had sent me also 540 stamps, and said he would get me some more and also crests. Did some Greek with Mama and went out for a walk, it was fresh and very nice. After dinner arranged my stamps, and Papa was greatly astonished that Allen had not come a little after three, he came about half-past 5 o'clock and said he had been on a paper chase for about 10 miles and was very tired. I sent a Valentine to Grandmama,[82] because it was her birthday tomorrow. A man came from Mrs. Senior to know if Papa would like to go to a concert there was going to be at Colston Hall, as he had a ticket to spare, but of course he did not go. Allen being so very tired I lent him my slippers, and when he came to put his boots on, on going, his feet were so swollen and sore he could hardly put his boots on.

February 6th 1874 Friday

Letter from Gerard Oakes, a very short, stupid one, and also there was a letter from Aunt Emily[83] saying she was not well enough to come. We had before written to her to ask her to come and stay a week. Papa and Mama decided that one of them should take me up to Windsor for Dr. Harper[84] to examine me on Monday, because Miss Tucker is coming here tomorrow and going to Windsor on Monday. She is going to be Grandmama's housekeeper. It was very foggy and cold so I did not go out.

---

82 Matilda Lomas. Grandmother of HRP lived with John Lomas, brother of Thomas Lomas
83 Emily Bulteel nee Shore
84 James P Harper, medical practioner, Windsor

February 7ᵗʰ 1874 Saturday

Papa had a letter from Mr. Walton[85] saying that the houses we spoke of were £120 a year, so Papa that morning wrote about some more. I hope very much we shall go to Buxton.

After dinner, read till about 4 o'clock, when Allen came.

Among some other stories, he told us that a boy sitting next to him at dinner, when he saw an apple pie come in, he clapped his handkerchief to his nose and walked out of the room, his nose did not really bleed but he wanted to go out and fetch some sugar as there was never enough in the tarts. There are fixed days for tarts but this was a day when they did not generally have them. Also he would have had his sugar with him. I think it was cleverly done.

Sunday February 8ᵗʰ 1874

Went to Christ's Church, not so full as generally because there was a collection. A foreign Bishop preached, not a good sermon, he was very affected, with his bags of sleeves it was enough to make one laugh. I was shown into a very small pew so that I nearly broke it on the other side, but the old woman who gives people their seat gave me a better one, very comfortable. After dinner Papa gave Miss Tucker some of Mr. Govett's[86] books to look at and we had a conversation about his book "Infant sprinkling and the Prayer Book".

February 10ᵗʰ 1874 Tuesday

Dr. Harper came and after a little talk said that I'd better not go to school which I was very glad of.

February 11ᵗʰ 1874 Wednesday

There was a letter from Mama to say Mrs. Senior had given to her for me a beautiful cameo set in gold. I wrote that night to thank her for it. She had sent down a large book of paintings of England which Grandmama said Papa was to have.

February 13ᵗʰ 1874 Friday

Dr Harper came and said I was to go on with the same medicine.

February 14ᵗʰ

Uncle John went off to town by the 9.05 train. The letters were very late. Grandmama told us to take a beautiful card basket which she had, with us. About 10 Papa went to the station, and said I was to wait till the man came down for the luggage. When I got to the station I found that Prince and Princess Christian had just gone. They had gone just too late for the 10.25, and when they came to the station their horses were all over foam, they went off by a special.

---

85 Isaac Walton, banker in Buxton
86 Robert Garrett, English pastor was against infant baptism and for a full immersion before baptism, as a result resigned his curacy

When we started it was five minutes late and there was only one carriage to the train, and we went so fast to Slough that I thought every minute we would be off the line. We could hardly keep our seats it shook so. Soon after we got to Slough the train came for us. We got a very nice carriage. Uncle John having lent me a book called the *"Rob Roy Special"* I read it all the way down, this time we only took three minutes to go through the Box Tunnel. Arrived at Bristol a very little after time, on getting home found Alan was there, he was very pleased to see me. Mama showed me my cameo, it is the most beautiful I have ever seen. It is Shakespeare's head.

February 15ᵗʰ Sunday

Papa went off to Christ's Church, but Mama and I went later and I got a nice seat after standing for a good time, not much of a sermon. Alan came, I went to the church just behind the house. I do not know the name of it. It is rather high church, the choristers had black dresses on that buttoned up tight to the neck and over that a short vest to slip over the head, white, not coming down to the knees.

February 16ᵗʰ 1874 Monday

Told the tayler to send for my clothes because they did not fit properly. Allen came, went out for a walk.

February 17ᵗʰ 1874 Tuesday

Went out by the Suspension Bridge with Mama. When we came home she was very tired.

February 18ᵗʰ 1874 Wednesday

I went out with Papa to Jeffery's old bookshop. We were there about an hour and I bought a book called *"The Jist Book"* by Mark Lemon, and Papa bought for me a book called *"Proverbs of all Nations"*.

February 19ᵗʰ 1874 Thursday

Went out with Papa to the old bookshop. I bought Pope's Homer, four nice little volumes for two and six. Papa gave me a large black gold morning ring.

February 20ᵗʰ 1874 Friday

Mr Lemon came. Went out up the downs, went to his house, had dinner, after dinner had talk then went for a little walk.

February 21ˢᵗ 1874 Saturday

Packed and sewed up Papa's books Allen came about 4 o'clock. Went to the museum, enjoyed it very much..

February 22ⁿᵈ 1874 Sunday

Papa went to Christchurch, but Mama and I stayed at home, I began to read

"Josephus". Allen came and had a talk. About half past 3 o'clock went to St Paul's Church, it rained hard all the day. When Allen left he seemed very sorry we were going.

February 23ʳᵈ 1874 Monday

After breakfast finished packing. It was so hot that we were obliged to have the window open. About 11 o'clock a man came to carry the boxes downstairs Got to the station and started in good time, got into an empty carriage, took five minutes going through the Box Tunnel. Got to Reading in pretty good time, found our other train waiting. There was a very peculiar dog, a sort of bulldog but it looked just like a man sometimes. Got to Windsor. Found Grandmama looking very pale and weak. Had tea and Grandmama said she would like to go to bed then, so very much unlike her. I wrote and read , had supper and went to bed. The dog seemed very uneasy as if something was wrong.

February 24ᵗʰ 1874 Tuesday

Grandmama better.Went out about half past 11 o'clock with the dog. It was a sort of falling dog. Dr Harper said I was better, a thing which I knew before.

February 25ᵗʰ 1874 Wednesday

Went out to see White the carpenter because I wanted something done to my jewel case.

February the 26ᵗʰ Thursday

It rained, and kept on raining all day. Went up Staines to see Grandmama, she was better.

February 27ᵗʰ 1874 Friday

Uncle John said he was going to Slough to get some flower seeds from Turner so I said I would go too. Played and went off about 12 o'clockUncle John told me the Queen was coming back that day so I asked him to find out what time. He found out it was about 5 o'clock. Asked Miss Tucker if she would like to go and see the Queen. She said we would like to do so very much, so we both went off together. We got there about half-past 4 o'clock, got a very good front place. There were about 80 people to see her come in. She came in about half past 5 o'clock, but she looked most extremely cross, of course she had John Brown there. Their railway carriage was a beauty. I saw J Llan there, shook hands with him, came home. Grandmama was a good deal better that day.

February 28ᵗʰ 1874 Saturday

Went to the market to get some flowers for Uncle John. After dinner went out in the garden and helped Uncle John to plant the flowers. Miss Tucker went out for a walk and when she came in, the dog was wanted to be washed and Uncle John and I had raced all round the garden a long time before we could get it in the kitchen. I went down to see it washed. They first washed it in a small footbath, then dried it and wrapped it up in a blanket on a stool before the fire to get it dry.

March 1ˢᵗ 1874 Sunday

I went (to church) by myself to the old church, got a very nice seat in the gallery. The municipal corporation were there and also the volunteers. Where I sat I could only see half of them and I saw one who did not turn round at the Creed, he was the only one.

Went with Miss Tucker to go to St George's. It was very full, Mr Tucker got a seat but I had to sit on some steps. Came home, had tea, after tea went off to Trinity, on getting there found a crowd at the door. It was late and also extremely hot, at last I got to Uncle John Bulteel's seat and got in. I was very nearly suffocated, it was so hot. The singing was very bad. The anthem was three-quarters solo by a man with a very quaking voice, the sermon was by Mr Robins,[87] not bad, but nothing much. On coming out Aunt Emily said they were going to drive out to Ascot on Monday and if I liked to go I might

March 2ⁿᵈ 1874 Monday

Uncle John had gone to London and would be back for tea. Read, gave the dog a brush, went to Aunt's and drove off to Ascot. It is a large place but was empty then. We had a very nice room. Had dinner, mutton chops, omelette cheese and Miss Cornwall and Aunt had a cup of tea. Went out for a little walk and at 4 o'clock started back. Just before we got to Dr Harper's house the wheel came off the carriage and Miss Cornwall who was that side went down with a bump, but none of us were hurt. We had to walk home and had a good laugh over it. After tea read "*the Tulkborne*" which said he was in Newgate for 14 years.

March 3ʳᵈ 1874 Tuesday

Went to the station and by chance saw a train in which brought Prince Leopold and Princess Beatrice.

March 4ᵗʰ 1874 Wednesday

Went to the South railway station. It was decorated very nicely but not finished

March 6ᵗʰ 1874 Friday

Uncle John went off early. Practiced and went out with Mama to the South Western Railway Station to see the decoration. I counted 285 flags, inside 73 flags, also inside 93 flowerpots with very nice flowers and two fish glasses with bits of coral in. They were put one each side of the door. The Royal Party fit in between very nicely. Covered all round with ferns. The wall was covered with a yellow and white sort of

---

87 Rector of Holy Trinity and Chaplain to Her Majesty's Household Troops at Windsor for 25 years. *The Times* 8th October 1898

cloth in wide stripes and round the door and sides a lot of sham flowers, very well done. One old woman behind me said she had never seen the like in Windsor for the last 40 years and along the roof on every other bar a flag and very nice wreathes of green hanging from the roof.

I heard that at the White Hart they had spent £18 on borrowed things, flags etc. Outside the station were about 43 different painted Coats of Arms and inside eight, and on the arches which the carriage will go under at the station in the middle there was a large crown and flags on each side. At the bank in Thames street there are pipes all round the windows and corners of the houses for gas to be lit at the Illumination. At the station round each stone there are a lot of those little glasses to be lit with oil, and also all round Gardeners' Square the same sort of glasses, some thousands. At the Town Hall each side one of these glass things with a large crown on the top and a man in the middle, and in front of the same sort one with our Arms and the other with the late Bussean. Went down to the Great Western Railway Station and there were about 40 people standing about waiting for the train because they expected some of the Royalty, but none came and they all looked so silly.

March 7ᵗʰ 1874 Saturday

Found Captain Jackson who lives in a house nearby opposite, had put five flags out and a lot of candles in the window for Illumination. I went with the dog up the Clewer Road to see where the fireworks were to be.

Went to look at the Artillery in the Long Walk and came back and took our places a little lower down than Doctor Turrell's house. We had a beautiful view because we could see half way up the High Street. We stood with our back to the railings so that we could stand on the coping stones when they passed and see over everyone's head. We had not been there long before the Footguards had come and lined the street in front of us half way up High Street. They were not properly settled before the Guard of Honor came with its band, passed us and went up to the castle. At the same time the Highlanders went with their band up High Street to line the station and part to Thames Street. The rest of Thames Street and part of High Street were lined by the Volunteers. Then the Horse Guards went by with the band in court dress, they looked extremely nice. About a quarter to one the Queen went past in state with the Prince and Princess of Wales and the rest of the Royal Family in carriages afterwards escorted by about 200 Horse Guards. The Queen looked rather cross. We waited about half an hour and then she came back in the first carriage drawn by four grays. With the Queen, by her side the Duchess and Duke, in front of her were the two bouquets of flowers which were presented to him at Gravesend with gold round the stems. By his side, in the second carriage there were the Princess of Wales, Princess Helena, Princess Christian of Schleswig Holstein, the Prince of Wales and Prince Arthur. The third carriage conveyed Princess Louise, Princess Beatrice, Prince Leopold and the Duke of Cambridge.

The 4ᵗʰ carriage conveyed the Duchess of Wellington (Mistress of the Robes) Princess Weasemky, Prince Waldemin Rapiatinsty and the Earl of Bradford (Master of

Plan of Windsor

the Horse). The 6th carriage conveyed the Lady Emma Osborne M. Oyerow the Clerk Marshal, Lord Alfred Paget and Colonel Lymedack Gardiner. The 7th carriage contained the Equerry in Waiting to the Queen, Lord Charles Fitzroy, Colonel Hon. W. Colville, Mayor General Probyn and Colonel Tynwchitt.

The eighth carriage conveyed Mayor General H. Ponsonby, Captain Campbell, Captain Hague and Lieutenant Ramsey. His Royal Highness Prince Arthur attended by Mayor Pickard ,and Lieutenant

Buchanan who had accompanied the Duke and Duchess of Edinburgh from Gravesend to Windsor. While they were passing there were very well received with shouts and handkerchiefs from nearly every window. The Queen looked very happy and was smiling nearly all the time, but the Duchess looked extremely pale as her dress, she was dressed all in white. Just as they entered the castle gate there was a royal salute from the Artillery. After that there was a rush to the park gates to see the procession go up to the castle.

We then up walked a little down Sheep Street. The road was nearly full of cabs. We waited there a little, then the Foot Guards went past to go to the barracks. A little after, the Guard of Honour and then the Horse Guards.

Had tea, read, about half-past 7 o'clock started to go to see Gardiners Cottages and then the fireworks. The effect was very pretty. On the cottages it was those little oil lamps all the way round. When we got to this end of Clewer road we found we could not go up it well, it was such a crush, so we got a place this side of the ploughed field only having that between us and the fireworks. They began rather late. There was one a very pretty colour, a sort of mane. I'd not seen it before. There were set pieces, on one, "*God bless Our Sailor Prince*", another, "*God bless them both*", and another "*Gardiner MP., the poor man's friend*". He gave all these fire works himself, they cost about £400. Directly it was over we walked as hard as we could to go round the town before the people could get there. On going there, a woman half-drunk knocked into Uncle who was smoking a cigar. Most likely she thought the cigar was a firework and ran up against it, and rolled flat over it in the road.

We walked through Peascod Street and down Thames Street to the South Western Railway Station. It was very nice. On coming back, met Mama, Aunt Emily and Miss Cornwall in a cab taking a view. When we passed Peascod Street we saw the crowd was so dense that we could not have got down. Went to look at the bonfire which was blazing well, before it was lighted it was 50 ft-high.

March 8th 1874 Sunday

I went to church but Mama and Papa and Uncle went to All Saints. The place was rather full; the sermon was by Mr Robins and was about five minutes long, not worth hearing. The text was "*Fear God and honor the King*". After tea I went to All Saints with Uncle John. Came home. Mamma told me that when Mary went out she by mistake let a beastly little dog in and they had to send for a man to take it out. He took it out between two mattresses. It would always try to bite.

March 10ᵗʰ Tuesday 1874

Mary gave notice to leave, so Mama wrote to Mary Critchlow to see if she could come. It snowed on and off all the evening and morning. Went out, saw off the train, the Marquis of Lorne and Princess Louisa, and on coming down Peascon Street, met the Duke and Duchess of Edinburgh in an open carriage. He took off his hat to me.

March 12ᵗʰ 1874 Thursday

Miss Cornwall's carriage called for Miss Tucker to go and see the Duchess go off by train and I walked, it was snowing very hard. I stood by the Battons because they did not go through Park Street, not many people. They passed in shut carriages and they had the Scotch greys as escort.

March 14ᵗʰ 1874 Saturday

Was just going to start to go to Slough when a letter came from Miss Cornwall to say that she was going to the Gold Pantry that morning and she would be very pleased to take me if I should like to go, so of course I did not go to Slough. They called for me about half past 11. Miss Cornwall, a young lady and I walked up the town and waited at Bird and Allen's for another old lady. When we got to the castle we had to wait some 10 minutes, after which a policeman, a very nice man, came and took us a through a great many passages. It was quite a long walk to get to it and the passages were very dark.

When we got there, the policeman left us and we went to a room where the Plate was all round the room in cases. The most beautiful of all was a large gold Eau de Cologne fountain. It was a large dome supported on silver pillars and underneath the fountain, round outside the basin of the fountain, silver horses being led by Arabs to drink. There were piles of plates, also 300 and about 200 salt cellars and a very great many things which I cannot tell of. On coming back we were led by the policeman who took us into the servants who showed us where the table was laid for about 150. I was there offered some beer, which I am very sorry I did not accept.

Then he took us to the House Keeper's Hall were the table was laid for about 80, then to the kitchen. Each end of it there was a very large open grate about nine feet wide and 7 ft high, they could roast four or five dozen joints at a time. There were six sirloins of beef being roasted at each side. There were two large gas stoves and in the middle a very large hot-water table to keep things warm. There were two cooks making potted meat. Beside the kitchen there is a room entirely for boiling potatoes. The basting ladle has a handle longer than a broomstick.

On coming out, met Aunt Emily in the carriage. We all got in. She drove to a man's when she got an order to say that we might go to the memorial chapel near Saint George's Chapel. It is a very beautiful place, pictures of our Lord in inlaid stones all the way round and images of the Royal Prince's and Princesses. In the middle is a statue of Prince Albert. At his feet there is a beautiful dog and at his head two angels bending over his head and one had a black rain through her face and it looked as if she had dirtied her hands and daubed her face.

Came home, after dinner went out. Saw a crowd at the station, waited and found the Queen was to come down at 10 past five. Got there about five. The stand and station was full. Then I got a place so that I saw the train come in and then saw her get into her carriage. There was a little cheer; the Princess of Wales was there too.

March 15ᵗʰ 1874 Sunday
Went to walk up the Long Walk. On coming back met the Queen who waved to me and of course John Brown.

March 17ᵗʰ 1874 Tuesday
Found Uncle, Papa and Miss Tucker were gone to the station to see the Ministers come in. Waited a little and then they came; there were only six. Disraeli was there and took the seat of honor. Came home, had dinner, went to the station, and was there just before the ministers who left by the next train. Both times I had a very good view. When they got into the carriage Disraeli said something and they all began roaring with laughter.

March 18ᵗʰ 1874 Wednesday
Mama told me she had seen the Lord Mayors of London, Dublin and York and that they were going back about 3 o'clock, so after dinner I went and stood up on Castle Hill. I was just in the sun and it was very hot. Waited about a quarter of an hour and then 32 walked in detachments, some had maces dressed in black, some dressed in red, some dressed in blue and one dressed in black velvet with a large white fur thing behind. All flowing robes. They had only just passed when in the procession came two Lord Mayor's carriages. They came dressed out very grand with men in silk stockings. There were about six and 20 carriages and most of them from the White Hart Hotel. All of them had pairs of horses, and the City Marshall rode first dressed very grand on a beautiful horse.

They went to the South Western Railway Station, and I walking quickly got there as soon as they did. They were about half-an-hour getting seated. There were about 90 in all in the train. It was a special. After they had gone I saw the horses and carriages put in the train. There were altogether four carriages that went. I put my hand inside the Lord Mayor of London's carriage. It was lined with white and yellow silk. Came home, had tea, after tea wrote, had music. One young lady, while the possession was going passed, said, *"why are they all old men?"* in a very mournful tone. And also while I was seeing them get into the carriages, there was a little crowd, and there happened to be a gentleman in front of me who I was pushed against, he said to me *"you are making a leaning post of me"*, so I said, *"I am sure I am not."* So he said *"do not tell me a lie"*, so I said, *"I am not doing anything of the sort"* and stared him out. I think it was extremely rude. He was dressed as a gentleman, but he certainly did not act as one.

March 19ᵗʰ 1874 Thursday

Went up the town with Mama to pay for the books. When we finished we went to Taylor's, the bookshop opposite the parish church and saw in a sort of Panorama the private apartments in the castle. After that, some fine oil paintings of the private gardens and then about 50 photographs done on glass in a foreign way taken instantaneously. The water was beautifully taken, when they first came out they were black and the man got a patch for it. It is a great deal better than we can take then and it can take objects miles further away then we can.

March 20ᵗʰ 1874 Friday

Went with Mama to get a fowl for Grandmama, also got two of my photos, one for Paddock and the other for Allen. Came home, left Mama and went a walk in the fields by the river. After dinner Gramdmama was not so well, so I took a note to Dr Harper to ask him to come. There were races going on just by his house and a great many people.

Came home, found the house full of smoke. Uncle John's fire had been smoking. We opened both doors, both back and front. I went to post my letter and on getting to the box found people standing around. I put my letter in without looking at it, but a woman told me it was full, so I pulled my letter back again. Some boy had been stuffing 30 or 40 circulars in and stuffed it full.

March 21ˢᵗ 1874 Saturday

Went out for about half an hour with the dog, but when I wanted to chain him to bring him home he would not come but kept about six yards in front of me all the way. Let the dog in, and I chased him up and down the stairs three or four times before I could get him downstairs to have his tub, then I had to push him down by force. Went out again, the town was very full because of the races. I heard that Lord Bathmore fell from the horse and was thrown and died about 2 o'clock. Helped Uncle John in the garden. Went out and saw they were coming home very early from the races, and found some of the horses did not run because of the death of Lord Bathmore. Saw three of Prince Christian's children come home from it. Saw a lifeguard drunk.

March 22ⁿᵈ 1874 Sunday

After breakfast went with Mama to William Street Chapel, a very good sermon. Went for a walk in the park, met the Queen, she looked very cross. After tea went with Mama to Trinity. Went to Aunt's seat, it was very full, but not a good sermon.

March 23ʳᵈ 1874 Monday

Had the window open, it was extremely hot. Went out to the station and found the Queen was just going to start. She was dressed in black velvet. She was with Princess Beatrice as they were going out of the station. John Brown was in the Queen's compartment putting the box together and laughing and talking with the Queen. The sun was very hot, went up the park and sat down for a time.

March 24ᵗʰ 1874 Tuesday

Last night it was 65 degrees when we went to bed in the bedroom. Went into the park and saw some soldiers drilling.

March 25ᵗʰ 1874 Wednesday

After breakfast went to see Dr Harper. I had a rash which he said were heat spots. Saw Sangers Circus[88] parade through the town. There were about 70 horses and four milk white mules, and also 8 milk white small ponies.

March 26ᵗʰ 1874 Thursday

Saw the procession of the circus. On a high sort of cart drawn by four horses were two horses with riders on them. Went to the circus. I saw four horses stand on their hind legs, and a boy[89] riding a horse without any saddle and stirrups and sitting sideways on it, and he was jumping off and all the time it was galloping, and a good many rode standing and jumping about and jumping through hoops. There was one boy, who jumped head over heels on horseback, and a lady came in and her horse danced and plunged and stood on its hind legs, but she looked very comfortable. Also four ladies and four gentlemen danced the Paris Quadrells on horseback very well, and a man stood on his head on a high pole without holding. Went to bed earlier because we had to go to Chatham tomorrow.

March 27ᵗʰ 1874 Friday

Went by the 8.10 train to Bishops Road. Got out there and walked to Praed Street.

Went on to Gillingham, a small village where the property is just outside the fortification. It is more than I thought. There had been a great flood there and the land lay by the water, some of it. A great many people had their houses floating. Our sea wall was a little damaged, but very little. One man said his calves were almost drowned, so he gave them some gin which revived them.

After dinner walked to the station. The town was all hung out with flags and an arch erected because they expected some of the Ashentee troops to come down from Portsmouth in the afternoon. Started by the 8.45 train. On coming back, saw the Crystal Palace and went underground. Also saw the dogs' home. The underground rail-

---

88 In a nine months' season Sanger's circus visited 200 towns, giving 2 shows a day, every day except Sunday. Their road train between sites was said to be 2 miles long and had at least 10 wagons to carry the tent and seating, a lamp wagon, 8 or 10 living wagons, a foal wagon, 10 wild beast wagons full of lions, tigers, bears and others, a harness wagon, a portable blacksmith's forge, property wagons, wardrobe and dressing wagons, a band carriage and at least six great tableau cars for the parade. "O what a circus" Berks FHS Historian September 2000

89 Initially circuses had concentrated on equestrian displays and that remained part of their programme. By the mid-1870's growing concern was expressed about the welfare of the child acrobats who were performing in them, and particularly about the early age at which their training began and the harsh treatment they received. "Lord" George Sanger declared that not only did he never have more than half a dozen young people under training at any one time, but claims that they had been purchased were absurd. He had been offered premiums as high as £100 by parents anxious for their children to be trained. Legislation was however passed in 1897 forbidding children under 16 to take part in dangerous performances. Pleasures and Pastimes in Victorian Britain-Pamela Horn 1999 Sutton publishing p89.

way was very full at Paddington. We got into a saloon carriage. There were a great many people went down. At Slough a porter, very respectfully, touched his hat to me. I was sitting with my head out of the window. He most likely took me for one of the Royal Family.

March 29th 1874 Sunday

Went to Aunt Emily's to see if she was going to Saint George's. It was very windy and blew my hat off once. She was not going because she was afraid it would rain, so I went myself. When I asked Wise to get me a seat he said, *"who are you?"*, so I said I knew Mr Bulteel and he got me a stall directly. Lord Russell preached a very good sermon.

March 30th 1874 Monday

After breakfast got ready to go with Uncle to see the review of the Ashantee troops. We went to the long walk and after waiting about an hour, saw some Horse Guards go by and then some Foot Guards to line the ground.

In about half-an-hour, the 2nd Battalion Rifle Brigade went past. They were very much burnt by the sun and some looked very ill. Then the second Battalion 23rd Royal Welsh Fusiliers with a detachment of the Royal Artillery and the 28th Company of Royal Engineers, and the 42nd Royal Highland (Black Watch) with part of the 79th Royal Highland, and a detachment of the Army Service Corps and the Army Hospital Corps.

We waited about half an hour when the Queen drove past escorted by some Royal

Review of Ashanti troops at Windsor
Illustrated London News

lifeguards. The first carriage conveyed the Queen, the Princes of Wales, the Princess Christian and the Duchess of Edinburgh. The second, Princess Louise, Princess Beatrice, Prince Leopold and Lady Churchill. The third, the Countess of Macclesfield, Lady Caroline Barrington, the Earl of Dunmore and Lord Cardwell. The 4th, Lady Princess Bailey, Lady Susan Melville and Lord Coleville. The Prince of Wales, the Duke of Edinburgh, Prince Arthur, Prince Christian, the hereditary Grand Duke of Mecklenburg-Strelity, the Grand Duke of Teek, the Marquis of Lorne, and Count Gleichen attended their respective suites preceded the Queen on horseback to the entrance of the Great Park, and joined the procession at the double gates and the long walk.

Then we ran off and saw in the park the Queen received by field marshal his Royal Highness the Duke of Cambridge commander-in-chief and his staff, and Major General his Serene Highness Prince Edward of Sasce-Weimar, commanding the Home District.

"On arriving on the Review Ground her Highness was received with a Royal salute by the troops in time under the command of Major General Sir Garnet Wolseley K.L. M .G.and C.B.[90] The officers specially employed on the gold escort were also present and were placed on the right of the line. Several were, however, prevented by illness from attending.

The Queen then drove down the ranks and on her Majesty's return to the saluting point, the troops were formed into a hollow square, when her Majesty presented Major General Sir Garnet Wolseley with the insignia of the Order of the Grand Cross of St Michael and Saint George, and of the Knight Commander of the Bath and Lieutenant Lord Gifford with the Victoria Cross, Sergeant Samuel McGawl of the 42nd, having been wounded and being ill, was unable to receive the Victoria Cross. Sir Archibald Alison, Colonel of the Staff, was also presented to her Majesty. His Royal Highness the Duke of Cambridge, by command of the Queen, then expressed her Majesty's thanks to the assembled troops for their gallant services during the Ashantee Campaign, after which the troops marched past in the following order: – The Royal Artillery, the Royal Engineers, the 23rd Royal Welsh Fusiliers, the 42nd Highland (Black Watch), part of the 79th Ditto, the Rifle Brigade (Prince Consort's own), the Army Service Corps, and the Army Hospital Corps. The Queen then left the Review Ground in the same order she came.

Sir Garnett Woolsey may well have felt a proud man when through the Royal Park of Windsor, before the eyes of shouting thousands, he led his army past their Queen. Not a year has gone since in the same place the Sheik of Persia sat by the Queen of England to see the English troops march past, but both the hour and. the men were different then. It was a fine spectacle – a splendid pageant which passed before the eyes of the Persian King beneath that bright June sun, but this sight is something more than the flower of the British Army. The chosen Corps of the service were brought out to show the stranger how English soldiers looked and marched, as they looked and

---

90 In 1883 Sir Garnett Woolsey contributed an article to a publication entitled *The Channel Tunnel and Public Opinion,* in which, amongst others, he warned the country of possible ways through the tunnel if it was ever built. HRP and 700 other dignatories signed the document

marched he might well have guessed so would they fight. But now the people of England were looking on their own country men – on men who, but a few short weeks since, had been face to face with the foe, and in the teeth of dangers, worse even than those which are born of every battlefield, having done the work that had been given them to do, had now come back to claim their just reward.

It was a wise forethought to change the ground of the Review. There can be no question that had the original choice of the Home Park been adhered to, considerable inconvenience would have been felt. As it was the site was a good one. It was the large open space between Queen Anne's Ride and the Long Walk, halfway down the latter. Along the East Side of the Ride, looking onto the Long Walk, were ranged the carriages, and there the crowd was thickest, though it stretched far away in an unbroken line northward right round the ground, down almost to the trees that fringe the walk. Towards the southern end of the line was the Royal Standard, where sat the Queen as the troops went by and on either side of this point were two enclosures, wherein certain of the privileged were allowed to be members of both Houses of Parliament, of the Royal Household, of the Press and last, though of course very far from least, the Eton boys.

Time had not admitted for more perfect arrangements, but such as they were the preparations were complete enough. The Second Life Guards, the Sixth Dragoon Guards (carebiniers) and the first Battalion of Grenadier Guards kept the ground, assisted by a large number of police both Metropolitan under Mr Superintendent Mart, and Windsor under Mr Chief Superintendent Lloyes.

At the saluting point stood a guard of honor of the Grenadiers. Between 11 and 12 the troops were to arrive, some from Portsmouth, some from Shorncliff, some from Winchester and others from Woolwich and Chatham. As they arrived, they were at once to march by the Castle Hill and through the high street, both bright with flags and lined with an enthusiastic crowd, to their respective stations. At 1 the Queen herself was to be on the ground. But the regiments had far to come, and trains will reasonably be behind their time, and, fortunately for a considerable part of the crowd who were somewhat on the scene, it was to 2 o'clock before the bugles called the troops to attention. But few could have fretted at the delay. Looking from the royal flag northward towards the castle, the eye saw a bright and varied scene. Out in front little lines of colors on the open green of the park, stood the heroes of the day.

On the extreme right was a small handful of men, clad in different colors, red, blue, even in black; these are the special service officers, each in the uniform of his own regiment, a few in the sober grey and pith helmet of the campaigning dress, those in black are the Chaplains who went up with the little force to Coomassie. Then came the artillery and the engineers a mere handful of men, even together; then the 22nd Royal Welsh Fusiliers with their new goat, sent them by the Queen herself from the Kashmir flock in the park. After this the 4th Highlanders, the Black Watch, the third Battalion of the Rifle Brigade, and lastly, the men of the Commissariat and the Army Service Corps.

Right and left, two sides of the square, stretched the thick black wall of spectators relieved by the scarlet of the guards, and flecked here and there by the white plumes of the Household Cavalry; while off to the north, so right round the ground, shone the brass helmets of the Carabiniers. When, too the eye grew tired of roaming so far afield; it might turn to a little group nearer home. Close to the saluting point are gathered a little knot of Scarlet coated white plumed officers of the staff. Among them is one in a uniform which we now know is a Scarlet clad Hussar with a white felisse lined with scarlet and stiff with golden embroideries. It is a Russian uniform we are told and the wearer is Prince Barcatinsky.

But there is among them a white horse, an Arab, as it seems, carrying one on whom all eyes are turned; his breast is covered with medals, and his face is familiar now to nearly all there, for it is the hero of the day, Sir Garnett Wolseley himself. Around him are his staff of whose good work every successive dispatch has told us, and with them is Prince Edward of Soisce-Weimar, in command of the guards. It is nearly two o'clock now, still no sign of royalty, and the crowd are beginning to wax somewhat impatient. Suddenly a bugle rings out and then again sergeant calls the troops to attention; arms are shouldered and Sir Garnet Wolseley and his staff ride off towards the north corner of the ground. Following them with our eyes we can see a bright mass of color moving swiftly down the Long Walk, and soon the cheers that came rolling up along the line announce the Queen.

In an open carriage drawn by four greys, she came up at a smart trot. At her carriage wheels ride the Prince of Wales as Colonel of the Rifle Brigade, the Duke of Edinburgh in the uniform of the Volunteer Artillery of London, Prince Arthur, of course, in the dark rifle green tunic of his own regiment, and the Duke of Cambridge, commander-in-chief of the army. Before and behind rides an Escort of lifeguards and all around the staff, a bright show of scarlet and gold, dancing plumes and glistening steel.

All present noticed how well her Majesty is looking, and how proud of her soldiers, as with such a sight before and such sounds around her, she may well be. As she comes to her Standard the cheers are merged in the strains of *"God Save the Queen"* and all uncover as her carriage stays a while till the music ceases. Then the horses' heads are turned and slowly the procession passes down the ranks. Beyond, a bright mass of color, grey horses passing slowly on, and the plumes of the staff waving in the brisk breeze, the spectators packed close behind the guards cannot see much now.

Still less can they see the next movement, for now either of the line closes in on the Highlanders forming a hollow square unto which drives the Queen. From a distance we can see Sir Garnett and his staff ride forward, and the General dismounts. That the Queen is speaking we can see, but what she says it is of course impossible for us to hear. This much however we learn – that when the square is broken Lord Gifford wears upon his breast the Victoria Cross, and not a man there upon that ground, be his coat red or black, but he is glad for the young soldiers sake, and for the honor so gallantly won.

But now the square breaks, the carriages come back, the Queen is ready beneath the shadow of her own royal flag, The bands of the different regiments come forward to the centre of the ground; with too, comes, or rather his brought, the goat, for he is evidently a stubborn or perhaps modest animal, and then, as the well-known strains of the "*British Grenadiers*" rise on the air, the March Past begins. In columns of companies regiments come. First ride the staff, next to them, alone, at the head of his little band of heroes, Sir Garnet Wolseley. As he carries his sword to the salute he turns, and, reigning up by the side of the Queen waits there to see his soldiers pass.

First come the Fusiliers and in front of them Sir Archibald Alison, Brigadier-General of the army of Comassie. It is somewhat strange, we think at first sight, that the Brigadier-General should be on foot, but we soon see the reason. Sir Archibald brought back but one arm from India and that arm is now in a sling. Then the line changed, the bagpipes strike up, and to the quick tune of the "*Highland Laddie*", the Black Watch come on. The men of the last companies are in the trues, and tartan is of a different colour, for these are the men of the 79, another Highland Regiment who volunteered to fill up the ranks of the 42nd when they sailed out from Portsmouth in December.

Again another strain, livelier, and quicker still. It is the old air of "*95* "and we know that the Rifle Brigade, the old 95th Regiment, are passing. After them, came the men of the Army Service Corps and of the Control, good fellows and true, who though hard fighting may not fall to their share as often as they can wish and generally get even more than their share of hard work. This ends the procession.

But the day is not over. Once more the troops are formed into line, the staff in the centre, and the General alone, set at the head of the staff. Slowly in unbroken order the long column advances. When, within 50 yards of the Royal Carriage, the men are halted, and the arms are ordered. Clearly we can see Sir Garnett turning to the right and left to see that all is ready, calling for three cheers for the Queen. He waves his plumed hat in the air, and from end to end of a few de joie, the cheers ring out. They are sent back again from the crowd, and are continued again and again till they die away in the strains of the national anthem and we know then that all is over and done."[91]

We then went and took our places in the Long Walk and saw the Queen go past. We walked up to the gates, there were crowds of people all down the park. We stood at the top of Sheep Street and saw lots of cabs and carriages and people go past. Into one cab got a policeman with his head bandaged up, and another we saw a young man who was so ill he could not sit up. He had an Ashantee hat and dress on. We then walked home and were told that three men had broken into a house close by and had been pursued by a London policeman and two Eton boys. The man who the police pursued took a pistol and shot at him five times, but only once took effect and after that he broke the pistol about his head, but between them they caught two.

April 2nd 1874 Thursday

Went to the station to meet Uncle William and Aunt Sarah who were coming from

---

91   Probably taken from a newspaper article

London to see Grandmama. Came home with them, then went out the town, and then on finding a crowd by the Town Hall I went in and found the two burglars being tried. I saw the jemmies they opened a door with and a pistol that was broken over the policeman's head and the purses and things they had stolen, and Mr Hayes the police superintendent asked for them to be remanded for a week, because the policeman was not well enough to come as witness, and it was granted. As they were being led through the streets handcuffed to one another and also to a policeman, they were hooted by a crowd of people and more policemen had to go to keep order.

April 3rd 1874 Friday

Went to the old church. It being Good Friday, there were no decorations. In the second lesson it was about the cock who crew. Just as he was reading it, a cock outside did crow and some people laughed. The communion table and stools were covered with black.

April 4th 1874 Saturday

When I came down I found I had a swollen face. The doctor came and said I only had a little cold.

April 5th 1874 Sunday

My face had swollen a great deal more, so did not get up to breakfast but I got down about 12 o'clock. Uncle William was not well and Grandmama was not so well. Had dinner. Uncle William was worse and thought he would like to go home, so he did so.

April 6th 1874 Monday

Mrs. Harper came with a telegram for the Doctor as he was going to call that morning saying that Mrs. A Davies at Wilton Park, Slough was very poorly. I went out to meet Dr Harper. He said he was going to call this morning and I told him there was a telegram for him.

Went up to the Castle and saw a lot of people going to the stables so I thought I would go too. I had to sign my name in a large book, and put what town I came from. I was shown around by a very nice groom. They were about 65 horses altogether and two ponies the Queen drives in the private grounds. We saw the carriages, also one called "*a charabanc*" given to her from France and a Russian sledge with bearskin rugs and two other small Russian carriages she had given her. Also we saw the perambulators of the royal family. The old ones were made of wickerwork lined with cushions. The stables were whitewashed and ventilated. Very nice and clean. We also saw the riding school where all the royal family learned to ride.

London Zoo – lions
Illustrated London News

London Zoo – elephants
Illustrated London News

April 8ᵗʰ 1874 Wednesday

Alfred[92] and I went to the zoo.[93] We went in a cab. A man there gave a sort of deer a book about quarter the size of a Bradshaw, which the animal, after a great deal of munching, swallowed. And another man gave some monkeys a match which it lit and struck setting the straw on fire. The monkey was very much afraid and ran away. The whole cage would have burned down if it had not been that the keeper happened to be close by with some water which he put it out with. I saw the sea horse come out of the water and kiss the keeper's face, also the two white polar bears playing in the water and pushing each other over. I saw a very large elephant, the largest one I have ever seen. About half past two, had dinner at the buffet. Papa met us about three. I saw the bears dance, and the hyena laugh as if it was going to split its side.

April 15ᵗʰ 1874 Wednesday

Mama called me at half past 10 o'clock and came in and gave me a locket, as it was my birthday. Then Papa gave me a nice hatbox.

April 19ᵗʰ 1874 Sunday

After breakfast got ready and went to Bridgetown church. We waited about for Field, the pew opener, and the clergyman, Mr Watkins,[94] saw us and asked us if we wanted a seat. When we said *"yes"*, he said *"I will give you one, the Duke's seat is always empty in the morning, you can sit there"*. Of course, we were stared at very much sitting in the Duke's seat. The man read very nicely and did not preach badly. After tea, went to Totnes Church. The clergyman, Mr Burrows, preached very well. He got very excited against the priests and I quite agree with him.

April 27ᵗʰ 1874 Monday

After breakfast got ready to go to Teignmouth. First we had a walk in the town, then on the beach, the sea was rough. Then we went to the sea wall to eat our lunch and then sat on the sound for a long time. There were some very amusing dogs playing about. We saw them draw in the mackerel line. There were not many fish. Some launce and some fish they called Sting fish I had never seen them before. They are like small roach and when they sting anyone they sometimes send them mad. Then we sat down on the esplanade and saw one steamer go out of town while tugging a ship, and another in the distance tugging three large ships. Then we went to the station, the train was three minutes before time. I forgot to say I found a piece of pumice stone – a nice large piece.

May 8ᵗʰ 1874 Friday

I forgot to say that yesterday evening we saw the Seymour Brake[95] start with four

---

92 William's son and HRP's cousin, later to become a co-director of Buxton Hydro
93 London Zoo at Regent's Park was opened in 1828
94 Mr Watkins took forward a James Shore
95 Brake belonging to Seymour Hotel

horses and about 23 people. They were Rose[96] the Linen Draper's assistants who with some friends were going for a picnic to Torquay. Papa heard them come back a little after 12 o'clock. The Ostler drove it, he is the best manager of horses. They went at that time because they only shut the shop at 5 o'clock and that only once a week.

Went for a walk and came up a sort of wood which I went in. It looked like an ill-kept garden. When I went on a little, I came to a sort of house, very bare and cold. In front there were 17 windows and a door. The door was small and had no porch and on the other side 13 windows and the same sort of door. I did not much like the look of the house so I walked on and came (in the Wood) to six or seven mounds, just like graves, with grass growing over them. I forgot to say that I only saw one blind in all the windows and no curtains of any sort. Emily says perhaps it is the Barrachs' or Bowdens' house.

May 12ᵗʰ 1874 Tuesday
Went up to see the cattle fair. It was very poor. Went to the Planes to see the horse fair. Once one of the horses stood on its hind legs and seven or eight more followed the example. All the people ran away shrieking and screaming and howling, and there were two ladies and gentlemen in a gig. One lady screamed and hid her face and would have got out while the whole thing was on the move, only they would not let her.

May 15ᵗʰ 1874 Saturday
After breakfast went out on the Pier at Penzance. Saw them loading the Scilly steamer with chairs, bread, sugar, meat and all sorts of things. There were also about two dozen passengers. The wind was coming from the sea and it was rather rough. At high tide the water splashed against the embankment and sent the spray right over it. Later walked to Newlyn. There were crowds of fishermen basketing thousands of mackerel. There were about 60 ships with them, and one I heard had two thousand.

May 18ᵗʰ 1874
I forgot to say that till 12 o'clock on Saturday night and after, I was kept awake by carts constantly going by with mackerel packed in baskets coming from Newlyn and a fishing town about half-a-mile distant and going to the railway station, and again I was woken on Sunday morning by them, and while I was dressing eight different carts went by. They go full and come back empty. On inquiring I found that they ran all night and they kept on till one or two o'clock midday on Sunday.

Went to the railway station and got in for Marazian Road station, that being the nearest station to St.Michael's Mount where we were going. When we got to Penzance Station the whole of the yard was full with fish baskets, some empty and some full, and they were packing them away as fast as they could. We got out at Marazian Road station and walked to Marazian about half a mile, then we walked about Marazian town, it is quite a small village. Then we walked across to St. Michael's Mount which

---

96   James Rose, draper

you can do at low water.

When we got to the Mount we walked straight up to the top where we went into it. The doorway is very low. We first had to sign our names in a book and then the woman showed us round. She had a very squeaky shrill voice. The rooms are nicely furnished. The dining hall was large and the drawing room very pretty. We went into the chapel. There was a very good organ and they showed us the way down to a vault. They discovered an uncoffined body in it, but papa would not go down. Then went up the steeple. It was a small spiral staircase. It was so narrow that it touched the sides and so low that I had to stoop. Afterwards Papa came up. He took a very long time in going down. I went first and was down two or three minutes before Papa. He somehow sprained his leg and he felt it for days afterwards. Then we sat on the grass and had our lunch and then walked home along the sands.

Tuesday 19th 1874

Went down to the boat, the same boat that belonged to the Baths and had a very nice man. On coming back I took an oar a little. Had dinner, after dinner went to the boat again. We had a fishing line. I took an oar. We caught three whiting pollock.

Wednesday 20th 1874

It was too rough to go on the water so went to see after a carriage to take us to Lagan Stone and Lands End. Got a very nice carriage and drove off. It was very dusty and exceedingly windy. We stopped at an Inn called *"The Lagan Inn"* about half-a-mile from the Stone and we had a guide to take us. It was exceedingly windy. The Stone is close to the sea and a pile of stones called Castle Treren and very hard to get at. The guide said it was left for the young gentlemen to get to it, and very few of these did. I went up. You have to climb up nearly perpendicular rocks, and I also moved the Stone by myself. It weighs between 70 and 80 tonnes.

Then we walked back, you had to sit down and somehow slither down. When we got to the Inn, we took the carriage and drove to Land's End. It was a great deal more windy there and you had quite to struggle to get along and one time when I was turning a corner the wind took me and carried me some feet to one side. The wind being from the land, you had to take care you did not get blown off the cliffs into the sea. The coast was very pretty and there were a great many ships. Papa sat in a carriage before the horse was put in and the wind was so strong that it moved the carriage nearly a foot uphill, then it rolled back. Coming home the wind and dust was so strong that we had to go some of the way with our eyes shut. At last we got home, our clothes quite brown from the dust and our faces black as if we had been packing in the coalhole.

21st 1874 Thursday

Today was rather cloudy and the sea was rather rough. I went on the St.Ives road and on coming back happened to find out the cattle market, there were pigs and cows. The pigs made an awful noise It rained in the afternoon and the sea got rougher. After tea the sea got quite rough. We saw the ships come into harbour and the Scilly Steamer came. We heard afterwards that it had terrible weather on the voyage.

May 23rd 1874 Saturday

It was so nice and calm that I went to order the large boat with sails. We got along very slowly as there was very little wind and it got so hot that we came back. After dinner walked to Newlyn. After tea, went out in a boat fishing but caught no fish. We saw hundreds of fishing ships coming in that had been out all the week near Scilly.

May 24th 1874 Sunday

Went to a Baptist chapel. It was a very grandly decorated place but small. The men singers were whispering and playing nearly all the time. The chapel is in the same street as St. Paul's Church, on the same side, not so far up After dinner walked to Paul, a village about two miles and a half off through Newlyn. There is a very old church there. Very low but large. There were a great many people about, and there was a christening going on so I saw the parson, an old man. I saw in the churchyard the name of the last old woman who spoke the old Cornish language. She died about 1765.

The fishermen had been busy all the day carrying the fish and Saturday night too. After tea went to St. Mary's, the large new church. We were put in one of the corporation pews, the singers being just in front of us. They all had their white night gowns. The parson did not intone. We had a very bad sermon from a man with a very bad temper. He had very thin lips and gnawed his nails. Came home, went on the esplanade, there were some two or three thousand people walking up and down.

May 25th 1874 Monday

Breakfast at half past seven, as we were going up by the coach at 8 o'clock to the Lizard. The coach came up to the house so we had nowhere to walk. It came empty with four horses but gradually filled as we went along the town. It looked very funny everybody opening their shutters and some getting dressed. We went on to Helston where we had to change coaches as the one we went in went on to Falmouth. It was Helston fair and the street was filling with shows etc. We were the only two that went on to the Lizard. We got there about 12. It was 24 miles altogether. We stopped at the hotel and walked to Lizard Point and saw the lighthouses.

There had a week or two before been a wreck of a vessel of 400 tonnes laden with corn. It was in a fog, the sea was quite calm and the men only just saved their lives. We saw them carrying away the wreck. It was very fine and hot and we had our lunch which we took with us. We walked about a little then came back and found we had not seen the very best thing which is Kynance Cove. We went into one of the shops where they sell the serpentine stone and he told us all about the place. The serpentine stone is found in great plenty there. We got a few things, had tea at the hotel and came away in the coach with two other gentlemen. When we got to Helston, which is 11 miles from the Lizard, we found the town crowded and the coach that we came back in; we had about 30, left seven behind. The horses could only just drag us up the hills and he kept on putting out and taking in the whole way. We got to Penzance about 20 to 10 0 clock.

May 27th 1874 Wednesday

After dinner a sort of falling fog came and thick steam like smoke came from the asphalt path, and looked very funny. It was because it was hot from the sun. Went out, saw the guide steamer in. It was filled with fish. It was built for a tugboat and is hired in the fishing time to carry the fish from the Lizard. I inquired what time it started because we thought of going on Thursday. He said it started at 5 o'clock. After tea went out, saw the Queen Steamer in, which is a better and larger steamer, also filled with fish, mostly mackerel. I will say that we are very comfortable here, and I should recommend anybody. Here is the address:- Miss Norton, The Baths, Esplanade, Penzance. We have a room on the first floor looking over onto the sea. In rough weather the waves go right over the house.

May 28th 1874 Thursday

After dinner went to the market when butter was going at 11d per pound. There is a market on Tuesdays, Thursdays and Saturdays. Then went down to the steamer the Guide; it had just brought 900 baskets of fish in. Had tea abd got ready to go to the steamer. It did not start till a quarter past. There were two other gentlemen on board with us, young clerks from Manchester on a holiday trip. It was nice and smooth when we started and a strong wind but as we got to move out it got rougher, and as we got to the Lands End there was what they call a race to tide meeting. It was very rough and we could see the waves coming in over the fore part of the boat and washed the deck and good many others did the same. We had to stand on the bridge or sit on the fish baskets all the time. We saw the Lands End Wolf Rocks, Bishop and Scilly light houses alight at once, all but Land's End were revolving lights. The Wolf Rock is white and red. We did not see more than half a dozen ships all the way. About half past eight they lit the ship's lights. The two compass lights put a white light on the fore-mast and a green one the right paddle and box, and a red one on the other.

We got to St Mary's about half past 10; it is very hard to get in, as there are so many rocks. The harbour smelt very badly of fish. When we got out of the boat a man asked us if we should like to have a boat the next day. We said we should call at 10 next morning. We went to Tregarthen's Hotel, the principal one and they showed us a room with two beds in it very nicely furnished. When we came down to the harbour we saw the two that came and the steamer were there.

May 29th 1874 Friday

Two other men had breakfast with us. We heard afterwards that they were under-writers to wrecks. After breakfast went down to the pier and got a boat to go to the island of Tresco because there were some very beautiful gardens there belonging to the Governor of the islands. We sailed over in about 10 minutes. When we got there we went to the Lodge and the head gardener was there and showed us around. We saw a great many flowers in bloom, and a mush plant standing from eight to 10ft high, and a camphor plant about 6 ft high, and a plant about a foot high with a flower about eight inches long and six wide, the shape of a pig's ear and it smells like bad meat. It looks just like a real pig's ear. It had just opened that morning and was covered with flies and the gardener said in a few days it would be covered with maggots. You could smell it yards off and we also saw many houseplants growing outdoors in great plenty.

We went to one of the hills on the island and had a very fine view of nearly all the islands. We had to row back as the wind was against us and it took us nearly an hour and a half. Had dinner, with the two gentleman we came with. They intended to have gone that morning but the steamer did not go, as there was no fish to carry. After dinner we all went to town to see a sale by auction of the things from one of the wrecks. It was carried on in a very grand style. There was a railing put round to keep the people from the auctioneer. All the things went very dear. We walked round Penannis point. The rocks were very beautiful. After tea went to the citadel and around by the fortifications.

June 2nd 1874 Tuesday
Saw some caravans for the fair which was to be on Thursday and last three days.

June 3rd 1874 Wednesday
Saw a lot more caravans in Days Menagerie,[97] performing dogs, chief Jacks in great quantities. After tea went to Menagerie. It was not small. Then to the performing dogs which was very good. There was an omnibus drawn by two dogs full of Mouchie and a dog dressed up as a milkman with two pails walking on its hind legs and lots more. Quite worth seeing.

June 4th Thursday
After breakfast finished packing. Went and had a look at the fair. I went in to Sanders's Animated Waxworks. After dinner the bus came and we went off to the station. When we got to Falmouth we took a cab to drive about for apartments. The first place we went to was a large house and rather dirty. There are no houses at all close to the sea and very little beach. We went to other houses but did not suit us altogether. The last house they showed us had a very nice sitting room with a fine view and two nice bedrooms. When Papa asked the charge she said if we came for one week it would be more than if we came for several. For one week 16 shillings a week including everything. We thought it was too cheap to be good so we did not take them. We were so disappointed with the place that we went to the hotel to go on by the train. The man took us to the Falmouth Hotel, the very best and near the sea. We ordered tea then went round Pendennis point and had a good view of the harbour.

---

97 Travelling menagerie, also known as the "beast show" or "travelling zoo". Popular in Victorian times. Day's menagerie contained a collection of 500 animals including lions, tigers, leopards, bears, hyenas, pack of wild wolves, ostriches, pelicans, vultures and other animals. Oxford Chronicle 24th September 1889

June 5th 1874 Friday

Went to the station. Had to change at Truro. The train was very full and we had not to change at Plymouth. Just as we passed Totnes, about two miles out to the station, we saw where an accident had been. A long truck train with two engines, one of the trucks ran off the line and dragged two of the engines. We saw the truck all smashed and the engine with the funnel broken off and the sides smashed in. The other engine was not damaged. We got to Dawlish about four and got apartments at 3 Marine Parade with the railway between us and the beach. The trains made a great noise at night and disturbed Papa as he slept in the front. I slept in the back and did not hear them. There was only the road between us and the rail. Went to the beach and saw them draw the fishnets in. Not many fish. There are about 1000 militia here for a month. They live in a camp.

June 6th Saturday

After breakfast went with Papa and got a boat and we went out and fished for dabs. We caught three very fine ones. I caught two at once.

June 9th 1874 Tuesday

It was very hot, so after breakfast went and got a straw hat and put on my puggaree. We had a boat and went out fishing but it was so hot and disagreeable so we came in. We got some very nice strawberries for 5d. a pint and had them every day after dinner.

June 12th 1874 Friday

I was just coming into breakfast when Papa showed me a letter saying Mama was not at all well so we decided to go to Windsor.

(Note from A.W.H. Lomas to say that several pages removed; *"during this period they moved to Buxton and ran the hotel; later to become The Hydro. They had an organ and HRP played it for services"*)

January 17th 1876 Monday

After breakfast went a walk with Harry. Unpacked an old box that had not been undone since it had come from Totnes. Found in it the old crocodile and a lot of books. Afterwards unpacked two of our Chinese boxes in Papa's room.

January 18th Tuesday

Went a walk with Harry. After dinner we went down to the Pavilion to see them skating on wheel skates.[98] It was the second day it had been opened. Harry Stamper was there making a great fool of himself. Waited for about an hour and then I tried. I felt very funny on them. At first my feet kept running away from me. I tumbled down five times. Walter tried too and he tumbled down as well. Harry said he would not

---

98 See Appendix 3

make such full of himself. He said he did it at Oxford. We all had to leave off at 5 o'clock.

January 19th 1876 Wednesday

Went down to the skating and met Harry, the Shiptons,[99] the Pilkingtons[100] and others. I skated for an hour and only fell down once and that was when I was pushed down.

January 20th 1876 Thursday

Went down to the Pavilion to skate. Did not fall down. After tea took the Pilkingtons up to my room to show them my egg shells and book.

January 21st 1876 Friday

Went skating, was pushed down once. Later the Pilkingtons came up to my room and we had a game of whist.

January 22nd 1876 Saturday

Went a walk with the Pilkingtons and we tried some skates from Furnesses with the wheels in a line. They were very common ones. Went skating all the afternoon. It was very full. I was knocked down three times.

January 23rd 1876 Sunday

Played the hymns. There were very few to service. After dinner went to Fairfield church. After service, walked with Mr. Pettit, Maude Harry Hunter and Miss Flickers to Mr Pettit's house. There saw Mrs. P and the baby. Came home, had tea, after tea played the service.

January 25th 1876 Tuesday

Was down early to see the Pilkington's off.

January 26th Wednesday

Went down skating. Met Mr.Pettit who invited me to a game of whist after tea. played till 9 o'clock.

January 27th 1876 Thursday

Went up to Mr. Pettit's to study.[101]

January 30th 1876 Sunday

I had a little cold so I did not go out. At 3 o'clock went across to 42 to read to Mama

---

99 Local medical family
100 Local legal family
101 Mr Pettit ran a school which also had boarders

who was not very well. Had tea there. Was a very good evening congregation.[102]

January 31st 1876 Monday

Took Jesse, my big dog, down to the billiard room to show Mr. Henderson. He said it was worth a good deal.

February 1st 1876 Tuesday

Went with Mr. Goldring to the Pavilion rink, but we found it was for ladies only in the morning so he took a pair of skates home to try them and he tried them in the yard. Then we went down and had a game of billiards at St Anne's. He gave me some points and I beat him. After dinner we went down rinking for two hours. Tomkinson being at Manchester and Newbald looking after the skates, we went down the two ends which was very jolly. I managed from one end to the other in a quarter of a minute. Later watched them skating from Kenilworth[103] window with an opera glass. I could see easily who was there.

February 2nd 1876 Wednesday

Mr Pettit called, went out for a walk. After dinner went down rinking and met the Pettit's children and boarders and had a very pleasant rinking for two hours. After tea there was a prayer meeting and I had to pray and some of them prayed awfully loud. Afterwards went into the drawing room and showed Mrs. Hardwick my stamp album. She was very much pleased with it.

February 3rd 1876 Thursday

At 12 went to the Pavilion to read the papers. Later sat up in Kenilworth watching them rinking. Brought Reggie Matthews to tea. Showed him my eggs. After tea went down rinking for two hours. It was very rough but not too hot.

February 4th 1876 Friday

Moved all the ornaments in my room as it was going to be thoroughly cleaned, and about 12 o'clock Martin came up and took the carpet up and carried my bookcase down stairs, and Fanny came about 1 o'clock to wash it. After dinner I went up and painted my conservatory and about 5 o'clock the men came up and put the carpet down again. Had tea, after, brought some of the things back.

February 5th 1876 Saturday

I went down to the Pavilion to ask the man what he would charge if I took my own skates and he said 6d. and I might skate as long as I liked, so I came home and in about five minutes Lawrence came with the bookcase. He said he was sure it would not go in and I said it would. We put it up and it just touched the ceiling and looked very

---

102 At Malvern House
103 Probably an extension at Malvern House

handsome. Then I had my old bookcase brought up and I used the top for old china. Put a few of my books in. After dinner old Isaac would come and help me put the rest in.

February 8th 1876 Tuesday

Went up to 33 to watch old Isaac. She first came out with a shovel of ashes and looked first one way and then the other, then carried them into the next room. Then she came out with coals, then she took matches and lit the gas in that room, then went on to the next, lit the gas and brought out as many coals as she could carry in her hands.

At supper there was a new gentleman, a Reverand Chapman. Jane, Alice's sister, asked him what he would like, so he said, "*a pint of Bass's pale ale*", so Jane grinned and looked up at Eliza who was standing by and when she asked what it was Jane said "*is he all as he ought to be?*"

February 9th Wednesday 1876

Rose's[104] man came and put a pane of glass in my bookcase.

February 11th 1876 Friday

Made arrangements to send Old Isaac a Valentine, a little box with coals in and written on paper "*A preventative against heat*", and also a little box inside the other with "*For ashes*" instead of "*Grate next door*" written on it. After supper read "*Lena Rivers*" by Mary J. Holmes.

February 13th 1976 Sunday

After tea chose the hymns. After service sat in the drawing room. Dr. Lyster was denouncing the Roman Catholic priests and Mrs. Ferguson and Mr. Chapman were for them. Mr. Chapman was very high church but he had been a Methodist. He was nasty and quizzing. I disliked him very much.

February 14th 1876 Monday

Had one nasty Valentine about "*Pleasures to come*" from all the servants. Eliza, a 4 /6 one from Nadin and a doll dressed in an old duster and all blacked supposed to be her six months after she has become Mrs. Nadin, which came from me, Evans and cook.

February 15th 1876 Tuesday

Looked at all Valentines. After dinner saw Lawrence about dog fancier's address; Mr Cuss, Whittle House, Bradford, Manchester.

February 19th 1876 Saturday

Played duets with Mrs. Hayes till half past 12 o'clock. Rinked for an hour, came home, had dinner. After dinner rinked for two hours, learnt to go on two front, two back or

---

104 Local plumber

any two wheels perfectly and backwards a little. Mr. Hayes was there, he trembled all over while skating.

February 25th 1876 Friday

The organ man came about 10 o'clock. We sent for Lawrence and began moving the organ. I hardly ever saw anything so dirty. Helped him all the afternoon, played to him.

February 26th 1876 Saturday

Helped the organ man, and about dinnertime he began to tune it. Finished tuning about 4 o'clock and went back by the next train. Mrs. Pettit called and tried the organ. In trying it afterwards, found notes out of tune so I had to have the front taken down again.

March 2nd 1876 Thursday

Repotted about three dozen plants and have only lost seven out of over 100.

March 3rd 1876 Friday

Went down to Hully's etc. Rinked for an hour, had tea, sat in the drawing room till Papa came back. He brought me Uncle's likeness and one of Willie's Masonic breast frills and three silk handkerchiefs.

March 4th 1876 Saturday

Lawrence came with the organ curtain and Sturges to put the curtain up. Rinked for two hours and brought a pair of skates home. Had tea, played duets with Miss Best and about half past eight went to No.6 and took up the carpet and skated till supper. After supper skated half an hour more.

March 7th 1876 Tuesday

Went to put plants in No. 7.

March 13th 1876 Monday

Lawrence was here and did sundry little things. Also Airman James was here putting up shutter in dining hall. F Bowland has been very ill. James and Martin changed the drawers from No.2 to my room, 22.

March 14th 1876 Tuesday

Boiled dusters and made toffee. Helped Miss Isaacs to move her things as the room was going to be papered etc. the next day.

March 16th 1876 Thursday

Chapman was here and about 11 o'clock sent one of the men down to paint my bedroom. My bedroom being finished, I helped Sarah move the bed into No.20 as the room smelt too much to sleep in. Chapman finished Miss Isaacs's room. (Mrs. Ferguson quarrel.)

March 18th 1876 Saturday
Lawrence brought my new hearthrug – green. Then Chapman came and finished the window and painted the inside of one of my cupboards. He left me some paint to do the other with. Mr. Pettit came with May and Harry Hunter who had come back from Oxford that morning. My room smelt of paint so that they would not stay. I painted the other cupboard.

March 20th 1876 Monday
Said goodbye to Fanny, my housemaid, who was leaving to be married. Slept in Windsor.[105]

March 23rd 1876 Thursday
Went to Hutchenson sale in Spring Gardens, most things went very cheaply. I bought a picture for 10d.

March 24th 1876 Friday
Went down to Hutchinson's sale and bought three Wedgewood jars with some other little things.

March 25th 1876 Saturday
Looked over and watered the plants. Went to a sale at Fairfield but there was nothing there nice but a cage of birds and that was very dear.

March 28th 1876 Tuesday
Moved all my plants from 7 to 18, as 7 was engaged for Thursday.

March 29th 1876 Wednesday
Studied from 10 till 12. Pottered about, rinked for an hour. Took a great fancy to two boys who had sealskin caps with two elder sisters and younger brothers.

March 30th 1876 Thursday
Studied from 10 till 12. Played, rinked for an hour. Made acquaintance with the two boys I had taken a fancy to. They are very nice.

March 31st Friday.
After dinner rinked for two hours. Those boys were not there.

---

105 Another extension at Malvern House

Milligan's, Buxton
Courtesy of Derbyshire Local Studies and www.picturethepast.org.uk

April 1st 1876 Saturday

I went to the cattle market and saw those two boys were there with their Mama and sisters, but they did not seen me. Had dinner, afterwards rinked for an hour. Those two boys were there, I went off when they did and and strolled about the town. After tea went down to the Pavilion and into the Reading Room. The two boys, their name was Hall, soon came by and I walked about with them till we met the Stampers. Willie was very rude. Then met Tomlinson who had some books to sell called "*Rinks and Rollers*", so I bought one.

April 2nd 1876 Sunday

Mama played for service so I went to St John's. Got into our pew and took Milligans[106] shopkeeper's case. The prayers were gabbled awfully by the new young curate and the sermon, 9 minutes and a half, by Eddy. After dinner met the two Halls as I arranged at the Old Hall and went for a walk down the Bakewell Road which we enjoyed very much.

April 3rd 1876 Monday

Went to the Gardens and met those two boys and we pottered about. Had dinner, afterwards met them again and walked up by Bishop Spencer's House[107] and the Manchester Road.

April 4th 1876 Tuesday

Late for breakfast. Afterwards studied for two hours. Met the Halls at the Pavilion. Had dinner, after dinner went a walk with them along the brook at the foot of Fairfield Church Hill. Came in had tea, after tea went with the Pilkingtons to the Spelling Bee at the Court House. The younger Hall, Tom, was there. It was very full and amusing. After he was turned out he came and sat by me. Came home, had supper with the Pilkingtons and went to bed.

April 5th 1876 Wednesday

Met the Halls at the Pavilion. Went a walk along the brook by the new Mortar mill and brickfield. We went up it a good way, passed where they were making a railway, to a small plantation and on coming back found a crow which had not been dead long. I cut off the best wing and brought it home. Went with them to their house, Hawthorn Villa,[108] and saw Pilkingtons coming down the road so I walked home with them. After tea met the Halls at the Pavilion and about half-past 7 o'clock brought them to my room, then took them down to show them the organ, then went to the Pavilion again.

---

106 Haberdashers in Spring Gardens. Mr Milligan was the leading draper in the town
107 Famous Bishop of Madras living at a large house around Edgemoor on what is now Bishop's Lane
108 Private lodging house at St John's Road

April 6th 1876 Thursday

The Halls came and as Charlie's eye was worse, we took him to Lomas the surgeon,[109] who said he had had a blow on it and gave me some stuff to bathe it with, and also said he might lose the sight of that eye. After tea the Halls came up and we all put our catapults to rights as we were going out shooting the next day. About eight went to the gardens and saw them home at 9 o'clock.

April 7th 1876 Friday

At 10 o'clock the Halls came and we took lunch to go out. For the first, we went by the Palace Hotel and along the brook by the new Mortar mill and when we had gone about a mile we thought we heard the fire bell at Fairfield, so we went straight across to it and found it was only a bell for the litany. So having come so far we took a road which led us into the Bakewell road taking us into it just by the old saw mill.

We got there about 12 o'clock, then went down the road and about 10 o'clock, just as we came to a waterfall, we went up the hill a little into the wood and had our lunches. Then we started on and just at the bottom of the long hill we turned to the left and went by the river having it on our left till we came to a long wooden bridge which we went across and there were houses that side.

We went along with the river to our right all the way but a very little. I do not think I ever saw anything so beautiful as the rocks were so very grand. The day was very warm and cloudless. About half past 3 o'clock we came to Millers Dale and walked through the town and got to the station from the other side. We stayed at a farmhouse half way to have a glass of milk, which was very nice. We got to the station at 4 o'clock and found we had to wait nearly an hour and a half so we went and laid down on the grass outside.

While we were lying there we saw Miss Buckles and Miss Thompson with walking sticks who been there for the day. When we went into the station Miss Shipton (Mrs. Mitchell) was there and borrowed a threepenny bit off me for a porter. Our train was very late. We got into the same carriage as Mr. Ferguson. We took just three and a half minutes running down to Buxton. The Halls came and had tea in my room and afterwards we had a game of whist and about 8 o'clock went down to the Gardens.

April 8th 1876 Saturday

The Halls said they were going to Monsal Dale by train and walk home from there to Millers Dale. They wanted me to go but I was very tired so I did not go. About 12 o'clock I went and sat in the Gardens. It was very hot, being over 60 out of doors. At 5 o'clock went to meet the Halls who were coming by the half past five train. Walked home with them and arranged to meet them at 7 o'clock, as there was the Band benefit concert. We went to the concert which was very poor. The Halls left about 9 o'clock and I left at half past. The Pilkingtons were there and so were the Stampers.[110]

---

109 Walter Lomas, veterinary surgeon and farmer
110 Father John GH Stamper, Vicar of Burbage

The dog's eye is no better and I think he is sure to lose the sight of it.

April 10th 1876 Monday

About 11 o'clock went to the Pavilion. There was snow on the ground and it was very cold. Met the Halls there. They were tuning Adams's[111] piano as he was going to begin with the season band that day. Harry Hunter came and brought me the second volume of Pucket which is from Robins library. We went down to the Pavilion, there Adams was having a practice with the new band. We went down to the Orangery, then we went to the Halls where I left them. After tea it snowed very hard so I went and sat in the drawing room where we had a spirited debate about rinking. I said the head was of so much use.

April 11th 1876 Tuesday

Thick snow on the ground. Went to the Pavilion where I met the Halls and Harry Hunter. Sat there for a little, then went home. After dinner the Halls came and a had a game of bezique with the older one while the other went turning out my eggs. About 4 we went out down Spring Gardens and I went into the new sweetshop. Went with the Halls to their house, then after tea went to the Pavilion and read in Blackwood's Magazine a piece called "1895" which was very good. Afterwards met Mr. Fletcher junior, he was staying at Malvern House. Broke dining room glass door.

April 12th 1876 Wednesday

11 o'clock the Halls came and we went down with Papa to Hulbys. Then myself and the Halls went to the Gardens; the Pavilion was very hot and outside very cold. The Halls asked me to go there to tea tonight. Saw the Halls home then came back and heard Adams and the violinist who played a duet, which was very nice indeed. Mr. Poulter come, and Mr. and Mrs. Master and Miss Alexander .

After dinner Goddard[112] came and took away part of my musical box to mend it. Then the Halls came and I had a game of bezique with the elder. Then went down the town. Went to their house and was introduced to Mrs. and the two Miss Hall's and Miss Gladstone, the governess. The house smelled awfully of gas. There was something wrong with the meter. I played with Miss Hall. Then I had to leave as I was going to have an organ practice at 7 o'clock. The two Halls came with me. We had a very good practice. Evans Rowland and Wright were there and we finished at half past 8 o'clock. The Halls sing very nicely. Then we went to the Pavilion where I looked at the Illustrateds, then I walked home with the Halls.

April 13th 1876 Thursday

Had a game of Le Grasse with Arthur Pilkington and we kept up 347. The Halls came and we had a game of whist and bezique and they stayed to dinner as it was snowing

---

111 Conductor of the Pavilion Gardens Band
112 Fredk. J Goddard, professor of music

hard and there was three inches of snow on the ground. After dinner Mr. Jones came with his curtains and about 4 o'clock we went up to his sale room where I bought four very old-fashioned salt spoons and looked at many other things. Then went down to Bright's.[113] Came in, played at races. I showed John Hall my book "*The A of F*" and when we were at the sale we had both dogs and John was very green. The Halls left at 9.

April 14th 1876 Friday

Went up in my room and wrote, and read "*Pucket*". We were just 24 for dinner and one upstairs. After dinner the Halls came and we went out to the Pavilion. It was very full and so was the reading room. Met Miss Hall, then went down and saw some men playing bells at the Crescent. Then came in, it was awfully cold. We played Goose and rules. Had tea, the Halls staying after tea. At 9 o'clock we had supper, then I walked home with them. There was no snow left and it was quite warm.

April 15th 1876 Saturday

The Halls came, then we went to see Harry Hunter at Fairfield to fetch the third volume of "*Pucket*". Today is my birthday. I am 17 years old.

April 16th 1876 Sunday

We were 34 for dinner. Afterwards we went out for a walk up Solomon's Temple way and home by the quarries. We met Tomkinson, the skate man, who had just found a stalactite which he gave us. We carried it a little way then hid it, as it was too heavy to carry home. Came in, chained up the dog. Saw Miss Isaacs promenading. We went to the Halls to tea. Mrs. Hall was away and the governess, so we were a small party.

April 17th 1876 Monday

The Halls came and we went down to the Royal and had a drive in a carriage down the Bakewell road. Then came back and fetched Mama. Came back again, then walked with the Halls to their house. Then the Halls came again and we fetched Jesse[114] in and sat about till teatime. They came down to tea, after I went out and Tom Hall fell over Jesse and cut his hands badly. I plastered his wounds up and had a game of bezique. Then they went home I with them. They were singing in the Pavilion when I passed.

April 18th 1876 Tuesday

Had a letter from Aunt Emily with a birthday present. A very nice gold pencil case. Then went down the town with the Halls. Took my book back and paid sundry bills. The Halls stayed for dinner, after dinner went out down the town again and got another book to take with me. Had a game of bezique with John then walked home with them. Met the Stampers and said goodbye to Harry as he was going back to

---

113 Shop in Crescent
114 HRP's second dog

Cambridge. Saw a funny thing in the road with a fire at each side. Packed as I was going to Windsor tomorrow.

April 19ᵗʰ 1876 Wednesday

The Halls came and helped me to pack. I said goodbye to Miss Atkins. I said I supposed she would be gone when I came back. Then we walked down calling at Robins for a book, then to the station were the Halls bid a very sorrowful goodbye. Between Buxton and London we only stopped at six stations. At one time going an hour and a half without stopping. We stopped at Millers Dale, Derby, Trent, Leicester, Wigston, Luton. We got to London only three minutes late. Then drove across and got to Windsor at 5 o'clock. We were met by Uncle John and Cousin Alfred. Walked home and met Grandmama.

April 21ˢᵗ 1876 Friday

Breakfast at half-past 7 o'clock as we were going to Chatham. We went by the 8 o'clock train and left Papa to go about 10 o'clock, only he was going to have his photo taken. We got there about 11 then we went round to see the property. First we went to Hawling and saw the church and one baker's shop. We then came back and went about Chatham. Then we went to the Sun Hotel and had dinner about 3. Fish, soup, foul, tart and cheese.

Then we went a walk eight miles on the Luton Road. Then we came back and got ready and went call upon Uncle John Baker.[115] When we got there they were at dinner. They live at Nile Terrace, Rochester. When they had finished dinner we went in and had desert. There was John Baker, his son Frederick, and three daughters. When we had finished desert they brought very strong coffee. Then we went into the drawing room and they made tea. They had some nice silver but the tea service was very poor. There were some nice Indian things and old silver in the drawing room. The middle sister sang, then I played a very grand piano.

April 22ⁿᵈ 1876 Saturday

Had face ache. Mr. Watchouse came and then the fly, then we drove to Gillingham. It was a beautiful day. We went over all the property. There are 16 acres of cherry orchard and it was in full bloom, a beautiful sight as if they were covered with snow. There are over 30 houses altogether. We saw all the convicts working at making a new bridge. We got home about 12 o'clock. They have an old organ in the coffee room at the Sun, which I tried there. Went up to Uncle Baker's for lunch. We had fillets, cold beef, tartlets and apple jelly which was very nice and made of Normandy pippins.

We started from there for the 2.20 train where we saw a very nice engine driver who asked us if we should like to go in the engine, so we got on at the next station and got out at the third afterwards. It was very nice. We went sixty miles an hour. The man told me all sorts of things about the engine. He had been driving six years and was 27

---

115 Matilda Lomas's brother

years old. When we got to Paddington we had to wait half-an-hour and we got to Windsor a little after 6 o'clock. The Queen was coming in about an hour, home from Germany. But I was too tired to go and see her.

April 23rd 1876 Sunday

Went into the conservatory and started for All Saints Church. We had a very poor sermon and had music afterwards. After dinner Alfred and I went to St. George's. We got a seat in the front row of the middle. Princess Christian was there with one or two naval knights. We had a beautiful anthem. There was a very nice looking young fellow stood in front of me. After tea Alfred and I went to Trinity. We waited a few minutes and Uncle and Aunt Bulteel came so we went into their pew. The anthem was very poor and the Church not very full. One of the minor canons of St George's preached. Walked home with Aunt, then walked round Clewer.

April 24th 1876 Monday

About half-past 10 o'clock went to my Aunt's as we were to go for a drive that morning. When we got there we found William the coachman had got a bad cold so we could not go. We sat there till 10 o'clock then we went in the town and had dinner at 2 o'clock. After dinner went for a walk and we made up our minds to go to a negro entertainment at the theatre. It was to begin at 8 o'clock. We were there by half-past seven. It was very full and we did not get out till 12 o'clock. There were some very good songs and a play at the end and also a piece called "*Shedadle*".

April 25th 1876 Tuesday

Went down to Hills and Saunders to have my likeness taken. It was a very hot day. I had it taken 10 times. Had a walk across the Thames and up the opposite bank. Came in, and found a letter from Dr. Harper asking me to go up there to tea on Wednesday night.

April 26th 1876 Wednesday

At half past 10 o'clock we went up to my Aunt's as I was to have a drive. Alfred went on the box. We went in the park and by Prince Christian's house. After dinner Alfred and I went up to Aunt's to have a game of croquet. It was the first game that had been played upon that lawn. I won. Then I went to the Harpers and had tea. Afterwards the doctor left and they had prayers. Then I had three games of chess with Jimmy and won the last two.

April 27th 1876 Thursday

We went out to get an order to see the memorial chapel but we could not get one till 11 o'clock, so we went to Laytons to have an ice. First got our ticket, then the relief guard came up played by the bagpipe and they played some very nice pieces. Then we went into the chapel. It is very fine indeed, especially the figures of life and death, one each side of the door. There were a great many people. There was one very fine picture at the right of the communion table, a light angle on a dark green. There are also the heads of all the Royal Family. After tea started for the concert at St. Mark's. We got there a nice place in the gallery. It was awfully full. A little before it was going to begin I went back for the opera glasses with which we saw beautifully. They sang the whole of the Elijah, about 120 singers, and Sir George Ely leading.

Everybody there was in full dress. The Princesses Christian and Beatrix were there.

April 28th 1876 Friday

Saw the Royal Stables. There are between 90 and a hundred horses altogether. Everything kept in beautiful order. We also saw the Queen go for a walk with Princess Beatrix in the private park. After tea I went for a walk in the Long Walk by moonlight. It was beautiful. forgot to say last Thursday, as we were at tea, the Queen drove by with a very broad brimmed straw hat and grinning tremendously.

April 30th 1876 Sunday

The Foot Guards went by at 9 o'clock to have an early service, as the Life Guards' band was to play for the 11 o'clock service and it was expected there would be a great many. After breakfast went up to Uncle's and Aunt said she had a postcard saying I might go to the organ gallery at the Chapel Royal. Then we started for Trinity, it was very full, two rows of chairs up the middle aisle and a great many standing. The band played *"Eiyius anumuni"* first. They read the Psalms but it accompanied the chants and the hymns. One hymn was *"Onward Christian soldiers"* which they joined in very heartily. Then Mr Robins preached a sermon, he is very common looking, and his father is an auctioneer. The sermon was very peculiar. He accused people in the town of accusing him of speaking honeyed words to the soldiers. He also referred to them following Christ's banner. Then they played while the collection was going on a very loud piece but they did not use the drums.

We went to Aunt's and had dinner at quarter past 10 o'clock. Then I went to Grandmama's and had another dinner, mutton at one and lamb at the other. I went to the organ gallery where I met Sir George Ely the organist and we had a very pleasant talk. He played the service very nicely. Brought out the thunder beautifully in the Psalms and played the Coronation Anthem from *"Zadoc the Priest"*. There are between 40 and 50 stops in the organ and three rows of keys. Some of the pedal pipes are 2 ft square.

I forgot to say I saw the Abyssinian King's son there with Lady Bidddolf. He is quite a dark colour with greying hair. Then Uncle John Bulteel came and I went to the old church and got a seat in the front row of the gallery. Had a good sermon from an old man. Later went down to the kitchen to catch black beetles[116] which we did every

---

116 Amongst the vermin which infested Victorian houses were black beetles, fleas and even crickets. If the struggle against them was not waged with commitment, they would "multiply till the kitchen floor at night palpitates with a living carpet, and in time the beetles would collect in corners of the kitchen ceiling, and hanging to one another by their claws, would form huge bunches or swarms like bees towards evening and as night closed in, swarthy individuals would drop singly on to the floor, or head, or food…" *The Victorian House* Judith Flanders Harper Perennial 2003 p76

night. We got a bowl of water and picked them up and put them in. They would not go in the traps properly. I forgot to say that on Monday last Alfred and I went to an old theatre which was used for rinking and we had a try but the skates were very bad and I could not manage it at all.

May 1st 1876 Monday

Got to Stokes about 4 o'clock where I heard I was to come for lessons on Tuesday, Wednesday, and Thursday.

May 2nd 1876 Tuesday

Went by the 9 o'clock train with Harry Bulteel to go to the Royal Academy. It was very full when we got there at quarter to 11 o'clock and you could hardly move. Afterwards Harry left and soon after I found Miss Kay. Went about with her for a little then walked out with her part way home. We passed Buckingham Palace and I left her at Victoria Station as I had to go to Portland Road to be at Stokes at three, but before I left she asked me to come and see her, so I said I would go on Thursday morning. She also gave me her address. I got to Stokes a little after time, had my lesson, I was the only pupil. Then I went to the Crystal Palace bazaar for half an hour. You can get almost anything you want there. There are some very nice second-hand shops of all sorts in Great Portland Street.

May 3rd 1876 Wednesday

The Blues went away at 8 o'clock but I was too tired to see them go. Was just in time for the 9 train. There was one of the new broad gauge carriages. The one which I got into was very lofty and broad. The best railway carriage I have ever been in. The train was very full and it was as much as the engine could do to start us. It groaned very much. I had a carriage to myself all the way. When I got to Paddington I could not open the window of the carriage so I had to open the window the other side and ask a man standing by to unlock the door. Then I had to cross the line. I went to Praed Street and got in for Baker Street and sauntered about till I got to Madam Tussauds where I went in. At first it is quite dazzling, so much looking glass and so many figures you do not know who are real and who are not. I went through the room of horrors but the part that interested me most were the relics of Napoleon. There were several old things of all sorts. Also the heads of all the murderers.

I left about half past 12 o'clock and found my way to Oxford Street and got my dinner at the Somerset hotel and coffeehouse and got a very nice dinner. Then found my way to Margaret Street passing Marshall & Snellgrove. I was again the only one at Stokes. I left there at 4 o'clock and went to the Crystal Palace bazaar, which is close by. I bought one or two little things there.

Arrived at Windsor at 6 o'clock. Came in, had dinner, then went to Aunt's. There was a parcel came for her and in the railway book there was one for the Queen and she had one and nine penny to pay.

May 4th 1876 Thursday

Uncle came up to my room at 25 minutes to 9 o'clock and as I had to leave the house for the station at 10 minutes to, I had to make haste. I was just in time for the train. There was one of the new carriages on so I got into that I took a handsome to Dr. Kay's house, 68 Charlwood Street, about half a mile. I met Miss Kay there and after playing her a tune I started with her for Victoria Station as we were going to Addison Road for the skating rink. The rink is just outside the station, a splendid one. Miss Kay had not been on often so I had to help her a great deal but she improved wonderfully. There were a good many on the rink but none were very good at it.

We left about 1 o'clock having had two hours at it. I went with her to Victoria and walked half way home with her. I walked to Stokes and got there a few minutes late. There were six of us altogether. After the lesson I walked to Oxford Circus and took the bus to the Strand. We passed two fountains and several monuments. I walked about there till 7 o'clock. I passed the Gaiety Theatre and two or three others.

May 6th 1876 Saturday

Took my book "*The Moonstone*" into the park and sat there. I saw the Queen and the Empress at a distance going to the mausoleum. Then saw Harry coming up, but when he saw me he turned back by the third young tree from the lodge going to Fragne. This side there was a log lying and a rat hole. Walked through the town which was very full.

May 7th 1876 Sunday

Went up to Aunt's house. They were just getting ready to go to Trinity so I went with them. The more I hear of Robbins the more I dislike him. The sermon had nothing worth hearing in it. Went back with them, went to see Bobby in his stable. It was a very nice little stable and William left it very clean.

About five minutes to 5 o'clock the Empress of Germany came in with two ladies of her suite and also Lady Biddulph with her son and daughter were there. They had the anthem "*Hear my prayer*". I do not think I ever heard anything so beautiful. It made one's blood run cold when that boy sang the solo part. It was like an angel, and he pronounced his words beautifully. The place was crammed. When I came out of there I went down to Eton Church. I had never been in it before. It is a good-sized church and very lofty. The organ is very funnily fixed, somehow in the steeple. There was a large choir but they sang very badly and I do not think I ever heard a man intone so badly. The main point of the sermon was that the communion was everything, the same that Robbins of Trinity says.

May 8th 1876 Monday

I went passed the new chapel they are building at the corner of the Clewer Road. They were laying the foundation that afternoon. An M.P. was doing it.

May 10th 1876 Wednesday

The Queen with the Empress of Germany and Princess Beatrice were going away at half past 10 o'clock, so I went down to the station to see them off. They had a splendid saloon carriage. They were very punctual. The Empress came first, she had a fine figure but she is getting old. She also has a lot of black hair. She had on a velvet jacket trimmed with beads and the Queen had a very shabby velvet jacket. Very old fashioned. The Princess Beatrice had a very handsome embroidered slate color dress. Though the shortest and fattest of the lot, she is by far the most stately. She looks as if she was Queen. John Brown of course was there.

I forgot to say that yesterday morning in Uncle's back garden we could hear the bagpipes being played at the castle.

May 11th 1876 Thursday
Went up and finished packing. Helped Uncle to pack a few flowers which I was to take with me. Went up to Aunt's to say goodbye and took some of my photos for her to choose one from. I also begged her very much to come and see us at Buxton. As I was coming back I met such a lot of people going to the Horse Guards barracks and the town was nearly empty. I learned afterwards it was an army doctor's funeral and when I got home I found Uncle was going to it. I said goodbye to Grandmama. Then the carriage came and Uncle went to the station with me and saw me off by the 1.15 train.

I was in one of the new carriages and when we got to Paddington I took a handsome to St. Pancras. There was one very good-looking porter. My train started at a quarter past 3 o'clock. I got a seat by the window as I like and a gentleman opposite and a gentleman and a lady at the other end. I had a very pleasant journey, no rain at all and I got here a little before 8 o'clock. Papa met me at the station and we had a cab up. Mama was waiting at the door. I came across, unpacked some of my things, then had tea in Kenilworth. My leaches travelled very nicely.

May 12th 1876 Friday
Attended to my plants and arranged them all. After dinner went to Lawrence and Rowlands for some biscuits.

May 15th 1876 Monday
Went up to Mr. Pettit to study. Then went and tried cricket with them as they were going to have a match next day.

May 16th 1876 Tuesday
Went off to the cricket field. They would not let me play. They said I was too big so I scored. The other side won.

May 19th 1876 Friday
I did not go to Mr. Pettit but practiced duets with Miss Jones, a lady in the house.

May 20th 1876 Saturday
Went and played with Miss Jones. I had a headache. As I was going through the

dining hall met Dr. Webster and Mr. Farmer who had just come. They were here about this time last year. After tea went down to the Pavilion with the doctor. Then to Robins for a book and took "*The toilers of the seas*". Went back to the Pavilion and found Miss Atkins[117] there. I believe she had come after the doctor. One of the first questions she asked him was whether there was a Mrs. Webster.

May 21ˢᵗ 1876 Sunday

I had a very bad headache. My headache was very bad so I went out after service.

May 22ⁿᵈ 1876 Monday

We sat and talked Mr. and Miss Wilson, Mrs. Hollingshead, Mr. Farmer, Dr. Webster and myself and also Miss Jones. We talked for about two hours asking riddles etc. and we arranged to have a game of "*Blind Man's Bluff*" after tea. We separated about 5 o'clock. As I was going to my sitting room I found Mrs. Hollingshead had taken the key and locked the door. The key had only been in an hour but I would not say anything about it. We began "*Blind Man's Bluff*" and two ladies, fresh arrivals, were just having their teas, Mrs. Kendall and Miss Neil, but they joined us when they had finished. We played for about an hour and then went into the drawing room and had a game of "*Proverbs*".

May 23ʳᵈ Tuesday 1876

After tea had a game of "*Post*" for about an hour. Then went into the drawing room and played at "*Proverbs*" and "*How When and Where*". There is a gentleman called Mr. Albany who walks on two sticks who is very nice at games.

May 24ᵗʰ 1876 Wednesday

After tea had a game of "*Spinning the Trencher*" and each person being a flower. Then we went to the drawing room and played "*How When and Where*". Then had supper and went down beetling with Dr. Webster and caught 113.

May 25ᵗʰ 1876 Thursday

Being Mama's birthday went up to Kenilworth and gave her a scent bottle I had got for her. Papa had given her an inkstand. After dinner Mrs. Hollingshead came up to my room and we arranged a Charade for the evening. I also read her a few bits of Mark Twain. We arranged about the Charade and we all met dressed at half past 9 o'clock. It was only a small one and it was over in a very short time. The word was "*dumb founded*". Mr. Albany guessed it. Then we undressed and had a game of "*The Stool of Repentance*" which was very good. Went beetling again with Dr. Webster and caught 164. After we catch them we put them into the fire. We first pop them into a bowl of hot water.

---

117 Manageress for Shore and continued after his death

26th May 1876 Friday

We agreed about a Charade in which I was to be Mrs. Perkins, housekeeper. So I went and got my dress. Miss Weston lent me the dress and I made a cap and had a wig. Miss Neil took the part of Alice the lady's maid. Miss Wilson, Amelia the housemaid, Mrs. Hollinshead, Emellien the lady's maid from over the way and Mrs. Kendall Lady Eleanor, and Dr Webster Jiggs the baker's young man.

We learned our parts before dinner and after dinner decided to have a rehearsal about 5 o'clock in No. 10 B. At 5 o'clock we were all there and we had great fun. Dr.Webster had to say, *"you do me proud ladies"*, but he could not pronounce the *"r"* so it sounded very funny. We had tea, I did not go in as I had the drawing room to get ready, but had mine in the kitchen. After tea we all met as arranged to meet dressed in the dining room at half-past 7 o'clock. When I went down there were roars of laughter and we finally began at 8 o'clock.

When I went into the room there was a great deal of laughter and I was asked by many afterwards who was Mrs. Perkins. They did not know me and Mr. Ferguson said I could not have done it better. It went off altogether very well and was very much liked. The proverb was *"when the cat is away the mice play"*. Then we had a game of *"How When and Where"*.[118]

May 29th 1876 Monday

When I woke up I found I had a large swelling on my face so I did not get up till after breakfast. Papa went to Matlock this morning to have the money paid over.[119] About 12 o'clock went to the dining room and Miss Jones and Miss Neil played. After dinner we sat talking and about 5 o'clock I was told that Walker was here, Mr. Owen's old nurse. So I went out to see him. He is much thinner. We had a game of billiards and I beat him. After tea, had a game of *"French Blind Man's Bluff"* then *"Object and subject"*.

May 30th 1876 Tuesday

My face was better but not well.After tea had a game of the *"French Blind Man's Bluff"*, then *"Proverbs"*, and had supper.

May 31st 1876 Wednesday

Went for a walk with Mrs. Kendall, Miss Neil, Mrs. Hollinshead, Miss Jones and Master Shipton. We went up Solomon's Temple way to get ferns. In coming home we got a good many and the others got much in front of us, but I knew a quicker way so I took that and was home first.

June 1st 1876 Thursday

I got up before breakfast and went down to the well with Mrs. Hollinshead.Went down

118 37 guests staying at Malvern House at this date
119 To repay Shore's mortgage

to Mr Hailly's to order a new suit. After tea went to the Pavilion with the others.

June 2ⁿᵈ 1876 Friday

Went to the well before breakfast with Mrs. Hollinshead.

June 3ʳᵈ 1876 Saturday

Went to Mr. Pettit and arranged to score for a cricket match that afternoon between themselves and Fairfield. I forgot say that after breakfast I went with Mrs. Hollinshead to Fairfield to see Emma Miller married. It was a very quiet wedding. Mr. Ferguson and Mr. Tong were there with Jess and Charlie. I had dinner at 1 o'clock and was at the field by 2 o'clock but as none of the Fairfield boys were there and it was rather cold I went back for my coat. We had been playing for about 20 minutes and it began to rain so we left off and came back.

June 5ᵗʰ 1876 Monday

It was very wet so we decided to have the Charade over again. Mr. Evans took Mr. Jiggs' part. We all learned our parts in the morning and at dinnertime arranged to have a rehearsal in Pomeroy at 5 o'clock. I watered my plants and at 5 o'clock went to Pomeroy.[120] We had the rehearsal and after tea we went up to dress. I had not Mrs. Perkins dress, so I had to make up the best I could. It went off very well and afterwards we decided to have a Grand Charade on Wednesday and ask all the Royalists up to tea.

June 6ᵗʰ 1876 Tuesday

Went out before breakfast with Mrs. Hollinshead and Miss Neil to the well Asked Miss Weston to write to Manchester to fetch back the old dress that I had for Mrs. Perkins. Then we arranged about the Charade. Mr. Albany wrote a note of invitation to the Royalists. It was in poetry. Had the rehearsal and agreed to have another after supper.

June 7ᵗʰ 1876 Wednesday

After breakfast got my dresses together as I had to change 4 times. Took the note down to the Royal. Then went to Mr. Pettit to ask him to come. Learned *"Betsy Waring"*. The answers came from the Royal which also was in poetry, though not so good as ours, and they said there were about 15 coming up, so we laid the table for 56 and there was just one chair too many.

About 6 o'clock they all came up with Mr Bailey at their head, just like a school. Lawrence came up to my room to help me dress. In the first scene I was Betsy Waring. I went in with a nightcap on and a nightgown. In the room there was a kitchen table, two chairs and a bucket. I go in with a candle broken in a dirty candlestick and a black bottle with some water. I go in first and sing *"Betsy Waring"*, then a lady and a little girl come in and ask me how I am and speak to me about temperance. Then I sit down on the bucket and I let the black bottle fall out and I say it is only lotion for rubbing

---

120 Extension

my joints, I sometimes have to rub the joints of my throat. She gives me some soup, then she says she must be going, and I say I will see her to the end of the lane, as it is such a dark night. We go out and I put on a shawl and a bonnet and take an old lantern and we grope our way along the room when a ghost appears and we are all very frightened and finally run out.

I change my dress and the next scene is one where I am Mrs. Boniface and I have a henpecked husband. A pair on their honeymoon come in and asked if this is the ship in distress. They engage a room and make a great fuss about everything, then an old gentleman comes in and engages a room and they have supper. Then the old gentleman goes to his room and does his right and left hand wrong. He goes to the wrong room and puts on a dressing gown and nightcap and tucks up his trousseau. Then the lady says she would go to bed, and when she goes to her room and finds the old man in it she screams and the old man comes out with his nightcapped head and finally they agree then to go to their right rooms and so that scene ends.

The third scene, we are all on board ship in a gale and some are ill and call for mops and basins and finally come to our journey's end.

Then the 4th. I was Mrs. Perkins house keeper and there was Mr. Jiggs baker's young man and house maid and lady's maid, and lady's maid from over the way and we have a party and I dance with Mr. Jiggs and sing. They say I sing like a nightingale and then we hear one outside. That is the end.

June 8ᵗʰ 1876 Thursday

We went to the Pavilion and Miss Neil said it was a pity I did not learn the violin. She was learning it so I said I would go and get one next day. Went star gazing with Miss Neil, Miss Jones Mrs. Kendall and Mr. Tong.

June 9ᵗʰ 1876 Friday

Went about the violin and it was to come down about 11 o'clock. The bow was no good so I had to go and fetch another. The flower man came and I got a rose, a geranium and a scented verbence from him.

June 10ᵗʰ Saturday

Miss Neil asked me to go with them to Axe Edge so we went down the town and took a carriage to drive there. We walked to the top and got a few ferns,[121] then walked back, had dinner. After dinner went to the station to see Mrs. Hollinshead off. Then Miss Neil, Mrs. Kendall, Mr. Tong, Master Shipton and myself went along the wood by the new water works to get ferns. Mr. Tong had to carry Miss Neil over the brook once, and I got over my ankles in bog.

---

121 "Pteridomania" or fern collecting was one of the most popular drawing room crazes in the 1850's. It was an inexpensive hobby. Judith Flanders p.163

June 12ᵗʰ 1876 Monday

Miss Neil, Miss Jones, Mr. Tong and myself went to Millers Dale by train and walked through the dale home. We waited a long time in the dale getting ferns. We got some very good ones. Mr. Tong went across the river nine times. Just before we came to the road there is a cottage where we got beautiful eider and when we got to the third mile stone we had three-quarters of an hour to do it in. We did it all but half a minute, just in time for dinner.

June 16ᵗʰ Friday

Mr. Albany arranged a Charade for the evening. The word was '*pilgrimage*' and the actors were Miss and Mrs. Nunnely, Mrs. Hills, Mr. Albany, Mr. Hills and Charlie Shipton and myself. It was not very good.

June 18ᵗʰ 1876 Sunday

Chose hymns had service, Mr. Bailey preached. After dinner the tent was opened and Charlie Shipton and I went down. While we were there Mrs. Doig, a very fat lady, came down and she could not get through the stile so we had to haul her over the wall which was a great undertaking.

June 19ᵗʰ 1876 Monday

Mr. Albany arranged a drive to Errwood Hall that afternoon and one to the Cat and Fiddle for the next day. The weather was very hot. After dinner the brake came and we started for Errwood Hall. The rhododendrons were out in full bloom and were very beautiful. There were quite walls of them each side. Came back about 7 o'clock. I rode on the doorstep most of the way back as there was a great deal of up hill and I could jump out and gather the ferns.

June 20ᵗʰ 1876 Tuesday

17 of us went to the Cat and Fiddle. It was a very heavy pull up the hill for 2 horses. When we got there we found a great many brakes there. We all got something to drink and after a short time started back again. We were home before tea.

June 21ˢᵗ 1876 Wednesday

Got ready to go to Castleton when Mrs. Pilkington and Mrs. Vickers sent to know if they might come, so I said yes. We started about half-past 10 o'clock. It was very hot. We went through Millers Dale where we stopped to see the old church.. It was a very fine old church. I went up to the top of the tower. It was a very hard way up but there was a good view from the top. We waited there about half-an-hour and then went on. It was awfully hot and we got to Castleton about 2 o'clock.

   After dinner we all went to Peak Cavern except Mrs. Pilkington and Mrs. Vickers who said they would rest. We sauntered there and after watching the stoning makers a little went through the cavern. We all had our candles, the day was intensely hot and so the cavern felt very cold and on coming out of the cavern it was enough to make

Cat and Fiddle, Buxton

one faint. We sauntered back to the hotel and ordered the carriage. When the ladies went upstairs they found Mrs. Pilkington and Mrs. Vickers in bed asleep, so roused them up and got off in the carriage about 5 o'clock.

Just on the way home is the Speedwell Mine. Some of us went down that and the carriage went on up a steep hill and we were to meet it at the top. First you go down 106 steps, then you get into a boat and go along the tunnel for some a hundred yards, then get out on a platform and see a wonderful cavern and a very deep hole. We came back and walked up the Winnets, a vale between rocks. When you have got up a little it is a grand view to look back and thunder was rolling deeply which made it grander. When we got over the hill to the Blue John Mine, some of our party were waiting for us, so we then went down the Blue John, in all, three of them. We have to take our candles. The mine was very fine indeed but I could not get hold of any Blue John stone.

When we came out it was pouring with rain and thundering and lightning very fast, so we waited in a little house that was just outside the mine where they sell the Stone cut etc. There was just a field between us and the road and a large shed by the road where the carriage went. It was half-past 7 o'clock before the storm abated at all Then the storm came on worse than ever but I was well wrapped up and did not get wet. As we went on a thick mist came on and we could not see half a dozen yards in front of us.

When we got to Dove Hole we stopped at an Inn and all the gentleman got out to get something. I got some hot brandy and water and just as I was going to enjoy it they

Buxton Wells Dressing
Courtesy of the Board Collection and www.picturethepast.org.uk

said the storm was coming on again, so I swallowed it off and jumped into the brake. Others who were not so fortunate got their seats wet and the green off the cushions died into their trousers. We got home about half past 9 o'clock and just as we got to the door one of the horses fell down dead beat.

June 23rd 1876 Friday

After tea went to the Gardens, then up to the Well dressing which began the day before. The wells were very nice but there were no shows in the fair. I forgot to say, on Thursday morning last eight of us went up to the fair to have a photo taken in a group, Mr. Kirkley, Mr. Tong, his elder brother, Mrs. Nunnerly, Miss Nunnerly, Mrs. Seebohne, Miss Phillips and myself. We were taken pretty well. It was rather wet this evening so there were not many at the fair.

June 24th 1876 Saturday

Went up to the fair and strolled about. Came across the Stampers and went on the roundabout but they would not come. I'd taken a great fancy for the man that attended to the large roundabout. I went on them a good many times. There were a great many people. Elijah was there with Edith, a private lady's maid and the butler that was at Thompson's. They went on the horses, and then Elijah came on with me. Then I saw Lawrence and he came on with me. It was the first time he had been on.

He liked it very much.

June 25th 1876 Sunday

Went for a walk with Miss Neil and her sister who had come over from Saturday to Monday. We went down by the brook by the brick kilns.[122] Mr.Tonge went with us. When we got to the pretty wood, we left the brook and went up to the new reservoir. Then we came home by Corbar wood and got home just in time for tea.

June 26th 1876 Monday

Went with the Miss Neills and Mr. Tonge to the Gardens. The rink was to be opened at 11 o'clock. It was very hot. Dr. Robertson[123] made a speech and declared it was open then. I was the third on. It was a very nice rink, part covered but the part covered was not quite dry so we had to rink in the sun. I persuaded Miss Nunnerly to come on and we skated till 1 o'clock. I went home and got something to drink, then went to see the frases of the circus which came in today. The frases in was not much. It is Pinders Grand Continental Circus. After dinner went to the circus, which was rather good, but they were not many there.

June 27th 1876 Tuesday

Went and sat in the Gardens with Mr. Tonge, Miss Phillips and Miss Nunnely. We saw two of the circus men there, Mr. J Pinder and another. After the band had stopped I went down the town with the ladies and Mr. Tonge asked me to go to dinner with him at the Old Hall. As we were going through Spring Gardens we met the circus.After dinner I went to the circus and met Harry Hunter there. We went and sat just by the band and took a fancy to one of the bandsmen.

Then went down the town with Harry, came in, changed my clothes and went down to the Old Hall. There were only 14 at table and a very sober lot. After dinner I went up to Mr. Tonge's room which was very small. Then we went up to the circus. It was very good and very full. Mr. J. Pinder's bareback riding was wonderful and when the horse was going at full gallop he would give a leap and jump straight onto its back standing up. It was over about 10 o'clock. Then I went and spoke to the bandsman I had taken a fancy to; he was a very nice fellow. Then went with Mr. Tonge to the St. Anne's Billiard Room where I had an iced brandy and soda and I left about a quarter to 11 o'clock.

July 5th 1876 Wednesday

Had my French lesson then Goddard came and gave me my violin lesson. Took Miss Phillips and her sister to the rink. It was the first time either of them had the skates on but they did wonderfully well, especially the young one. It had been raining that morning so the floor was very slippery. They had not many tumbles.

---

122 Lightwood brickyard and reservoir

123 WH Robertson, the well-known doctor

W. & G. PINDER'S

CONTINENTAL GRAND

HIPPODROME AND CIRCUS,

will visit Tideswell, Saturday, June 24th; Buxton, Monday and Tuesday, June 26th and 27th; Bakewell, Wednesday; Matlock, Thursday, with the Greatest Company of STAR ARTISTES, the most Costly and Beautiful

PROCESSION.

The SPACIOUS MARQUEE is constructed of the best material, combining the elegance and magnificence of design of a summer pavilion with the stability and convenience of a stationary building.

MADLLE. REBECCA,

The distinguished Continental Horsewoman, whose daring bird-like flights over and through various objects, is the theme of public approbation. The greatest, Female Bareback Rider in the profession.

MR. J. W. PINDER,

Unquestionably the Premier Horseman in the World, in his exciting Sporting Act, "The Newmarket Jockey," in which he will Leap from the centre of the Arena on to the bare back of his horse, while at full speed.

FOUR GOOD CLOWNS.

TWO PERFORMANCES, the first taking place at 2.30. The last at 7.30.

Doors open half-an-hour previous to each Entertainment. For the convenience of Country Friends and Families, residing at a distance, Full Programme on each occasion as excellent as in the evening. Notwithstanding the enormous expense, and to give all parties an opportunity of witnessing this brilliant Amalgamation of Novelties, the following will be the low Prices of Admission:—Reserved Seats (carpeted), 3s; Boxes (select) 2s.; Second Class, 1s; Third Class, 6d. Children under 10 years admitted at Half-price (except to Third Class).

Sole Proprietors - Messrs. W. & G. PINDER.

Advertisement for Pinder's Circus
Buxton Advertiser

July 6ᵗʰ 1876 Thursday

Arranged to go to Longnor that afternoon, 15 of us, so I and Mr. Tonge went down to see about the brake. We were the only two gentleman of the lot. When we had ordered the brake, it being very hot, we went in St.Anne's bar room and got iced brandy and sodasThe brake which was to come at 3 o'clock.

July 10ᵗʰ 1876 Monday

Had French lesson then practiced the piano till 10 o'clock when I went down the town in a carriage with Maurice. Mother stayed at the Royal for dinner, so I had to take the head of the table. After dinner I went to the rink. It was cold and windy and there were not many there. I learned the outside edge and crossing feet, then went into the reading room for a few minutes, then came back home. After tea went down to the rink and when I had been there a few minutes the Miss Phillips came down and said they were coming on. It was their second time but they did it beautifully and the Wax girl also came on. After supper Mrs. Leaky, Mr. Holmes, Miss Pratt, and the Miss Phillips sat outside the drawing room door all evening playing each other pranks.

July 11ᵗʰ 1876 Tuesday

Went to the rink. I was introduced to two sisters in black to help them round. They were very nice. Also there was a Miss Nathan and another lady from the Royal, also Miss Holmes from here, and it was as much as I could do to hand them all round in turn. My arms ached tremendously. After dinner sat in my room reading and about 4 o'clock Harry Hunter came. He stayed a little then I went up to Fairfield with him where he changed his things as he was going out to dinner. Then back with him. Went to the Pavilion where we saw a lady who died her hair so badly that you could see the parting, quite a dark color, and the hair golden. Also you can see the dark color under the eyebrows.

July 19ᵗʰ 1876 Wednesday

Captain Barton told me about a sale there was to be that day at Whaley Bridge of his brother's house, so I went with him. At the station we met Dr. Holmes and he came as well. When we got there we got a gig and drove there about a mile. When we got to the house Captain Barton met his nephew, about 17, to whom he introduced us. He took us round the house. It is a nice house but the house looks more like a chapel than a house.

There were some very nice china and oil paintings. There was a landscape of Gainsborough. Dr. Bennett bought the pictures. About 10 o'clock we went to a small cottage and had dinner. We all had to help ourselves from the leg of mutton. The cottage was very old and so were the people that lived in it. After dinner we went back to the sale. There was a pony and carriage sold for £16. A very good pony.

I went up to the house and found a very old clock with three weights and three bells and three little men with hammers, two to chime and the other to strike. It had not gone for years. I got it brought down and it was put with a table and a wooden box and I got

SALES BY AUCTION.

Overleigh, near Whaley Bridge.—The residence of W. P. Barton, Esq., who is leaving the neighbourhood.

T. W. BRITTAIN has the honour to announce that he has received instructions to dispose of by AUCTION, on WEDNESDAY, July 19, 1876, at 10 a.m., the Whole of the most superior, costly, and Modern Dining, Drawing, and Bedroom FURNITURE, in Suites; Kitchen Requisites, Glass, Breakfast, Dinner, Dessert, and Tea Services, Pony, Gig, Harness, Prize and Prize-bred Poultry, Ducks, &c., &c., comprising splendid rosewood pianoforte, 7 octaves, by Collard & Collard; magnificent drawing-room suite, in black ebony, inlaid with pollard oak, in crimson rep; two walnut occasional tables, rosewood workstand, with worked bead top; case of choice ferns, with bronze stand; eight days time piece, with glass shade and marble slab; walnut canterbury, Brussels carpet, 13-6 by 17-6, with border; fender with polished steel top bar, polished steel fire-irons, coal vase, pair of lustres, with vases to match; three pair of plain muslin curtains, with brass cornice and fringe; a quantity of engravings and water colours, oil painting, interior of Amiens Cathedral by Keops; ditto, Virgin and Child by Castelli; ditto, Landscape by Gainsborough; ditto, unknown; large solid oak bookcase, with six shelves and cupboards underneath; oak dining table, with velvet cloth; six carved oak chairs, with upholstered backs, in blue leather; mahogany easy chair, round stand, bronze statue, black marble vase, clock, Brussels carpet, 11ft. by 17ft. 9in., with border; oak pedestal sideboard, with slides and cellarettes; damask curtains, with polished pitch pine poles and rings; large oak hat and umbrella stand, with marble top; small umbrella stand, two modern oak hall chairs, Fitzroy barometer, skin and cocoa-nut mats, office table, oak secretaire, oak corner cupboard, brass tudor and French bedsteads, with spring mattresses, upholstered and other ottomans, iron French bedsteads, blankets and quilts, painted enclosed washstands and dressing chests, large and small sets drawers, mahogany sets drawers, mahogany washstands, maple painted and polished pitch pine wardrobes, with mirror doors; toilet glasses, with birchwood frames; double and single toilet services, with bottles and glasses; towel rails, slop pails, child's mahogany high chairs, child's cribs, rocking chairs, tapestry carpet for the whole of the bedrooms, dressing-rooms, nursery, landing, &c., all one pattern; hearthrugs to match, cane-seated chairs, indiarubber water bed for invalids, linen press, plated venison dish, with cover; set of plated dish covers, ditto decanter stands, cruets, candle of plated dish covers, ditto decanter stands, cruets, candle-sticks, sugar basins, cream jugs, fish knives, cutlery, about 1,000 vols. of books in good condition, brass microscope in mahogany case, with slides, &c.; white and gold hand-painted breakfast and tea services (Minton ware), dinner services, hand-painted dessert services, cut glass decanters, wine, ale, and spirit glasses, earthenware, filter, cans, kitchen dresser, round stand, windsor chairs, fender, clothes horses, fish kettles, saucepans, cans, buckets, coal boxes, hastener and jack, plate and dish rack, a quantity of home-cured hams and bacon, and numerous other effects; also, bay pony, 11½ hands, seven years; yearling bay filly, pony gig, set of silver-plated pony harness, set brass-mounted horse harness, child's pony pad, box of croquet, hay rakes and forks, step ladder, corn bin, & quantity of prize and prize-bred black-red game fowl, Rouen ducks and drake, Aylesbury ducklings, several hundred yards wire netting, wheelbarrow, tools, hive of bees, and numerous other effects.

In calling attention to the above Sale, the Auctioneer would neither be doing justice to himself nor his employers if every possible and available effort were not made to impress upon the public the special value of the above furniture to be submitted to competition. To describe its various qualities and excellencies would be out of place here, suffice it to say that the whole has been bought new within the last three years from the first London and French houses regardless of expense, and is now in as good condition as when it was bought.

Catalogues, price 3d. each, will be ready seven days before the Sale, and can be had at the place of sale; the Railway Hotel, Whaley Bridge; the Royal Oak Hotel, Chapel-en-le-Frith; the Manchester Arms, Stockport; the Swan Inn, Disley; or the Auctioneer's, Fairfield, Buxton.

On view the day before the Sale, by catalogue only, which will admit two persons.

N.B.—On account of the great number of lots which must be disposed of in one day, the Auctioneer, to prevent disappointment and loss of time to his friends and customers, begs to inform them that the Sale will com-mence at the time advertised to the minute.

Advertisement for WP Barton's auction
Buxton Advertiser

the lot for 6/6. The Stampers were there, some of them, and Mrs. and Fred Walton. Mrs. Walton bought the pony and trap. I left the place and was just in time for the train where I met the other two. After tea began cleaning the clock.

July 25th 1876 Tuesday

Had a good practice on the violin. Had dinner at the Royal. Sat next to the Spencers, then came up and helped move Mother's things from 21 to 20.

July 26th 1876 Wednesday

Had a practice on the violin, then straightened my room.

July 27th 1876 Thursday

Took Jess out for a walk and watched them rinking. After dinner Lawrence came and we set that clock going. Then I went and sat in the Gardens with Mr. Nightingale and others. I sent my advertisement of Jess to the Manchester Guardian.

July 28th 1876 Friday

In time for breakfast. Mother was not very well so I had to take the head of the table. Then showed Uncle my album.

After dinner went to the rink. It was very wet in some places. Then came and met Harry Hunter. He had tea with me. Then Mr. Nightingale and myself went to the rink where we met the Stampers. It was very jolly. I have never liked it so much before. I went backwards quite well and cut figures and did not care what I did.

July 31st 1876 Monday

Went with Mr. Nightingale and Mr. Ferguson to Manchester. First we went with Ferguson to the police courts and he showed us three Courts going and we sat on the bar and sentenced the prisoner. They were very nearly all for drunkenness. It is a wonderful place. There seems to be doors everywhere. Then Ferguson gave us an order for the Assize Courts. We went there first. There is a splendid roof and it is all very fine.

Then I went to Philips and Son, Dean's Gate, where I got some very nice boots, much cheaper than I get them here. Then we went to the Exchange. It is a very fine room and it was very full. Between 1 and 2 o'clock is the best time to see it and on Tuesdays. We had our dinner at a Stewards dining room which was not bad and very cheap, but the Exchange rooms are the best. Went to the police courts but Ferguson had gone so we went off to the station.

August 1st 1876 Tuesday

Met Laurence in a dog cart at the end of Spring Gardens. We went the old road seven miles. It took us two hours. I never was on such a road. We got to Tideswell and had a very nice lunch at the King's Head. Then looked at some horses. It rained nearly all the way coming. I never was out in such rain. It streamed down inside the umbrella and I had to hold it with both hands.

We started to go to the farm at half past 12 o'clock. The name of the farm is Wetstone. When we got there we had the horse taken out and started back at a quarter to 2 o'clock, getting to Fairfield at half-past 3 o'clock where I met Harry Hunter and walked down with him. Then I went to the courtroom to see some pictures there were to sell, but I did not care for them. After tea went to the rink where Lawson[124] of the Old Hall Hotel fell down and sprained his ankle and broke a small bone in his leg. It was the first time he had been on and he had been on over an hour.

August 3rd 1876 Thursday
Went to see Harry Hunter off with his Aunt who were going on toLeascale before us.

August 4th 1876 Friday
Made friends with a young fellow here of the name of Masters and we went out together.After tea went to the rink with Masters. He is only beginning.

August 5th 1876 Saturday
Went down the town and on going to the station saw two Pullman cars, a sleeping car and a drawing room car. We learned that they were hired by 16 Americans who were taking a tour through England and one of the ladies had a salmon and brick red dress on. They were all dressed out. They slept in the cars at night and had their meals there.

After tea went to the rink with Masters, then to the fireworks. We stood by some of the Americans and we could hear all where they had been. The fireworks were very good. There was a lace pattern in the different colours which was very pretty. There were over 2000 in the Gardens.

August 7th 1876 Monday
Saw Mr. and Mrs. Hole off. Went to the rink with Masters. Then went to the station to see Miss Rityerow off.

From August 9th to August 15th I had not time to write as I was packing up to go to Seascale. From August 15th to September 16th is written in Holiday Book Number One.

September 17th 1876 Sunday
Felt very funny not knowing anyone. There is a black servant belonging to some Americans in the house named Turner. Miss Turner is very nice. The Black's name is Abna Gay. After breakfast it rained so I stayed in for service. The organist played better than I thought he would do. Mr. Carpenter preached. After service I went up and spoke to the organist and arranged to play the chants for the evening. After dinner I took the dogs out for an hour. Came in and tidied out my conservatory. Some of the things had grown wonderfully.

---

124 Nephew of Brian Bates – hotel keeper of the Old Hall and wine merchant

September 18th 1876 Monday

The deeds of valour etc. done by me between September 18th and 19th are in obscurity being as how it was too much trouble to write them except that we have a very good lady singer here called Miss Currie. She is very stout and says she has had 22 offers."

APPENDIX 3

SKATING ON WHEELS

"*Skating On Wheels*. (By a Beginner). Perhaps the preponding sensation which one for the first time equipped in skates with wheels, and standing on the rink, is able to distinguish is that of anguish about the ankles. The pivot upon which the body is balanced seems suddenly but decidedly to have got down into the ankles, and after a few desperate plunges, and the accomplishment of a sort of heel-and-toe step consequent upon frantic endeavours when falling forward to throw the body back-ward, and when falling backward to thrust himself forward, the skater is exceedingly glad to grasp the friendly rail, and so to steady himself. After a while he makes the discovery that this violent plunging is a work of supererogation, and that, on the whole, it is rather easier to stand still them to gyrate in the uncomfortable and unnecessary manner indicated. The next conviction gained is that the wheels of the skates being so planted as to form an oblong, it is just as easy to stand upon them as in an ordinary boot. This acquired, the pupil goes slowly forward, and if he has learned his skating on the ice will not improbably become acquainted with a tendency on the part of the skates to turn aside, toe to toe, the progress attained being not altogether dissimilar in style from the walk affected by a clown on the stage. This is got over in time – *o e runnabilis experienta me docuit* – and the struggle would be much shorter if it had only occurred to the managers of the skating rinks which are now springing up over town and country to adorn their establishments with a few simple and a neatly framed instructions to the beginner. Reading and writing, may as Dogberry will have it so, come my nature. But skating on wheels does not, and a few elementary instructions would not be out of place. For example if the novice knew when putting on his skates that the wheels are mounted on an indiarubber axle, and that if he presses on one side of his foot the skates will move backward, and that he if he leans on the other side a contrary direction will be taken, it will be the saving of at least half an hour's tribulation of spirit.

The hold which skating rinks have taken upon the affections of the people is surely one of the social phenomena of the age. Possibly the acceptability of the new recreation may in some measure be traced to the circumstance that it was introduced in this country under what is called distinguished patronage. It was at "*Prince's*" that skating on wheels first found a settled home in England, and that "*Prince's*" can do no wrong is an axiom as firmly established in fashionable society as is that other round which our constitutional law is built, and which claims a similar immunity for the monarch. For a long time those sections of society for whose membership the precincts of "*Prince's*" were too narrow were content to peer in at the palings, like Peri at the gates of Paradise and watch others skate. In course of time it occurred to the enterprising gentleman who are the business managers at Prince's Club, and who have, I believe, secured a temporary monopoly of the sale of wheeled skates in England, that their operations might be extended by giving license to use the skates at rinks to be established elsewhere. As a consequence London has now several skating rinks, whilst there is hardly a watering -place of any size on the coasts where visitors who go down to bathe may not, if they please, remain to skate. "*Prince's*", as the mother establish-ment, still holds the palm of skill and grace in skating, and it must be confessed that when the pain in the ankles has vanished, and when one gets accustomed to the skates, there are few sports that afford further opportunities for the display of skill and grace. With the exception of cutting "*the inside edge*", an expert can do with the skates on wheels what may be done by the skater on ice. Of course there are obvious advantages connected with skating on asphalte as compared with skating on the ice. If the thing had been invented in Mr. Pickwick's time, we should never have had the painful picture of Mr Winkle with his face and hands blue with cold forcing a gimlet into the soles of his feet, putting his skates on with the points behind, and with the assistance Mr. Snodgrass, who knew rather less about skates than a Hindoo, getting the straps into a hopelessly complicated and entangled state. We have changed all that with the introduction of skating on wheels, and if there is any colourable inconvenience arising from the state of the temperature it is rather that we are red with heat than blue with cold. The happy skater is, in fact, wholly independent of the weather, and, as he "*lightly flashes along*" may liken himself, as Coleridge did his youthful body, to;

> Those trim skiffs unknown of yore
> On winding lakes and rivers wide,
> That ask no aid of sail or oar
> That fear no spite of wind or tide.

This perfect immunity from a conspicuous influence to which the English nation are peculiarly subject, is a strong recommendation for skating on wheels; another being that it is one of the few outdoor pastimes in which both sexes may join. In this respect the skating rink is not without its value as a practice ground for the exercise of those qualifiers which make men gentle and women trustful, there being perhaps few sights more touching than the spectacle of a gentleman who has become an adept in skating, guiding across the treacherous asphalte the faltering footsteps of his sister or his cousin.

In his life of Dickens, Mr Foster gives prominence to a theory held by the subject of the memoir, that the circles of life are actually very narrow; and that in new and unexpected scenes we are constantly coming across the same people. My brief experience of skating rinks is wholly in favour of this view. There are certain people I always meet wherever the rink may be situated. There is the young lady who is "*sure she will fall*" if she moves a step by herself, and who is content to pass a long summer's afternoon in the enjoyment of the bar at the end of the rink, which bar she clutches with an altogether unnecessary sterness of grip. Sometimes, with an intense expression on her face that speaks of the height of enjoyment, she slowly and cautiously travels a few paces, always holding on to the iron bar. Once I saw her brother, on pretence of carefully guiding her, inveigle her out half-a-dozen paces on to the rink, which done he basely deserted her, and she, with mortal terror painted on every line of here face, sidled and hobbled and crept back to the faithful bar. There is the young man who, having got his skates on, determines to skate and goes flinging himself about the rink like a delirious semaphore. One gets odd glimpses of the young man in various attitudes, sometimes with his arms wildly tossed aloft as he struggles against the tendency of his skates to go up in the air, and his body in various postures on the ground. But oftenest he is discovered swinging with curved body over the bar at either end of the rink, his favorite device of stopping himself when he reaches the limits of the rink being to throw himself violently on the bar. He is always red in the face, is generally marked with dust on the knees, shoulders and back and on the whole is not desirable company. Still, I infinitely prefer him to the young man in a check suit, who with long, slow, but not graceful curve, goes skating round and round with his thumbs in his trouser pockets, and a look of smug satisfaction on his face, that plainly says "*If you want to see how to skate, here you are*". I met that young man at Brighton, at Eastbourne and in various quarters of London, and have never seen him without there coming unbidden to my heart the wish that the semaphore would accidentally get in his way. There is the young lady with the fan, which she uses in place of a parasol as she glides up and down unattended. There are the two young ladies will always skate together, with hands crossed and locked in an affectionate embrace. There are scores of young ladies who skate hands across with their brothers or cousins, and who skate so well as to suggest that they might trust themselves alone. There is a tall, slim gentleman, who with hands lightly folded behind his back, cut figures of eight, and other figures, to the admiration of the crowd. And always there are the children, some of whom, the girls especially, skate better than any of us, making the air the while musical with their merry laughter as they skim in and out, bewildering the semaphore, and sending him floundering with wilder gait to hang out his signal "*all right*" across the friendly bar."

EXAMPLES OF TREATMENTS AT HYDROS

Advice given to bathers in Bradshaw's 1894 Dictionary of mineral waters, climatic health resort, sea baths and hydropathic establishments is as follows:

"In selecting a bathing place, not only should the chemical composition of the waters be taken into account, but also the climate, altitude, resources of the station, habits of the patient, and his moral proclivities.

The family medical adviser should select the station most suitable for his patient, should furnish him with an introduction to the resident doctor, and should indicate the proper moment for departure. The warm months, which suit some persons, are not equally advantageous to others. Englishmen, owing to the high temperatures prevailing in July and August, often prefer to make their visits to watering places in May and September. There are, however, many patients, – for instance, the lymphatic, the scrofulous and the rheumatic, – who require the direct heat of the sun quite as much as the thermal action of the waters. Such persons will, of course, prefer the warmest season for the mineral waters. Our ancestors would appear to have made some systematic preparations before going to the baths. We are a little too indifferent now, perhaps, to such preliminaries. We content ourselves generally with complementary treatment. The Germans, on the other hand, employ both. They have the preparatory treatment and the after treatment, and deem the one not less important than the other.

To regain health, it is not sufficient merely to take a course of water; it is also necessary to observe certain hygienic precautions. As regards treatment, there are perhaps no fixed rules. The indications must vary according to each individual case, for where one requires tonic, another may require alternative treatment. Medical men are naturally the best qualified to decide what is good to eat it in each individual case – whether, for example, an animal or vegetable diet is in any given instance more suitable of the two.

For some patients Bordeaux, for others a lighter wine is most suitable; the table water will also vary, from Carlsbad to Apollinaris, Pougues Oriel, Condillac, Vals or Bourboule as the case may be.

Many invalids find in exercise, and, if necessary, in massage and gymnastics, a complementary hygienic treatment. The want of exercise engenders disease, and is one of the most potent factors in the production of gout, gravel, obesity, anaemia, dyspepsia, and many other affections. Digestion is aided almost as much by the legs as by the stomach. It is by proper exercise that the appetite is sharpened, the digestion strengthened, nervous energy developed, and sleep induced.

Concerning wearing apparel, it may be remarked that as a rule, mineral-water stations are situated in mountainous countries, where the temperature and hygrometric conditions of the atmosphere are subject to change every hour. For a patient who has experienced the depurative action of the waters, and has thereby been rendered more liable to take cold, a light woollen overcoat, worn as required, is always advisable.

The stimulating effects of the thermal treatment, the life led, the exercise taken, the obligation of early rising, all conduce to make sleep even more imperatively necessary than under ordinary circumstances.

It is not assuredly by leading in watering-places the same life which a man has led elsewhere – not, for example, by turning night into day – that he can expect to regain strength and nervous energy. Early rising and early retiring to rest must be the rule for all who wish to benefit by the waters.

Amusement is not absolutely necessary to the good efects of the mineral water-cure, nor is it true that it is its principal element. Bordell is said to have treated horses successfully with mineral-waters, and as "amusement" or "imagination" are unknown to such animals the most incredulous must allow that mineral-waters have a curative power due to their own specific principles. On the other hand, it is not less true, as Zimmerman remarks, that "certain diseases can only be relieved by medicines acting on the mind, and therefore, amusement and recreation play an important role in Hydro-mineral medication". Persons, therefore, interested in the success of any particular spring should bear this fact in mind, and remember that as there are patients to whom quietude, tranquillity, the contemplation of nature, promanades on hills, in meadows and so forth, may suffice so there are others, with less bucolic tastes, who may prefer a good orchestra to the song of birds, and to whom the varied amusements of society, enjoyed in just measure, are alike useful and profitable.

The selection of an hotel is also an important matter. If an invalid is thrown among those whose conversation and habits are agreeable, and whose tastes and feelings are in harmony with his own, his sojourn will become a pleasant one. He may be induced to prolong it, and may separate with great regret from his new acquaintances. How often has a friendship formed at a watering-place exercised a happy influence over the whole of after life!

Hints to visitors at watering places. Drinking the water. It used at one time to be the custom to drink mineral waters by the gallon. Of late years, however, this practice has more or less declined, and it is now the rule to administer waters in graduated doses of one glass, half a glass, quarter of a glass, or even, as at

Eaux- bonnes, by the tablespoonful. The quantity should be diminished or increased in accordance with the indications of the disease, and the degree of tolerance shown by the patient. The waters are generally taken best in the morning, and their absorption is often promoted by a short walk. To go directly from the spring to the bath, or to drink the waters while in the bath itself, frequently disagrees, causing a sensation of weight in the stomach, or even nausea. Strictly speaking, all mineral-waters might be taken internally. In practice, however, the hypothermal are reserved exclusively for external use.

Baths.

In the present state of our knowledge it is scarcely possible to say how mineral baths exactly act. It is reasonable to attribute their action to absorption through the skin. This however, is denied by some physiologists. M. Durrien, for instance, maintains that the weight of the body is unchanged after a bath of moderate temperature, but that it gains or loses weight in proportion as the bath is under or over a mean temperature. Scontetten maintains that the mineral water bath acts less by the mineral principles contain in it than by the electricity liberated. He suggests a study of the magnetic needle as a means of judging the efficacy of a spring. A bath of from 50 to 76 degrees Fahrenheit is considered tepid, and 76-92 degrees f. warm, from 92 to 112 degrees f. hot. A mean between the two latter is the temperature of the reservoirs in the thermal establishments. It is of course impossible to give any one temperature which will be applicable to all cases. Some individuals will be affected by a temperature 70 degrees more than others will by one of 82 degrees. When, how - ever, the temperature of the bath is unsuited to a particular case less benefit is to arrive from the waters. A patient should therefore note accurately the thermometer before entering his bath, and not, as is so often done, rely on his own tactile sensibility, or on that of his attendant. As a rule, to which, however, there are exceptions, the stay in the bath should not exceed one hour; nor should it be continued after the temperature begins to fall to lukewarm, for a bath should either be hot or cold. If a warm bath be continued too long it is apt to produce determination of blood to the skin; if the cold bath be so continued, it is apt to produce a revulsion of blood towards the internal organs.

Shower baths and douches.

The douche bath has only been prescribed systematically of recent years. Its chief advantages are that it can be used so as to impact a shock or stimulus, that it requires less time, and that it can be administered at what are comparatively extreme temperatures. The douche consists essentially of a jet of water, which as it were encloses the whole or any given portion of the body. Its effects can be modified by altering the temperature, direction, power, or form of the jet d'eau.

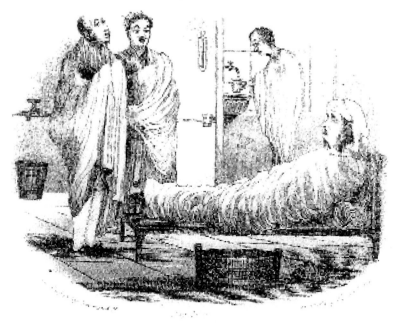

THE WET SHEET PROMENADE
WAITING TO BE UNWOUND

Figure 1. The wet sheet treatment. From *The water cure illustrated*, London, Newman, [n.d., c. 1870], unnumbered engraving. (*By courtesy of the Wellcome Trustees.*)

Wet Sheeting.

The patient takes the waters wrapped in wet linen sheets.

Massage or "Kneading," is a method of treatment which has prevailed in the East from time immemorial. It is now common enough in most balneal establishments in Europe. Long abandoned to quacks and empirics, who owed to it much of their success in treating joint affections, it has at length taken its place as a recognised method of treatment. Massage consists essentially of a series of acts of pressure and traction alternatively to the skin, muscles and sinews. This manipulation can be combined, as desired, with the douche, the sweating baths, the simple bath (wet massage) or without water at all (dry massage). From a physiological point of view it may be said that the douche and massage act by augmenting the quantity of blood passing through a tissue or organ in a given time. The process organic exchange thereby becomes more active, and nutrition is stimulated.

Gymnastics form a useful addition to the Hydrotherapeutics. The gymnastics have here spoken of have of course nothing to do with professional gymnastics, but are simply and solely medical exercises. Their object is to restore the body to its normal form by suitable and continuous motion, and to compel feeble or undeveloped organs to undertake their fair share of physiological work. To this system of treatment the illustrious Delpech gave the name of "orthomorphism".

Mineral research from a therapeutic point of view. The term "mineral waters" is applied to those waters which hold in solution a variety of mineral substances at various temperatures. Some writers have denied the therapeutic efficacy of mineral waters, basing their opinions on the minute quantities of mineral matter held in solution. In many cases, however, the waters act with so much energy that no scepticism as to their power is possible. Thus at Eaux- bonnes a season rarely passes without some sufferer inducing haemoptysis by an indiscreet use of the waters. At Ax, Dr Carrigon has known death to occur from the injudicious and excessive use of the Vignerie spring. The Carlsbad waters, if taken by persons of a plethoric and sanguine habit of body, may occasion dangerous symptoms. Many of these mineral waters are of much more complex character than the older chemists, with their less perfect methods of analysis, supposed. Quite recently Dr Thenard has discovered arsenic in the waters of Mont-Dorel, while in other springs existence of rare elements, such as rubidium, can now be demonstrated."

Electrotherapy.

Priessnitz's regime began to look fairly primitive when faced with the challenge of electric baths, gas baths, agitation baths, oxygen baths, ozone baths, pine needle baths, borax baths, hyssop baths, creosote baths, carbolic baths, lavender baths, iodine baths, mercurial baths and sulphur baths. The Bathman was becoming a technician who watched dials as well as turning on taps. Prominent among new cults was electrotherapy, an art which had been much abused by quacks and was by no means free of them. It was used to apply heat to joints and to stimulate muscles and nerves.[125] It claimed to be good for rheumatics, arthritics and amongst others for those suffering from gastric disorders.[126]

The tainted word hydropathy was now replaced by hydrotherapy. This was defined as a science based on mechanical thermic action of water in disease, irrespective of the source of the water. It was not to be confused with balneology, which was concerned with the chemical and diluent action of mineral-waters.[127]

In his Plain Guide to the Water Cure published in 1872 Dr W T Fernie (Dr Gully's successor at Malvern) explained, more or less, how the electric bath worked. The patient immersed himself in an ordinary hot bath, the water of which had been *"chemically acidified"*, while the attendant fastened one pole of an *"electrical apparatus"* to the metal side of the bath then handed the other to the patient. *"In this*

---

125 Turner p.245
126 Havins p.142
127 Turner p.246

way," explained Dr Fernie sceptically, *"it is professed that whatever metallic, mercurial or other poisonous inorganic principles are lying embedded within internal structures can be painlessly removed, and visibly deposited, in the case of mercury, as a bright mirror on the side of the bath or upon the surface of the plate attached there - to".* However a *"leading and most competent electrician"* had told the author that the system was both useless and injurious. Dr Fernie agreed that it was sheer charlatanism to show the patient bright mercury on a pole at the side of the bath, since any such quantity in his body would have killed him. He explained how, in his opinion, the trick of producing bright deposits was performed. The usual form of electrical bath, in Dr Fernie's view was *'unphilosophical'* but he thought it might be useful, in some circumstances, for drawing drugs from the patient's system.[128] This was naturally enough not recommended for children or for those of a weak constitution!

Nowhere were faradisation (the patient sat with his feet against a large electrode while the attendant passed the other electrode about the various parts of his body) and galvanisation(the passing of an electric current through the patient's body via an attendant-electician who was first instructed to try the strength of the electric current on himself) practised more intensively than in the great Hydro founded by John Smedley at Matlock (the rules were strict; *"no form of supper shall be deemed light"*, said the prospectus; *"discussing maladies one with another is a mischievous and foolish practice"*). Many of the shock treatments were administered while a patient sat in a chair. He was dabbed with an electrode under his clothes by an "electrician" who was under strict orders to test the strength of the current on himself before applying it to the patient. When the prescription was *"endorsed"*transmitted the operator had to pass the current through his own body and apply it by hand. For general faradisation the patient sat with both feet on a large metal electrode which was wrapped in wet flannel and kept warm by a hot-water bottle, while the other electrode was moved by decrees about his body; three minutes to the neck and spine, four to the abdomen and so on.[129]

The Inhalatorium.

For the respiring of medicated, rarefied, compressed or natural airs, also gases, vapours and sprays. Inhalation was said to bring the medicament in direct contact with the affected part, thus taking some of the strain from an over-drugged stomach. All known brands of healing incense were to be had in the Grand Ducal Inhalatorium opened in 1899 at Baden-Baden. Inside, fastidious gentleman sat in cubicle sniffing away scented vents or holding to their mouths nozzles linked with tall cylinders. Unique among inhalant resorts was Mont Dore, perched over warm springs in the Auvergne, where the salles de vapeurs were filled with man-made clouds, continually renewed. In the salles d'aspiration sat asthmatic patients, fully clothed for periods up to an hour and a half, after which they were carried away in a kind of sedan

---

128 Turner p.249
129 Turner p.251

chair to their hotels for an hour's rest. In the ominous sounding salles de pulverisation jets of water were driven with great force against heated metal discs and the resulting mist was inhaled by those with nose and throat complaints. Mount Dore claimed to have started the inhalation of concentrated vapour in 1833. It was much resorted to by clergymen, actresses, singers and others who over-used their voices.[130]

The Emantorium.

This differed only slightly in function from the Inhalatorium. It is described in Stedman's Medical Dictionary as "*an institution where treatment is supplied by radioactive waters and the inhalation of radium emanations*" Early in the 20th century spa doctors were discovering radioactivity and thermal waters everywhere; it was the exciting new ingredient which could bring back prosperity to a resort. According to a Buxton guidebook of 1911 the Buxton Hydro Hotel had "*a well-equipped Emanatorium for the inhalation of Radium Emanations combined with Oxygen*". This radioactivity was liberated by the Buxton waters, and according to sir Charles Cameron continued to enrich the atmosphere of the Peak, that healing air for which Buxton was renowned. The Empire Hotel, Buxton, now claimed to be "*the only hotel in England with an open-air restaurant,*" here guests could absorb the precious emanations as they dined. Not to be out done by Buxton, the City of Bath in 1912 also installed a species of emanatorium for the "*inhalation of radioactive gases*". No other spa had so much vitalising nitrogen in the air, according to a 1916 guidebook; the whole city was virtually a radium bath![131]

Douche.

The application of a single or multiple column of water against some part of the body. Various types of hose and nozzels were used and treatments varied in relation to temperature, pressure and mass of water used, according to the type of complaint being treated. The douche was a widely used form of treatment and many variations existed eg horizontal jet, vertical jet, fan, broken jet. Special applications of the douche to particular parts of the body or internal organs were separately named e.g.dorsal, lumbar, cerebral or gastric douches.

Wet douche	Douche applied when patient is immersed in a bath (some times referred to as the undercurrent)
Dry douche	Applied directly to body of patient, usually erect.
Descending douche	What we now know as a shower.
Greville heat treatment	Superheated air was applied to the affected part of the body

130 Turner p.254

131 Turner p.55

THE ASCENDING DOUCHE "NOW SIR, DO SIT STILL."

Figure 2. The douche. From ibid., engraving no. 11. (By courtesy of the Wellcome Trustees.)

	prior to immersion in a warm bath.
Medicated bath (pine, brine and sulphur)	A bath prepared with the type of additional medication as described. It is possible to conjecture that such baths were replicating the kind of treatment found elsewhere, brine for example, at the Nauheim baths or sulphur the baths at Bath in Somerset.
Moor (or Peat) Bath	Moor peat was mixed with water and heated by steam injection to a temperature of 90 to 105 degrees F.(32 to 40 degrees C) to form a paste. The recommended time of immersion in the bath was about 20 minutes, but because the hot mixture could induce drowsiness some patients bathed for lesser time. After emerging from the peat the patient was hosed down by the bath assistant and wrapped in hot towels for a further 20 minutes. The treatment was considered effective for skin disorders, rheumatism and sciatica. The peat bath induced profuse sweating and often resulted in a temporary loss of weight. The peat was obtained from the moors surrounding Buxton. A variation of this bath was that peat sitz bath which immersed the lower torso and thighs in

	a small bath filled with the peat mixture.
Mustard bath	As the medicated baths but containing mustard powder.
Mustard pack	Mustard and water mixed to a thick paste and applied to the affected area.
Nauheim bath. Nauheim (Bad Nauheim) now Germany.	Effervescent saline bath found naturally in the resort of The water there is heavily charged with carbonic acid gas (carbon dioxide) and contains, in solution, a large amount of calcium chloride. The bath was artificially prepared in Buxton and elsewhere by the addition of several chemicals, including carbonate of soda and hydrochloric acid, in particular proportions, to the natural mineral water. It was felt to be very effective in the cure of cardiac and renal cases.
Russian bath	In this bath the patient lay on a slab in a small room filled with steam. The temperature would range from 115-120 degrees F (46-48 degrees C) and the length of the bath 10-20 minutes. The treatment might include alternate heat and cold with the patient moving between the steam room and a cold shower. In a Russian bath the patient would be rubbed by an attendant to promote the early appearance of perspiration. Ailments treated by this method include rheumatic pain, diabetes, dyspepsia and sciatica.
Schott exercises	Swedish medical gymnastic exercises adapted by Drs. August and Theodore Shchott of Bad Nauheim into a programme suitable for the treatment of cardiac disease. These could be used either in conjunction with the Naauheim bath or alone.
Sitz bath	Small portable bath made of metal, porcelain or wood of such a form and size that the patient could be seated in it by leaving it the feet outside the bath. The lower trunk and upper thighs only were immersed in the sitz bath and could be taken hot or cold and with or without a douche. Used for the conditions of the lower spine and genitalia.
Vapour Bath	Essentially a steam bath. In some cases the patient was enclosed in a cabinet with only the head protruding. Alternatively the half vapour bath enclosed the lower trunk and lower limbs only. Local versions of the apparatus were available to treat individual limbs.[132]

---

132 Langham p.95-99

FAMILY TREE

All-in-One Tree of William Lomas

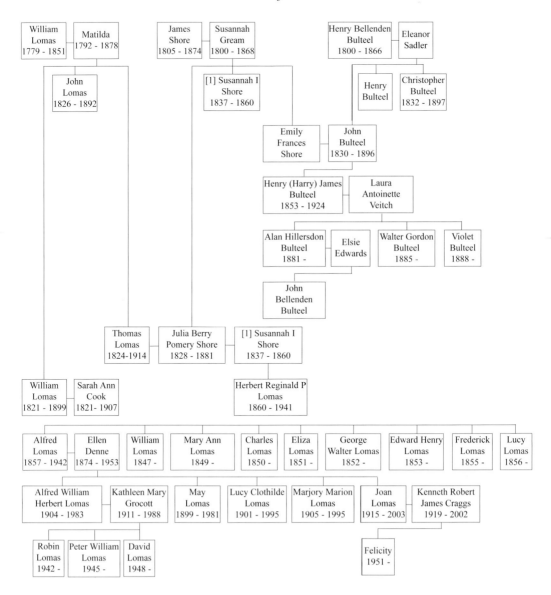

BIBLIOGRAPHY

Anglican evangelicals: Protestant Secessions from the Via Media, c1800-1850 Grayson Carter Oxford University Press 2001

History of the Free Church of England. The Free Church of England 1960

The Cobbett of the West R S Lambert Nicholson and Watson 1938

Victorian Exeter 1837-1914 R Newton Leicester University Press 1968

Henry Phillpotts GCB Davies SPCK 1954

The Oxford Dictionary of National Biography HB Bulteel Timothy C F Stut

The Bulteels the story of a Huguenot family Vivien Allen Phillimore 2003

Weymouth's Spas Nottington and Radpole DMH Reeby 1994

Taking the Cure E S Turner London 1967

The Development of Buxton and Matlock since 1800 Trevor Marchington unpublished

Buckley's Modern Buxton 1886

The Hydropathic Establishment R O Allsop Spon and Chamberlain 1891

Buxton and its Resources James Croston 1876

British Spas from 1815 to the Present Phyllis Hembry Athlone Press 1997

Pleasures and Pastimes in Victorian Britain Pamela Horne 1998 Sutton Publishing

Buxton – a pictorial history Mike Langham and Colin Wells Biddles Ltd. 1993

Spas and health resorts of Great Britain Luke 1919

The Victorian House Judith Flanders Harper Perennial 2005

Soft Answers Richard Adlington Penguin 1949

Spa Hotel Jean Askew 1973

Parrotts Guide to all the Establishments of Great Britain 1889

Buxton as a Health Resort Dr J C Thresh 1883

W H Robertson's *Buxton and the Peak* Ward Lock 1897

Metcalfe's *The Rise and Progress of Hydropathy in England and Scotland* 1912

The Peak Thorough Guide M J B Buddeley 1903

Divining Rod: Its History, Truthfulness and Practical Utility John Mullins and Joseph Mullins Kissinger Publishing 1927

Michelin Guide to Great Britain 11th edition .1930

Canadian War Diaries www.collectionscanada.ca

Ramsgate Raid Records Chas A F Austen 1915-1918 The Addiston Publicity Bureau

Music's Great days in the Spas and Watering places Kenneth Young MacMillan 1968

Illustrated Guide to Buxton John Heywood Manch &c.1906

Early Memoirs of Ottoline Morell Faber and Faber 1963

Taking the Water Cure: The Hydropathic movement in Scotland 1840 to 1940 James Bradley Marguerite Dupee, and Alastair Durie Business and Economic History volume 26 No.2 Wellcome Trust 1997

The Spas of England Peter J Neville Havins Hale and company 1976

The Business of Hydropathy in the North of England 1850 to 1930 Alastair J Durie University of Leeds

Derbyshire Portraits Clarence Daniel Clapham 1978

English Spas William Addison B T Batsford 1951

The Golden Age of British Hotels Derek Taylor and David Bush Northwood Publications
    1974

Bradshaw's Dictionary of Mineral Waters 1894

Venice Rediscovered John Premble Clifton 1994

Buxton A People's History Mike Langham Carnegie Publishing 2001

Handbook of the Bengal Presidency with an account of Calcutta City Eastwick. John Murray
    1882

The Channel Tunnel and Public Opinion J.Knowles. London 1883.

Closely Guarded: a life in Canadian Security and Intelligence John Starnes University of
    Toronto 1998

Periodicals and newspapers

Buxton Advertiser

High Peak News

Caterer and Hotel keepers Gazette

The graphic

London Illustrated News

Punch

The Free Church of England magazine

The Times

The Scotsman

Norwich Union magazine

ACKNOWLEDGEMENTS

I owe a debt of gratitude to the late Mike Langham for his encouragement to proceed with this venture and taking the time to read the first draft.

I would also like to thank the following:

Jean Askew for responding to my request for information in the Buxton Advertiser and for taking such an interest in the project; the staff at Matlock Local Studies and Buxton Museum; Jen Edgar for her work in editing the manuscript; my sons, Andrew for his practical help and advice and Christopher for the loan of his flat enabling me to make numerous trips to the British Library; finally my wife, Ros, for all her support and encouragement in bringing this work to publication.

INDEX